Fourth Edition

HEALTH CARE ETHICS

Principles and Problems

Thomas M. Garrett

Harold W. Baillie

Rosellen M. Garrett

University of Scranton

Prentice Hall

Upper Saddle River, New Jersey 07458

Library of Congress Cataloging-in-Publication Data

GARRETT, THOMAS M., [date]
 Health care ethics : principles and problems / THOMAS M. GARRETT, HAROLD W. BAILLIE,
ROSELLEN M. GARRETT.—4th ed.
  p. cm.
 Includes bibliographical references and index.
 ISBN 0-13-019448-4
 1. Medical ethics. 2. Medical ethics—Case studies. I. Baillie, Harold W., [date] II.
Garrett, Rosellen M., [date] III. Title.
 R724.G35 2000
 174'.2—dc21   00-028573

VP, Editorial Director: *Charlyce Jones Owen*
Acquisition Editor: *Ross Miller*
Associate Editor: *Katie Janssen*
Marketing Manager: *Don Allmon*
Editorial/production supervision: *Edie Riker*
Prepress and Manufacturing Buyer: *Sherry Lewis*
Cover Director: *Jayne Conte*
Cover design: *Bruce Kenselaar*

This book was set in 10/12 Palatino by East End Publishing Services, Inc.,
and was printed and bound by RR Donnelly & Sons Company. The cover was
printed by Phoenix Color Corp.

© 2001, 1998, 1993, 1989 by Prentice-Hall, Inc.
A Division of Pearson Education
Upper Saddle River, New Jersey 07458

Printed in the United States of America

10   9   8   7   6   5   4   3   2   1

ISBN   0-13-019448-4

Prentice-Hall International (UK) Limited, *London*
Prentice-Hall of Australia Pty. Limited, *Sydney*
Prentice-Hall Canada Inc., *Toronto*
Prentice-Hall Hispanoamericana, S.A., *Mexico*
Prentice-Hall of India Private Limited, *New Delhi*
Prentice-Hall of Japan, Inc., *Tokyo*
Pearson Education Asia Pte. Ltd., *Singapore*
Editora Prentice-Hall do Brasil, Ltda., *Rio de Janeiro*

Dedicated to the memory of

Thomas M. Garrett
Teacher, Friend, Husband

CONTENTS

3   Principles of Beneficence and Nonmaleficence   57

4   The Ethics of Distribution   83

5   Principles of Confidentiality and Truthfulness   111

PROBLEMS OF HEALTH CARE ETHICS

6   Professional Standards and Institutional Ethics   136

7   Ethical Problems of Death and Dying   165

8   Abortion and Maternal-Fetal Conflict   198

9   New Methods of Reproduction   229

PREFACE

Tom Garrett's passing on New Year's Eve 1997 has dramatically altered our expectations and experience in writing this new edition. This book was initially Tom's idea and while his illness progressively removed him from the labor of writing subsequent editions, his intelligence and spirit nevertheless continued to animate our work. This edition has been accomplished without his presence and guidance, and for the two of us there is an incompleteness to this text that no amount of our time or effort could satisfy. We dedicate this text to his memory in the happy acknowledgment of his continuing influence.

The fourth edition embodies several improvements over the third, but contains no dramatic structural alterations. Work has been done to clarify and improve the philosophical reflections that provide the context for the discussion of both principles and problems in the field. Further, we have attempted to provide a natural and unified discussion of the problems associated with the still contentious issues surrounding the end of life. To give added perspective we have provided occasional interludes on insights offered from cultural traditions that are not usually understood to be part of the mainstream discussion of American medical ethics. We have also enlarged the discussion of genetics research and, of course, updated information on many issues.

As always, there are many people to thank for their contribution to this text. Several colleagues in the field offered their advice and suggestions regarding the revisions in a symposium organized by the University of Scranton. We thank them and the University for this opportunity. Dr. Baillie would also like to thank the University of Scranton for a sabbatical, during which work was completed for this edition. Our work on genetics research has been aided by the support of the Northeast Regional Cancer Institute, which received funding from the Department of Energy's Human Genome Project. We appreciate that support. Our students have provided a continuing opportunity to test the clarity of our thinking and have challenged our presentation with questions and problems that have enlightened and invigorated us. The medical and health care management communities in Scranton and in the Republic of Slovakia have been both teachers and students for us, providing us with anchors in the school of hard knocks. Thank you to Tom Hickey of the University of Michigan, Ann Arbor for his careful review. We would also like to thank Jennifer Ackerman, Emsal Hasan, and Edie Riker at Prentice Hall for their continued confidence in the book and their untiring efforts to bring this edition to completion. Several scholarly presses have provided us with permission to quote from their material, and we appreciate their continued generosity. Finally, and for the fourth time, we would like to thank Eleanore Cooper for her secretarial support so crucial to producing a manuscript, and for her persistent good humor throughout the trials of the last two years.

Harold W. Baillie, Ph.D.
Rosellen M. Garrett, R.N., Ph.D.

1

ETHICS, PROFESSIONAL ETHICS, AND HEALTH CARE ETHICS

This is a book about health care ethics, that is, a book about applied ethics in various professional health care fields. It is also about the ethics of the health care consumer, since the patient must make the most serious ethical decisions of all.

Ethics is that branch of philosophy that seeks to determine how human actions may be judged right or wrong. When the study of ethics is applied to a professional field, it becomes necessary to discuss not only basic ethical positions, but also the nature of the profession and the conditions under which that profession operates.

The study of ethics as a branch of philosophy implies that the human mind is the fundamental means by which actions may be judged. The judgment itself may arise from the nature of or principles of reason (as in Kant) or from experience (as in J. S. Mill). Thus, ethics is not the same as moral theology or religious ethics, since ethics uses common human experience as its point of departure. For its final determination of right or wrong, religious ethics ultimately appeals to a revelation to a particular group, while philosophical ethics does not, or at least should not, invoke particular religious belief as a justification of its conclusions.

Ethics need not be taken as an attack on religiously founded morality, which for the believer has a superior validity. Ethics is not, after all, capable of judging the claims of divine revelation. Yet, since they are both concerned with how a human life ought to be lived, ethics and religion often consider the same problems and share important insights. Occasionally during the course of this book, we will refer to various religious traditions in order to broaden our discussion by providing alternative views or a different perspective. These references are to illustrate the complexity of the problem under discussion, and do not provide a full discussion of that religious tradition. The core of our approach will remain philosophical.

Nor is ethics the same as law, although the law is an important expression of social judgment about the rightness or wrongness of actions that seriously affect the public good. This social judgment is the result of a loosely organized, society-wide ethics discussion (of which ethics books and ethics classes are a small part), and the law presents certain conclusions of this discussion. Whereas law is largely concerned with the public good and the protection of individual rights, ethics not only includes these topics but goes beyond them to look at the obligations of individuals to themselves, as well as to others and to society.

Because it attempts to look beyond the opinions of the group to the history of critical discussions regarding more fundamental issues about human nature and the nature of human activity in general, ethics is not sociology or a mere description of what a given group thinks is right or wrong. At the same time, ethics must recognize that contemporary public beliefs may point to very important insights about the rightness or wrongness of particular activities. In the context of professional ethics, public opinion has a great deal to do with defining the role of the professional and in setting up expectations for the profession. In chapter 4, which discusses justice, we will even see how public opinion has a decisive role to play in the fair distribution of health care.

THEORIES OF ETHICS

Ethical theories, that is, theories about the characteristics of human activity, can be grouped in many ways. We will look at four particular versions: consequentialism, Kantian deontologism, natural law, and virtue ethics.

Consequentialism

The first class of ethical theories, *consequentialism*, sees the rightness or wrongness of an action in terms of the consequences brought about by that action. These consequences are generally evaluated according to the extent to which they serve some intrinsic good, that is, a good that is good in and of itself independent of any further consequences. As such, this good is usually considered to be external to the actions that bring it about.

The most common, but not the only, form of consequentialism is *utilitarianism*. Utilitarianism, or social consequentialism, holds that one should act so as to do the greatest good for the greatest number. For example, the good as defined by J.S. Mill would be the presence of pleasure and the absence of pain, so that for Mill determining the proper action involves adding up the aggregate of pleasures and pains suffered by the members of the community. Mill allows that there are different qualities of pleasures and pains, which are determined by the preferences of those who have experienced a wide variety of both. The state of affairs that yields the greatest amount of preferred pleasures and the least amount of pain is taken to be the best.

There are several different problems with this position. First, the notion that human good consists of the aggregate of pleasures and pains seems an inadequate presentation of the varieties and depth of human good. Second, the idea that the consequences may be seen as external to the actions that bring them about seems to contradict the idea that what is good for humans makes them more complete as human beings, not just "better off." Third, the utilitarian principle tends to overlook the good of the individual and to concentrate on the aggregate of individual goods (although utilitarians attempt to overcome this difficulty). Finally, utilitarianism is tied to a claim that the aggregate consequences of an action are clear enough to be accurately measured and tallied in some way. This dependence on the clarity of the consequences of an action is considered by many ethicians to be largely insupportable. As will be apparent throughout this book, many ethical dilemmas are dilemmas precisely because the larger consequences of actions are not clear at all. There are, however, many areas in health care ethics in which society may rightfully judge that the utilitarian approach is the most reasonable approach available (for example, in issues concerning distribution).

Kantian Deontologism

The second class of ethical theory, *deontologism*, is very powerfully expressed in the work of Immanuel Kant. The basic idea is that an act must be done because it contains certain characteristics such as universality or conformity with the moral law. Kant used the principle of universality to identify appropriate actions: if the maxim or statement of an action could be universalized as appropriate for everyone, that action would be ethically permissible. This universality is then basis for considerations such as duty or justice or respect for an individual's autonomy. As a result, the deontologist considers the rightness or wrongness of at least some acts to be independent of their consequences; that is, some acts are good or evil in and of themselves. Unlike utilitarians, deontologists hold that lying is wrong even if a lie would accomplish great good for individuals and society. They use formal rules in judging the rightness of an act, such as "Do unto others as you would have them do unto you" or "Act in such a way that you always treat humanity, whether in your own person or in the person of any other, never simply as a means, but always at the same time as an end."

One strength of the deontological position is its emphasis on the moral significance of the individual, in the form of rights or equality. Although we sympathize with that emphasis and accept the moral centrality of the person, we feel that contemporary deontological positions are so extreme in their emphasis that community becomes a nonexistent moral category. The individual is so exalted that it becomes impossible for there to be any moral significance in the other. To the authors, this simply does not accord with experience. Our experiences with friendship, marriage, and community living indicate that these realities are central in the moral development and moral life of the individual. As we will make clear, society is for us the means by which the individual is educated to right reason and trained to social roles. Any position that does not give a large place to this fundamental moral relationship between the individual and society is inadequate.

Natural Law

Classical (or scholastic) natural law takes the position that rational reflection on nature, particularly human nature, will yield principles of good and bad that can guide human action toward human fulfillment or flourishing. Since it is concerned with human flourishing, that is, the actualization of potentials inherent in human nature, classical natural law is teleological. Where Kant emphasizes the universal demands of reason, natural law focuses on our ability to recognize the structured complexity and coherence of nature. For example, central to a natural law ethics would be a definition of human beings, such as Aristotle's suggestion that we are rational animals. The study of nature would provide other definitions as well, such as the family, or a natural death, or natural reproduction.

Thus, where Kant finds the simplicity of universality, with its rights and equality, natural law finds moral significance in family, friendship, and community. But it then has the problem of producing and defending a clear definition of these natural realities and their fulfillment. This is a difficult requirement to meet in the face of a pluralistic society in which the nature (or definition) of even apparently simple relationships (like marriage or the family) can be the subject of intense dispute (see chapter 9 for a discussion of new methods of reproduction). So much of what we once thought to be natural has been shown to be also social (for example, the dominion of master over slave) that the task of adequately defending the classical natural law position is difficult, if not impossible. (This point is also illustrated by one of the most significant fruits of the natural law theory, the principle of double effect; see chapter 3 for a discussion of beneficence and nonmaleficence).

As in our criticism of utilitarianism, we find that both deontologism and natural law rely on an assumption that moral dilemmas can be made clear and, consequently, that we can reason ourselves out of problems. This escape is accomplished through the use of a formal criterion or perhaps a definition of a nature that in large measure denies *or at least misunderstands* the role of consequences in our moral thought. The suggestion is that by looking to the formal properties of an action we can escape the limitations of our knowledge of the consequences of that action. We suggest that this clarity is misleading, because it is attained at the cost of denying the role of social experience in understanding both the dilemmas we face in daily life and the way in which our understanding of our own good can grow.

Virtue Ethics

The third class of ethical theory may be labeled *virtue ethics*. Virtue ethics is, unfortunately, a somewhat confusing term, because it is used as a label for two different approaches to ethics. What we call virtue ethics, *narrowly defined*, states that "a virtue [is] a dispositional trait of character that is considered praiseworthy in general and in a particular role." In this narrowly defined approach, "a virtue ethics [is] a systematic formulation of the traits of character that make human behavior praiseworthy or blameworthy" (Shelp, 1985, p. 330).

This view of virtue ethics reflects the tradition of the mentor in medical education. The mentor would take a student under his wing and be the model for the student's education and career, while the student would pattern his behavior after that of the mentor. But, virtue ethics narrowly defined does not go far enough in setting up a framework for evaluating the rightness or wrongness of individual activities. After all, how does a student recognize whether his mentor is a good or bad role model? Or, what happens when the student faces new situations never confronted by the mentor? Thus, although we would agree that health care professionals should be compassionate, truthful, and unselfish (traditional elements in physician mentoring), these emotional dispositions do not guarantee correct decisions regarding what is done to the patient. Such decisions must appeal to the knowledge and the reasoning ability of the professional and rest on a specific relationship with the client in a specific social context that identifies the nature and goals of their relation. We turn then to virtue ethics broadly construed.

Virtue ethics *more broadly defined* involves not only the virtues, but the integration of the virtues with what has been variously called practical wisdom or right reason. This practical wisdom is the ability to choose patterns of action made desirable and revealed as desirable by reasoning that has been informed not only by habits of emotional experience or virtues (Baillie, 1988), but by consideration of the widest possible range of experience for the human person situated in society. Reasoned consideration of this wide range of factors and the emotional dispositions are both influenced by cultural traditions about the common understanding of what would be a good and complete life, and so need to be tempered by both logic and a healthy skepticism about those traditions.[1] This cultural background, made a real part of the person's life through training to the virtues of that society, is the basis from which action and thought arise. For example, we try to be courageous because we have been taught that we ought to be courageous through models that our society presents. These models are presented because our society understands them to embody elements of what a good and complete human life would be. Practical wisdom thus requires as a foundation the development of virtues, that is, dispositions concerned with both the emotions and the intellect. But as we grow in ability our dispositions open up to reflection, that is, we take over the responsibility of perceiving and thinking about what is good and bad.

The perceiving and thinking involved with practical wisdom involves a developing recognition or intuition of what a human being is, and what is good for that human being (Aristotle, Bk 6, ch. 5). This involves not only the recognition and application of patterns of action shown to be appropriate by past experience, but the study and evaluation of all the reasonably known proximate and remote consequences for the person and society. To act properly in a given set of circumstances involves knowing how one's actions might affect these circumstances, the societies of which one is a member, all of the persons involved, and ultimately oneself. This knowledge is incomplete and provisional, yet, because it is rooted in experience, it remains the soundest basis of action. Furthermore, because it is incomplete and provisional, this knowledge is capable of development, both in the sense that we can both learn more through more experience and improve our understanding of patterns of action by continuing to reflect on them and their results. In particular, their results can deepen or alter our understanding of ourselves and what it means to be human.

What distinguishes practical wisdom from consequentialism is that, by evaluating entire patterns of action, practical wisdom not only examines actions and their consequences but also questions why we understand particular events to be significant at all; that is, why is this action or result important for us as humans? Practical wisdom grows as a result of the ability of additional experience to enrich or alter our intuitions, which have themselves been the product of previous experience and training. For example, in chapter 2, we will discuss living wills as a means of protecting patient autonomy. This raises questions such as these: What is it about the patient that a living will protects, and how is it that this protection can fail even when all the formal or legal requirements have been met? Or, in chapter 9, we will discuss how new methods of reproduction can fail to protect autonomy even when they succeed in providing patients with what they want. In our view, everything is judged in terms of its ultimate as well as immediate effects on the total development of the individual person living in a community; yet our understanding of this total development constantly changes and grows.

We also wish to stress the fact that ours is not an individualistic position, for what harms other persons ultimately harms the agent. One's own dignity means very little if other persons do not have a similar value. As we shall see, in discussing the common good, the basic reason for limiting one's own freedom is the preservation of the dignity of others. This preservation of the dignity of others is not merely a question of one-on-one relationships, but of harms to society, which ultimately result in harms to individual dignity. For this reason, social effects, that is, effects on the various communities of which the individual is a member, are extremely important. What destroys such social goods as the family, communication, clean water and fresh air, or the health care delivery system, is ultimately if not immediately and directly of great consequence for the individual.

The effects in question are not simply material effects, such as the loss of a leg or of property or even of life itself, but of such intangible but extremely important aspects of the person as human dignity and freedom of choice, as well as freedom from unnecessary restrictions. Although it is not always easy to specify everything that is demanded by human dignity, the authors, like American culture itself, see attacks on freedom of choice and freedom from unnecessary restrictions as attacks on human dignity and so as *prima facie*, or presumptively, evil. That is, such attacks are seen intuitively to be wrong, unless the opposite can be clearly established.

This broader definition of virtue ethics includes a consideration of the emotional dispositions and cultural factors that influence dispositions, as well as the development of reason so that it is capable of balanced consideration of the consequences for the individual person in society. This holistic approach pivots on practical wisdom as the *primary virtue* for ethical decision making. The present work might then be called a virtue ethics in this broader sense. To avoid confusion, however, we shall call it the approach of practical wisdom.

Emotions and the Ethical Life

As argued previously, emotions influence our ability to perceive ethical values and to make ethical judgments. Our concern for ourselves and for others lies at the heart of ethics, and particularly at the heart of the ethics of the health professions. Without fellow feeling we would not be so ready to acknowledge that others have the same moral value as we do. Love urges us to go beyond the minimum in helping others. Yet, without compassion, we might help others as if we were dealing with blocks of wood to be moved around in line without expertise. Arrogance might lead us to paternalism and to domineering behavior, even as we pretend to help others. Hatred, envy, and resentment can distort our perception of reality and our decision making.

We will soon be discussing the difficulties in surrogate decision making, many of which originate in the conflicting emotions felt by the surrogates. It is painful to ask worried loved ones to make decisions on behalf of a patient. Yet, who would feel comfortable allowing a person to make a surrogate decision for a spouse for whom he had no apparent emotional attachment or for a parent whose death was treated as just another daily hassle? For practical wisdom, emotions color our perception of the world and inform our judgments of actions in that world. Although they cannot be the sole, or even most reliable, guide, they remain a fundamental element of ethical deliberation and action.

KEY ISSUES

Having located our theory relative to broad categories of ethical theory, we now wish to stress some of the key notions that underlie our position.

The Dignity of the Individual

At the heart of this book is the assertion that the individual person is the central value in terms of whose dignity all consequences are to be judged. To begin with such an assertion is to begin with an intuition, that is, implicit knowledge gathered from our society's traditions. With this assertion, we have not proved anything about human dignity; rather, we have named a starting point for discussion. The authors believe that this is a reasonable starting point because of the emphasis American and Western traditions have placed on this issue.[2] Other traditions may locate the central ethical concern elsewhere, for example, on community or service. This book, then, will be a discussion, with particular focus on the American tradition, of how human dignity is made present in medical care and how medical care can help us to define dignity.

Consistent with the broad range of concerns under the review of practical wisdom, this dignity resides not merely in the capacity for pleasure nor in the ability to make free choices, but in the capacity for warm human interaction, friendship, and family relations and for the most broadly based social life, as well as for union with the whole of reality. Although these capacities are not likely to be completely fulfilled, they are, nevertheless, at the core of the dignity of the human person.

The individual person is not an abstraction that can be labeled simply as "an autonomous being" or "a bearer of rights," but is a concrete individual whose life involves shared experience in a particular community and sharing in a specific set of social roles in that community. Thus, individual and society are not opposing concepts. They can be understood only in terms of one another. Individuals are not simply individuals; they are also fathers, daughters, nurses, teachers, and wage earners. All these roles that entangle the individual in the lives of others and in the life of the community specify consequences that must be considered.

It is important to note that, partly because of the interdependence of the individual and society, the concept of human dignity is not static. History has affected the concept as it has revealed further dimensions of humankind and given deeper insights into what that dignity demands for the full flowering of the person. Only in the nineteenth century did American society recognize the full evils of slavery and child labor. In our own generation, we have seen progress as our society came to consider sexism, racism, ageism, and the like, as affronts to human dignity. The recognition of these evils has not removed all of them but has begun the process of reform. Unfortunately, society can forget the consequences of such insults to human dignity. Unfortunately, too, as resources become scarcer, societies are tempted to downgrade the dignity of the sick, elderly, poor, and powerless. Sometimes this happens because of selfishness and shortsightedness. Sometimes it is a regrettable manifestation of the tragic in human life. We will return to the tragic dimension shortly.

For these reasons, it is difficult to define precisely what is included in the concept of the dignity of the individual. At various points in this book, we will return to this question. For example, the implications of freedom of choice as part of human dignity will be developed in chapter 2 in our discussion of the principle of autonomy. Our developing understanding of the demands of human dignity are crucial in the consideration of the distribution of health care, abortion, death, and dying, as well as in the rationing of organs and the use of new modes of reproduction. Each of these problems, which will be treated in subsequent chapters, will reveal other aspects of human dignity.

The Role of Society

Society plays a necessary ethical role in that it is impossible for an isolated individual to meet the full requirements of practical wisdom for most if not all decisions. After all, it is unlikely that there would be any developed practical wisdom without society. This is true not only because of the fundamental opacity and ambiguity of ethical issues, but because of the limits of individual experience with regard to consequences, as well as the individual's dependence on society for language and education. The society, on the other hand, although not free of opacity and ambiguity, makes possible the education and training of the individual and brings to this education the wealth of experience and knowledge that it has amassed. It also brings society's particular perspective on this experience and knowledge.

Before proceeding, a few words need to be said about the words *ambiguity* and *opacity*. The *ambiguity* of which we speak refers to situations in which the clarity of the facts does not dictate the decision to be made. Thus, nothing in nature tells us whether we should drive on the right or left side of the road, although it does tell us we must do one or the other if we are to avoid disaster. Society can remove the ambiguity by law or custom. When there are potentially dangerous ambiguities about the relationships between key individuals and institutions, society by custom or law defines the roles and relationships. In short, in the ambiguous situation, problems can be resolved by choice, especially social choices. This social removal of ambiguous roles is particularly important in applied ethics.

Opacity refers to situations in which our knowledge is so limited and the situation so structured that we cannot arrive at an answer even with a social choice. In such situations, no matter what choices we make, serious moral questions remain unresolved. Society may attempt to treat the situation as merely ambiguous and attempt to clarify it by a decision, but the problem remains, since a mere decision does not solve it. We shall see examples of this with regard to the moral status of the fetus and the distribution of health care. The opacity of some situations is part of the tragic dimension.

Although society cannot eradicate opacity, it provides a knowledge base and a social decision-making mechanism. Among other things, this decision-making mechanism removes many problems of ambiguity. The customs and traditions of society encapsulate vast amounts of practical knowledge that influence the individual. This involves, in part, the formation of habits through the influence of role models, peer pressure, and family life. Whether we like it or not, we are all formed by social customs. These range from major principles, like the claim that we are innocent until proved guilty, to minor issues, such as the proper way to thank a host for dinner. None of us ever escapes this influence of our society, nor could we if we wanted to.

Moral Ambiguity, Opacity, and the Limits of Practical Wisdom

All the previous considerations point up the complexity of life as we must live it. This lived complexity gives rise to a moral complexity that often involves us in moral opacity and ambiguity. Indeed, it is in our acceptance of moral opacity and ambiguity that this book differs from other approaches to ethics. While recognizing the value of certain aspects of both deontologism and utilitarianism, we nevertheless see ourselves as offering an important and different perspective. These other ethical positions assume that some clear and unequivocal ethical principle or ethical consequence is not only possible, but is the source of any acceptable ethical evaluation. These positions suggest that, if clarity is not possible, ethics is not possible. As is clear from our discussion, our ethics presupposes no such clarity. Ethical reasoning cannot always be assumed to start from clear and distinct principles. The starting principles are often so general and vague that they can give little practical guidance. First principles such as "do good and avoid evil" may be valid, but are of little value in decision making. When we strive to develop secondary principles that are more applicable, we are adding to the primary principle material that may not be absolutely certain. We are often dealing with short-term probabilities, while remaining ignorant of the long-term consequences. Thus, as we shall see in chapters 2 and 3, the medical form of the principles of autonomy and beneficence incorporates social judgments that remove ambiguity by embracing the specifications of American society. We run the danger, then, of going from the overly general to the overly specific.

When the matter is truly opaque, society must resort to law to preserve the social order or the value of the individual person. In such cases, law is a practical determination, not the truth. No matter how useful, such laws do not remove the opacity and do not resolve the underlying moral problem. As we shall insist in our treatment of abortion, the opacity remains and the tragic dimension of life hits us with full force.

Occasionally, we are tempted to believe that our practical compromises are true solutions. This temptation springs from an uncritical acceptance of our implicit knowledge. Our beliefs about the nature of the world and the ultimate meaning of life influence all our judgments. This influence occurs whether these beliefs are philosophically or theologically founded, or even unfounded. An implicit belief in divine providence or in modern science affects our evaluation of a medical problem. Similarly, the assumption that the fetus is a person or that the authority of a particular church is supreme will also have major effects.

In addition, implicit knowledge about underlying truths as well as implicit knowledge of appropriate circumstances and of the means of applying such truths to the circumstances are always there, although not always consciously. For example, the competence and rationality of patients can generally be assumed, but in many settings a conscious evaluation needs to be made. Assumptions taken over from the culture may never have been examined critically. For example, many assume that modern health care is scientific and that the doctor knows best, when in fact, as we shall see in many sections of this book, some practices have little scientific justification. As a result, when an individual thinks that he or she knows clearly and unambiguously what is right in a situation, especially an opaque situation, this person might be wrong because of implicit, unexamined assumptions about action. This, too, may be part of the tragedy of human life.

None of this is to say that society is always correct or should be accepted uncritically. Our own society once approved slavery, the oppression of women, and the disregard of the handicapped. What we are saying is that society has an important role in evaluating and even creating consequences, as well as in forming our perspectives on the world and our character. In the tragic dimension, we face problems for which there is no satisfactory solution.

Society and Moral and Legal Rights

Most Americans are acquainted with the discussion of social ethics through the language of rights. For example, the Constitution speaks of the right to life, liberty, and the pursuit of happiness. Sometimes, particularly in popular or rhetorical discussion, the term *right* is no more than a means of expressing a set of ideals or goals for human social development. For example, the United Nation's *Universal Declaration of Human Rights* (1948) is best understood as an expression of hopes, rather than realities. We will not make use of this sense of "rights."

There is, however, a second use of the term *right* that plays an important role in the discussion of ethics in contemporary society. In this sense, a right is a moral or legal claim that an individual may assert against someone else. Thus, there are two types of rights: moral rights, in which the claim is based on moral principles, and legal rights, in which the claim is based on law. Any such claim imposes an obligation on another person (whether an individual or a corporate person, such as a company). For example, if you have signed a contract for a service, you have a legal and moral right to have that service performed by the person (or by the company) with whom you signed the contract. Conversely, this person (or the company) has a legal and moral obligation to perform that service for you. Or, if you promised your friend you would meet her at four o'clock this afternoon, then she has a moral right to expect you to be there, and you have an obligation to show up.

Rights are accepted when they have been justified or made valid by an appeal to the proper set of principles. For example, a legal right may be asserted when the appropriate legislation has been made law or when a judicial decision confirms an interpretation of law. Clearly, legal rights appear, change, develop, or disappear according to developments in a society's code of law.

Moral rights are very different. They exist as part of a moral perspective or as a set of moral principles and, as such, they can be understood in as many ways as there are diverse moral positions. For example, a utilitarian will understand rights to be generated within the experience of a society as a statement of what the society finds most basic in the treatment of the individual. A deontologist will understand a right to be a moral claim that in a sense preexists the society; that is, the individual gets rights from a source other than, and more important than, society. For example, a right may be a consequence of God's creation, or it may be another way of expressing the autonomy of the person.

In this book, we will speak of rights in both the legal and the moral sense. When speaking of legal rights, we will be referring to legal rights granted by American law. When we speak of moral rights, we will speak of rights to things that are demanded by the dignity of the individual inside a particular community. To put it another way, we see rights as claims to things that are necessary to protect and advance the particular person in that basic dignity. And, as our understanding of dignity grows in depth and insight (or perhaps withers under stress of catastrophes), our identification of rights may grow (or diminish) as well.

We admit, however, that rights in their specific as opposed to their general form are structured by the society in which the individual exists. Thus, although there may be a general moral right to food, the right to a specific food will depend on the resources of the community and even on its culinary customs. This point will have particular importance when we discuss the general right to health care in chapter 4.

Public or Common Good

We have insisted that practical wisdom considers the direct impact of actions not only on the individual person but on society. Our reason is simple: The good of society is one of the chief means to the protection and growth of the individual. Without the public good or common good, all other goods would be difficult to attain.

The common good is understood to be the collection of goods that, having been produced by the broadest and most inclusive form of social cooperation, belong to society as a whole, as opposed to belonging to individuals, and that benefits every individual directly or indirectly. In modern times, much of this cooperation is managed by the government, but key parts of the common good, such as the language and the culture, are the result of even more widespread cooperation. However, when we say that the common good belongs to the society, we do not mean that it belongs to the government. Society owns the language, one of the most important of the goods in the common good. The language is *not* the possession of either the government or any individuals or group of individuals. Indeed, when a government acts as if it does own the language, we are almost certainly dealing with tyranny of the worst sort.

The particular goods that form part of the common good are not written down in some easy-to-find handbook. Over time, the list has grown from such things as the judicial system and the economic infrastructure (roads, canals, etc.) to include the educational system, the welfare system, and police and fire protection. Today we are debating whether the health care system (or nonsystem, according to some) is or should be part of the common good. This last question cannot be answered *a priori* because it depends on the social evaluation of the entire system. In short, it depends on the values of society and the resources available. We shall return to this concept in chapter 4.

Each particular part of the common good is justified only insofar as it contributes directly or indirectly to the good of every individual in society. In other words, the common good is not some great god to whom all is to be sacrificed. It is a means to the perfection of all individuals in the society. A public sewer system, for example, directly serves not only those who are hooked up, but, by preventing the spread of disease, it serves everyone in the society. The public educational system serves the students directly, but it serves everyone by preparing people capable of carrying on the essential functions of society.

Ultimately, the public good exists for the good of individual persons, rather than the other way around. For grave reasons, minor goods of the individual can be subordinated to the public good. Thus, most of us pay taxes to support large parts of the common good. But our very personhood does not belong to the society, and it would be unjust for society to demand that we sacrifice our life or our sanity for the common good. In short, the common good cannot justify destroying the individual human person, which is the central value and so the justification of the existence of society and the common good.

In the chapters that follow, we will often consider conflicts between individual and public goods and the conditions under which one is subordinated to another.

The Tragic in Human Life

We have referred to the tragic in human life frequently in the previous pages. By *tragic*, we mean the consequences of human limitations in knowledge and resources (Nussbaum, 1986), leading to two types of problems: (1) the chance of being wrong despite the best knowledge and intentions; and (2) the need to make morally wrenching decisions in the face of incomplete information or with inadequate resources. The central issue is that human beings are limited in their ability to know by ambiguity and opacity and in their ability to act by space, time, and resources. For example, when a health care professional performs triage, that is, rations care at the scene of an accident, some are helped and some neglected. This is the "damned if you do, damned if you don't paradox." This is the essence of the human tragedy. We will address the topic of tragedy in this book, without pretending to have the wisdom or resources to avoid or overcome it.

APPLIED ETHICS

When the principles of ethics are applied to a situation, more than principles are required. Because the application of principles is to be made in a particular society with its particular role definitions, customs, and laws, these must be taken into consideration.

Ultimately, the consequences of health care for the individual must be considered, since the consequences vary in particular social situations and change over time as techniques are improved. The factual study of consequences is thus a necessity. For practical wisdom ethics, this factual information is concerned with the generalizable effects of an activity and with the probable effects of the activity in the particular case (Jonsen and Toulmin, 1988). Thus, while everyone agrees that it is wrong to kill innocent persons, before we can pass ethical judgment in a concrete situation, we need to know whether the person is innocent and whether the particular activity will kill. Whether pornographic material causes violence is a question that must be answered before we can condemn pornography on that ground. In medicine, we will have to look at the effects of medical treatment not only on the body, but on the spirit, lifestyle, and pocketbook of the patient, as well as its effects on society. In short, applied ethics looks to the concrete and the practical and thus demands more than theory.

In medical ethics, the consequences change as techniques and conditions change. One hundred and fifty years ago, before blood typing and matching, blood transfusions were almost universally fatal and so generally unethical as well. Twenty years ago, the risks were small and blood transfusions generally posed no ethical problem. Today, with the spread of AIDS, there are again ethical problems with the system that supplies blood for transfusions. Sometimes our knowledge of the consequences and alternative treatments change, with the result that both the medical and ethical status of a treatment must be reevaluated. We shall see further examples of this with regard to radical mastectomies, tonsillectomies, and medical circumcision.

In the real world, we need a mutually acceptable way to decide on the consequences and evaluate them. For example, in determining the effects of lead poisoning on children, we have certain canons of scientific procedure that, when followed, will answer this question (to the best of our ability). Or, in determining who is innocent and who is guilty in these particular circumstances, we have the court system and the legal code. In short, applied ethics looks to the concrete and the practical and, in so doing, it involves socially developed institutions and socially accepted techniques that aid the individual in evaluating moral issues.

For these reasons, when we present material regarding problems that are very much rooted in ambiguous circumstances, such as the appointment of a guardian for incompetent patients or the definition of death, we will rely on court decisions, laws, and even statements by professional associations for what is at least a reasonable starting point for arriving at explicit content for an ethical decision. Sometimes the law even dictates what the decision should be. This is because these sources represent the thinking of interested parties who have a collective experience greater than that of any individual. These institutions are the socially developed schemas, the means by which a particular society applies ethical principles for itself and its members to specific circumstances. This is not to say that we agree with, or even ought to agree with, each of these decisions and statements. The value of the individual provides us with the perspective from which critical evaluations of these procedures and decisions may be generated. Indeed, it is the task of the individual to develop these critical evaluations as his or her experience suggests the need for critical considerations. In the pages that follow, we will be exercising this critical function to suggest ways in which law and custom might be made to better defend and promote the dignity of the individual in the context of health care. At the same time, the collective experience of the society as a whole and of significant professional groups is a precious resource.

THE PROFESSIONS
AND PROFESSIONAL ETHICS

In an ideal situation, we would start the following discussion with a definition of a profession, apply it to health care, and then draw out its implications. Many people, including those in the professions, think in precisely this way. Unfortunately, there is no unchallenged definition of a profession, and the whole idea is thought by some to be outdated. For example, the Federal Trade Commission treats a physician as an entrepreneur, an individual engaged in economic activity for the sake of self-interest. This impression is enhanced by the formation of physician unions by physicians who come to see themselves as employees of, for example, health maintenance organizations, or the advertising of medical services such as elective cosmetic surgery. Although we recognize that professionals work for pay, traditionally we have expected more from those who bear the label professional, especially clergy, lawyers, educators, and health care workers.

A profession, in the traditional sense, seems to involve the following elements: (1) a dedication to a particular way of life supportive of a particular expertise; (2) a deep involvement in activities important to the functioning of society; and (3) a commitment to place service to society and often the individual ahead of, or at least equal to, personal gain. In the health care fields, this service to the individual is of central importance.

Traditionally, a profession also controlled entrance into its membership and set educational requirements (see chapter 11). In addition, professions were supposed to have and enforce ethical codes on their membership.[3] These powers are given to the profession by the society for the sake of the profession's service to the society. The trade-off is beneficial to both parties: power and exclusivity in return for healing.

The Purpose of Medicine and the Health Care System

This trade-off of service for exclusive power is not without its problems, however; for while we may all assume that we know the purpose of medicine, nursing, physical therapy, and health care in general, a little reflection reveals difficulties that have ethical implications.[4] Let us look at the medical profession as the currently most powerful professional group in health care.

Is the overarching purpose of the health care professions the prevention of death or the alleviation of suffering (May, 1983)? If it is the alleviation of suffering, does this embrace not only a cure of the cause of the suffering, but also the comforting and care of the sufferer who cannot or will not be cured? Another possibility is that health care, in the context of a specific illness, is only the attempt to optimize the patient's chance for a happy and productive life as defined by the patient (Robin, 1984).

If the purpose of health care professionals is the prevention of death, then physicians are professionally correct when they keep people alive in a vegetative state. If their purpose is the relief of suffering by either cure or care, physicians who use "heroic measures" with a person in a permanent vegetative state are cruel and unprofessional. The appropriateness of curing the patient seems obvious, but an emphasis on comforting the sufferer can quickly lead to the possibility of assisted suicide or euthanasia, contentious issues that we will discuss in chapter 7. If the purpose of health care professionals is to optimize the patient's chances for a happy and productive life as defined by the patient, then treatment that dooms the patient to an unproductive life is perhaps unethical even though the physician and society think that the unproductive life is good.

Pellegrino (1979b) holds that the purpose of medicine is a "right and good healing action taken in the interests of a particular patient." Kass (1983) also emphasizes healing as the primary purpose, although elsewhere (1975) he suggests that the pursuit of health is the primary purpose of medicine, with the prevention of death and the alleviation of suffering secondary pursuits. Positions that put healing at the center provide a way of judging when to stop treatment because death is imminent or because healing is no longer possible. At that point the alleviation of pain becomes primary as the only humane and ethical possibility that remains.

It is impossible to define the purpose of either medicine or health care in general so that it can be engraved in stone. In the first place, the immediate, practical purpose of health care changes as the condition of the patient changes. In the second place, the general purpose changes as the agreement between the patient and the health care provider changes. Finally, the society's needs may change, altering the social purpose of the profession. Medicine and health care have several purposes, and all need to be considered in line with the condition and wishes of the patient and the needs of the society.

The idea that medicine has as one of its purposes the pursuit of health (Kass, 1983) recognizes that the physician is also concerned with preventing as well as healing disease and that the individual physician seeks to maintain health at an optimal level for the particular patient. This can also have great social implications for the physician, who is then placed in an advocacy role regarding questions of public health.

The health care professions as a whole should have as their purpose the prevention of disease and the maintenance of the health of the whole population. The fact that such tasks are often relegated only to public health officials, sanitary engineers, and the Centers for Disease Control does not mean that the social dimension is not part of the purpose of the health care professions.

In the United States over the last few years, the development of managed care as a model for the delivery of health care has added the concern of efficiency to any discussion of the purpose of health care. Because efficiency is a very powerful criterion of action, discussions of health care's purpose can be easily sidetracked by evaluations of efficiency. Indeed, when economic costs become a primary concern, the effective treatment of a patient may suffer.

This variety of purposes can create a complex role for the physician who is responsible to the patient, to his or her profession, and to the society. This has led to several descriptions of the role of the physician, ranging from a patient advocate interested only in what is good for the patient to a gatekeeper who will limit access to scarce medical resources.

Many suggest that the physician is in a no-win situation in which there are too many limits and too many expectations to allow the physician a reasonable opportunity to perform her or his task. One alternative is to suggest that the best the physician can do is to withdraw from these larger issues into a world limited by the technical proficiencies found in medicine. However, all the difficulties we have described are inescapable. As is clear from the day-to-day operation of the hospital, a technician's responsibility is to a performance, a machine, or a test. For a physician to retire to technical expertise is to abandon the real responsibilities that he or she has to the patient as a fellow human being. The very nature of medical practice demands that the physician be at the confluence of the difficulties we have described.

A Definition of Medical Practice

This brings us to our sense of the definition of medical practice. The physician is one who draws on training and experience to advise patients on ways to obtain the best care or, if necessary and possible, to restore their physical well-being, and the physician correlatively represents that patient to the social institutions that exist to help patients care for themselves.

We are intentionally not emphasizing specialized expertise or skill. Important as these are, they are the means to accomplish one of two things: (1) an accurate picture of the patient's problems, or (2) the end that the patient and the physician have already determined that they want. The real issue in the practice of medicine is the advice the physician gives the patient. This advice is based on training and skill, and although it is loaded and biased by several complicating issues (see chapter 4), it is the center of the physician's practice.

The authors thus assume that in most encounters the primary purpose of medicine is the care of patients. When healing is not possible, the alleviation of suffering by ethical means becomes primary. When healing is not necessary, the prevention of disease and the maintenance of health are the proper focus. The prevention of death and the prolongation of life may be the result of all the activities designed to achieve the above purposes, but these are not goals in and of themselves without further consideration. As we shall see in chapter 7 in our discussion of death and dying, the value of life and the prolongation of life can become problematic.

We have oversimplified the issues here, because key words such as *health* and *disease* and associated terms such as *cure, restore,* and *maintain* are all ambiguous. In chapter 4, when we discuss the distribution of health care, the nature of disease and health becomes an important issue. We shall also return to the problem in chapter 6 when we examine, however briefly, the obligation to evaluate health care.

Professional Ethics

Professional ethics are a special type of applied ethics. Moreover, there are different views about the nature of professional ethics. First, a set of rules might be called *professional ethics* because it is articulated by the members of a profession or, second, because it is concerned with the ethical conduct of the profession. The first type of professional ethics, the professionally articulated ethics, is found in codes of ethics promulgated by the professional group. Occasionally, such codes are also found in authoritative rulings of the professional association. We will refer to these codes and rulings throughout the book, because they often indicate careful thought based on long experience with the problem. Some of these codes were originally a mixture of what may be called rules of etiquette and professional courtesy, as well as of rules about matters of deep ethical concern. Indeed, at times, the professional articulated codes have been self-serving, rather than truly ethical, or at odds with more general social values. In this time of enormous change in health care in the United States, professional codes are receiving closer scrutiny as they are asked to do much more in defining the profession and the purpose of health care (Wolf, 1994). Much of this book can be seen as a commentary on, and suggestions for, professional ethics in health care.

The idea of the professionally articulated ethic lingers on, since some professionals claim that only they know enough to judge the ethics of their own group. This claim disregards the fact that their clients or patients and society as a whole are affected, so others have a right to participate in formulating and imposing the professional ethic. As a matter of fact, the society and clients are part of the force that forms the role ethics of a particular profession and so have a great influence on its ethics.

The socially accepted purpose of the profession has a preponderant influence on the definition of the professional's role, as well as on the specification of rights and duties. A profession such as the law is set up and approved for the promotion of justice according to the constitution and laws of a specific society. In the society of the United States, with its adversarial system of justice, the lawyer has a duty to represent the interests of his or her clients to ensure a fair trial, even though that might result in some perpetrators of crimes going free. Similarly, health care providers have specific obligations that depend on what is approved as the purpose of the profession within the culture.

Furthermore, society decides formally, through licensing laws and even court decisions, what the profession will and will not be allowed to do. Less formally, social movements, such as the patient's rights movement, change expectations, and so relationships, such that ethics changes with them even before they are enacted into law. If society expects health care professionals to stop and treat people involved in accidents, this will become part of the obligations of the professional role even before it is incorporated into the law. The development of the doctrine of informed consent, which will be treated in chapter 2, is a prime example of how expectation and law have changed the roles of physician and patient, thus radically influencing health care ethics.

This influence works both ways. The profession has an obligation to society to assist in the development of social attitudes and policies that govern not only the operation of the profession, but also the expectations of the public. The public's excessive confidence that medicine will cure all illnesses and perhaps indefinitely postpone death is due to the overconfidence of the medical profession as much as to other social sources. The expectations that testing will reveal all problems or that there is always something that medicine can do for a patient, no matter how frail, are public issues that the professions ought to address. Recently, with the question of physician-assisted suicide, the medical profession has taken a more public role in ethics discussions; but if they are the experts, they must contribute to the public discussion of all issues affecting health care.

THE HEALTH CARE PROFESSIONS

Membership in a profession or the adoption of the role of practitioner of a profession brings with it obligations specific to that profession or role. The importance of the role definition for professional ethics is crucial. It determines what duties are specific to the members of the profession and which rights will be granted by society. Despite the difficulties raised regarding the purpose of medicine, we will (tentatively) seek to establish the roles of some of the key professions involved in American health care and to specify the roles that they play. By focusing on roles, we will be able to see what the options are for health care professionals in advising and treating patients.

The roles defined are not uniformly delineated in all societies. Indeed, the roles change over time even in a given society. This should surprise no one, for the role assigned to the health care worker is influenced by the values of a given society, as well as by the goals and aspirations of the profession. Socialist medicine is more committed to the service of the collectivity, rather than merely to the good of the individual. Medicine in the United States has always focused on the well-being of the individual, rather than on the social good. American medicine, for most of its history, was in the Hippocratic tradition, which paternalistically saw the physician in charge of everything. Indeed, it is only in the 1980 version of The American Medical Association's *Principles of Medical Ethics* that there is a mention of patient's rights and societal obligations (Veatch, 1981a, p. 25; see also American Medical Association, 1996). The patient's rights movement, with its insistence on liberty and equality in line with the Western liberal political tradition, has had much to do with this change. The changes are still going on, with the result that at present there are competing versions of the role of the physician. Parallel changes are occurring in the profession of nursing as it seeks to define and obtain social acceptance of new and expanded roles for nurses. Here, too, there are competing models and so conflicts with what is ethical and what is not.

Models of Nursing

The models of nursing are concerned not only with the nurse patient relationship, but with the nurse physician and nurse institution relationship. These concerns are part of the women's movement as well as nursing's need to obtain proper professional recognition. The struggle becomes more acute as nurses increase their educational level and expand their practice roles. For this reason, we include some detail on changing nursing roles that illustrate the dynamics involved.

Murphy and Howard (1983) propose three models for nursing: the bureaucratic, the physician advocate, and the patient advocate. In the bureaucratic model, the nurse is supposed to concentrate on the details of institutional coordination. She or he may not go against the physician. Loyalty is the prime virtue and the rapport of the team takes precedence over the patient. This model hardly makes sense when nurses enlarge the scope of their practice and often work outside institutions as nurse practitioners. In hospitals, however, patients still experience themselves as sacrificed to the organization and the needs of the health care staff.

The physician advocate model sees the nurse as an extension of the physician, that is, a physician's extra hand. In 1973, the International Council of Nurses explicitly rejected such a role. The Judicial Council of the American Medical Association (1996) has since 1984 held that in emergencies a nurse's disregard of the physician's orders should not be looked on as a breakdown in professional relationships.

The patient advocate model calls for the nurse to be an independent although interdependent professional whose ethics cannot be dictated by others. The nurse's primary obligation is to provide the best possible care for the patient and not merely to serve institutions and physicians. The authors are in favor of such a model, but, in the absence of agreement about it, nurses, like physicians, cannot always be clear about their roles.

These models indicate that there can be ethical problems within health care based on a failure to agree on the roles to be played by physicians and nurses, as well as by other health care professionals. The models also indicate that changes are occurring in nursing. The same may be said of all other health care specialists who operate in the American system. Physical therapists, respiratory therapists, medical social workers, occupational therapists, and medical technicians all have roles to play, and these often-changing roles have ethical implications.

Models of Medicine

In the 1970s and 1980s, many writers on medical ethics stressed the importance of the model as a means of describing and even dictating the relationship between physician and patient. Veatch (1972) proposed four models: (1) the engineering model, (2) the priestly model, (3) the collegial model, and (4) the contractual model. Later, Veatch (1981a) added and May (1983) developed a covenant model. In the 1990s, with the growth of the physician as businessman or even as bureaucrat or employee in a managed care setting, it has become clear that this list itself might not be adequate.

The *engineering model* makes the physician an applied scientist, if not a technician. Like the scientist, the technician, or the engineer, the physician in this model tends to be interested in facts, not in values. In this model, the health care professional is likely to speak of treating a disease rather than taking care of a patient. Indeed, the ill person can disappear under a pile of supposedly objective test results.

The ethical implications of such a model should be obvious. The technical goal to be accomplished is likely to become the important thing, regardless of the psychic and social costs to the patient. There is a narrowing of the physician's decision-making process, so key human factors are left out. In particular, religious and value preferences tend to be neglected in favor of more technical considerations.

The *priestly model* is based on the fallacy of generalized expertise. That is, the model assumes that, since the physician is an expert in medicine, he or she is also an expert about life in general. The physician assumes a moral dominance over the patient. This leads to physicians who make pronouncements such as "That is a risk you should not take," or "Your family should be your first consideration." The main principle of this model is the traditional one of "Benefit the patient and do no harm." Unfortunately, because the priestly physician treats the patient as a child, the traditional principle often neglects other principles that command the physician to respect the freedom of the patient, to protect the patient's dignity, and to contribute to the good of society.

The ethical implications of this model will be seen constantly throughout the first part of this book as we discuss the conflict between the obligation to do good and the obligation to respect the autonomy of the patient.

The *collegial model* sees the physician and the patient as colleagues cooperating in pursuing the common goal, which may be the preservation of health, the curing of illness, or the easing of the pain of the dying, depending on the situation. Such a model demands confidence and trust from both parties in the relationship and calls for long, continued conversation between the two so that they will be sure of the goal and in agreement about the means. Ethically, this is perhaps an ideal relationship, as it recognizes both the autonomy of the patient and the expertise of the physician. But in day to day reality, this ideal is often unobtainable. The demands of a busy practice, rooted in limits of time and energy, make this model difficult to establish and maintain in even a few cases.

The *contractual model* sees the relationship between the health care provider and the patient as a business relationship governed by a contract or a free agreement entered into for consideration, that is, for specified goods that are to be exchanged. In a purely contractual relationship, each encounter between provider and patient will in theory start out with negotiations about the conditions of sale and the warranties expressed and implied. Although there are some virtues in clarifying expectations, most providers and most patients want the relationship to be more than contractual in this sense. Indeed, with Pellegrino and Thomasma (1981), we insist that there are obligations that arise from roots deeper than the contract. As we insist throughout this work, ultimately it is the dignity of the individual human being that is the primary ethical consideration.

The *covenant model* attempts to recognize those elements of the health care relationship that go beyond mere contract. In the covenant model, the dedication to an ideal and the privileges granted by society impose obligations on the physician and nurse quite aside from a contract. This becomes clear in emergencies when the health care provider must help even in the absence of a contract. The covenant also supposes a permanent relationship, or at least an open-ended one in its duration. This aspect is illustrated by the fact that a physician may not terminate a relationship at will, but must provide for the continuing care of a patient. The covenant relationship is also seen in the tradition that the physician or nurse has to provide at least some care on the basis of patient need, independent of merit or ability to pay.

Emerging Models and Roles

Although we still speak of a physician patient relationship as being a personal and professional relationship, the rise of managed care corporations has created a potential for several new models with profound consequences for both health care and health care ethics. Health care providers are increasingly employees in businesses scrambling for customers, employing marketing strategies, and attempting to increase their profits. This new activity is dramatically altering both the health care system and the public perception of it.

As the surplus of physicians becomes a reality and the for-profit sector of health care grows larger and larger, more and more physicians join nurses and physical therapists in the ranks of employees (noted as early as Starr, 1982). This shift can be expected to produce changes in the roles of physicians. They too will face the problems of the bureaucratic model that nursing has had to cope with. In particular, they will enjoy less autonomy in the practice of medicine. They will, for example, find themselves under pressure to increase income and decrease costs (Mechanic, 1986) by, for example, functioning as gatekeepers for access to resources. There will undoubtedly be more regulation of the pace and routines of work. Most important of all, physicians may find themselves used as replaceable units in a service delivery system that allows less time for the personal relationship with the patient and so more of a temptation to act on the basis of the engineering model. One thing seems certain: Employees in a bureaucracy will be under pressure to produce profits, and the health care provider will be caught between the ethic that says that the patient comes first and an "ethic" that replaces the patient with the bottom line of the annual report. At the very least, there will be tension between the traditional advocacy of the interests of a particular patient and the duty to allocate resources in the interests of society and all patients.

Although this book operates on the basis of a more idealistic role for the physician, nurse, and health care institution, the reality of the market-place and of changing American values will need to be taken into consideration. This will be particularly true when we consider the principle of justice and the problem of health care distribution in chapter 4 and professional standards in chapter 6.

Provisional Summary

In practice, the medical relationship becomes whatever the physician and the patient negotiate within the limits of their contact with one another and their individual assumptions about the purpose and nature of health care. Thus, when contact is brief with a focused purpose (such as a hernia repair), it can be simply contractual and quite impersonal. When developed during a long relationship, as with a family physician, it can be characterized as truly personal, with mutual sympathy and shared values. The negotiation of the relationship can be difficult. Some physicians still want to operate as if they were appointed to rule the patient, a situation acceptable to some patients but not all. Other physicians, however, may see themselves as collaborators with their patients, which can make patients nervous if they are desperate for clear and certain answers.

The changes that have occurred and the difficulties we have described in the previous paragraph are reflections of the deep and continuing changes in American society. These changes make the very notion of a profession somewhat problematic. In the chapters that follow, we will not concentrate on models, but on the principles and the dynamics by which they are applied to concrete situations. These principles and dynamics should be present in any model that is negotiated.

The Patient's Role

Everything said thus far should indicate that we do not see the patient's role as the sick role. The sick role calls for the patient to be passive and subordinate to the physician, because the physician has a built-in institutional superiority. We believe that the role of the patient should be a more active one that respects equality of persons. All too often, health care providers succeed in forcing patients into the sick role, but this does not mean it is right or good health care. We will, in fact, go on to argue that the patient should take the opportunity to evaluate the physician prior to any illness and that the patient's choice of a physician is one of his or her key acts of autonomy.

In line with what has been said, we see the role of the patient or the patient's surrogate as that of a partner in health care or at least that of a contractor who gets to specify key conditions of the relationship. The exceptions that occur in emergencies are discussed in chapter 2.

Ethical Diversity and Health Care

The previous pages discuss the roles and goals of health care professionals in terms of the culture of the United States. It should be obvious, however, that other societies can and do define the roles and goals in different ways. The differences are not only a result of differences in philosophy and religious belief, but of the history of the professions in a particular culture. A belief in fate, for example, makes some cultures less liable to approve of aggressive intervention to save life. Some cultures are more insistent on equal treatment than others. The positions of the family in general and health care in particular also vary and affect the ethics of familial relations. Numerous volumes (such as Veatch, 1989) present these cultural differences, which work their way into important variations in practice. In Israel, for example, decisions about caring for newborns are influenced by a religious tradition that stresses the sanctity of life, by memories of the Holocaust, and by concerns about the population (Eidelman, 1986). In the United States, the tendency is to treat any baby who is potentially viable and continue until it is almost certain that it will die, whereas the British are more likely to start treatment but, then stop it as soon as it appears that there is extensive brain damage (Rhoden, 1986). Although the culture should not be decisive, it is a factor that must be considered.

The diversity in cultural differences in health care ethics should make us particularly sensitive to the fact that the United States, as a pluralistic society in rapid change, presents particular problems. The discussion of ethics is always difficult in a pluralistic society that permits a wide diversity of opinion on every conceivable subject. The difficulties on the theoretical level are heightened when the society is debating the roles of professionals and the obligations that flow from these roles.

Because there is no complete agreement in America about the purpose of the health care professions and the role definitions of the various professions, health care ethics is often in turmoil. At the very least, it is in transition as new roles emerge and society places new restrictions on and grants new privileges to health care providers. The authors have taken a stand on what the roles ought to be. This has been done to give some coherence to the treatment of health care ethics, but also with an awareness that the debate is ongoing.

SUMMARY

The present book follows the approach of practical wisdom, in which the individual person in a concrete community is the intrinsic good. All actions are judged to be good or evil in terms of their consequences for the individual person in that society. The practical wisdom of such an approach demands that all dimensions, individual and social, be considered in assessing consequences. Particular attention must be paid to the impact on the persons and society as a whole.

Although we follow a practical wisdom approach in which the principles that guide actions are formed by consideration of the general consequences of various activities, we are conscious that changing circumstances change the consequences and so the principles. We are even willing to admit exceptions when the evidence in an individual case shows that the general consequences are not present and the good of the individual and society will not be harmed by the exception.

Professional ethics, and health care ethics in particular, involves a specification of obligations in terms of the purpose of the profession, as well as the general and particular practice role of a given health professional. The purpose and role are the result of agreement between the profession, patients, and society. The society part in this definition is influenced by the society's philosophy, religion, and history in short, the entire culture. In the United States, a pluralistic society in rapid change, the cultural factors are not always harmoniously integrated, so there are many disputed areas in health care ethics and, as seen in chapter 6, even the nature of the disputes can rapidly change.

NOTES

1. It is useful to note that common sense and practical wisdom are not the same. Common sense, or what people are accustomed to, rests largely on the comfort produced by existing practices, rather than on critical thinking. Existing practices tend to be firmly ingrained because they have been developed over time and consequently are comfortable, both emotionally and intellectually. These practices are the basis of what might be called common sense, because most people in the society are accustomed to the set of practices and have their expectations and presumptions established by it. Practical wisdom has a much broader scope, requiring that "all things be considered and considered critically." Practical wisdom tries not to take things for granted, but to examine them from all sides, since every event is like a pebble thrown in a pond, with tiny waves moving outward from the center. Even so, practical wisdom is not infallible, as we shall see when we examine the American health care delivery system.

2. As evidence to support this starting point, we note that many different ethics positions take seriously the issue of dignity. For example, Kantianism treats dignity on the basis of our pure rationality, while natural law finds dignity capacity to

know the natural order or for theologically based natural law in our status as creatures (cf. Vatican II, *Dignitatis Humanae*).

3. Perhaps there are no professions if all these requirements must be fulfilled. More likely, however, there are various stages of professionalization. See Garrett (1963, pp. 159-162) on the idea of stages of professionalization and Baumrin and Freedman (1983) for various ideas on professions.

4. Consider, for example, "The Goals of Medicine: Setting New Priorities," a special report in *The Hastings Center Report*, 26.6, Nov.-Dec. 1996.

2

PRINCIPLES OF AUTONOMY AND INFORMED CONSENT

GENERAL FORMULATION

The dignity of the person commands us to *respect individual persons*. In theory, we respect individual persons by recognizing their social uniqueness and their moral worth. In practice, we have become increasingly aware that respect for the dignity of individuals involves allowing them to make their own choices and develop their own life plans, all in the context of their particular society and in dialogue with that society. As we mentioned in chapter 1, the individual is not isolated from society and so is not absolutely individual or absolutely unique. Thus, when a person acts as an individual, that person brings a newness and spontaneity to a collection of social roles that probably have a long tradition in the society. For example, when a person becomes a parent, that person as a social being takes on an age-old social role, but as an individual she does so for the first time and may act in ways that are fresh and that may bring renewed life to that task.

When we allow individuals to make their own choices and develop their own lives in the context of a particular society and in dialogue with that society, we allow individuals their autonomy. To put this negatively, autonomy means that *one human person, precisely as a human person, does not have authority and should not have power over another human person.* This means that individuals should not coerce others or limit the activities of others or impose their will on others. Even society and its instrument, the government, must respect the freedom and privacy of individual persons and can interfere only when it is necessary to protect others or for very serious and overriding social concerns.

We stress that, since this respect for freedom and privacy is ultimately rooted in the dignity of each individual person, the principle of autonomy also calls for respecting even those persons who are not at a given moment capable of free choice. In short, persons do not lose their dignity because they are unconscious or in a coma or out of contact with reality. Even though such people present special practical difficulties, they must be respected. Dignity does not depend on a person's ability to function in a specific setting; rather, the setting ought to accommodate itself to the individual's limitations, as in providing a proper surrogate for an incompetent patient.

Specialized knowledge, even a license to practice, does not authorize professionals to control any aspect of another's life or to limit the freedom of others. Although it is true that professionals may have a great influence over decisions made by or for individuals (such as a physician offering medical advice), influence through expert advice is not the same as authority to decide for another. Society may grant such authority to professionals, but only rarely and often only under court supervision. This, then, brings us to the formulation of the medical version of the principle of autonomy, informed consent.

PATIENT AUTONOMY: INFORMED CONSENT

The health care formulation of the principle of autonomy can be expressed as follows: *You shall not treat a patient without the informed consent of the patient or his or her lawful surrogate, except in narrowly defined emergencies.* The principle clarifies the meaning of respect for the person and his or her freedom in the context of health care. It not only seeks to prevent medical tyranny and to preserve freedom, but also to encourage rational decision making by the patient, who in the last analysis must live with the consequences of medical treatment or the lack of it. In law, this principle is connected with both the right of privacy (right to noninterference) and with the law on assault and battery, which forbids not only unwanted touches but even the expectation of an unwanted touch. In law, as in ethics, *informed consent* is a crucial concept in medical practice.

Informed Consent

The concept of informed consent is not only complicated and easily misunderstood, but relatively recent in American medical ethics. Indeed, many older health care professionals find it strange, since their tradition calls not for informing the patient, but for concealing things from the patient. They do not seek to gain the consent of patients, but control of them. Hippocrates (after whom the Hippocratic Oath is named) would find the concept of informed consent particularly strange, for he felt that most things should be concealed from patients while they are being cared for and that, in particular, nothing was to be told the patients about their present or future condition.

The great Greek physician obviously did not believe that he needed the patient's consent. Those who use the priestly model of the physician discussed in chapter 1 will still tend to view the relationship with the patient in this paternalistic way. Those who follow the collegial model and see the patient as a full partner in the healing process understand that informed consent is not only an ethical necessity, but a necessary component of health care. Within the contract model, informed consent is the act by which the contract is specified.

Regardless of the health care professional's attitude, the law in the United States insists on informed consent, especially for any invasive procedures, such as those involved in surgery, or treatments with considerable risks involved. In short, to disregard informed consent in the United States is to risk lawsuits. The law in other countries is different, but in the United States, at least since the 1960s, the law has tended to say that the role of the health care professional requires respect for the freedom of the patient and, in particular, that this respect demands informed consent.

The Key Concepts

For informed consent by the patient or, when appropriate, by a lawful surrogate, the following conditions must be present: (1) The patient or appropriate surrogate must be competent or have decision-making capacity, that is, be capable of understanding the consequences of the consent and be free from coercion and undue influence that would substantially diminish freedom; (2) the health care professional, within the demands of his or her particular role, must provide the necessary information and make sure that it is understood. In general, if any one of these conditions is not present, there is no patient-informed consent and so no authorization of treatment. At times, the permission of a court is required before the patient can be treated. It must be stressed that the health care professional does not have a right to treat the patient who is incompetent because she or he is unconscious or drunk or severely retarded. Authorization based on informed consent is required, if not from the patient directly, then from a surrogate. If there is no authorization, this generally means that the health care professional cannot proceed. The exceptions will be discussed after the conditions given previously have been explained more fully.

Competence and Understanding

By *competence*, we mean the ability to perform a certain task. In the context of health care ethics, we mean the ability to make choices based on an understanding of the *relevant consequences* of that choice on oneself and others.[1] The ability to understand the relevant consequences is to be judged by commonsense, rather than a technical or professional standard. According to the common sense standard, the patient must be able to understand such things as the fact that he or she will die or get sicker without treatment or that the treatment will be painful and will result in the patient being out of action for a number of weeks. The competent patient is not to be judged by his or her educational level, nor does the competent patient have to understand everything about the condition or the treatments proposed. Often even a highly trained specialist does not understand everything about a disease or a treatment. Indeed, the physician may not *fully* understand how a common drug like aspirin works. In any event, the *exact how* of the treatment is not always in itself ethically important, whereas *the consequences* are crucial. We are, then, speaking of substantial common sense and not complete medical or scientific understanding. More will be said about this later when we discuss what must be revealed to the patient.

The competent patient must understand the consequences of her or his decision to accept or reject a particular treatment. In particular, the patient should understand that she or he is authorizing or refusing to authorize treatment (Faden and Beauchamp, 1986). The effects of the treatment on the patient's health, life, lifestyle, religious beliefs, values, family, friends, and society are all factors that bear on the ethical decision to accept or reject treatment. So the patient must be capable of understanding consequences in these relevant areas.[2]

The fact that the patient makes a decision contrary to that recommended by the health care professional or even contrary to the general norms of society does not prove that the patient is incompetent because of a lack of understanding. The patient may prefer to suffer the pain from the disease rather than the pain from the treatment. The patient may prefer to die rather than put her family through long agony that leaves them penniless, as well as emotionally drained. This is an important point, since health care providers, like all human beings, must resist the temptation to impose their values on others. Worse yet, the health care provider may forget that medical values and even the value of health and life are not the only valid values in ethical decision making. Physicians are taught, "First, do no harm," but they must remember that the patient is the one who, in most cases, best understands what is truly a harm to her.

Most of this is neatly summarized in the following statement from a publication of the American Hospital Association (1985, p. 9):

> Decision-making capacity is the patient's ability to make choices that reflect an understanding and appreciation of the nature and consequences of one's actions and of alternative actions, and to evaluate them in relation to a person's preferences and priorities. A patient's decision contrary to a physician's recommendation does not in itself indicate incapacity.

Classifying the Incompetent

Because a patient may decide contrary to a physician's recommendation, it is important to recognize that *all physician-patient encounters must begin with the presumption that the patient is competent*. The issue here is the protection of the dignity of the patient, which includes protecting the patient from the interpretation of disagreement as incompetence. Nevertheless, there are times when our intuition clearly tells us that this person ought not be making important decisions for himself. The problem is establishing when our intuitions are correct and when they are self-serving.

There are no handy labels that can be used to classify those who are incompetent to understand the consequences of their decisions. Each case is to be judged individually. People may be unable to perform many tasks, and may not even know what day of the week it is, but still understand the consequences of their decisions. Someone under the age of 18 is not legally competent in most cases, but she or he may well be ethically competent to judge the consequences of health care decisions. People who have been declared legally incompetent to manage their financial affairs or who have been involuntarily committed to a mental institution might still be ethically competent to make a decision about accepting treatment. Many people who have been classified as retarded are quite capable of understanding that they will be in pain if they accept or refuse treatment. Health care professionals cannot ethically treat such persons against their will unless the courts have appointed a guardian specifically to make decisions about treatment. The permission of a parent may protect the health care provider legally in these cases, but when the child is judged competent, the health care professional still has the ethical need for informed consent. We will say more about this problem when we discuss surrogates.

Unconscious people are temporarily incompetent. People under the influence of alcohol or drugs may, to a greater or lesser extent, be temporarily incompetent. A few patients have so permanently lost contact with reality that they may be incapable of understanding any ordinary consequences of their actions. In general, as stated earlier, the assumption is that adults are competent unless there is clear evidence to the contrary. A publication of the American Hospital Association (1985, p. 10) puts it very clearly: "In the absence of indicators to the contrary, hospitals and health care professionals should assume that the adult patient has adequate decision-making capacity."

There are, of course, cases in which the person is incompetent or temporarily incompetent. Residents of long-term-care facilities who are often labeled "pleasantly confused" are probably incompetent, although they may have lucid moments or days in which their ability to assent or dissent must be respected. On the whole, however, the "pleasantly confused" need a surrogate to consent for them. When there are none of the usual surrogates, a guardian needs to be appointed. A surrogate or a guardian alone may suffice for informed consent, but not for the broader tasks of protecting these patients. We will return to the problem of advocacy and protection of patients in chapter 3.

Competency and Freedom

Competence requires not only the ability to understand the consequences of one's decisions, but freedom from coercion and such undue influence that would substantially diminish the freedom of the patient. There is not only a question of coercion, undue manipulation, or ordinary persuasion (Faden and Beauchamp, 1986, p. 337), but also of natural reactions to illness and normal circumstances of health care. High fevers and some drugs can leave anyone temporarily incapable of understanding anything.

Coercion may be seen in the use of force or of drugs equivalent to force. These will invalidate any consent. More often, however, the problem is not one of force but of undue influence. Physicians who threaten patients with the withholding of treatment in the future unless the patient consents here and now are guilty not only of blackmail, but of invalidating the consent obtained. Although such cases exist, they are not the common source of undue influence. Family pressures may constitute undue influence and substantially reduce freedom. The sick person is often dependent on his family and so susceptible to their pressure that he or she cannot envisage bucking the relatives. This pressure is particularly great on children, who are completely dependent on their parents.

Not only outside pressures but normal and natural factors can strongly affect our freedom. All the strong feelings that accompany a serious illness or a hospital stay also have an impact. The exaggerated fears of the timid and the magical hopes of the desperate both distort understanding and affect competence. In addition, the influence of the unconscious and the individual's personal history also affect the decision-making process. These factors do not, however, take away the ability to understand the consequences of one's actions or constitute undue influence or coercion.

It is obvious that no one is ever completely free. The question the health care professional must answer is whether any of these influences, external or natural, substantially diminish the person's freedom so that there is inadequate capacity for a valid consent. There is no easy answer to this question. The evidence of competence or incompetence should be obtained by reflective conversations between physician and patient in which the physician is aware of her or his own biases as well as those of the patient (Katz, 1984, p. 133). In short, the physician and all health care providers are obliged to spend time getting to know the patient and determining the state of the patient's mind and understanding. With Katz, we would stress that "short of substantial evidence of incompetence, choices deserve to be honored."

The Information in Informed Consent

In this context, it should be noted that we are dealing with the need for an explicit consent. The mere fact that a patient seeks the assistance of a health care professional or enters a hospital does not constitute even implicit consent in all cases. In minor matters, however, implicit consent may be present and may suffice for the purpose of informed consent. Thus, a patient who goes voluntarily to a hospital grants implicit consent for a temperature and blood pressure reading. Since nothing is at stake, this is sufficient. By the mere fact of entering the hospital, the patient does not give implicit consent for intrusive procedures such as the taking of blood or the administration of an enema, let alone for an operation. When any real danger or an invasive procedure is involved, the patient needs to know what is being proposed and what the consequences might be. An explicit consent should then be given. In any event, it should be kept firmly in mind that even implicit consent can be revoked. The patient has the right to refuse to have his or her blood pressure taken, even though the patient has already submitted to the procedure a dozen times.

If the patient is to make a mature, free choice with an understanding of the consequences, the health care professional and the physician in particular must provide information about these consequences. The type and extent of the information to be given depends on the criteria for disclosure. There are four conflicting rules or criteria for the disclosure of information to the patient: (1) the patient preference rule, (2) the professional custom rule, (3) the prudent person rule, and (4) the subjective substantial disclosure rule.

The *patient preference rule* dictates that the health care professional tell the patient what the patient wants to know. This rule does not make much sense. Some patients will want a lot more information than they need and can end up wasting time. Others will want no information and so avoid their own responsibility for decisions affecting their health and life. More often than not, patients will not even express a desire for information. Many patients do not know that they have a right and a duty to ask for information. Regardless of the cause of a patient's refusing information or at least not demanding it, patients will end up with inadequate data for a decision. In short, such a rule does not promote autonomy and so is not truly respectful of the patient.

VanDeVeer (1986) defends the idea that the competent patient can delegate the physician to make medical choices about specific forms of treatment under one condition: It is clear that the patient has merely delegated his or her right to make informed choices *about the manner of treatment and not about whether she or he will be treated in the first place*. The authors feel that, in general, this absolves the patient from too much responsibility. It makes sense, however, when the patient has a personal relationship with a health care provider who fully understands the values and desires of the patient. If such a relation exists, the physician *may* know enough to act in accord with the values of the patient, and the patient *may* also have enough experience with the health care professional to trust in this person. These conditions are not to be assumed but established.

The *professional custom rule,* also called the professional community standard, says that the health care professional shall tell the patient what is normally or customarily told patients in similar situations. For a long time this was the operative rule. It is still the rule used by many physicians. There are two major objections to this rule. First, it leaves the health care professional free to abrogate the rights of the patient by suppressing very relevant information. Such suppression can be the worst sort of manipulation, even though it is intended for the good of the patient. Indeed, in some cases it was customary to suppress information that might cause the patient to refuse treatment. One study (Rosoff, 1981, p. 326) notes that as many as 50 percent of the patients would have refused treatment if the potential complications had been revealed to them. As we shall see when we discuss therapeutic privilege, this motive for suppressing information is neither ethical nor legal. Second, research indicates (Rosoff, 1981, pp. 313-457) that the professional custom is a myth. In other words, there is no such thing as a professional standard. In practice, then, the rule means that the physician is using her or his own bias or ignorance as the standard.

The *prudent person rule,* also called the reasonable patient standard, rests on the assumption that the physician's disclosure to the patient should be measured by the patient's need for information material to the decision to refuse or accept treatment. Thus, the rule would have the health care professional provide the information that a prudent, reasonable person would want before making a decision about treatment or the refusal of treatment (Meisel, 1989, p. 27). In practice, this is generally understood to include the first six items below (Rosoff, 1981, p. 318). We have added a seventh, since a reasonable person will want to consider those factors as well.

1. The diagnosis.
2. The nature and purpose of the proposed treatment.
3. The known risks and consequences of the proposed treatment, excluding those eventualities that are too remote and improbable to bear significantly on the decision process of a reasonable person or are too well known to require statement. Included should be the both the provider's and the institution's success and failure rates with the proposed procedures.
4. The benefits to be expected from the proposed treatment, with an assessment of the likelihood that the benefits can be realized.
5. All alternative treatments that might reasonably be used. All the information mentioned in items 3 and 4 is to be given about the alternatives as well.
6. The prognosis if no treatment is given.
7. All costs, including the amount and duration of the pain generally involved, the potential impact on lifestyle and ability to resume work, as well as the

economic costs of both the treatment and aftercare. The patient should also be told whether or not insurance will cover the bills.

The *subjective substantial disclosure rule* (Faden and Beauchamp, 1986) calls for the health care professional to describe to the patient everything that would be material or important to the particular patient and not merely to a fictional reasonable and prudent person who makes the decision. A factor would be material or important if it could change the decision of a particular patient. This rule brings in the subjective and objective factors important to the individual patient and not merely those important to a hypothetical objective prudent person. The application of this rule demands that the health care professional really get to know the patient and determine what is important to him or her. This in turn calls for real dialogue between patient and professional or between surrogate and professional.

We favor a combination of the prudent person and substantial disclosure rules because, together, they best assure that the particular patient will have the information needed for a sound decision from the patient's point of view. Thus, the patient should be informed of all the things a prudent person would want to know, plus the things that are of importance to this particular patient.

The consent forms used in many hospitals do not provide the information required by any of these principles. They are too close to blank checks to have any moral or ethical value. In the authors' opinion, they do not suffice as ethical authorization of treatment, even though the law may occasionally give them some weight.

Making the Information Understandable

Because the purpose of the information is to enable the patient or the surrogate to make choices based on an understanding of the consequences, there is an obligation to present the information in such a way that the patient or surrogate does indeed understand the consequences. In short, the obligation to obtain informed consent before proceeding involves an *obligation to actually communicate and not merely an obligation to spout facts* (Hartlaub, Wolkenstein, and Laufenburg, 1993). A recital of all the technical details and the use of technical language may not only fail to increase comprehension, but may actually destroy understanding. The mere fact that a patient has signed a consent form saying she or he has been told the facts does not mean that informed consent has been given. To be content with a mere recitation of the facts and the signing of a form makes a mockery of the patient. Even when the law accepts such forms as proof of informed consent, ethics demands that the health care professional make sure that the patient understands the consequences in terms of the things that are important to the patient. If there is no understanding, there is no agreement and so no authorization to proceed.

Difficulties with Informing the Patient

We have already spoken of the obstacles to effective communication with the patient. At this point, it is necessary to mention a very real professional problem that occurs both because of the nature of medical knowledge and the emotional blocks of health care professionals and of patients.

Uncertainty and the Need for Continued Discussion

Although medicine speaks of itself as being scientific, knowledge in the field is anything but certain (Bursztajn et al., 1981; Duncan and Weston-Smith, 1984). To a very large extent, the health care professional knows only the general probabilities for classes of patients. When it comes time to apply these probabilities to individual patients, the probabilities lose much of their predictive value. That is, the odds that a cure will result or that a certain side effect will occur are largely unknown in the case of a particular patient. Further, as treatment progresses more information will be available. What works or does not work, how much improvement or continued decline the patient is suffering, and what other problems are appearing, are all factors which must be considered.

There may be difficulty in deciding how much of the health care professional's uncertainty should be shared with the patient. This is an emotional problem for the physician, the nurse, the physical therapist, and other members of the health care team, since sharing uncertainty may take away some of the professional mystique as well as upset the patient who wants reassurance. Although too much uncertainty can paralyze the ability to act, the refusal to face uncertainty and ignorance has sometimes led to irresponsible treatments (Katz, 1984). In other cases, certainty is purely subjective, a result of the physician's personal preferences or hopes, rather than of scientific research.

Uncertainty can also be a problem for the patient, who does not want to face the ambiguities of the situation. Although no one wants to cause the patient additional suffering, if the patient is to be a full participant in his or her treatment, the patient must be informed (see chapter 1 on the collegial model and the discussion later in this chapter on therapeutic privilege) and kept aware of his developing medical condition. It can be argued that sharing the uncertainty can ultimately build trust and that, in any event, the failure to share uncertainty is inimical to shared decision making between physician and patient. Informed consent calls for just that sort of continual discussion and sharing.

Is Informed Consent Possible?

All the difficulties and distinctions made thus far can call into question the very possibility of informed consent. If we add to this that the health care professional is often an authority figure with power and the patient a more or less powerless individual under great stress, the question of the possibility becomes more serious. Before attempting to answer the question of the possibility of informed consent, let us first clarify the point at issue.

Informed consent does not demand full freedom of choice. Indeed, few human acts are ever fully free, and certainly no human acts are made without the influence of many factors. Second, although impartial presentation of the facts and perfect understanding of the consequences is the ideal, this ideal is seldom reached. People under stress, both patients and health care professionals, operate at less than optimal levels of rationality. It follows, then, that a perfectly informed consent is impossible.

If one assumes that perfectly informed consent is perfectly rational, that is, objectively and unemotionally derived from certain premises, in the manner of geometry, then a perfect informed consent is not necessarily desirable. Ethics is concerned with good and evil. Of necessity, then, it is bound up with love, fear, hate, ideals, ambitions, and other emotions. In such situations, the ethical health care professional will be trying to persuade the patient even as she or he provides information as honestly as possible. The concern and convictions of the health care provider are important and need not be suppressed, only controlled. On the other hand, the fears and ideals of the patient need to be respected, because they are connected with the patient's values and history and are not merely annoying obstacles to communication. As mentioned earlier, it is the patient who identifies what is truly harmful to him. In short, informed consent involves a conversation between patient and physician that allows the exchange of relevant information, a shared analysis of that information, and, ultimately, a decision by the patient (Meisel and Kuczewski, 1996). It must not be forgotten that this is a conversation that must continue as new information about the patient's condition emerges and new decisions are to be made.

PATERNALISM: WEAK AND STRONG

The difficulties in informing the patient can be very frustrating, and may lead to the desire to simply move forward with treatment for the patient's benefit. This conflict between respect for autonomy and the desire to help the patient brings us to the problem of paternalism. The word *paternalism* is derived from the Latin word *pater*, meaning "father." In its dictionary meaning, it refers to a ruling or controlling of others in a way that suggests a father's relationship with his children. In the context of health care ethics, paternalism involves acting without consent or even overriding a person's wishes, wants, or actions in order to benefit the patient or at least to prevent harm to the patient. There are two elements here: first, the absence of consent or even the overriding of consent and, second, the beneficent motive (the welfare of the patient).

It is not paternalism when the health care provider acts to prevent the patient from causing serious injury to others. This is a delegated exercise of the police power of the state and is authorized by law. There is also no question of paternalism if the health care professional overrules the patient for the convenience or profit of the provider. The nurse who, in a desire to finish her charting, gives a painful treatment before a narcotic has taken effect is not being paternalistic. Such cases constitute pure tyranny. Nor is paternalism at work if the health care professional refuses to go along with the patient's wishes because these wishes are against the conscience or professional standards of the provider. In this case, the professional is acting for the sake of his or her own conscience and not specifically for the welfare of the patient. In any event, the health care professional is not the mere servant of the patient.

Paternalism exists, however, when the health care worker intervenes to prevent patients from harming themselves in some serious way. This paternalism is authorized by law in the case of those attempting suicide. Whether it is ethical depends not only on the factors discussed in this chapter, but on deeper issues of life and death, which will be discussed in chapter 7.

It is useful to distinguish between strong (also called *extended*) paternalism, which attempts to overrule or override *the wishes of a competent person*, and weak (or limited and restricted) paternalism, in which consent is missing or the health care provider overrules or overrides the wishes of an incompetent or a doubtfully competent patient. Weak paternalism is sometimes called *cooperative paternalism* when one of its purposes is to restore the person's competence so that the patient may give informed consent.

Strong paternalism involves the usurpation, that is, the coercive seizure, of the patient's right to make decisions. As noted at the beginning of this chapter, even the government does not have the right to overrule its citizens except when necessary to protect the rights of others or when there is an overriding state interest.

In practice, many governments, including that of the United States, practice paternalism. Strong paternalism on the part of the government is justified only for the promotion of substantial state interests and the protection of the rights of others.

The government more frequently engages in weak paternalism, although the justice of this is debatable. The law recognizes the right of parents over their children on the assumption that the children are not fully competent, although the extent of even the parent's right to be paternalistic is debated. Also, most states authorize involuntary commitment to a mental institution of a mentally ill person whose actions are dangerous to herself (Beis, 1984, pp. 114-135). If we make the judgment that mental illness is an indication of doubt about competency to give informed consent, this is a form of weak rather than strong paternalism. Even so, this weak paternalism is surrounded by all sorts of legal protections, including the right to counsel.

The government, however, *has not authorized health care providers to use strong paternalism* and appears to authorize weak paternalism in only a limited number of cases.

From an ethical point of view, writers generally reject the right of health care providers to use strong paternalism. Quite aside from the fundamental issue of authority over others, there is the basic question of the competence of an individual to decide what is best for another person and, in particular, for a competent adult. Competence to make such decisions requires knowledge of both the values of others and all the factors influencing their lives. Health care providers and patients do not necessarily share the same values. The health care professional, for example, may believe that life is precious no matter what. The patient may believe that life without the ability to move about is meaningless. Health care professionals certainly do not have the right to enforce value judgments on the patient on the grounds that "Doctor knows best." Finally, it would be a rare health care professional who knew all the factors influencing the life of a patient. In short, professionals lack the competence to decide what is best for another and so have no right to use strong paternalism.

Sometimes those who justify strong paternalism in health care act as if there were only one correct decision in every case. It is good to remind ourselves that more than one good decision is often possible, especially when we are operating not in a world of certainty, but in one in which probabilities are often all we have to go on. Most of all, we must stress the fact that decisions about health, life, and death are not merely medical decisions, but involve the good of society and the good of third parties, as well as the values of the patient. Although the health care provider is competent to give advice about the medical aspects and even the medical odds, the patient has the right and obligation to make the decision and lay bets.

Although it appears impossible to justify strong paternalism in the health care setting, the problem of weak paternalism remains. As we noted in the discussion of exceptions in nonemergencies, the courts have sometimes allowed treatment without informed consent to relieve serious pain or suffering. To the extent that this treatment will remove doubts about the competency of the person and allow informed consent, we tend to think it is justified. Here the treatment is directly in the service of autonomy.

Another example of weak paternalism may be found in the use of restraints. In the hospital setting, the temporary use of restraints is often justified on the grounds that the patient is confused and disoriented and so likely to injure himself. Hospitals recognize the dangers of this policy and typically accompany the use of restraints with various safeguards, such as periodic visits to the patient, approval of supervisors or the physician if the restraints are to be used over a long period, and written justification of their use. Granted all the proper institutional safeguards, restraints may be justified by weak paternalism.

The problem of paternalism is even more complicated in the mental health setting. The American Psychiatric Association (1995) urges that the law permit at least a short period of involuntary confinement and treatment if *all four* of the following conditions are present: (1) Evidence must indicate that the person's mental illness is treatable and that the treatment is available; (2) the person must be obviously so mentally ill that he or she is incompetent to make medical decisions; (3) evidence of mental deterioration, such as delusions or hallucinations, must be clear; (4) the person must obviously be suffering.

Although the authors are not completely at ease with this approach, it is a genuine example of weak paternalism and appears to be ethically justified as long as time limits are placed on the involuntary hospitalization. Although we admit that weak paternalism is justified in some cases, we insist that there is *no general authorization* for even weak paternalism.[3] Each case needs to be studied, and exceptions should be made carefully.

The principle of autonomy and its relationship to paternalism cannot be fully understood until we have studied the principle of benevolence. We note that the struggle between paternalists and those who put autonomy in first place is a struggle about whether benevolence or autonomy is primary. This will appear more clearly after the consideration of benevolence in chapter 3.[4]

Therapeutic Privilege

Physicians have long claimed and the law has often recognized an exception called the therapeutic privilege (Rosovsky, 1984, pp. 98–102). Therapeutic privilege is *the privilege of withholding information from the patient when the physician believes that the disclosure will have an adverse effect on the patient's condition or health*. This is a specific form of strong paternalism in that the physician is making a decision for a competent person on the grounds of an anticipated emotional difficulty.

Even those who justify the privilege limit it by placing three conditions on its use. First, use of the privilege must not be based on generalities, but on the actual circumstances of a particular patient. That is, it must be used on a case-by-case basis. Second, the physician must have a founded belief, based on an intimate knowledge of the person, that the full disclosure will have a *significantly adverse effect* on the patient. The mere fact that the patient will be disturbed by bad news is not a sufficient justification for the use of the privilege. Third, reasonable discretion must be used in the manner and extent of the disclosure. The physician may not be justified in concealing all the information. For example, although a physician might argue that even the word *cancer* would seriously harm the patient and justify concealing the diagnosis, this would not justify concealing the fact that the treatment was extremely painful. The same general principles apply to all health care professionals, although it is not clear that the law will protect them.

According to Rosovsky (1984, p. 101), the privilege cannot be legally used in a case in which the reason for withholding the information is the belief that the patient will refuse treatment if told the whole story. In short, the privilege does not justify denying a person the ability to choose just because one suspects the patient might choose differently than the physician. Rosovsky also notes that the privilege is not a justification of the misrepresentation of significant facts or fraud or willful misrepresentation. It is one thing to withhold information, but quite another to deceive the patient. Additional discussion of the problem of deception is given in chapter 5 in the discussion of confidentiality and truthfulness.

Although the therapeutic privilege may sound reasonable enough at first glance, there are two serious problems with it. In the first place, research fails to find cases in which the disclosure of information has a significant adverse effect on the patient's condition or health. In the second place, it is a denial of patient autonomy.

THE CONSENT OF CHILDREN, ADOLESCENTS, AND INCOMPETENT PATIENTS

There is not enough time in an introductory text to treat all the problems involved in the ethics of consent of children and adolescents. Interested parties should consult Morrissey, Hoffman, and Thorpe, (1986). Their treatment of the law in this area also raises key ethical questions. It is important to recognize that the ability of the child or adolescent to consent depends on both the actual and legal status and the need of the patient, that is, the seriousness and nature of the health problem. Moreover, because society does not appear to have a uniform outlook on the matter, no easy solution is possible. The law, whether in statutes or court decisions, gives social specifications of rights and obligations. Unfortunately, in the case of health care for children, the law is a blend of older theories that gave preference to the rights of parents and later theories that gave first place to the child's welfare and, more recently, to the rights of the child.

Surrogates

The previous sections have made it quite clear that surrogates are important in health care ethics. Surrogates or substitutes are people who are authorized by law or custom to make decisions when the patient is incompetent or doubtfully competent. There is, however, no handy list of surrogates that can be relied on with certitude. Ordinarily, parents are considered surrogates for their minor children, spouses for one another, adult children for parents when parents are lacking, grandparents for grandchildren, and, when sons and daughters are lacking, adult grandchildren for grandparents, not to mention brothers and sisters as well as uncles and aunts. In our society, the surrogates follow the kinship lines on the assumption that these relatives are likely to know the values if not the desires of the patient and can be trusted to act in the best interests of the patient.

Assumptions, however, yield to the facts (Emanuel and Emanuel, 1992). In many cases, health care providers find themselves caught in a crossfire between two or more potential surrogates. The father of the child may consent to treatment while the mother refuses. The wife may say yes while the brothers and sisters of the patient shout no. Equally difficult is the situation in which the provider suspects a conflict between the interests of the patient and the interests of the surrogate. For example, the surrogate may want the patient to die in order to make life simpler, even though the patient could still have a reasonable life if treated. As noted in the previous section, the health care professional may know that what the patient desired when competent is at odds with the decision of the surrogate. The patient may have expressed a desire to have life-saving measures omitted when he or she becomes terminal, while the spouse may want heroic if futile measures continued. If a quick decision is necessary, these conflicts may not be resolvable, and the physician may need to refer to hospital policy or law to identify a surrogate in the crisis. When in doubt, the first concern is to do no harm. When there is more time before a decision is necessary, it can be hoped that a longer discussion between the health care provider and the family will reach an agreement (Kuczewski, 1996). In chapter 3, we will devote time to the principles that govern the obligations and so the decisions of surrogates.

In all these cases, the health care professional must proceed with caution and be ready to seek court intervention when the desires of the patient or the patient's apparent best interests are being neglected. In short, surrogates do not and should not always have the last word.

Who Shall Inform the Patient or the Surrogate?

Most writers on medical ethics assume that the physician has the obligation to inform the patient or surrogate. There is no doubt that the physician has the primary and principal obligation to inform. Other health care providers, especially those who are legally independent practitioners, like nurses and physical therapists, also have obligations in this area. Finally, hospitals and other health care institutions appear to have at least supervisory responsibility to make sure that their employees have informed the patient when it is their duty to do so (Annas, 1981). One root of the obligation of informed consent is the legal idea that an unwanted touch constitutes battery. As a result, everyone who touches the patient needs the patient's informed consent (Graber et. al., 1985). Although it may be assumed that the signature on a consent form gives consent or that the physician has obtained such consent for treatment, nurses, physical thera- pists, medical technicians, and respiratory therapists will encounter cases in which this is obviously not true. When the patient asks what is going on, what drug is being administered, or why an enema is being given (a proce- dure that invades the body, if only in a minor way), the question should be answered *within the limits of the expertise of the particular health care provider.* That is, providers should not go beyond their own professional compe- tence. If a patient does not even know that she or he is being prepared for an operation (and such cases do occur), supervisors should be informed, more formal procedures instituted, and formal, detailed written proof of informed consent obtained.

The report of the American Hospital's Committee on Biomedical Ethics (American Hospital Association, 1985, p. 8) notes the following obligations of the hospital with regard to informed consent:

1. ensure that informed consent has been obtained for diagnostic and therapeu- tic procedures performed in the hospital
2. develop educational programs that teach effective ways of obtaining ethically and legally acceptable informed consent
3. make certain that patients are aware of their right to consent or reject pro- posed procedures and treatments.

The AHA report also suggests that hospitals may wish to have mate- rials available that can be understood by patients or to have arrangements with libraries for obtaining such materials. Such suggestions are in line with the spirit as well as the letter of the law in the area of autonomy. Indeed, they indicate sensitivity to the need for a provider-patient coopera- tion that not only respects patients but improves health care in general.

EXCEPTIONS IN EMERGENCIES

The obligation to obtain informed consent before proceeding to treat a patient included in its statement an exception for emergencies. For there to be an emergency justifying treatment without informed consent, three con- ditions must be present (Rosoff, 1981, p. 14).

1. The patient must be incapable of giving consent and no lawful surrogate is available to give the consent.
2. There is danger to *life* or danger of a *serious impairment of health.*
3. *Immediate* treatment is necessary to avert these dangers.

The authors believe that, from an ethical perspective, the first condition should be modified to include the words *and the wishes of the patient are not known*. If the wishes of the patient are known, that is, if a living will or a clear directive exists beforehand, the fact of incompetence does not destroy the wishes of the patient. Both the surrogate and the health care professional should follow these known wishes, since one is not dealing with a narrowly defined emergency.

Although the authors' clear support of advanced directives is not universally accepted, we base our support on two basic ideas. First, health care professionals need informed consent in order to lay hands on the patient. This consent is not to be presumed when the patient has given advanced directives to the contrary. Second, the authors' basic stand on the relationship of the individual to society demands the principle enunciated by the New Jersey Supreme Court in the *Jobes*[5] and related cases. This principle stresses the general primacy of the right to self-determination over the state's countervailing interests. Exceptions to this general rule should be determined by the legislature or the courts, since only the society is competent to decide when its interests are preeminent.

The need for treatment must be so immediate that even a delay to get a consent or to find a surrogate would endanger the patient's life (Meisel, 1989, p. 36). In most cases, this condition will not be met.

A careful look at these conditions indicates that most visits to a hospital emergency room do not involve the sort of emergency that justifies treating without consent. For many so-called emergencies, treatment can be delayed (without danger to life or a risk of serious impairment of health) until the person regains consciousness or until a surrogate can be reached.

This narrowly defined emergency exception is justified on the ground that consent can be safely assumed in those cases in which a reasonable person who accepted the ordinary community view of things would consent if properly informed. This is a reasonable assumption and is probably verifiable in the vast majority of emergencies in this narrowly defined sense. Thus, no one raises serious questions about the use of the exception. The question of whether similar assumptions hold when the person is of doubtful competence and in a nonemergency situation requires separate consideration.

Exceptions in Nonemergencies

In line with what has already been said, the following statements can be made. If the person is competent and refuses treatment, there should be no treatment in either emergencies or nonemergencies. If the patient is doubtfully competent and refuses treatment in a nonemergency, the benefit of the doubt goes to the patient, unless the health care provider seeks and obtains a court order. Problems arise, however, with clearly incompetent persons in nonemergency situations.

We must at the very start recognize that there is a temptation to justify treatment of the incompetent patient, because any decent human being, especially one dedicated to the healing arts, finds it difficult to stand by and let another person suffer when something could be done. The emotions seem to dictate that the principle of benevolence "Do good" (see chapter 3) takes precedence over the principle of autonomy and the necessity for informed consent. Traditional medical ethics based on the priestly model certainly gave benevolence the first place over autonomy. That this is the correct answer is not clear either legally or ethically. Some law courts have held that a physician can treat without consent not only when there is serious danger to life or health, but when it is necessary to relieve great pain and suffering (Rosoff, 1981, p. 16); however, this appears to be the exception today. Indeed, Rosovsky (1984, p. 90) simply states that "when patients are incapacitated but do not require life—or health— saving treatment, practitioners cannot proceed." Legally, then, health care providers generally proceed at their own risk when they treat incompetent or doubtfully competent persons in nonemergencies.

Ethically, it remains questionable whether the mere fact that it is possible to do some good *authorizes* a person to treat an incompetent or doubtfully competent person when no surrogate is present to give or refuse consent. At this point, basic attitudes toward life and one's neighbor enter into the picture. On the one side are those who believe that they are their brothers' keepers and see the possible good as justifying intervention. On the other side are those who, like the authors, hold that we are *not* our brothers' keepers and so permit no additional exceptions to the need for informed consent.

The position of the authors can be stated very simply. As a rule, one individual does not have authority over another. If the health care professional feels that action in nonemergencies is required (1) when competency is nonexistent or doubtful, (2) or when there is no advanced directive such as a living will (see chapter 7), the legal system should be used to get a guardian who can give a consent. In short, the freedom of individuals should have the protection of due process and the law even in health care settings. We note in passing that at least one court (Meisel, 1989, supp. 1991, p. 27) has determined that a surrogate of a nursing home patient treated without consent did not have to pay the nursing home for unpaid bills. Further developments in this direction will certainly make health care institutions more careful about obtaining informed consent.

When in Doubt, There Are Courts

In the preceding discussion, it is assumed that no surrogates were available to give or refuse consent for the incompetent or doubtfully competent person. In serious nonemergencies, it is always possible to seek the help of the courts, which can, on brief investigation, appoint a guardian *ad litem*, that is, a guardian for this specific instance. The court-appointed guardian is, then, the lawful surrogate who can consent to or refuse treatment in line with the best interests of the patient or the rational choice principle. This procedure can also be used when the health care provider thinks that the surrogates are not acting in the best interests of the patient. In any event, recourse to the courts protects the health care providers from lawsuits even as it keeps them from assuming unjustified authority over patients.

The courts are not the ideal place to make such decisions, for the intrusion of the legal system into patient care can be cumbersome, expensive, and insensitive. But in the absence of patient competency, proper surrogates, or clear legislative directions, societal protection of rights through the courts is both necessary and appropriate. Even the American Hospital Association (1985, p. 13) suggests that the courts should be consulted in the following five cases:

1. The incapacity is great and likely to be prolonged, and there is no obvious surrogate.
2. The capacity of the patient is questionable, and the decision to be made is significant.
3. The views of the surrogate are strongly at variance with the medical judgment or the patient's known views.
4. The choice of the individual to serve as surrogate is controversial, and all efforts to resolve the matter at the hospital level have failed.
5. Family members radically disagree about the course of action in the case of a patient who lacks adequate decision-making capacity.

Although no one wants the courts to practice medicine, it is clear that the suggestions given by the American Hospital Association recognize that human rights, and not merely health care, are involved. The courts are rightfully concerned with human rights.

The Role of Institutional Ethics Committees

In some institutions, Institutional Ethics Committees (IECs) are now consulted in cases in which surrogates are involved. Institutional Ethics Committees are multidisciplinary groups of health care professionals, frequently with community representatives, set up in health care institutions to educate the public about biomedical ethics, to help in policy development, and to act as consultants in difficult cases (see chapter 6). The consultation function is controversial because in some cases it has led to the committee's making decisions or unduly influencing decisions that are more properly the province of the patient, the surrogate, or the individual health care professional (Siegler, 1986, and Olson et. al., 1994). In addition, although the legal status of these committees is not at all clear (Wolf, 1986), some writers (Lo, 1987) feel that the courts will respect committee recommendations. Meisel (1989, p. 473) notes that neither the courts nor statutes create an obligation to follow the advice of an ethics committee.

The New York State Task Force on Life and the Law (1986) proposes using the ethics committee rather than the courts in resolving conflicts and dilemmas about patient care. This would make the committee into a mediator. Although this sounds admirable, the following cautions seem in order (Lo, 1987). First, since the goals of the committee are not always clear, some committees dominated by health care professionals might end up confirming prognoses, providing emotional support for health care professionals, or reducing legal liability, rather than protecting the rights of patients. Second, many committees limit participation by patients and families so that the most important actors in the ethical drama are left out. Indeed, many committees have no nurses on them, even though nurses are the professionals in most frequent contact with patients and their families. If, in addition, the committee is loaded with physicians, the mediations and recommendations may reflect the value of the medical profession, rather than the values of the patients. Finally, the tendency of some committees to operate in secrecy, to omit recommendations and reasoning in the medical record, and to refuse to permit review of their recommendations casts doubt on the integrity of these committees. All committees should keep in mind that they may become legally liable for their decisions and recommendations (Meisel, 1989, p. 480).

The Hastings Center *Guidelines* (1987) contain a valuable section on ethics committees. In their treatment of review of ongoing cases (prospective review), the *Guidelines* stress points that, as a matter of policy and sound ethics, should be made clear to patients and surrogates. Among other questions that demand clear answers are the following:

1. Is consultation of the committee optional?
2. Are recommendations merely advisory?
3. Must the patient or surrogate consent to a committee review?
4. Does the committee consider only ethical problems?
5. What constitutes a quorum of the committee?
6. Do recommendations require a consensus?
7. Will a written record be kept in the patient's record?

Every one of these questions demands serious thought, because each involves an ethical issue. Since we do not have easy answers to the questions, it should be clear why the ethics of the Institutional Ethics Committee are still being debated. Only experience and time will allow us to form a final judgment about the utility and the ethicality of particular features of the committee.

Despite the problems, the authors would like to insist on three points. First, from an ethical point of view it seems clear that the IEC is not a surrogate and so is not authorized to make decisions for incompetent patients or their surrogates. Only the law can give such authorization. Second, even though the IEC is not a surrogate, when consulting on ongoing cases, the ethics committee can and should act primarily as a guardian of patient's rights. Third, the functions of the committee should be clearly and publicly announced and its recommendations and decisions open to review.

Along with the growth of ethics committees, we have seen the birth of medical ethics consultants who may or may not be part of an ethics committee. Their ethical problems are treated in Fletcher, Quist, and Jonsen (1989).

THE RIGHT TO REFUSE TREATMENT

The principle of patient autonomy clearly implies that the patient or the surrogate has the right to refuse treatment. The right does not depend on whether the refusal makes good sense to someone else, but only on the competence of the patient. Mental patients have the right to refuse treatment, although the exact scope of the right is sometimes blurred (Beis, 1984, p. 153). Even in a psychiatric facility, the right to refuse treatment remains unless it is specifically ordered by a court.

The American Hospital Association's Bill of Patient's Rights (1992) summarizes this right rather neatly:

> 4. The patient has the right to refuse treatment to the extent permitted by law and to be informed of the medical consequences of his actions.

This right to refuse, however, does not imply that the patient is ethical in refusing treatment in any and all cases. Whereas the health care provider is not ethical in forcing treatment on the patient or, with rare exceptions, in treating without informed consent, the patient, like the health care professional, must respect the principles of beneficence and nonmaleficence, which will be discussed in chapter 3. This becomes a particularly emotional and difficult issue when a patient refuses life-sustaining treatment. This can easily require a health care provider to stand by while a patient dies, and few are comfortable with that. As we shall see in chapter 7, this tension has led to many disputes, a lot of thought, and significant court cases, as the ethics dilemma spills over into law.

For example, Israel has taken the unusual step of disassociating *consent for treatment* from a *refusal of treatment* (Gross, 1999). Consent demands the discussion and respect for the patient we have just presented, but when any patient refuses life-sustaining treatment the agreement of an ethics committee is necessary for that refusal to take effect. This committee may force treatment over the patient's objection if the patient has been appropriately informed, the treatment is expected to provide significant improvement, and "there is a reasonable expectation that after the treatment the patient will give his/her consent" (Gross, p. 15). The main objection to this approach is that it deprives the patient of significant control over his treatment; if the patient cannot refuse, what is the point of consenting? There is so much turmoil over any refusal of life-sustaining treatment, however, that this is how the Israeli legislature has tried to defuse the problem. We will return to this issue several times during the course of this book.

PROBLEM AREAS

The principle of autonomy poses special problems in psychiatric facilities. The same is especially true of nursing homes (Uhlmann et. al., 1987). Since nursing homes have an ever-increasing number of residents, the ethical problems will only increase rather than decrease. Many of the residents of these homes are threatened by dementia, physical frailty, and prejudices against the elderly. It is estimated that as many as 50 percent of the residents are intellectually impaired. In many cases it is hard to find out what the resident values or wishes, while the usual surrogates such as spouses and relatives may not be easily available.

In the face of these problems, nursing home administrators and health care professionals should take at least the following steps to protect autonomy. First, before or shortly after admission, the resident, or, if the resident is incompetent, his or her surrogate, should be informed of various decisions that may have to be made in the future. They should then be asked for a written directive, if not a living will or a durable power of attorney, that will specify their wishes in important medical decisions. It is understood that these directives are subject to change. Since December 1, 1991, any health care agency receiving either Medicare or Medicaid money must follow the federal *Patient Self-Determination Act* (Omnibus Budget Reconciliation Act, 1990), which requires among other things that, on admission, institutions must ask patients whether they have advance directives. The agency must document such directives and, if there are none, tell the patient about the living will and durable power of attorney, as well as inform the patients of their right to refuse treatment in line with the appropriate state law. The act also requires the health care agency to tell patients about its policies for implementing these laws (Hudson, 1991). (We will return to the living will and durable power of attorney in chapter 7.) Second, a surrogate should be appointed by the resident if the resident is competent or by a court if the resident is incompetent. All this should be attached in writing to the medical record.

A fuller development of these ideas, along with a sample form and policy that present both principles and applications, may be found in Uhlmann et. al. (1987).[6]

SUMMARY

The principle of autonomy demands that a health care provider not treat a patient without the informed consent of the patient or the patient's surrogate except in narrowly defined emergencies. To follow this principle, the health care provider must decide whether the patient is competent to understand the consequences of the consent to or refusal of treatment and is free enough to give consent. To help the competent patient or the surrogate in making a decision, the health care professional and, in particular, the physician must give the diagnosis, the prognosis with and without treatment, and reasonable alternative treatments, as well as inform the patient of the economic, psychic, and social costs of the treatment. In addition to the emergency exception, cases exist in which weak paternalistic intervention can probably be justified. In cases of doubt, a court order should be sought. These obligations created by the principle of autonomy often seem to be in conflict with the principle of beneficence, which will be treated in chapter 3.

Special procedures are needed to protect autonomy in places such as psychiatric facilities and nursing homes.

CASES FOR ANALYSIS

The cases following each chapter illustrate the issues discussed in the chapter. Although actual events and sometimes the public record supplied the raw materials for these cases, they have been edited to illustrate ethical problems, rather than as actual detailed reports. In most cases we have changed names. We have retained actual names only when the case is so famous as to require that identification.

Because some of the events described took place many years ago, the state of health care reflected is not up to date in all cases. The ethical problems are real.

At the end of each case, we pose questions to help the reader identify the ethics problems presented. We also note when a case can be readily used for another chapter. We stress that the fact that an ethical principle cannot answer the ethical questions without reference to the particular facts in the case and a review of all conditions necessary for the application of the principle. In short, the reader must reason about both facts and principles in order to answer the questions in a reasonable way.

1. Mrs. G. has an aneurysm in her brain, that if untreated by surgery, will lead to blindness and probably death. The surgery recommended leads to death in 75 percent of all cases. Of those who survive the operation, nearly 75 percent are crippled. Mrs. G. has three small children. Her husband has a modest job, and his health insurance will cover the operation, but not the expenses that will result if she is crippled.

When informed of all this, Mrs. G. is in great turmoil for a week or so until she makes her decision. She refuses treatment because she does not like the odds. There was, after all, only one chance out of sixteen for a real recovery. In addition, she could not come to grips with exposing her family to the risk of having a mother who would be a burden and not a help.

Can a patient with serious social obligations, such as a family, refuse treatment? What odds for recovery would be good odds?

2. Mrs. Ursula Stack, a 75-year-old housewife, becomes aware of breathlessness and is easily fatigued. She is known to have had a heart murmur for two years. She consents to come to a research hospital for cardiac catheterization, which confirms the presence of severe, calcific aortic stenosis with secondary congestive heart failure.

Because of the unfavorable prospect for survival without surgical intervention, the recommendation at the combined cardiac medical-surgical conference is for an operation. The physician explains the situation to Mr. and Mrs. Stack and recommends aortic valve replacement. It is noted that the risk of surgery is not well known for Mrs. Stack's age group, and that early mortality is usually around 10 percent, with 80 percent good functional results after three years. Her lack of other obvious disease makes her a relatively good candidate for a successful surgical outcome despite her age.

Mrs. Stack appears to understand the discussion and recommendation, but requests deferral of the decision and shows signs of denial of the problem. She has no other medical problems, her husband is in good health, and their marriage appears happy. They are financially secure and enjoy a full set of social and recreational activities. She returns on three subsequent occasions for simple, supportive attention. The physician decides not to employ psychiatric assistance or other measures to reduce her denial and begins to use conversation to reduce her anxiety associated with her decision.

Does Mrs. Stack's apparent denial of her condition make informed consent impossible? Is the physician ethical in reducing her anxiety about her apparent refusal of treatment when the physician believes treatment is medically indicated?

3. John, 17 years old, is seriously injured while jumping from a train on which he had been hitching a ride. Taken to a nearby hospital, he is given emergency treatment by Dr. Lycanthropus, who judges that the boy's right arm will have to be amputated below the elbow because it had been crushed beyond repair. Two other physicians are consulted and agree that the amputation should be done immediately to protect John's life.

John is unconscious as a result of an anesthetic administered to allow the suturing of a head wound that was bleeding profusely. Attempts to contact the boy's parents in a neighboring town are unsuccessful. Dr. Lycanthropus amputates.

Should the physicians have obtained informed consent before they gave the anesthetic? Even superficial head wounds tend to bleed profusely and the pain could have been stopped with a local anesthesia. Is this a case for the emergency exception?

4. Charlene is a devout Jehovah's Witness. A teaching of her religion is that is it wrong to accept blood transfusions, because they are understood to be equivalent to eating blood, a practice prohibited by the Bible. She is pregnant, and insists to her obstetrician that if she hemorrhages during her delivery the physician cannot give her any transfusions. The obstetrician objects, because of the small but real risk to her and her baby. Even if she is willing to accept the risks involved, can she make this decision for her baby? Should the physician try to overrule her refusal, by either going to the ethics committee or the courts?

5. Jerry, age 11, is hospitalized and diagnosed as having schizophrenia. His parents are told that he should be given an antipsychotic medication to clear up his thoughts. Having been told that only this medication will help, the parents give consent without any additional information. Jerry is given prolixin. After being on the drug for two months, he starts to develop strange movements. Without warning, his arm jerks straight up over his head, or his foot and leg jerk from time to time. These movements are uncontrollable. This was diagnosed as tardive dyskinesia. These are side effects suffered by most patients who use the drug for a long time. In 1 or 2 percent of the cases, the side effects severely incapacitate the patient. Some experts argue that there is virtually no danger if the antipsychotics are used for only a short time.

Should the physician have informed the patient of the side effects, which are serious and always occur with continued usage? Does therapeutic privilege apply here?

6. Mary, confined to a wheelchair, has no living relatives and no friends. She is a very lonely 19-year-old woman. She seems to have no interests in life except taking care of her long red hair and reading *True Confessions*. She has been diagnosed as having small-cell cancer of the lung. This cancer sometimes responds very well to chemotherapy. If it does not respond to the treatment almost at once, it is fatal and the patient dies within months. The treatments leave a person very weak for a long time and cause hair loss. The physician tells Mary of the diagnosis and prognosis without treatment but tells her nothing about the side effects, lest she decide to refuse treatment.

Is therapeutic privilege properly and ethically invoked in this case? Quite aside from concealment of the side effects, has the physician revealed sufficient information for an informed consent? Is Mary competent to consent or to refuse?

NOTES

1. Buchanan and Brock (1989) argue that the standard of competence must include both self-determination and patient well-being. Unfortunately, *all things considered*, others cannot judge the well-being of the patient. When we attempt to make such judgments, we end up imposing our judgment or the group's judgment on the individual. We insist that this is tyranny except when done for overriding state interests.

2. Some writers make the conditions for competence so strict that, if applied, most people would be judged incompetent most of the time. Thus, Feinberg (1975) wrote that, for a fully voluntary assumption of risk, there must be calmness and deliberation, an absence of distractions and disturbing emotions, and no misunderstanding or neurotic compulsions. If drugs or alcohol are involved, there would in this view be less than perfect voluntary decisions. Although we might agree with Feinberg in theory, in practice perfectly voluntary decisions are not required. This is true especially in the medical sphere, where there is nearly always some emotion disturbing a person's philosophic calm.

3. In the context of paternalism in general, VanDeVeer (1986) has developed a principle of hypothetical individualized consent, which would permit and justify interference with a competent or doubtfully competent patient if the following conditions are met. First, the health care provider knows the values of the individual in question so that the interference would promote the values of the particular patient. Second, in view of the first condition, the provider knows that the patient would validly consent if (1) he were aware of the relevant circumstances or, (2) his normal capacities were not substantially impaired. Third, the interference would involve no wrong to the provider or third parties.

Especially in a medical context, the first condition assumes that there is a truly personal relationship such that the values of the patient are well known and not merely assumed. In the health care setting, the first part of the second condition must also assume that there is not sufficient time to inform the patient of the relevant circumstances. The assumption of substantial impairment makes this and the theory of weak paternalism very similar.

4. One of the best explanations of the conflict between benevolence and autonomy is found in Engelhardt (1985). For other views, see Beauchamp and McCullough (1984) and Culver and Gert (1982).

5. The Jobes case may be found in *BioLaw*, 1987, pp. 571-580.

6. Although the authors praise the Uhlmann article, they disagree with his idea that the institutional ethics committee is a suitable surrogate. As noted earlier in this chapter, ethics committees are for educating and advising, not for making decisions. We are also concerned with, although not completely opposed to, the idea that the physician may be appointed as surrogate. Actually, a nurse who knows the patient better would be a more suitable health care professional surrogate in most cases. In the last analysis, a nonhealth-care professional is more likely to have the comprehensive view that the patient should have. We will discuss the patient's comprehensive view in chapter 3.

3

PRINCIPLES
OF BENEFICENCE
AND NONMALEFICENCE

INTRODUCTION

In its most general form, the principle of beneficence says no more than "do good." Similarly, the principle of nonmaleficence tells us to "avoid evil." Unfortunately, these formulations are so general as to be useless. This becomes painfully clear when we realize that we cannot do all good or avoid all evil. The tension between autonomy and beneficence is a difficulty here as well. It is a very difficult experience for a physician or nurse to be prevented from aiding a patient because the patient has refused consent to the very good that the health care provider has spent her entire life learning to provide. These tragic conflicts show us why we need more specific formulations to help us to sort out the possibilities and make ethical choices.

The Impossibility of Doing All Good

The impossibility of doing all good arises from the nature of time and space, which create the context for our own limitations and the limits of the instruments available to us. There is just so much time in a day. Indeed, there never seems to be enough time to do all that we want to do or plan to do. The limits of time restrict us no matter how efficient we become. Space, too, hems us in. We cannot directly and immediately do good to those who are far away. Indeed, because we can only be in one place at one time, most of the people in the world are beyond our direct touch, and so we cannot help them personally.

Our own limited talents further limit our ability to do good. Not everyone has the intelligence to be an atomic physicist or a designer of supercomputers. Some have better health than others, some greater strength, some better coordination. The relative strength of intellect, body, and coordination thus puts limits on what a person can do. It should be noted, however, that even those who have enough intelligence to master any given task do not have enough time to master all tasks. The person who is both physician and lawyer is rare; the person who is physician, lawyer, electrical engineer, mechanical engineer, nuclear physicist, biophysicist, anthropologist, chemist, paleontologist, carpenter, plumber, bricklayer, and agronomist seems as real as a winged horse. Even if such a person did exist, time and space would still limit the good he or she could do since one cannot do all these activities at once.

Finally, our ability to do good is limited by the state-of-the-art in a given area, as well as by the availability of state-of-the-art tools. Not every health care facility can afford to have all the up-to-date technology, and often decisions have to be made regarding what can be afforded and what will be let go. Some treatments are easily done by nurses or general practitioners, while others require highly trained specialists. Not every facility can have highly trained specialists in all the specialties.

Our obligation to do good is also limited by our obligation to avoid evil. In other words, the principle of nonmaleficence limits the principle of beneficence. The sight of a child drowning in a raging stream filled with floating ice urges one to attempt a rescue. But one stops after realizing that a rescue attempt would threaten one's own life, and one would probably not be able to save the child in any event. The evil involved is a price to be paid for attempting a rescue, but in these circumstances the evil is too great and too likely to warrant the rescue. Although we might praise the rescuer as a hero, we would not say she or he had a duty to jump in. Indeed, we call such people heroes because they do *not* have a duty, but do more than could be normally demanded. In health care ethics, this is the basis for the distinction between *ordinary* and *extraordinary* care, where ordinary care does not present excessive risks or burdens for the patient, while extraordinary care might help the patient, but the odds are poor or the risks and burdens are very high (see discussion later in this chapter).

Clearly, more specific formulations of the principle of beneficence are needed to help us decide what we should do. It should be clear, too, that doing good and avoiding evil will not simply be a question of principles, but of practical wisdom weighing the relevant aspects of the factual and social situation, as well as the concrete meaning of human dignity in a particular time and place.

The Impossibility of Avoiding All Evil

Nearly everything we do has some undesirable side effect or at least the risk of some evil. When you cross the street, you run the risk of being hit by a car. When you take aspirin, you risk stomach problems or possibly Reye's syndrome. When you undergo major surgery, you risk your life. Life is inherently risky. If we tried to avoid all risk of harm, we would have time for nothing else. Indeed, if we tried to avoid all risks by staying in bed, we would risk bed sores, muscle deterioration, and stationary pneumonia. There is no escape from all risk, and so there is no escape from all evil.

Quite aside from the inherent riskiness of human life, we must also face the fact that, because life is social, we are involved in actual evils to a greater or lesser extent. We are members of a society that, despite considerable progress, still oppresses minorities and women. Many people work for companies that are destroying the environment. Some teach in schools where at least some professors are grossly unfair to students. A few are employed in hospitals that tolerate incompetent physicians or nurses. By continuing to cooperate with groups that cause or permit evil, we are to some extent tainted by evil. Yet we cannot avoid all this evil. If we isolate ourselves as hermits, we cut ourselves off from the benefits of social life and increase the risk to our lives and even our sanity. Worse yet, our flight from evil often leaves the villains in charge and the victims in worse shape than before. There is no easy way out. We need specifications of the principle of nonmaleficence that will enable us to make at least rough judgments about what evils to avoid.

SPECIFICATIONS OF BENEFICENCE

As noted in chapter 1, the individual person is the intrinsic good, and all other things are to be judged by their effect on the individual. In practice, some things are *necessary* for the dignity of the human. Other things, such as gourmet foods and designer clothes, are merely desirable. These merely desirable goods, not necessary for human dignity, may, under certain conditions, be subordinated to the good of other persons and of society.

The things necessary for the person to remain human and maintain dignity are at the top of the list of goods to be done. Ordinarily, the list of necessary goods includes nourishment (including both food and water), shelter, and clothing, as well as memberships in social groups necessary for the psychological growth of the person. Many people would also include health care, as defined by their society, as a necessary good. For example, the constitutions of many countries, particularly in Eastern Europe, include health care as a right to be protected and ensured by the government. Of course, asserting such a right does not by itself explain which aspects of health care are necessary and which are only desirable. This is a problem of the manufacture and distribution of health care (see chapter 4) as well as a problem of defining "necessary." For example, we say that things such as food and health care are "ordinarily" necessary for the person to remain a human being, since in medical ethics we will encounter cases in which even the provision of food or the continuance of medical care may be destroying human dignity and maintaining a human being in what is often called a "vegetative state" (see chapter 7).

Often, however, it is not merely a matter of deciding which goods are necessary and which are merely useful for ourselves, but of situations in which the effort to better or to preserve ourselves may conflict with the good of other persons. In these cases, our betterment is often subordinate to their survival. At times, the obligation to respect others may limit the obligation to attain even these basic, necessary goods. At the very least, humans are generally free to sacrifice even basic goods for themselves in order to preserve basic goods for others. Thus, a person may forgo medical care to avoid impoverishing the family and depriving it of basic goods.

As we have already seen in chapter 2, particularly in the discussion of paternalism, even the health care provider's right to help is limited by the respect due to the freedom of the patient and by the need for informed consent from the patient or a lawful surrogate. A tension exists here between respecting freedom and securing what a health care professional may consider in the best interests of the patient (Engelhardt, 1985).

The societies we belong to are among the most necessary of goods. We depend on society for nearly every conceivable good and so are obliged to be members of various societies and to participate in and contribute to these societies, as well as to observe their rules. The necessary goods of these societies place obligations on us. In line with the demands of practical wisdom, we must consider these social obligations when deciding which goods must be done. This assumes that the society is just and does not seek to subordinate the individual totally to the group.

In practice, most of the goods we have to do are specified by social agreement, whether through law or custom, as well as through relationships, roles, or agreements. These specifications result from the acts of both societies and individuals. As a result, considerable variation may exist between societies and individuals. Thus, although all societies have common general obligations, specification between societies varies considerably. All societies must demand contributions from their members, but they exact different contributions, such as taxes or personal service, depending on history and the form of government in a particular society. Again, although all people need to have an income, they vary greatly in the way they choose to acquire that income. Some hire themselves out and acquire one set of obligations; others enter into individual contractual relations with a series of customers and so have different duties. As is evident from these remarks, how a society distributes its resources is a powerful expression of what the society thinks of as good or necessary. The discussion of justice and distribution is extremely important for understanding how the good of health care is made a practical reality. Less dramatically, but no less importantly, the marriage contract sets up a relationship and specifies a set of obligations that excludes certain other relationships. The relationship of father and mother to their children creates specific obligations that have priority over other obligations. Health care providers have similar roles to play.

In the health care professions, law, custom, relationship, and contract are particularly important. As we saw in chapter 1, the specific role of the provider determines the relationship to his or her patient. The professional, moreover, professes to do certain things implied in the purpose of the profession. These are the general goods that the professional is obliged to provide. On the other hand, the patient has obligations to his health and to those in his life which will take specific form through his consent. Thus, the agreement embodied in informed consent between professional and patient further specifies the particular good to be done in this case. Note that the physician or nurse cannot profess to do more than their particular education and skills permit, nor can they do more than the patient agrees to.

Health care providers are not sages capable of solving all problems and so should not attempt to, even if the patient were to let them. These two limits or specifications the one by talent, the other by agreement must be kept in mind at all times in health care ethics.

All these general and specific obligations in beneficence are also limited by the obligation to avoid evil. Before giving even more precise specifications for beneficence in health care, at least some general rules about the obligation to avoid evil must be considered, since we cannot avoid all evil.

SPECIFICATIONS OF NONMALEFICENCE

Because most people realize that it is impossible to avoid all evil, ethicists have devised various general rules to help people to decide what evils can be tolerated. A very basic one, included in the training of most health care professionals, is *primum non nocere*: first do no harm. This basic expression of nonmaleficence enjoins the professional to at least not make the patient worse off than before she came for help. The problem is recognizing what exactly is harm. This is part of the reason for requiring the discussion between patient and provider, since they may have differing opinions on what is harmful in the immediate situation. But given what we have said about human limitations, this discussion alone is not adequate.

The Principle of Double Effect

Perhaps the most famous effort to identify rules to identify tolerable harm is the principle of double effect developed by natural law thinkers.[1] The notions that the nature of actions can be clearly known and that some acts are good or evil independent of their consequences are quite prominent in the formulation. The *principle of double effect* provides that a person may perform an act that has or risks evil effects if all four of the following conditions are verified:

1. The action must be good or morally indifferent in itself.
2. The agent must intend only the good effect and not the evil effect.
3. The evil effect cannot be a means to the good effect.
4. There must be a proportionality between the good and the evil effects.

An example of this would involve a woman who discovers that she is pregnant at the same time she is diagnosed with cervical cancer. Treatment for the cancer would involve a hysterectomy, which would cause the death of the fetus. Can she and her physician pursue treatment? The action would be the treatment of the cancer, which would include the hysterectomy. The intent of the treatment would be to save the woman's life by curing her of cancer. The death of the fetus would be an unintended, even though foreseeable, *consequence* of the treatment; the surgery is the means to the cure, not the death of the fetus. Finally, there is a proportionality of results: the death of the fetus, which faced an uncertain future anyway, is balanced by the life of the woman. Treatment may be pursued.

A difficult example is found in an ectopic pregnancy, which is a pregnancy that occurs when the egg is fertilized and remains in one of the fallopian tubes. This situation poses severe health threats for the woman, and the fetus has no chance of survival. The preferred current treatment would be to end the pregnancy with methotrexate, a chemical agent that kills fast-growing cells and is often used for chemotherapy. But note the difficulties. The action itself, and the intention of the action, involve directly the death of the fetus. Indeed, the attractiveness of this type of treatment is precisely the point that only the fetus is destroyed, while the fallopian tube is preserved. Yet, because of the focus of the treatment on the death of the fetus, steps one, two, and three of the principle of double effect seem to be violated and the action would be ethically wrong.

The Principle of Proportionality

In line with the practical wisdom approach, which considers all relevant factors and looks at the consequences of acts, this book uses a different formulation, which may be called the *principle of proportionality*. This provides the following:

Provided the action does not go directly against the dignity of the individual person (the intrinsic good), there must be a proportionate good to justify permitting or risking an evil effect.

Note that as stated, the principle is not a consequentialist principle because of the priority given to the dignity of the individual. An action is evaluated in view of the effects it has on that dignity, in fulfilling it as well as giving or removing opportunities.

The proportionality contained in this principle, (as well as in step four of the principle of double effect) is to be judged by considering the following four factors:

1. whether there are alternative ways of attaining the intended good with no evil or less evil effects
2. the level of good intended and the level of the evil risked or permitted
3. the certitude or probability of the good or evil intended, permitted, or risked
4. the causal influence of the agent

Alternatives

If there are alternative ways of attaining the good with less evil or less risk of evil, common sense dictates that the alternative be chosen. Put another way, *the good is to be done with the smallest amount of evil possible*. In medical practice, this means not using a drug with harmful side effects if it is possible to treat the condition with diet or exercise. Here the possibilities would depend on the self-discipline of the patient, as well as on the effectiveness of the diet and exercise.

Recall from chapter 2 that the health care professional has the obligation to inform the patient of the alternatives and the relative benefits and risks involved. The patient has the obligation to consider these and to weigh proportionality.

The Level of Good and Evil

Everyone recognizes that not all goods and evils are equal. Losing a few hairs from one's head is generally considered very minor compared to losing an eye. Saving a human life is, for most of us, more important than keeping a pet well fed. At base, we recognize that some things are *merely useful* for the life of the person, while others are *necessary* for human life and dignity. However, there is much room for discussion as to what goods fall into which class, as well as to which is more or less useful or necessary. It is generally accepted that in the United States a formal education is necessary to earn an income, but there is no agreement about which level of education is necessary. People can agree that vitamin A is necessary yet still disagree about the best source of vitamin A. For all that, there is considerable agreement that certain things are seriously evil and others very minor.

The loss of life, or of freedom of choice, or even of movement, is considered a great evil; the loss of a favorite sweater or a small sum of money at cards is not. In short, what threatens basic human rights and dignity or what threatens life or physical integrity in a major way is considered serious. In practice, the hope of a serious good is needed to justify even risking such evils.

Certitude or Probability of the Good or Evil

Some serious evils are remote; that is, the risk of them is so small that in practice we treat the evil as not serious. Although you risk your life just about every time you cross a busy street, the risk is so small that you feel no moral uneasiness about crossing as long as you are careful. If the odds are very small that an operation will save your life and very high that it will leave you crippled, the lifesaving aspect becomes a lesser good and the risk of being crippled assumes more serious proportions. In practice, then, proportionality involves very complicated if not always precise balancing of the levels of goods and evils with the probability or certainty of these same goods and evils.

Certitude, Probability, and the Wedge Principle

In arguing about the certitude and probability of consequences, particularly evil consequences, ethical thinkers, implicitly if not explicitly, often invoke the wedge or camel's nose principle. The wedge analogy assumes that if you put the tip of a wedge into a crack in a log and strike the wedge, you will split the log apart and destroy it. The camel's nose analogy imagines that if you let a camel get its nose under a tent the rest of the beast will soon follow. In a general sense, both analogies operate on the underlying idea that in defending a given position even a small concession will destroy that position.

There are two forms of the wedge principle. The first or logical form is concerned with logical consistency and not necessarily with the actual effects. Assuming that ethical principles should be universal and cover all individual situations, exceptions are seen as the logical wedge that will undermine the principle. Thus, some religious thinkers argue that if you claim that contraception is ethical you must also accept homosexual activity as ethical. They say that this is logically consistent because both involve unnatural acts. The argument has no force, of course, with those who see no evil consequences in either contraception or homosexuality. Similarly, deontologists will argue that if you permit any justified lies you logically undermine the whole prohibition of lying. This version of the wedge principle does not say that you will increase lying, but only that you logically undermine the principle.

The empirical form of the wedge principle does not worry about logical consistency, but about the actual consequences of the act or the exception to the rule. Will the exception increase lying and so threaten social interaction? Will the practice of contraception lead to an increase or a decrease in abortions? Will sparing the rod spoil the child? These are questions of fact that must be answered by experience or careful studies. Often, however, the careful studies are lacking, and we are given general impressions or so-called common sense answers to questions of fact. This is an invalid use of the empirical wedge principle, since evidence and not opinion is needed.

It is not always easy to discover the consequences of such things as pornography, television violence, or the effects of cesarean sections or circumcision. Because answers are often hard to come by, decency demands that one investigate carefully before invoking the empirical wedge principle and then tossing around prohibitions on the basis of what you guess might happen. Again, all the rules on proportionality return as the good and the evil consequences are calculated. Even though an action may produce harmful consequences, even more harmful effects may arise from trying to suppress it. Prohibition, which aimed at suppressing alcoholism, not only failed, but contributed to the beginning of organized crime. Suppressing pornography, for example, might do great harm to freedom of speech and so not be justified. The justification, however, is a question of fact and not a matter of mere opinion.

The Causal Influence of the Agent

Most effects are the result of many causes, such that a particular agent is seldom the sole cause of the consequences. Lung cancer, for example, may have been triggered not only by smoking, but by conditions in the workplace and in the general environment, as well as by hereditary factors. The smokers and the polluters are responsible for the lung cancer to the extent that they caused it. They are not solely responsible, since hereditary factors also play a role.

In some cases the action of a particular agent may be a very minor contributor to the evil. For example, the cleaning staff in a hospital that is overcharging patients help to keep the place going, but hardly make any great contribution to the evil. The accountants, on the other hand, are more deeply involved. The board of directors is directly and largely responsible for the overcharging.

Although there is no excuse for the board, since it has the controlling causal influence, the cleaning staff needs no more good than their need of a job to justify their continued employment. The accountants, having tried to change the situation, can tolerate the involvement if they feel that they can prevent other serious evils by continuing to work for that particular hospital.

In this context, it should be stressed that in many cases there is no causal influence and no possibility for a given person to change the situation. In these cases, there may be no obligation to avoid or remove the evil simply because it is impossible to do so. We shall discuss this in chapter 6 on self-policing and the problem of whistleblowing.

Preliminary Summary

The detailed consideration of the principle of proportionality brings us to a reformulation of the principle of avoiding evil. The principle of nonmaleficence now reads as follows: "Avoid evil and evil consequences unless you have a proportionate reason for risking or permitting them."

This reformulation of the principle of nonmaleficence calls for a more precise working of the principle of doing good. The reformulation of the principle of beneficence now reads as follows: "Do good unless the consequences of doing good produce a disproportionate evil."

In practice, the good to be done depends on the seriousness of the matter and on the whole network of social roles and contractual obligations that defines the particular good that this individual should do. It is time, then, to return to the statements of beneficence and nonmaleficence specific to those involved in health care.

THE PATIENT'S OBLIGATION

We start with the patient's obligation, since the patient is the center of health care and the reason for its existence. Equally important is the fact that the patient must make health care decisions in a context that includes obligations to family, society, and the values of things other than health and mere biological existence. As noted at the end of chapter 2, the fact that a patient has a legal right to refuse treatment does not mean that there is also an ethical right to do so.

What is the patient's ethical obligation with regard to preventing disease and maintaining and restoring her or his health? In view of the fact that health is only one among many goods and the obligation to take care of health only one of many obligations, many medical ethicists have given the following summary statement: *Individuals are obliged to use ordinary but not extraordinary means of preserving and restoring their health.*[2]

The explanations of ordinary and extraordinary make it clear that this is really only a form of proportionality. Ordinary, for example, does not mean common, usual, or everyday. Rather it means *that which, all things considered, produces more good than harm*. Extraordinary does not mean unusual, rare, or exotic, but *that which, all things considered, produces more evil than good*. For example, the use of Valium, a minor tranquilizer, would be extraordinary in a patient whose adverse reaction to the drug is rage. On the other hand, the implantation of an artificial heart might be an ordinary means if that is the only way a person can prolong life long enough to put it in order.

The ordinary-extraordinary terminology may be confusing, and so it is better to word the principle as a special case of proportionality. The patient's formulation of the principle of benevolence in health matters, then, reads as follows: *Take care of your health as long as, all things considered, this does not produce more harm than good*. The phrase "all things considered" is important, because it distinguishes the patient's obligation not only from that of the health care professional but also from that of the surrogate. As we shall see shortly, both the professional and the surrogate do not have to consider all things.

The phrase "all things considered" also stresses the need to balance out all the obligations of the patient. The phrase includes not only the effects on the self, but also on the family and society; not only the pain, cost, and health benefits, but the meaning of life and the quality of life as the patient sees it. Health care that barely keeps a patient alive while its costs reduce the family to fiscal poverty and emotional exhaustion is not necessarily a good thing. Indeed, the patient can reasonably judge it an evil to be avoided. Similarly, treatment such as a blood transfusion that conflicts with a religious obligation would not be a good, let alone an obligatory good. On the other hand, neglecting exercise, proper sleep, and nutrition is nearly always wrong because such basic self-care procedures hardly conflict with other obligations.

In this context, it should be emphasized that the health care provider cannot make these decisions, if only because the professional does not know all things, much less all things that are pertinent to the decision of the patient. Above all, the health care provider is not competent to judge the meaning and value of life for other people. Certainly, the health care professional is never in the position of being qualified to say that the quality of life of the patient makes that patient unworthy of life or unworthy relative to other persons. The proper nature of the health care professionals' judgment of the quality of life will be treated later in this chapter.

Recent interest in the managed care delivery of health care has put an increasing emphasis on preventive medicine and good health habits. There is likely to be increasing social pressure on individuals to cooperate with these concerns or perhaps lose access to health care. This shift in the balance of individual and social power may lead to attacks on autonomy and a degradation of human dignity (Morreim, 1996).

THE HEALTH CARE PROVIDER'S OBLIGATION

Although the health care professional is not competent to make a judgment of proportionality *all things considered*, he or she has a professional role and is competent in a given area. In this area, the health care professional must judge the proportionality of consequences. In the case of physicians, we call the specific formulation of beneficence *the medical indications* principle. For nurses it would be *the nursing indications* principle, and so on, for each profession involved. Here we will discuss only the medical indications principle for physicians.[3]

The medical indications principle states that, *granted informed consent, the physician should do what is medically indicated such that, from a medical point of view, more good than evil will result*. To put it another way, the medical benefits are to outweigh the medical burdens on the patient. The following example, taken from Ramsey (1978, p. 182), illustrates the principle in action.

There are two groups of babies with spina bifida. The first group will die within a few days or weeks. The second group will live for months or years or more even if untreated. This second group of babies, who are not dying, is further divided into group A and group B. The babies in group A have such a wide wound on the back that it is not suitable for an operation. An operation might not heal and might leave the wound infected and the final condition of the baby worse than at first. Group B contains babies who were seen to kick at birth and so have some muscle power. In this case, an operation stands a good chance of reducing the handicap and improving the child's chances in life without making things worse.

Treatment is not indicated for group 1 because its members will be dead in a short time and nothing would be accomplished by the operation. In this case, the surgeon should not urge the operation. For group A, the operation is not medically indicated because the specifics make the child unsuitable for an operation; indeed, the specifics create a risk of making the child more handicapped. Treatment is medically indicated for group B because more medical good than harm should be accomplished. The surgeon should propose the operation and even make a strong case for it.

To see the significance of the principle more clearly, we will alter the case by supposing that in group B there is one child who is severely retarded. Is the operation for spina bifida still medically indicated for that child who is not dying and who has an operable condition? The answer is yes. There is *more medical good than harm* to be gained by operating, so the operation is medically indicated. Medically, the benefits of the surgery are greater than the burdens resulting from it. The fact of severe retardation is not a *medical* counter-indication, regardless of how one feels about retardation. A judgment about the value of life of retarded people should not enter in here because that is not a medical question. It is a profound personal or philosophic question to which there is no easy answer. We shall return to the quality of life problem in chapter 6 when we discuss the value of life to the person who possesses that life.

Let us look at a third case in which a severely retarded neonate is dying from pneumonia. The child's life can be saved with antibiotics. Is treatment of the pneumonia medically indicated even though saving the life will leave the family and society with a severely retarded child on its hands? Does the fact of severe mental retardation change the medical indications? The answer is no. The treatment of the pneumonia is medically indicated since medically it will produce more good than harm. The treatment is medically indicated unless the patient is dying of some other untreatable disease or unless the treatment will cause more harm than good from a medical point of view. The fact that the child will never lead a full life as defined by the physician or by society is not a medical counter-indication. Rather, it is once again the sort of quality of life decision that goes beyond the consideration of medical benefits and burdens and so beyond the scope of medicine and beyond the competence of the physician.

The impact of the decision on the family and the society is also not a medical question, although it would be part of the patient's consideration of benefits and burdens. Perhaps, as we shall see, it may at times be a part of the surrogate's decision. Indeed, an attempt to make such factors part of the medical indications approach would detract from the central idea that the health care professional, except in industrial, military, and some judicial settings, is to seek the good of the patient and not the good of the other parties involved.

The Baby Doe rule,[4] although it is still debatable (Newman, 1989), is an example of one attempt to apply the medical indications principle and speaks to these situations rather clearly (Murray, 1985). Two points should be noted in the following quotations. First, the rule speaks of life-threatening situations and not merely of patients in a terminal condition. Second, nutrition and hydration are considered part of treatment.

The Department of Health and Human Services rule (1985b, no. 4) condemns the *withholding of medically indicated treatment*, where "withholding" is defined as follows:

> the failure to respond to the infant's life-threatening conditions by providing treatment (including appropriate nutrition, hydration, and medication) which, in the treating physician's (or physicians') reasonable medical judgment, will be most likely to be effective in *ameliorating all such conditions* [italics added].

Three exceptions to the condemnation are listed, although appropriate nutrition, hydration, and medication must be provided even in these cases.

1. The infant is chronically and irreversibly comatose.
2. The provision of such treatment would merely prolong dying, not be effective in ameliorating or correcting all the infant's life-threatening conditions, or otherwise be futile in terms of the survival of the infant.
3. The provision of such treatment would be virtually futile in terms of the survival of the infant, and the treatment itself under such circumstances would be inhumane.

The requirement that appropriate nutrition, hydration, and medication be provided even in these three cases is questionable (Lynn and Childress, 1983). Nutrition, hydration, and medication may only prolong the dying process. Furthermore, although we may have strong emotions about something as commonplace as eating and drinking, nutrition and hydration in hospital settings are often painful and uncomfortable medical procedures, rather than simple, everyday acts. Nasogastric and gastric tubes need medical justification and are not to be taken as ordinary methods of feeding and hydrating. (This point is more fully developed in chapter 7 on death and dying.) We stress that keeping a patient alive at all costs is not automatically medically indicated.

Medical Indications and Medical Costs

Faced with a patient, the physician's primary ethical obligation is captured in the medical indications principle. However, the physician's obligation to do good extends to her or his professional contribution to society as well. As mentioned in chapter 1, the physician is a locus of information for society as well as for the patient. And, as we will see in chapter 4, society must make decisions about distributing scarce medical resources. A clear understanding of these resources and their possibilities is essential to an appropriate distribution. The physician and other health care professionals have an important obligation to society to provide the health care information and leadership to ensure that this distribution is accomplished in ways that allow the goals of health care to be achieved (Baillie and Garrett, 1991).

THE SURROGATE'S OBLIGATION

The obligation of the surrogate in giving or withholding consent depends on whether the wishes of a once competent patient are known or can be deduced, or whether the person has never been competent, or whether the wishes are unknown (Emanuel and Emanuel, 1992). If the wishes of a once competent patient are known either orally or in writing or can be easily deduced from a person's actions and values, the surrogate should decide in accord with the wishes of the patient. This is sometimes called the substituted judgment principle. To overrule these wishes would be a violation of the person's autonomy.

An important difficulty with substituted judgment is that research strongly suggests that in many cases surrogates simply do not know the wishes of patients even though they think that they do (High, 1994). When the need to have a discussion about end of life care is not pressing, the subject seems too awkward and often put off until later. When "later" comes, it is often too late, and the surrogate must act based on impressions and feelings, rather than on actual knowledge of the patient's wishes. In spite of how well we think we know our loved ones, it turns out we are not all that good at it.

When the person has never been competent or has been competent but never manifested his or her wishes, two principles have been proposed for the surrogate: the best interests principle and the rational choice principle. The best interests principle requires that the surrogate act in the best interests of the patient, *disregarding the interests of others*, including the interests of the family, society, and those of the surrogate. The best interests principle thus demands that the good of the patient and nothing else be considered.

The rational choice principle commands that the surrogate choose what the patient would have chosen when competent and after having considered all available relevant information and the interests of relevant others. The rational choice principle goes beyond the narrowly defined interests of the patient. It recognizes that patients are obliged to, and generally do, consider the interests of at least some others in making their decisions. The rational choice principle would allow the surrogate to judge that even a very painful treatment should be given, since many people depend on the patient for moral support. The principle might also justify refusing the treatment on the grounds that the treatment would impoverish the patient's family and leave the patient crippled.

Each of these principles entails problems. The best interests principle asks the surrogate to do what is nearly impossible—to judge what is best for another. Furthermore, it does not address the fact that the interests of the patient and the interests of the surrogate may be in conflict. Not all surrogates can surmount their own interests.

The rational choice principle assumes that we could know what the patient would have chosen when competent and after having considered every relevant factor. This is a very broad assumption. We doubt that anyone can know what a person would have done in certain circumstances. Among other things, we generally do not know what relative value the patient would have given to the interests of others. In practice, the rational choice principle probably leads to the surrogate choosing what, all things considered, the surrogate deems best. The difficulty of the task is illustrated by the following cases:

1. A wife faces the prospect of a husband who will be in a vegetative state forever or will be severely handicapped, requiring constant care at home if the treatment works. If the treatment does not work, he will die within a year.
2. A son who wants his inheritance as soon as possible must decide whether his father should be given care that will prolong life for years, even though the father will not know where or who he is most of the time.
3. A mother is faced with the decision of whether to treat a seriously deformed and profoundly retarded child who will never recognize her and will act as little more than a large animal in the house for many years to come.

In all these cases, the motives are mixed and the choice agonizing. Although we would all condemn the son for letting the father die in order to get his inheritance sooner, we also recognize that both the wife in the first case and the mother in the third have legitimate interests and concerns. The best interest principle, which asks them to disregard these concerns, seems to ask something unreasonable, if not impossible. The rational choice principle, on the other hand, is reasonable, but creates a fear that we will open up a Pandora's box of evils. The wedge principle reappears. We are left asking whether the rational choice principle will lead to surrogates violating not only autonomy, but also the patient's right to treatment or even to life.

The introduction of ethics committees may provide more advice to health care workers and even to surrogates, but it does not solve the problems of surrogate decision making, since the committees do not, barring a legal delegation, have legal authority to make the decisions. Ethically, the ethics committee might perhaps supplant the surrogates only temporarily and if there were evidence that the surrogates were not following one of the approved principles of surrogate decision making. Even in these cases, however, a court order should be sought as soon as possible. In any event, we need more experience with ethics committees, their composition, and their values before taking any definitive stand about them.

All these problems point to an underlying problem in pluralistic societies that lack a community consensus about what is right or wrong. Such societies end up substituting laws that set down the minimums, only to find that the minimums do not solve their problems. When the pluralistic society becomes increasingly infected with distrust, not only of professionals but of government, law seems to lead to malpractice suits and increasing demands for lay review and control of health care decisions. In the absence of a community consensus and its accompanying trust, everyone in health care must feel isolated and very alone when faced with the difficult problems involving incompetent patients.

The Quality of Life Problem

Health care providers, when using an indications principle appropriate to their particular profession, can and legitimately do make judgments about the benefits and burdens of medical, nursing, or respiratory care or their omission. The quality-of-life judgment has a different status when there is judgment about the value and meaning of life itself. An indications principle forbids health care professionals to make quality-of-life decisions about the relative worth of persons or their lives; such decisions are considered beyond their competence. Thus, a nurse may ethically judge that a given nursing intervention will leave the patient worse off. Nursing science, however, does not permit a judgment that a treatment should be omitted because this particular life is no longer worth living. This is particularly true in a pluralistic society in which there is no social consensus about such questions. In chapter 7 in our discussion of death and dying, we will have to face the related question of whether a given life is a human life.

Unfortunately, in a world of scarce resources, there will come a time when society and its instrument, the government, must make at least minimum decisions that indirectly judge what life and health are worth in monetary terms. Society will at least have to decide how much it will pay to preserve life or provide health care. The increasing cost of health care will ultimately force society to make a judgment to limit the good that a health care professional can do, because it will limit the reimbursement that the professional will receive for it. This will be discussed in chapter 4 which covers justice in the distribution of health care. Here we will stress some of the value issues other than justice.

At the beginning of chapter 2, we stressed that the individual person is the intrinsic good and not a good merely because he or she is useful to society or to others. In short, persons are valuable because they are human and not because they produce something. We must, however, ask what makes biological life valuable to the person. Mere vegetable or animal existence is surely not valuable to the person without qualification. That question will be considered in chapter 7 in the discussion of death and dying. We must also face the question of whether human life that has a potential for personhood has value. We will look at that question in chapter 8 which discusses abortion. All these problems are painful precisely because we do not have a community consensus about values. At the same time, they are crucial problems because they concern what have always been considered basic values.

Professional Power and Benevolence

Writers on health care ethics (Kass, 1983; Pellegrino and Thomasma, 1981) emphasize the ethical obligations that arise from the unequal power relationship between the patient and the health care professional. We must be concerned about this inequality in practice. Some evidence indicates that all relationships between health care professionals and their patients involve some problems of power and territory (Rosenthal et. al., 1980). This would not be the case in a perfect world, where both the principle of autonomy and the principle of beneficence would be perfectly observed and where the compassion of the care giver overcome all annoyances from the patient. In the real world and in daily life, the temptation to use power for one's own convenience and comfort is real and almost constantly present. We include a few examples of the abuse of power to illustrate the type of ethical problem that is generally not discussed. Once described, the following common abuses of power need no commentary.

1. To maximize income, the physician schedules three patients for the same time. If they all show up, two of them have to wait and so waste their time for the convenience of the physician. As the day goes on, the waits become longer, as long as three or four hours. Most patients are too intimidated to complain, let alone to bill the physician for their lost time.

2. The nurse, knowing that the orthopedic surgeon likes to move fast, uses hot water in preparing the casting compound since that speeds up the setting time. She disregards the fact that it also makes the cast very hot and uncomfortable, especially for children with tender skin.

3. The patient is told to take off all her clothes, put on a paper gown, and wait for the physician in a cold examination room. Two hours later the doctor shows up, making no excuse and giving no explanation for the inconvenience.

4. A small-town physician tells patients that he will never treat them again, not even in an emergency, if he ever hears that they went to the new doctor in town.

5. The patient in Room 5 does not wash himself when told to do so. The nurse punishes him by waiting twenty minutes to answer the patient's call bell.

6. The supervisor puts a family member out of the patient's room because the relative makes the nurse nervous when the nurse is taking the patient's pulse and temperature.

Medical Indications and Unnecessary Surgery

Studies indicate that considerable unnecessary surgeries are performed, that is, surgeries that are not medically indicated or not indicated because less-radical alternatives are available. Some studies in the early 1980s estimated that as much as 36 percent of all cataract surgery, 36 percent of knee surgery, 43 percent of hemorrhoidectomies, 31 percent of gall bladder surgery, 29 percent of prostate surgery, and 28 percent of hernia repair surgery are unnecessary (*Perspectives*, 1985). The fact that second opinions significantly reduce surgery indicates that some "unnecessary surgery" may be due to a difference of opinion among surgeons. At the very least, this indicates that medical indications are not precise, but are as much a matter of opinion as of scientific research. More disturbing is the fact that the second opinions indicate that many surgeons are too quick to take up the knife before less-drastic measures have been tried. The Wennberg variations, which tie the number and type of surgeries to the number and type of surgeons in an area, give some credibility to this interpretation. The most disturbing interpretation of all holds that some surgeons merely operate with or without medical indications. Such conduct involves exposing the patient to unnecessary risk, defrauding the insurance company, and wasting health care resources. Fortunately, this seems to be rare.

Conflicts of Interest

An actual conflict of interest exists when a health care provider subordinates the interest, including the financial interest, of the patient to the interests of the provider or a third party. The duty to the patient forbids actual conflicts of interest. A potential conflict of interest exists when reasonable people suspect that the health care provider will be tempted to subordinate the patient's interest. The necessity of protecting the profession's reputation forbids most potential conflicts of interest. We shall speak of the exceptions later.

Thus, there may be suspicion when a physician is both prescribing and selling the prescription to the patient. The same may be said when the physician owns a pharmacy, a store that sells medical devices, or a nursing home or private hospital. Some suspect conflicts even when the physician owns a large share or much stock in such enterprises. Law and professional codes can make even the appearance of conflict unethical. Medicare and Medicaid regulations forbid referring a patient to a physician-owned health care facility. In 1993, the AMA finally declared it unethical for physicians to refer patients to a medical facility in which the doctor has a financial interest. Unfortunately the AMA's motive appears to have been a public relations ploy aimed at improving the profession's public image.

Potential conflicts of interest are generally to be avoided but may be ethically tolerated when the enterprises connected with the physician actually charge lower prices. This is often the case with doctors in rural areas when there is no pharmacy and selling the drug is a real service. Here the price may even be slightly higher in view of the special services being provided in such cases. Those interested in pursuing the complexity of the issues involved should consult Abood (1989), Morse and Popovits (1989), and McDowell (1990).

The Health Care Provider as Patient Advocate

In chapter 1, we spoke favorably of the nurse as patient advocate. In light of the principle of beneficence as expressed in terms of medical indications or nursing indications and all parallel professional indications, we want to argue that all health care professionals have an obligation to be patient advocates in the area of their expertise. This advocacy does not authorize the health care provider to overrule patients or lawful surrogates, but it does, when everything else has been attempted, authorize or even oblige them to seek court protection for the patient whom they suspect is being abused or made the victim of a conflict of interest.

In chapter 6 we deal with self-policing and whistleblowing as part of the advocate's role. Here, we would like to stress the problems of patients who are particularly vulnerable and so in need of protection not only *by* health care professionals but *from* health care professionals. Problems in this area will grow as the population ages and long-term care, whether in the home or in long-term care facilities such as nursing homes, becomes more common.

Nursing homes often have a large number of patients who, if not confused, are weak and physically vulnerable. At times the nursing home patient may have been made confused or incompetent for the convenience of the staff. Overmedication or "snowing" of patients has been documented on several occasions (Cushing, 1984). The fact that tranquilizers such as Thorazine and Mellaril account for as much as 20 percent of the drugs prescribed in nursing homes gives rise to questions about induced incompetence.

The consent of such patients and the consent of surrogates can easily be overridden. They can be punished for failure to bow to the whims of the staff. The punishments can be as severe and obvious as the use of physical abuse or as hard to detect as withdrawal of attention and concern for the patient. Although federal and state regulations govern long-term care and require periodic visits from state inspectors, these do not provide 24-hour-a-day protection. Registered nurses, licensed practical nurses, aides, and administrators who are on the spot have the obligation to protect the patient and to provide, as far as possible, conditions that foster not only the health but also the dignity of the patient. This is an enormous challenge. The budgets are often low and the staffing may sometimes be inadequate in numbers and in training. Often, only a handful of professionals oversee numerous aides. The truly ethical health care professional, then, may find herself involved in a continuous and even losing battle for the proper care of the patient. At this point, the obligation to be a patient advocate can change to the obligation to support the political advocacy of the professional organizations that have the power to influence the allocation process (see chapter 4).

Beneficence and the Right to Refuse Patients

Except in emergencies, health care professionals and health care agencies do not have to accept all patients who present themselves for treatment. Americans, however, are shocked when they hear stories of the "dumping" of indigent patients or even of patients who lack adequate health insurance. Yet, even in 1982, it was estimated that about 1 million families a year were refused health care for financial reasons. In some cases, as many as 90 percent of the cases transferred to public facilities from emergency departments at other hospitals made the trip because they lacked adequate medical coverage.

All of us are shocked when we read such newspaper stories. At the same time, it is clear that health care professionals and institutions cannot treat everyone who comes along and can treat only a limited number of patients without payment.

The institutional problem and the problem of social justice involved in these situations will be treated in chapter 4. Here we will treat the basic principles covering the obligation of the health care professional practicing in a noninstitutional setting.

Before discussing the ethical issues, we want to point out the increasing concern of the law and lawyers in this area. So great is their concern that widespread changes are expected in the next decade. Already, federal antidumping legislation has been enacted in the amendments to the Comprehensive Budget Reconciliation Act (COBRA) (Krugh, 1990; Singer, 1989). There is also increasing legal concern about the gate-keeping function in health maintenance organizations (HMOs), which could lead to deterring access to even emergency services (Craig, 1990). Finally, there are legal efforts to increase access to long-term care through Medicaid antidiscrimination laws (Gilbert, 1991). Although the immediate impact of this is largely institutional, individual health care professionals will also be affected.

Traditionally, health care professionals, except in emergency situations, have had the right to select or reject patients who came for care. This was based on the idea that the professional-patient relationship was very personal and not something that could be forced on either the health care professional or the patient.

In more recent times, we have begun to see that the power to reject and accept patients can be abused. If the rejection or acceptance is not based on factors relevant to the professional-patient relationship, then unfair discrimination exists, which rejects the dignity of the patient. Our ideas of fairness no longer approve of an unqualified right to reject patients. At the same time, no one would say that health care professionals must treat all who present themselves for care.

There are legitimate reasons to reject certain patients. First, the physician may lack the skills to treat a particular patient. Second, the physician may lack the time because the practice is already oversubscribed.

Can a health care provider ethically reject a patient because of inability to pay at all or inability to pay as much as the physician requests? The answer is both yes and no.

The health care professional who never does charity work is certainly not practicing the profession of healing as much as operating a business. In our opinion, such a person is unworthy of the name of health care professional. During most of American history, charitable service was so much a mark of the life of the physician that the vast majority of them had very low incomes (Starr, 1982). At the same time, the health care professional has a right to earn a good living and so must have some discretion as to how many nonpaying clients should be accepted. Although the physician's role calls for charitable work, it does not call for becoming a charitable institution. We note that nurses in many parts of the country are still so underpaid that much of their work must be considered a charitable contribution to the sick and poor. We are left, however, with a problem of justice in the microallocation of health care, which will be treated in chapter 4. Although, ethically, physicians have wide latitude in selecting patients, they have less freedom in dropping a patient. Both legally (Annas, 1981; Cowdrey, 1984) and ethically, a physician is guilty of abandonment if, in a nonemergency situation, she or he does not continue treating a patient and so exposes the patient to danger. However, there are good reasons for terminating the relationship. Termination of treatment requires that the physician provide for continuity of care by handing the patient over to another qualified professional.

The appearance of AIDS has raised old questions about the right of health care professionals to refuse treatment to a patient because of danger to themselves. Two points need to be considered in answering the question. First, all the rules of proportionality apply. Second, because the professional professes to serve society and the sick, the risks of harm must outweigh that professional obligation, as well as the other goods involved. In short, it takes more than normal risk to excuse health care professionals because of danger to themselves. In this context, it should be noted that by 1993 researchers had unearthed less than forty cases of health care workers infected by patients who were HIV-positive.

Tegtmeir (1990) argues that it is difficult to establish a completely convincing ethical argument for the duty to care for an AIDS patient. He notes, however, that the antidiscrimination act probably creates such a duty in those employed in government health care facilities. As yet, this does not appear to impose any legal obligation on private physicians. Medical schools have created such an obligation for students and residents as part of the contract of employment or service. There will undoubtedly be continuing developments in this area.

In the case of AIDS, all current research indicates that the risk of a health care professional being infected by a patient is very small *if proper procedures are followed*. There is no danger if the health care professional with open cuts or breaks in exposed skin avoids working with the AIDS patient until the cuts and cracks are healed. Then there can be temporary ethical excuses for not working with AIDS patients. On the other hand, a refusal based on a dislike of some groups at higher risk for AIDS, such as homosexuals or drug users, appears contrary to the whole spirit of the health care profession.

SUMMARY

It is impossible to do all good and to avoid all evil. It is necessary, then, to have principles that specify which goods are to be done and which evils are to be avoided. In practice, this specification involves a judgment of proportionality between the good intended and the evils risked. In health care, there are different specifications for the patient, the patient's surrogates, and the health care professionals. For health care professionals, further specifications arise from the nature of the profession in question. The medical indications principle is a prime example of the principle of proportionality and the professional obligation joined in one principle. Quality-of-life judgments are not within the expertise of the health care professional.

A patient should not be turned away except for relevant reasons, nor should the relationship be broken even for relevant reasons without providing for continuity of care.

CASES FOR ANALYSIS

1. Joseph Saikewicz, age 77, IQ 10, mental age two years and eight months, has been institutionalized for forty years. Joseph can communicate only with gestures and grunts. He is unaware of danger. He becomes disoriented when removed from familiar surroundings. He has no living relatives.

His health had been generally good until he was diagnosed as having acute myeloblastic monocytic leukemia, which is inevitably fatal. In approximately 30 to 50 percent of these cases, chemotherapy can bring about a temporary remission that usually lasts between two and thirteen months. Results are poorer for patients over 60. The chemotherapy often has serious side effects, including anemia and infections.

In April 1976, the probate court appointed a guardian *ad litem* with authority to make the necessary decision.

What is medically indicated for the patient? Is the fact of his severe retardation medically relevant to either the doctor's or a surrogate's decision?

2. Angela is an extremely beautiful woman in the eyes of everyone but herself. Angela is convinced that she has a big nose that detracts from her appearance. Despite the assurances of friends and family, she persists in this belief. Angela goes to a plastic surgeon to remedy her condition. The surgeon points out that there is no need for the surgery and lists all the inconveniences to Angela and the expense of the work. Angela persists in her demands. Finally, the surgeon flatly refuses to operate on Angela's nose. Angela then goes to a second plastic surgeon, who believes that the psychological effects of the surgery justify the risks and the expense. The second surgeon performs the operation, modifying the nose so little that friends hardly notice the results. What is medically indicated in Angela's case?

3. Mrs. Selbstmord, age 55, has chronic asthma. Even though she is very allergic to cat fur, she keeps two cats to whom she is very attached, and she smokes a pack of cigarettes a day. She also insists on getting emotionally involved in all family squabbles. Her family physician lectures her constantly on the fact that all three factors complicate her asthma. He is reluctant to prescribe most asthma medicines because of the side effects, but most significantly because a change in Selbstmord's lifestyle will do more good than any medication. After a year of unsuccessful patient education, he refuses to treat her any further unless she does her part and changes her lifestyle.

Is the physician ethical in refusing to treat the patient until she reforms her health habits? Is he blackmailing her or is he making a last desperate attempt to make her face her real problems? Is the patient capable of handling all the factors that complicate her asthma?

4. James, age 14, is afflicted with a harelip and cleft palate and needs a common operation that promises to improve both his appearance and his speech significantly. The boy's father, a believer in mental healing, refuses to permit the operation. The physician explains the operation to James, who expresses a desire to "try for some time longer to close the cleft palate through natural forces."

Is the father acting ethically on the basis of any one of the three surrogate principles? Do not neglect the social implications of the decision. Should James' opinion carry some weight? Should the physician have sought a court order?

5. Brother Fox, age 93, a member of the Society of Mary, suffers a heart attack while undergoing corrective surgery for an inguinal hernia. He sustains substantial brain damage, slips into a coma, and is placed on a respirator in an intensive care unit. Two neurosurgeons state that there is no reasonable possibility that he will regain consciousness.

Father Eichner, who has been Brother Fox's close friend for nearly twenty-six years, knows that Brother Fox would want the respirator removed. In the past, the two man had discussed the Quinlan case, and Fox had stated that he wanted no extraordinary means used if he were ever to be in this situation.

Father Eichner would not ordinarily be considered a lawful surrogate. Is his testimony such that we could still consider there to be a sort of substituted judgment? Would this situation have been helped by a proxy statement? (See also chapter 7.) A court-appointed guardian ad litem?

5. Joe is 11 years old, is affected with Down's syndrome, and suffers from mental retardation. He has never lived at home and has been institutionalized since birth. He is in a home for nineteen multiply handicapped children and is attending a special school. He is able to write his name, has good motor and manual skills, can dress himself, is toilet trained, can converse reasonably well, and can participate in school and Boy Scout activities. It has been recommended that he be placed in the county's sheltered workshop following his education. This means that he can be occupied in some gainful employment.

When Joe was 6, a pediatric cardiologist made a preliminary diagnosis of a ventricular septal defect, a hole between the two chambers of the heart that elevates the pulmonary artery pressure. The pediatrician recommended cardiac catheterization to define the exact nature of the problem. The parents agreed. The tests showed a condition that, if untreated, generally leads to an average life expectancy of 30 years. About 25 percent of people with this condition die suddenly; the rest deteriorate slowly. Untreated children cannot run and play. The pediatrician recommended corrective surgery with a risk of death placed at 3 to 5 percent. He noted that he did not recommend the surgery for those with lower IQs, since little would be gained.

Joe's parents refused because they do not want Joe to outlive them. They believed that care for the disabled in the United States is terrible. They also believed that Joe would be a burden to their nondisabled children.

Is it ethical to not recommend the operation for those with low IQs? Is the physician using an unethical quality-of-life norm? Are the motives of Joe's parents consistent with their obligations as surrogates? Note that Joe has never lived at home and he might be a burden on the other students when he gets older.

NOTES

1. The principle of double effect is common among Roman Catholic moral theologians. Those interested in the complexities of it and the contemporary debate about it should read Richard A. McCormick and Paul Ramsey's *Doing Evil to Achieve Good: Moral Choice in Conflict Situations* (1978).

2. This ordinary-extraordinary means principle was originally developed by Catholic moral theologians as early as the sixteenth century. It originally arose because some treatments, even common ones, were so painful that it would be unreasonable to oblige a person to undergo them. In time, the principle became more general and became a proportionality principle. See McCartney, 1980, pp. 215-224.

3. Ramsey (1978) holds that the patient and the physician are both bound by the medical indications principle. Ramsey seems unwilling to trust the patient and is overly concerned with the wedge principle. We object to this approach, because it makes the physician the judge of what should be done and does not accept that decisions about health are not simply medical decisions.

4. The Baby Doe rule can be found in 45 CFR Part 1340, *Federal Register*, April 15, 1985, pp. 14878-901.

THE ETHICS
OF DISTRIBUTION

INTRODUCTION

The present chapter should be a book. The problems are complex, and even basic concepts such as need, contribution, disease, health, and health care are ambiguous. In addition, many if not most of the ethical problems of distribution involve the whole society and its common good. In this chapter, then, we attempt first to clarify these key concepts and then to provide a brief introduction to the problems of allocation of health care. Although we will attempt to establish principles for the distribution of goods and services, often we can only point out the complexity of the facts that society must consider in attempting to distribute goods in such a way that the dignity of the individual person is preserved.

A Definition of Health and Disease

The initial step in this evaluation involves understanding the psychosocial nature of health and disease. This requires, first, a definition of terms and, second, an indication of how variations in this definition can affect what is expected from the health care system. We are not attempting here to define any particular condition, but we wish to show how social expectations and habits influence what we perceive to be significant. What we perceive to be significant lies at the heart of particular health conditions and so ultimately determines society's recognition of a need for health care.

Health and disease can be understood only in terms of what is perceived to be significant, because to talk of health and disease is to assume a privileged position. From a global biological perspective, there is no health or disease; there are only different organisms competing for survival in the ways available to them. For example, a dog with fleas is not sick unless you care for the dog, which gives the dog a privileged position. If you are raising fleas, then the fleas have the privileged position and the dog is not sick at all. Thus, like justice, although perhaps more surprisingly, health and disease can be properly understood only in their social context.

In noting the social context of definitions of health and disease, we do not mean to deny the scientific nature of much of what contributes to health care. We simply mean that health and disease are not exclusively biological or physiological. On the contrary, health and disease are loaded with social and subjective concerns, as well as objective scientific criteria. Indeed, most scientific considerations are nested within larger and controlling social and subjective issues (Ehrenreich and English, 1979; Rosenberg, 1979; Oppl and von Kardorff, 1990).

These social and subjective considerations take several forms. Social conditions influence and may control the recognition of a problem and, once recognized, its determined degree of seriousness. In other words, people may suffer the symptoms of a disease without ever considering themselves to be ill. The point at which a collection of symptoms is admitted to be an illness varies greatly with social background (Spector, 1985; Starr, 1982). For example, some people will not admit that they are ill until they cannot continue to work. Others consider themselves ill if they feel any discomfort or pain. Even the type of symptoms counted varies with social background. Social conditions may also encourage the perception of a behavior, once accepted, as a disease. For example, the dramatic growth in the diagnosis of hyperactivity or attention deficit hyperactivity disorder is a study in the effect of changing cultural expectations regarding the behavior of children (Diller, 1996).

Because of the influence of social concerns on the recognition of disease, we define a disease as *any deficit in the physical form or physiological or psychological functioning of the individual in terms of what society wants or expects from that individual or in terms of what the individual wants or expects for himself.* As defined, disease involves a reference to the desires of the society and those of the individual, and not merely to physiological functioning (see Callahan, 1991).

This definition of disease emphasizes the role of the society and the individual in defining disease. Certainly, the biological and physiological elements are included. If a tumor causes such pain that the individual cannot get out of bed or even think, then it meets the criteria of a disease. On the other hand, an individual with arthritis may not consider himself as having a disease as long as he can function effectively. Similarly, society may consider the arthritis a disease only when it makes the individual unable to contribute anything to society. Thus, by recognizing or emphasizing (or by denying and de-emphasizing) particular physiological conditions, social and individual expectations and history influence the presence or absence of disease.

Although individuals and the society at large are the major actors in deciding what is a disease, the health care professions, acting as agents of society, have an important role to play. As we mentioned in chapter 1, health care professionals possess special knowledge and are thus responsible for mediating between the needs of the patient and the social resources available to care for that patient. Furthermore, the professions' social responsibility includes direct participation in the decisions about what constitutes a disease and its appropriate treatment. The health care professions have not always been helpful to society and may on occasion be self-serving. Despite these reservations, the health care professions are needed to help society and individuals to make informed judgments about what should be considered a disease and how to marshal our resources against it.

Given our definition of disease, health is easily understood as the *lack* of any deficit in the physical form or psychological functioning in terms of what the society wants or expects from that individual or in terms of what the individual wants or expects for himself. If you can do what you want or expect to do or what society wants or expects, then you are healthy.

Disagreement in Defining Disease

The conceptions of health and disease held by individuals and society may vary widely enough to allow two people to look at the same condition and evaluate it very differently. There are health authorities who argue that the low body fat levels, the enlarged heart, and the stress on muscles and ligaments characteristic of athletes indicate an actual decrease in their health, while many others argue that athletes who "suffer" from all these conditions represent the genuinely healthy individuals in our society. Not only is it necessary to understand the social circumstances and personal expectations of the individual in order to be able to understand their "health" or "disease," but it must be further recognized that one will bring to that analysis presuppositions, or prejudices, that will strongly influence the analysis. When a disease has its own lobbying group, the disease gets disproportionate attention. If the presuppositions and prejudices enlarge the scope of disease, they will create a demand for health care that makes it even more difficult to distribute scarce resources for the service of all members of the society.

Not only may there be differences among individuals in their understanding of disease, but there may be differences between the individual and society as well. As we have seen, both have different concerns, interests, and responsibilities, which may lead to conflicting evaluations. A father caring for his desperately ill son may not accept society's (i.e., the health care system's) judgment that his son should not receive the organ transplant that he needs. Whereas society sees a boy too ill to be likely to survive treatment and thus an inappropriate risk of scarce resources, the father sees only his son. Both are correct. Yet when it comes to the distribution of health care, the society's judgment will prevail when the individual cannot afford to pay for treatment or when resources are apportioned.

The tragic dimension of this conflict results from the irreconcilability of the two perspectives under current historical and material conditions. Only so much can be done and, given differences in perspective, the judgment of what should be done will be contested. Deciding against the desires of the individual and her or his definition of disease is not an attack on the dignity of the individual if there are socially significant reasons for doing so. This irreconcilability between the views and concerns of the society and those of the individual is not simple ambiguity: It is a genuine difference in interest and perspective that will remain in any system.

This conflict between individual and social definitions of disease can be a danger to a fair system of distribution in that the society's power can be used to silence the anguish of the individual. Fair distribution and even political stability require a continuing dialogue between the society and the individual on what counts. To maintain this dialogue, the potentially tragic dimensions of distribution must always be acknowledged, and the society must restrain itself and hear the individual (another way of explaining the need for autonomy). It is only by an honest attempt to mediate both concerns that there will be growth in the understanding of what fair distribution is all about.

The Goals of Health Care

As we discussed in chapter 1, there is some ambiguity about the purpose of health care. It is usually assumed, as part of our "common sense," that health care is a good. It is, however, an instrumental good; that is, it is not a good for its own sake, but a means that helps us to attain some other good. In the next paragraphs, we attempt to remove some of the ambiguity so that the choices and their implications for distribution become clearer.

One possible goal of health care is the prolongation of life. Modern medicine has been developed over the last 300 years in light of the hope that all human dysfunction can be eliminated, thus putting death off indefinitely. In other words, in our culture we expect medicine to help us to avoid or indefinitely postpone death. Yet every living, natural organism dies. Thus, the hope that health care may forestall death indefinitely is not based on any scientific evidence. This hope is a social intention that overlays the scientific investigation of life and disease. This hope creates in many individuals a socially induced need for medical care that may go far beyond what medicine can accomplish.

This hope, based on impossible roots, can have a devastating effect on human dignity and on a society's resources. There is now a wide variety of technical means to extend life: respirators, mechanical hearts, dialysis machines, and many other devices. But what kind of life is maintained under such conditions? The increasing number of well-publicized cases of mercy killing indicate a growing uneasiness with the vision of life hooked up to such devices. (We will return to this question in chapter 7.) It is also the case that such life-prolonging efforts are tremendously expensive. For example, one-quarter of all Medicare funds are spent during the last year of a person's life, and most of that is spent during the last month. Much of this money is spent prolonging dying and represents scarce resources that could be used to maintain and improve health. This purpose does not appear to serve any inherent need since we do not seem built to last forever. Furthermore, the socially induced need must be reduced if society is to distribute its scarce resources most effectively.

A second possible goal of health care is to alleviate suffering. Most of us will agree that people should live their lives as free as reasonably possible from pain. But what is pain or suffering? Pain is a personal or private experience, and it is very difficult to accurately comprehend the pain another individual is suffering. Also, what is the purpose of alleviating suffering? If we alleviate suffering without dealing with the cause of that suffering, we are simply masking the pain. Is it better to mask pain, or should we be left suffering so as to be forced to act to change the conditions that caused the suffering?

For example, painkillers are certainly useful and appropriate in many cases. A woman suffering from incurable cancer is aided by morphine in a way that many see as totally consistent with her dignity. But another woman, suffering from disorientation and loneliness, is kept sedated in an understaffed nursing home against all understanding of human dignity. Human beings ought to be spared senseless suffering, but ought not be warehoused like used machinery.

There are less dramatic examples of how the alleviation of suffering can be abused. Some drugs on the market, for example, are highly effective in treating ulcers by stopping acid production in the stomach and thus preventing pain. In most cases, such treatment does not deal with the underlying cause of the ulcer, such as stress or excessive use of alcohol or the presence of a bacterium. Thus, the drug effectively masks the true problem, allowing it to continue and perhaps cause greater problems elsewhere in the body.

These considerations make it clear that prolonging life and alleviating suffering are not always goods; that is, they do not always fulfill a need so as to protect the dignity of the person. As we will see in chapter 7 in our discussion of death and dying, there is a wide variation of estimates of what counts as too much suffering. If health care takes on the task of alleviating suffering, it is going to have to confront that variety and be responsible for judging private emotional as well as physical conditions.

The third possible goal is to optimize the patient's chance for a happy and productive life as defined by the patient. One problem with this suggestion, as we have already seen, is that society has a decisive role in defining health and disease. This is a role that society cannot abrogate because of its own need for survival. In the context of socially financed or socially delivered health care, the debate on the meaning of optimum health care would be endless and would probably lead to no improvement in government-sponsored health care.

The consequences of optimization for fair distribution are also quite significant. Enormous amounts of resources will be affected by even small gradients of change in the meaning of optimum. Take as an example mental health. Should we be free of only those anxieties that prevent us from functioning at all, should we be free of all but minor anxieties, or should we be free of all anxieties? An attempt to free the members of a society of all but minor anxieties would not only be fantastically expensive but probably impossible.

Optimizing the happy and productive life of a person is certainly a possible goal of health care. Unfortunately, the insistence on such optimization will cause grave problems in distribution. As we will point out shortly, it is probably safer and more realistic to speak of adequate measures of happiness and productivity.

Because of the social influence on ideas of happiness and productivity, it should be clear that the definitions of the individual must be reconciled with the ideas of the society. As already noted with regard to the mere prolongation of life, society may have to change the induced need in order to better address the problem of distribution.

We should also note a further problem in identifying the goal of health care. Not only may health care have an obvious, or generally intended, purpose but, in its instrumental capacity, health care can be used to serve several less obvious ends. In our economic and social systems, health care delivery not only takes care of patients, but it also pays the salaries of and provides social status and psychic satisfaction for health care providers. Any understanding of the purpose of health care is going to be influenced by the economic, social, and psychic concerns of health care providers. Such concerns are not the goal of the health care system, but can easily be treated as if they were.

For the present, we will proceed as if health care is generally a good, but with an indeterminate goal. Thus, we must recognize the possibility that there are cases in which it is not a good, and we will recall the potentially self-serving aspects of the role of health care providers in defining health and providing health care.

Health Care Has Its Own Limit

In light of these concerns, there is also a limit intrinsic to health care based on the limits of medical and health care knowledge. The knowledge of a health care professional is a combination of science, experience, and compassion. Much importance has been placed on health care as a science, but questions have been raised recently about what it means to say that health care is based on scientific knowledge.

According to Bursztajn et al. (1981), Americans have exaggerated ideas of the power of health care and medical knowledge, because they have a dubious concept of science in general and of medical knowledge in particular. Many people believe that health care is simply a matter of scientifically and certainly identifying the cause of a problem and treating it with a scientifically validated drug or procedure. They expect that this cause can be identified by a diagnostic procedure that will give a clear and unambiguous answer. They further expect that the treatment will be equally precise and straightforward. It is as though medicine, in particular, is a kind of magic that offers cures and restoration beyond the frustrations and limits we find in other areas of human life.

Medical advances and reports in the popular press seem to validate this attitude. The advances made during the twentieth century stem from identifying the causes of diseases such as influenza, polio, smallpox, whooping cough, and many others. Once identified, these diseases were treated with recently developed miracle drugs or vaccines, which drastically limited their destructive effects, leading to an increase in life expectancy and to a decrease in infant mortality.

But whatever their impact on the daily lives of people, these successes have created an impression about health care that obscures the nature of many health problems. For example, hypertension, a clinical problem that figures in many diseases, is apparently the result of several different factors: genetic history, health habits, and stress. Identifying the contribution of each of these factors, and even how they influence one another, is a much more complex problem than identifying the virus that causes smallpox. Health care for these problems must settle for diagnoses that are probable, rather than certain, because the diagnosis reflects the recognition that a disease may have many interrelated causes. Indeed, some causes of a disease may be beyond the reach of any health care.

The limits of medical diagnosis and of all forms of health care need to be acknowledged if we are to have a realistic view of the extent to which they can satisfy needs and should be supported by society. Indeed, the removal of exaggerated views about the magic of modern health care can do much to mitigate the demand for health care and so decrease the costs. Such realism should result in making it possible to serve more people with fewer scarce resources. This point needs to be stressed, since even the wealthy American society has arrived at a point where the cost of health care can no longer be disregarded.

Humane Health Care

Society will be working toward a distribution of basic health care that is adequate for the restoration and preservation of health as society defines it. This basic and adequate health care may be called humane insofar as it protects the dignity of the individual person.

When the absence of a certain type of health care leads to early death, disfigurement, or loss of the functions necessary to take one's place in society, we have certainly fallen below the basic minimum of health care for American society. In other words, the absent care is part of the basic and adequate minimum. It is basic because, in our society at our stage of ethical, scientific, and technological development, the dignity of the individual demands that we employ reliable and ordinary means to maintain a certain minimum level of treatment. This minimum requires that the individual gain relief from pain, which destroys higher human functioning, and that the individual be restored at least the minimum functioning valued by society; that the individual be spared a death that is the result of trivial or avoidable circumstances; that she be spared disfigurement that will make her repugnant to her society and herself; and that she be spared a loss of function that will make her unable to share the actions, burdens, and accomplishments that membership in society demands. A poorer society than ours might not be able to address many of these concerns due to its lack of abilities and resources.

In this area, the society has limited freedom to specify what basic needs are and how they will be met. What limits the freedom of society in specifying these needs are the demands of human dignity and the extent of the society's resources. Both concerns are limits, for the society must not only protect its members by protecting their dignity, but it must also protect itself by protecting its resources. Thus, the society must refer to considerations broader than those viewed by the individual, considerations such as the individual's contribution to society and the cost-benefit ratio of any treatment. It will not be obligated to treat a private in the army in the same way as the president, nor will it have the obligation to provide the most expensive false teeth if a cheaper pair will do the job. Granted a superabundance of resources, society might specify a right to all these things, but we can see no general right that would call for such specifications.

In these decisions, the functioning desired by the individual cannot control the definition of adequate care, since we know that resources would not permit satisfying all those desires. The distribution, then, will undoubtedly leave some individual sick in his or her own estimation, that is, below the desired level of functioning. As noted earlier, there is a genuine and irreconcilable difference in concerns and perspective between the individual and society. We cannot argue that a person who demands social payment for health care has a right to establish the level and type of treatment that will be received. Only the reasonable desires of the individual for health care need to be satisfied and then only if we understand that the *reasonableness of the desire for restored function depends on the judgment of society as well as of the individual.*

THEORIES AND THEIR LIMITS

Many theories have been proposed for solving the problem of distribution. Most of these theories fail because they disregard one or more of the reality factors that we mentioned at the beginning of the chapter.[1] In practice, however, need and contribution are the main factors in the just distribution of all goods. We have already developed the place of need in the process; after a brief consideration of the more likely, but still defective, theories, we will return to develop the importance of contribution as the second great norm of distribution.

The Basic Concerns: Need

A need is a deficit or a lack of something considered requisite (i.e., necessary). Many needs, if unsatisfied, will lead to the destruction of the human person. This brief explanation of the concept of need can be made a little clearer, albeit more complicated, by making the following distinctions.

Needs can be inherent, subjective, or socially induced. An inherent need exists no matter what the individual person may think about the matter. Thus, everyone has an inherent need for a certain minimal amount of nourishment. If food is not taken for a long time, the person will grow feeble, will be unable to function, and may even die. The amount needed may vary with the body size of the person, but it is rooted in the reality of living beings in general.

Subjective needs, on the other hand, grow out of the ideas and desires of the individual. These needs may be peculiar to the individual, as when someone in love claims that they "need" the other. Or they may be socially induced, as when anyone over sixteen who lives in a suburban area "needs" a car. Often, when these subjective needs are socially induced, they mimic inherent needs and must be addressed, as when adults say that they "need" a job.

Socially induced needs are a result of a historical development of material and social conditions coupled with a social consensus that some things are necessary for happiness, social life, or some other goal. In our society, indoor plumbing and running water are considered necessities. Most Americans would agree with this, although it is clear that societies survived and often flourished without these necessary goods. Even today, many societies lack the wealth and infrastructure to supply these goods to the majority of their people. Yet, Americans experience these and hundreds of other items as necessary, because their society both produces these goods and teaches their necessity. Examples include television sets, microwave ovens, showers in the bathroom, air conditioning, and a private phone line. The cellular phone and the personal computer with connection to the Internet are becoming socially induced necessities.

It is clear that socially induced needs grow historically and so create ever-increasing demands on individuals and society. The restless human being is forever discovering new and better ways to satisfy the need for shelter, food, education, defense, and health care. Each new invention creates a demand or a need for itself, and full participation in society often requires access to these new inventions. The existence of these socially induced needs and their relationship to human dignity can be adequately understood only in the actual circumstances of a given society. In short, what is necessary in one society is not always necessary in all societies. In view of this, there cannot be a definitive list of things that are needed. Indeed, the list keeps changing, creating ever-new demands for the goods in question.

It should be noted carefully that because individuals vary enormously in their natural endowments, desires, and social situations and sensitivity to social pressure, all needs are not equal in practice. Some need more food and health care than others. Others need less elaborate shelter and clothing. Very much to the point, a healthy population needs less health care than a sickly one. So, too, older people generally need more health care than young adults. These differences in need eliminate the possibility of a simple egalitarian solution to the problem of distribution.

Need will be one, but not the only, basis for the distribution of health care. Contribution to society will also enter into the distribution.

The Basic Concerns: Contribution

If there are no contributions to society, there is nothing to distribute; that is, no society produces anything without the effort of its people. For this obvious reason, all societies have found it necessary to base at least part of the distribution of goods, health care included, on the contribution of groups and individuals. This acknowledgment of contribution motivates contribution and so is essential to the functioning of society.

It should be noted that economic contribution is not the only form of contribution and payment not the only form of reward. Individuals create a variety of political and social goods that enrich society. The father and mother who raise good children, for example, may make the biggest contribution of all: the good citizen. Teachers make enormous contributions by training students for the key positions in society. The Veterans Administration, with its educational benefits, home mortgages, hospitals, insurance plans, and other programs, is designed to reward those who served in the military. These benefits are intended to be rewards for service and inducements to continued service. The political and social health of a society depends directly on continued contributions in key areas of the society. All these contributions should be weighed in a fair and prudent theory of distribution.

Distributive Justice: Needs and Contribution

The nuanced concepts of need, contribution, and health developed earlier in this chapter must be kept in mind in considering the ethical applications of these concepts. Our earlier treatment may even be considered as additional criticism of any theory that neglects one or more aspects of the problem.

A system of justice *based on need alone* holds that a just system provides goods to its members simply on the basis of their demonstrated need and their inability to satisfy it on their own.[2] The individual is the exclusive focus of this theory of distribution, and the individual is understood in his or her uniqueness, that is, in terms of his or her particular problems and possibilities. For example, an individual with allergies has a need for specialized medical treatment. Simply because the person has this need, this theory entitles her or him to receive treatment for it.

If the individual cannot get the treatment on her or his own, the individual has a claim for treatment against the larger society. A society that does not strive to supply what a person really needs attacks the dignity of the person. Thus, denying food to a starving person is an attack on his or her health and life and so on the dignity of that person. In line with our insistence on the dignity of the person, we may say that a person has a right to the satisfaction of needs connected with his or her dignity. Insofar as health care can satisfy such a need, a person can claim a right to it. When the individual cannot satisfy the need on his or her own, the right is a claim against society.

Two things must be stressed. First, the right to health care does not specify for whom or how the right is to be honored. Second, even when there is a claim against society for the health care, this does not specify how the society shall fulfill the claim. The fulfillment does not necessarily or always involve government intervention. Indeed, such government intervention may be a last resort to be used only after society has failed to set other mechanisms in place.

A theory of distribution based on need alone has an intuitive attractiveness, but it ignores not only contribution, but the power of society in defining and creating needs as it defines disease and health care. In short, it refuses to face the real world as outlined earlier in this chapter. Finally, it does not consider the scarcity of resources nor the importance of a differential in distribution in order to motivate contributions. Need, however, remains one of the principal factors in any just theory of distribution.

Contribution

The contributions of individuals to society must be acknowledged in practice. Failure to do so undermines a powerful motive for producing goods and leaves the society with less to distribute. Nowhere is this clearer than under communism, which believed "to each according to his need, from each according to his ability." The communists failed to recognize that neglecting to reward contribution, when added to other factors, leads to the economic problems that ultimately forced the collapse of many communist societies. The need to increase production of goods in short supply demands that contribution as well as need must be considered.

The provision of a return for contribution also helps to avoid paternalism and foster a respect for the right of the individual to make her or his own decisions; that is, it provides the consumer some freedom of choice. Although it is always tempting to say that everyone should eat certain foods or be sheltered in a certain manner and even to dictate how much medical care a person should consume, the fact is that people have different needs and tastes. This is a result not only of differences in biological and social needs, but also of differences in subgroup membership and individual choices. As long as individual choice, subgroup autonomy, and individual differences are valued in American society (and it is our position that on moral grounds they should be in any society), they should be respected in the distribution of the basic goods.

Practical Wisdom and Just Distribution

In short, a just distribution must consider both need and contribution. How is each to be judged and the distribution accomplished? It is the authors' contention that justice as distribution is accomplished through the application of practical wisdom to meet the demands (needs) of human dignity in the social and economic circumstances of the time. Justice thus involves respecting human dignity, satisfying human needs, and recognizing human contributions within the system and in ways that are characteristic of the system.

The specific definition of human dignity and the specific demands that flow from it fluctuate according to a number of factors: the traditions and goals of the particular society, the available economic and social resources, the current understanding of the meaning of appropriate social ideals, the power and persuasiveness of political authority, the consensus of the society in the distribution, and the preferences of individuals.

In attempting to promote human dignity, the traditions and goals of a particular society must take into consideration both the strengths and weaknesses of individuals. For example, in the United States the economic system tries to encourage industriousness and efficiency as socially beneficial ideals. It does this by rewarding the pursuit of selfish interests in the belief that such selfishness can be turned to the advantage of the common good by increasing productivity. Unfortunately, without the moderating influence of other social values, the system can isolate many individuals who do not fit the model well; their strengths might not be in industriousness or efficiency, but in artistic conception and expression or tender care for the sick and dying. As a result, these individuals who do not flourish under capitalist competition may not receive their share of health care when looked at from the perspective of other social values. This, in turn, raises questions about the adequacy of a pure capitalist market distribution of health care resources. For all that, most of the distribution should take place because people are able to purchase what they want and need. Where that is not possible, society as a whole must intervene directly or indirectly.

These questions illustrate how our understanding of the demands of human dignity evolve and why the actual practical principles of justice can be specified only through the historical circumstances of a society. Both the identification of general principles and the specification of these principles take place in a social tradition. There is a rough form of practical wisdom at work as the community faces the tasks of surviving through changing circumstances. This practical wisdom works through the history and language of this tradition; concepts are informed and understood in terms of the tradition, and social consciousness exists as its derivation. From the original doubts of the Founding Fathers about the institution of slavery, through the Civil War, to the civil rights movement of the 1950s and 1960s, American culture has evolved both an intellectual understanding and an emotional awareness regarding the practical issues of civil rights. This understanding is fragmented among different factors of the society and is changing (one hopes improving) as new issues are raised, such as hiring quotas and reverse discrimination. In short, justice in practice is not the result of the application of a few simple principles, but also a question of politics and social consensus. It is a ragged sort of justice, but all we have in the face of the reality of human existence.

In deciding difficult cases, the factor of contribution or potential contribution becomes important, even critical. When the basic needs for health care as previously defined have been met, society has discretion in the use of its funds for health care or any of the other essential goods, whichever promotes the public good. Here the utilitarian principle of the greatest good for the greatest number seems justified, within the general limits of human dignity.

Social Priorities

Political and economic realities force us to acknowledge that costs of basic goods, including health care, must be considered when dealing with scarce resources. One cannot simply say that cost should not be considered just because it is unpleasant to consider it. Here, as elsewhere, the basic dilemma of guns or butter remains prominent. No society can provide everything that everyone needs, let alone what everyone wants. Just as political considerations must be acknowledged to avert the danger of revolution, economic considerations must be acknowledged to prevent destroying the economy.

There can be no general right to the best a society can offer, because in an era of scarce resources (which will most likely be our permanent condition) a society would destroy itself if it tried to provide all of its members with the best of every material advantage.

Ethical distribution, then, must provide for *priorities* and a system of allocating resources that at least *regularizes expectations* in the light of what is politically and economically possible. Appeals to such norms as equality or equality of opportunity as a principle of distribution are useless if there is not and never will be enough to go around or if such appeals define their terms in ways alien to the society.

For these reasons, we emphasize the centrality of practical wisdom in ethical decision making. As our ability to recognize and tackle social problems, including health problems, develops, as our political understanding of such issues improves, and as our economic ability to satisfy human needs changes, we will be called on time and again to rethink our ethical decisions and commitments. Our practical wisdom must balance the shifting demands and possibilities that our changing circumstances present.

Health Care versus Public Health

Granted that health care is generally the focus of discussions of distribution, health care alone is not enough to promote health, long life, and reduced suffering. Health education and public health measures, such as sewage treatment, water purification, smog control, safety inspections at work sites, and school lunch programs, are equally if not more important. It is increasingly clear that a person's lifestyle and genetic endowment are key determinants of health. Thus, alcohol and tobacco use, secondhand smoke, asbestos in buildings, and illegal drugs, as well as nutrition and sleep habits, all affect health. The Environmental Protection Agency, the Occupational Safety and Health Agency, and school lunch programs are health programs that should not be neglected in the name of health care.

This distinction between health care and public health will pose a problem in the ethics of distribution. Society must decide how much it wants to dedicate to public health and health education, which will prevent disease in the future, and how much to health care, which seeks to cure or rehabilitate here and now. It is not obvious that one should always take precedence over the other. One major difficulty in making this decision is found in the fact that education and public health measures save statistical lives, rather than identified lives.[3] No one ever knows that she or he was saved from a disease by public health measures, even if the incidence of that disease has dropped significantly. On the other hand, anyone sick who is cured by a physician or nurse fully appreciates the influence of health care on her or his situation. The emotional difference between the influence of public health and that of health care must be recognized in forming a policy on public health. Once again, the actual situation, the resources available, and the definitions of a given society will have to be weighed and balanced to allocate efforts in a manner consonant with human dignity.

MICROALLOCATION: INDIVIDUAL AND INSTITUTIONAL RATIONING

A balanced distribution is not the result of society's efforts alone. The individual, as well as health care professions and institutions, must be present in the dialogue. That is, the distribution of health care is influenced not only by political and social decisions, but also by microallocation.

Although society can control macroallocation, individuals, both lay and professional, as well as institutions such as nursing homes and hospitals, are deeply involved in microallocation on a daily basis. Both the patient and the health care professional are engaged in triage or at least the allocation of their time and energies. Hospitals and health care institutions are faced with rationing decisions on the basis of their resources and the ability of the patient to pay. All these groups have a great impact on what health care is offered to an individual, but their influence is limited by the macroallocation of the society.

Triage and the Health Care Provider

The term *triage* originated in military medicine, in which it refers to the process of sorting sick and wounded soldiers on the basis of urgency and type of problem so that they can be sent to the proper treatment facility. The triage rules for emergency surgery in war call for giving first preference to the slightly injured who can be quickly returned to battle, with second place being given to the more seriously injured who need immediate treatment. The hopelessly wounded are treated last.

By extension, triage can be used for the prioritizing of treatment in catastrophes and emergency rooms. In a disaster, for example, rules like the following apply: Give first preference to those who need treatment to survive. Give second place to those who will survive without treatment, and give last place to those who will not survive even with treatment. Emergency room triage may introduce additional distinctions. First place might go to those who have life-threatening conditions that, if not treated immediately, will cause serious physical injury. Emergency rooms may well put the third-priority military group in this first position, even though they will not recover with treatment. Second come those who will require treatment within thirty minutes to two hours before being threatened with serious physical injury. Finally, there are those who at the time of examination are not critical and do not require treatment to survive.

Military triage and any other triage that is not based on individual need but on social concerns might be quite different. In military triage, the good of the group is given precedence over the good of the individual, so the contribution made by an individual to the group, rather than the need of the individual, is made the primary criterion of judgment. Jonsen, Siegler, and Winslade (1986) note that, when penicillin was scarce during World War II, it was given first to soldiers with venereal diseases, rather than to the wounded. Those with venereal disease could be returned to the battle much more quickly than the wounded.

Because most triage is done in emergency or crisis situations, it generally and correctly disregards everything but the medical indications and the good of the individual patient. Although emergency room triage sometimes disregards medical indications when it treats a hopeless patient, this is a reflection of a social belief in the magic of medicine, which suggests that no one is beyond help and that everything possible ought to be done.

We can expect current triage practices in emergency situations to change as cost factors make society aware that we cannot afford to use resources when no good can be accomplished. Cost factors and other considerations involving a recognition of the limits of health care are currently eroding the belief that no one is beyond help and that everything possible ought to be done (see chapter 7).

More importantly, this interaction between costs and hopes in the emergency room is paralleled by the system-wide discussion we have been outlining in this chapter. Efforts found in managed care corporations or in government, such as the Oregon plan for distributing Medicare and Medicaid funds, are essentially triage on a larger scale. Not only are we now seeing a more close social evaluation of the benefits expected from treatments, but we may also see a lowered priority assigned to those who have a life-threatening condition but little or no contribution to make to society. For example, should dialysis be withheld from diabetics who are also alcoholics and homeless? This is a shocking thought because it involves judging the value of human life in terms of social utility; that is, it is a matter of making social investments that will reap the best returns. Yet this type of judgment may become a fact of life as society is forced to give more consideration to efficiency under the constraints of scarcity. The dangers of this shift in attitude demand continued public debate about the tragic ethical conflicts involved.

Dangers of Social Power

The importance we have assigned to the social debate and social consensus is not without its dangers. As society assesses the extent of its own social needs and the limits of its obligations, there is a tendency to overlook the dignity of the person. This is especially true when resources are scarce. The society might stop listening to the needs and expectations of the individual, in particular powerless persons. But the dignity of each person requires that society listen to those who are potential patients. The dialogue must continue despite the conflict between social and individual definitions of disease.

Society may also diminish the dignity of the individual by labeling a person "diseased" without some clear and overriding social justification. Such a process is acceptable only when, all things considered, it is necessary to protect the dignity of other members of the society. Thus, quarantining an individual might be acceptable if he or she has a highly communicable disease. On the other hand, such labeling is not acceptable if it is done because the individual does not have the proper political ideas or does have a limitedly communicable disease associated with socially unacceptable behavior. Even though social concerns are legitimate factors in a decision, the needs of a society are not trump cards that simply override personal dignity.

In labeling or categorizing people for the public good, practical wisdom cannot avoid issues regarding the quality of life. These issues are beyond the scope of medical competence, as, for example, when contribution is included as a factor in awarding care. This opens up the possibility of abusing the dignity of individuals who do not fit the expectations or preferences of those making the political decisions. Thus, the practical requirement of establishing a hierarchy of health care needs raises issues that the society must treat very carefully, for they open the door for a potentially strong paternalism, or even political tyranny. At the same time, there appears to be no other even semiprincipled way of approaching the problem in a world where scarcity is a fact and the need to apportion resources is disregarded at the peril of both the individual and society.

Compounding the problem is the fact that the socially accepted concept of human dignity changes over time and reflects the circumstances of society. This changing social ideal of human dignity must be continuously and critically examined. The examination must involve the entire society in dialogue with all social and political authorities. After all, the demands of dignity do place some limits on what society can impose on the individual. At the very least, dignity requires society to listen to the individual in determining what human function and health care mean. This will be difficult and painful, because the discussion must always face the tragic dimensions of human life. If, however, the society fails to hear the individual, it has not merely neglected but destroyed the dignity of the individual.

The Economic Dimension
on the Institutional Level

As noted in chapter 3, health care providers, whether individuals or institutions, are not charitable institutions that can supply all services free of charge. Those institutions that received federal monies for certain purposes, such as construction, are legally obliged to care for a certain number of the poor free of charge. This obligation, however, does not call for free treatment of all indigent patients. The needs of the indigent poor would soon overwhelm the resources of any voluntary health care institution. Economics, then, becomes a central factor in an institutional distribution policy.

Up to the present, the American society has permitted economic considerations to enter into microallocation at the institutional level. To prevent such considerations from dominating admissions decisions, the society permitted differential pricing. For example, hospitals were allowed to charge one class of patients more so that it could subsidize the care of the poor. Changes in how medical bills are paid, such as by third-party payers (for example, Blue Cross and Blue Shield), have made such attempts to shift economic burdens ineffective. The health maintenance organizations (HMOs) have exacerbated the problem. They use their power to contract lower rates with the hospital and so decrease the hospital's income. This also slows down or stops cost shifting. Indeed, a hospital may have all beds filled by HMO patients and be losing money. Those persons without any form of health insurance or government help are thus more vulnerable than ever. The authors are not wise enough to know the solution to this problem, but clearly new mechanisms must be developed to cover those persons without the means to pay, while protecting the existence of these institutions needed to satisfy the needs for care.

Society is faced with two problems; the first concerns the extent to which society will require health care institutions to care for the poor without recompense. The second involves to what extent the society itself will pay for the care of those who cannot pay. In short, we are back to the problem of macroallocation. In the long run, problems cannot be solved on the institutional level without recourse to the societal level.

Microallocation: The Institutional Sphere

A fundamental distinction at the intersection between the societal level of allocation and the institutional level is between health care institutions that are for-profit groups and those that are not-for-profit groups. The not-for-profit groups can be further subdivided into those that are run by the government and those that are controlled by voluntary associations. These, in turn, can be classified as general community hospitals or specialized facilities devoted to only one illness or even to a single class of patients. Because each stands in a different relationship to society, the distributive ethics vary.

The for-profit institutions clearly operate under an entitlement theory and, at the present stage of history, this is correct insofar as they pretend to do no more. To put it another way, inside a socially approved market economy, they are as institutions ethical, if not admirable, when they take those who can pay and reject those who cannot.

Government-owned and -operated general hospitals should be open to all, with priority granted to the economically disadvantaged on the basis of medical need. These hospitals are paid for out of general funds and should be for the good of all citizens, but priority is to be given to the economically disadvantaged on the assumption that those with health insurance or sufficient wealth can obtain services elsewhere. Government hospitals for specialized populations, such as those run by the Veterans Administration, should distribute within the limits of their purposes. All this assumes that society has reached some consensus on the levels of need and how they will be satisfied.

Private, voluntary, not-for-profit groups are a more complicated matter. They do not derive their funds from the general funds of society, but they do have special privileges, such as tax-exempt status. In short, voluntary, not-for-profit hospitals are burdened with the public interest because they receive support and income from both the government and their communities. They also derive much of their income from government programs such as Medicare and from other tax-exempt institutions, such as Blue Cross and Blue Shield. These hospitals are, moreover, so much a part of the local community that they have special relations with and possibly obligations to that community.

Some specialized voluntary hospitals, such as those in academic medical centers, often give preference to interesting cases that are particularly important for teaching health practitioners and increasing knowledge in the field. This is allocation on the basis of potential contribution to society, rather than on the basis of patient need alone.

A Microallocation Problem: Institutional Allocation

No matter what manner of macroallocation is developed by society, the need for a principled method of allocation also exists on an institutional level. Some advocate institutionally fair allocation by the use of procedural rules that either eliminate bias or minimize its effects. Although these rules do not come to grips with the basic economic problem, they should be considered.

One set of procedural rules proposes selection by lottery or by some form of the first-come, first-served rule. Behind these rules is the belief that a strict equality should be the governing principle in allocation decisions. We reject these procedures for the same reason that we rejected the egalitarian view. The rules disregard the differences in need and the fact that the differences must be acknowledged because they are relevant to the dignity of the individual person. If all things were equal, which they never are, then the lottery or first-come, first-served principles might be applicable. In the real world of scarce resources and unequal needs, they merely dodge the issues. Fortunately, these rules are generally not used in practice.

A better proposal is that there be some sort of due process in the allocation of resources. Thus, the allocation might be done by a committee that represents a cross-section of the community. Such a method, it is argued, should prevent any one person from having too much power and so unduly influencing the decision in favor of his or her biases. This proposal has great merit precisely because it looks to the incorporation of a community judgment. The judgment of the local community, however, may not be enough in the face of the economic problem, which seems to call for decisions on the national level. In any event, it should be recognized that committee decisions can lead to trading and back-scratching as well as to balanced judgments. Thus, due process is a step forward, but not a final solution.

In the long run, only some sort of a national policy that represents the broadest possible community judgment will prove reasonably, although never completely, satisfactory. At every step of the way, there must be a dialogue between the society and its members about the nature and meaning of human dignity and how its demands may be met, given the abilities of the society.

Rationing

At the very beginning of this chapter, we noted that the distribution of any scarce resource involves rationing. This means that not everyone can have everything she or he wants. In short, it means limiting consumption and parceling out the goods that can be consumed.

In a society that assumes that everyone can have everything, such rationing is impossible except in times of extreme emergency. To change such a mentality, a society must both face the scarcity and evolve rules for the distribution, that is, the application of the concepts of need and contribution. We suggest the following controversial rules for discussion. Such discussion will illustrate the difficulty of the task of changing social evaluations of health and life itself.

In health care, basic needs such as the preservation of meaningful life must take precedence over mere wants and desires and acquired needs. Thus saving the leg of an otherwise functional diabetic woman has precedence over a treatment that might or might not prolong her life, and might or might not improve the comfort of a functioning individual who already has a fatal condition.

Priority should be given to the needs of individuals who have a chance to resume functioning over the needs of individuals who are never going to be functional in any way or who are already terminal. The dignity of the person demands that comfort care should be administered to this second group, but prolonged treatment merely to keep them minimally alive wastes not only money and energy but is often an affront to the dignity of the person. We shall return to this in chapter 7.

HMOs, Managed Care, and the Common Good

The health maintenance organization (HMO), the most common form of managed care, has been proposed as a solution to the problem of scarce resources. Typically a for-profit corporation, an HMO requires its members to enter the system of health care delivery through a gatekeeper, that is, a care manager (a physician-employee) of the HMO who provides basic care and controls access to other forms of care, such as testing and specialists. Thus, the patient's choices are limited so that he or she has little or no role in choosing or rationing health care. By stressing preventive medicine, the gatekeeper is, in theory, supposed to minimize the appearance of serious diseases and in the long run have healthier and less expensive patients.

In many cases, the gatekeeper-physician is rated as an employee, or even rewarded, on the basis of his or her ability to control costs. This creates a tension between the concern to treat the patient properly and to control health care costs adequately. In light of this manner of evaluation, HMOs have been criticized for substituting the goal of controlling costs for that of improving health care. In short, the task of rationing social resources has been put squarely on the shoulders of primary care physicians, who are not necessarily the people best suited for the task (Angell, 1993).

This issue is being addressed in several ways. There are several legislative efforts to limit how far HMOs may go in cutting care. For example, federal legislation now mandates that a woman and her newborn child may not be forced to leave the hospital earlier than forty-eight hours after delivery. This action was in response to concerns that cost-cutting efforts by HMOs had led to required discharges of new mothers and their babies in twenty-four hours before they were physically ready to go. HMOs and managed care groups themselves have been developing practice guidelines to provide guidance to gatekeepers to ensure a balance of both proper care and lower costs. Further, in October of 1999, Congress was working on a federal "Patient's Bill of Rights" which would give patients certain rights against HMOs and other health care insurance systems. These rights might include the ability of the patient to sue an HMO or other insurance companies if they have received substandard care.

This reveals a fundamental structural or systematic difficulty in HMOs and managed care groups. On the one hand, much of the burden of rationing care is put in the hands of the physician, whose personal stake as an employee may cloud his or her ability to make an appropriate social judgment. On the other hand, nonmedical groups, such as legislators and accountants, are becoming heavily involved in some important details of medical care. Whether an adequate adjudication of these roles can be worked out is both the promise and the danger of HMOs.

Some Concerns

All this *may* lead to a decrease in health care costs for the insurer, although some HMOs face serious financial trouble after a few years. Experience has also shown that HMOs meet rising costs by raising their rates as well as reducing care.

Unless the HMO also decreases the costs to those who pay for the insurance, that is, employers rather than individuals, an HMO will not flourish. When employees, especially unionized employees, complain, the company that pays the bill may force the HMOs to improve the quality of care, or the company may change HMOs or its whole insurance program. The employers cannot afford a high-cost benefit that produces morale problems. How employers respond to complaints may be just as important to the future of this version of health care as are the HMOs themselves. Moreover, until the system for accrediting HMOs is in place and mandatory, we will not know if HMOs improve health care or even maintain the existing level.

The existence of HMOs, by itself, does not lead to a better distribution of health care and so does not necessarily serve society as a whole. Those who are uninsured are still uninsured. The basic health care needs of these people are not met by the HMO system. Indeed, even those who currently receive Medicaid (for the poor) or Medicare (for those over 65) may find themselves with reduced benefits under state or federally mandated HMOs. Some poor people who currently qualify for Medicaid may even find themselves excluded from the revised HMO plans. In short, the allocation of health care can be narrowed and reduced in quality.

The Mechanisms of Distribution and Ideology

The furious debates about HMOs and other mechanisms of health care distribution rest on an underlying set of ideologies rooted in the economic concerns of contribution and need. Conservatives wanted to use the market as the main mechanism of allocation. This neglects the fact that the market disregards needs and supplies only those who have the money to purchase the service. At base, it is an overemphasis on contribution. Liberals, on the other hand, incline toward a system that, while it does not completely eliminate the market, tends to make the government the organizer if not the financier of health care distribution. In general, the liberal approach disregards or downplays the scarcity of resources and the necessity of rationing in favor of meeting needs. In so doing, the liberal position often overlooks the importance of contribution.

To avoid the worst effects of these ideologies, which tend to oversimplify the reality, it is necessary to return constantly to the principles and factors outlined in the previous pages. These principles may not solve the problem of what distribution mechanisms are to be used, but will alert us to the dangers to human dignity that result from the naive acceptance of one or the other abstract simplification.

Finally: Allocation of Resources by the Patient

The patient must make decisions about the allocation of his or her resources among all needs, including those of the family. For example, a parent under 65 with no medical insurance and no claim to Medicaid will have to decide whether to take a child to the doctor or hospital while taking into consideration not only the medical condition of the child, but also the potential economic damage to the family that might be incurred by the resulting bills. Patients are already constrained by the economic and social organization of health care and make decisions on allocation in terms of careful calculations of results and costs. In other words, the parent must ask if the child is sick enough to justify paying the doctor or going to the trouble of getting medical assistance. The uncertainties and trade-offs in this decision are so intractable that there appear to be no clear ethical guidelines for the individual except that all relevant factors must be considered within the context of the society's macroallocation of resources.

SUMMARY

A just society seeks to protect the dignity of its members and to satisfy their basic needs. Ordinarily, a society accomplishes these two tasks by giving its members the opportunity of satisfying their own needs in their own way. When members cannot satisfy their own needs, the just society specifies how it will attempt to satisfy these needs directly and humanely. In short, society must decide what constitutes a minimum level of satisfaction consistent with human dignity and the resources available. In making this specification and setting this minimum, the society is limited and influenced not only by the needs of members and the resources available, but also by the need to keep itself functioning. These concerns must be weighed and balanced within its own culture, values, and history. Because resources are always scarce, this direct distribution involves a judgment evaluating various sorts of basic needs and various ways of satisfying them directly. In particular, this judgment must recognize the need for rewards for those whose contributions keep society going or produce the surplus from which direct distributions can be made. The ideology of both liberals and conservatives, which would specify the mechanism of overall distribution, must be examined critically in this context.

Directly provided adequate humane health care should include the care necessary for the individual to avoid premature death as measured statistically, to function in society as a productive member, and, when such functioning is no longer possible, to be free of unnecessary physical pain in life and death. Society may decide that it has the resources to do much more than this minimum. That would be a desirable situation. It is not, however, a situation necessary for every society.

There are no easy answers to the question of what is the minimum in a given society and how it is to be attained. As we have suggested, human dignity is maintained only by consistent attempts to be consciously aware of its demands.

CASES FOR ANALYSIS

1. Clozapine (brand name Clozaril) is a drug manufactured by Sandoz for the treatment of severe chronic schizophrenics who are unresponsive to regular treatments. One study indicates that after a year of treatment 68 percent of the treatment-resistant patients were improved. In another study, 55 percent of those improved were able to work or go to school, and readmissions to the mental hospital were reduced by 88 percent (Meltze and Burnett, 1990, p. 892). A third study (Eichelman and Hartwig, 1990) in a state mental hospital showed that over two years the new treatment saved the state $20,000 a year per patient. In addition, clozapine has a low incidence of side effects, such as tardive dyskinesia, associated with other drugs for schizophrenics. It can, however, produce seizures and tachycardia, which can cause individuals to refuse further treatment. Unfortunately, unless constantly monitored, the drug often produces damage to the bone marrow, reducing immunity and exposing patients to all sorts of infection and even death. The proper use of the drug demands weekly blood tests of peripheral white cell counts. As a result, in the United States the combination of drug and tests costs $8,944 per person per year for the remainder of the patient's life. One study estimates that it would cost $1.2 billion a year to treat the 133,000 patients defined as *eligible* for the drug (Terkelson and Grosser, 1990, p. 866).

If the use of the drug is extended to groups other than the *eligible* group, Terkelson and Grosser (1990, p. 867) estimate that 186,000 patients could benefit. Under these assumptions, the treatment could cost $1.7 billion a year. The fact that most eligible patients are indigent makes these figures all the more significant.

Part of the cost seems to be explained by the fact that the manufacturers have insisted that the drug and tests be bought as a package, with the tests being administered by a for-profit home health company, Caremark, Inc. Many professionals feel that the price of the package or system is excessive and that there is good evidence both here and in England that the testing can be done by other laboratories (Reid, 1990). Sandoz later agreed to sell the drug aside from the whole package.

Does ethics demand that clozapine be authorized for all patients on medical assistance and all patients in state mental institutions? Are additional studies on cost savings necessary? Which principles are to be used here? Why? In answering the questions that follow, it will be well to ask what additional information would be useful or necessary to be more confident of the answer and then push for a decision on the basis of what is known.

Is this drug part of basic adequate care or is it, because of cost, a non-basic treatment? In answering this question, weigh the monetary costs, the side effects, and the fact that much of the drug will be wasted since a fairly high percentage will abandon the treatment. If it is basic, should the law stop Sandoz from increasing costs by insisting on its Patient Management System? Will the decrease in readmissions to mental hospitals and the return to the work force of a significant number of patients offset the costs of the treatment? If there must be a rationing scheme because the resources are limited, what should be the basis of that rationing since we do not know ahead of time who will benefit from the treatment? Can you think of other areas where the same expenditure would help more people and give a greater return to society? Discuss prenatal care, breast cancer prevention, free inoculations for children on medical assistance, alcohol and drug rehabilitation and antismoking campaigns.

2. Dr. Williams has his secretary ask new patients if they have medical insurance. If they do not, he refers them to other physicians. When accused of acting unjustly, he points out that he has an office to maintain, with staff salaries to pay, supplies to purchase, rent, and insurance bills, as well as his responsibilities to his family. He claims he has little choice.

Is Dr. Williams's method of rationing health care ethical? Why or why not? Does his reason justify turning away *all* who are not insured, or most of the uninsured, or only a few of the uninsured? What specific additional information do you need in order to judge the validity of his reason? Argue the case assuming he has no children and then twenty. Argue the case assuming that malpractice insurance and other professional expenses, including loans from medical school, leave him with a net income of $50,000, then of $100,000, then even more.

3. A debate erupts when Community Hospital announces that as a cost-saving measure it will close its emergency room from 10:00 P.M. until 6:00 A.M. The hospital explains that it is in danger of going bankrupt, and its emergency room is a very expensive hospital department. Patients will still be able to receive emergency treatment at the nearby State Hospital. Opponents argue that this will severely restrict indigent patients' access to care.

Granted that Community Hospital is in danger of going bankrupt, is its decision ethical? Is Community Hospital guilty of what is really a form of indirect "dumping" that is not covered by the law? How will the access of indigent patients to health care at State Hospital be limited? Will the poor be unable to get there because they do not have cars and there is no public transportation? Will State Hospital's emergency room be too small to handle the increased patient load? Assuming that the answers to the last two questions are yes, what should the health care community have done to make the general community solve the problem? Do health care professionals have any obligation to mobilize the community to remedy maldistribution? What are the limits of that obligation?

4. When, in the summer of 1996, reports were released on the success of protease inhibitors in treating AIDs, both the government and clinical directors were faced with new problems of distribution. Protease inhibitors were used as part of a drug cocktail that can drive the HIV virus *below the level of detection* and lead to a great increase in disease-fighting immune cells. But no one knew if the drugs could wipe out HIV lurking in the lymph nodes. Indeed, little had been published. Attention had been focused on dramatic turnabouts, but less attention had been paid to failures, or resurgences of the virus.

The treatments developed would cost between $12,000 and $16,000 a year at retail. The exact price would depend on the other drugs used in the cocktail (Waldholz, 1996). Although most private health insurance and managed care programs cover the treatment, some are restricting its use to the advanced stages of the disease. The treatment is not being given to people with the beginning of the disease since there is no evidence that it slows the progress of the disease. Indeed, there is debate as to when it is best to begin treatment with the new cocktail. Early treatment might make HIV cells drug-resistant and leave the patient with no drugs when the virus reemerges. Waiting for even the first symptoms to appear might take five to ten years, making clinical trials difficult.

When the announcements were made, the treatment was not being financed by the states' AIDS Drug Assistance programs, created for the uninsured. Clinical directors estimated that they would have to double their income in order to meet the demand for the new treatment. National estimates put the total cost of treating even half of the estimated 800,000 Americans infected with HIV at $6 billion dollars a year.

There are, moreover, problems with the treatment. The patient must take 14 to 20 pills per day on a very tight schedule along with dietary restrictions. In some cases the treatment will last for years and possibly for the rest of the patient's life. There is serious doubt about the ability of drug users, alcohol abusers, and many rootless people to maintain such a regime. This fear is reinforced by the side effects of some of the cocktails: nausea and headaches at the start of treatment. These effects cause some to stop treatment. If the patient starts and then stops, there may be serious social consequences. Specifically, a new drug-resistant form of HIV may develop and spread through the population. Already there are cases of patients who have sold their protease inhibitors in order to purchase street drugs. In July 1996, there were already eleven known mutations that may ultimately make the virus resist the drugs.

Even aside from the discipline required for the treatment, should the government increase payment for these new antivirals? What health care services or general public services should be reduced to provide this extra money? This is a political and social question that involves the opinion of the whole society.

Should clinic directors refuse to treat those who do not appear to have the discipline to carry through with treatment? If they do treat them, how can they justify the risk of producing new drug-resistant strains of HIV? How are the answers to these questions affected if the clinics receive no new funding?

NOTES

1. The utilitarian theory would call for distributing so that the greatest good for the greatest number results. Unfortunately, this tends to subordinate the individual person to some abstract aggregate. The egalitarian theory aims at an equal distribution of goods or at least the opportunity for goods. Unfortunately, needs are not

equal, so this would actually lead to a waste of resources. Justice as fairness (Rawls, 1971) is an attempt to balance the basic equality of people with the inequality of their needs and abilities. The inequalities result from a sort of natural lottery and may be tolerated so long as any pattern of inequality is evaluated by effects on the least advantaged members of society. Unfortunately, so many schemes of distribution can be justified by this theory that there is nothing to prevent the fox from ruling the hen house. The fairness theory also disregards the natural selfishness of some people who would forever produce new inequalities for their own profit. Justice as entitlement holds that goods ought to be distributed according to a system of contracts. Without such a contract, a person would have no right to health care or any other good. Most find this offensive, since it would deny basic goods such as food, shelter, and health care to those who do not have a contract or cannot afford one.

2. The communists advocated such a single principle when they preached, "To each according to his needs, from each according to his abilities." They failed for a variety of reasons, not the least of which was the failure to reward contribution properly.

3. In the previous pages we have insisted that in most encounters the primary purpose of medicine and the other health care professions is to treat the particular patient. Once having entered into a relationship with this specific and identifiable patient, the health care professional has an obligation to that patient. In the vast majority of cases, then, there is a moral claim of an identified life, that is, a specific person.

The health care professional, however, has obligations to others as well. As just noted, health care professionals, generally through their professional organizations, have obligations to society, that is, a duty to prevent disease, to maintain the health of the populace, and to oversee the delivery of health care. Such work in public health saves *statistical lives*. The people who do not get sick because of public health measures cannot be specified individually. But, in a sense, we know of them through the statistics that show that interventions had a good effect. Individual practitioners can satisfy this obligation to save statistical lives through their professional organizations or through their own actions.

5

PRINCIPLES
OF CONFIDENTIALITY
AND TRUTHFULNESS

Introduction

In medicine, as in the rest of human life, truthfulness and confidentiality exist in an often uneasy tension. On the one hand, all social cooperation depends on truthful communication. On the other hand, telling everything could lead to disaster. We do not go around telling everyone what we think of them for the simple reason that this would destroy human relationships and in some cases lead to violence. We soon learn two important and inter-related truths. First, telling the truth is not the same as telling the whole truth. Second, some truths should be kept confidential. It is difficult, however, to decide what may ethically be concealed and what must be revealed.

In chapter 2 we outlined the basic truths that a health care provider *must* provide the patient in order to get informed consent. In that context, the patient had a right to the information and so there was an obligation to communicate it to her or him. The context of informed consent, however, does not cover all the problems of truthfulness. In the present chapter, we will develop principles to cover cases in which it is not a question of informed consent or in which the physician is dealing with someone other than the patient or a lawful surrogate. For example, should a physician write on a death certificate that the patient died of AIDS? Should the physician tell the patient that he is sterile if this was discovered by accident and is not connected with the patient's visit? Finally, there are the cases when the nurse or physician is addressing the entire community by mass media.

In the second part of this chapter, we will develop principles to cover the cases in which the truth ought to be kept confidential, that is, concealed from people other than the patient. Must the physician conceal from a wife the fact that her husband has herpes? Must the nurse conceal from a parent the fact that a 16-year-old daughter had an abortion? When can a physician reveal sensitive information to a nurse or another physician?

TRUTHFULNESS

The ordinary ethics of truthfulness is generally summed up in two commands. First, do not lie. Second, you must communicate with those who have a right to the truth. These commands are too simple to come to grips with the complex problems met in real life. As a matter of fact, both of these are really hypothetical commands. The first really says, *"If you communicate,* do not lie." The second says, "You must communicate, *if the other person has a right to communication."* Neither says that you must tell everyone everything you know or everything they want to know. The first command leaves you free not to communicate—to remain silent or to evade the question or even to tell a falsehood, which, as we shall see, is not the same thing as a lie. The second command opens up the question of who has a right to communication of the truth.

Lying

There are many very different approaches to the problem of lying.[1] In line with our general approach, we will judge the ethics of lying in terms of its consequences for the individual and for the social system of communication.

Traditionally, a lie was defined as speech (communicative expression) against the mind; that is, a lie communicated something at odds with what the speaker believed to be true. A lie was understood to be wrong because it was contrary to the natural purpose of speech and subverted the community, which necessarily relies on speech. But when the varieties of speech are considered and the many ways in which they are used (such as, for humor, for play acting, for teaching, or for cooperation), it is difficult to see how speech simply against the mind universally or even generally has evil consequences. For this reason, we prefer to call such speech against the mind a falsehood and to define a lie as *a falsehood in those circumstances in which the other has a reasonable expectation of the truth.*[2] When the other has a reasonable expectation of the truth, a falsehood breaks down communication and renders the variety of forms of social cooperation extremely difficult, if not impossible. At the very least, a lie isolates the individual and in so doing harms her dignity.[3] Ultimately, the breakdown of social cooperation hurts every individual, including the liar. In this approach, lying is wrong because of its social effects and not because the other person has a right to the truth.

The revised definition of lying appears lax until the nature and range of reasonable expectations have been examined. These expectations vary with (1) the place of communication, (2) the roles of the communicators, and (3) the nature of the truth involved. All three of these are connected with both the obligation of confidentiality, which will be discussed later, and the right to privacy.

These three factors, which determine the reasonableness of the expectation of the truth, are in large part specifications of the obligation to minimize evil and to justify the tolerance of evil by a proportional good. All the factors studied in the treatment of proportionality in chapter 3 can be usefully reviewed at this point.

A person does not have a reasonable expectation of the truth if the communication would take place in circumstances in which people could overhear information that might be damaging. For example, if someone asks a professor about the faults of a student in a public place where others can overhear, there is no reasonable expectation that the professor will tell the truth and so hurt the student. The expectations would be different in the privacy of an office.

The role of the two communicators also helps to establish the reasonableness of the expectation of the truth. Ordinarily, the dean of the college asking a professor about a student would have a reasonable expectation of the truth. Even the dean of the college has no reasonable expectation of the truth if he or she asks for information that the professor obtained when counseling a student. The counseling relationship was confidential, and the obligation of confidentiality changes expectations. Similarly, if a stranger walks up to me and asks for the intimate details of my sex life, he has no reasonable expectation that I will share them with him. A person sensible to cultural norms would know that strangers do not even ask such questions, let alone expect a truthful answer.

Even a very good friend would not reasonably expect a truthful answer to a question about very private matters, such as one's finances, sex life, or secret ambitions, nor about such potentially damaging information as the fact that I have a criminal record, suffer from AIDs, or formerly belonged to the Ku Klux Klan.

A physician doing a health history in her office would have a very reasonable expectation of a truthful answer to all the questions bearing on diagnosis. The role, the place, and the nature of the matter all create the expectation in this case. The patient who goes to the physician for a diagnosis also has a reasonable expectation of the truth.

Many people have unreasonable expectations of the truth. In the ideal order, these people, who are frequently prying busybodies, should be rudely told to mind their own business. In practice, the demands of social life often require that we get rid of them in less abrupt ways. When they have no reasonable expectation of the truth, I retain my right to conceal the truth and to protect both my privacy and the good of myself and others. As we shall see in the section on confidentiality, people do not ordinarily have a reasonable expectation that a health care provider will tell them the truth about anyone but themselves.

Society recognizes that there is no reasonable expectation of the truth when someone is asked to testify against himself. It is for that reason that a person on trial cannot be forced to testify. On the other hand, the society through the law does specify certain situations in which an individual has a reasonable expectation of and perhaps even a right to the truth. The laws on truth in lending, fraud, and the revelation of latent substantial defects in a product provide examples of reasonable expectations of the truth. In most situations, however, the law says that buyers have an obligation to find the truth for themselves.

It is not a lie to conceal the truth, although it may be unethical for other reasons. If I keep my mouth shut or evade the question or give an ambiguous answer or even tell an outright falsehood when I am asked many of the questions mentioned in previous paragraphs, I have not lied. Indeed, because I used those means to avoid an evil, I have, granted proportionality, done something virtuous. It would be quite different if I told a falsehood to a person who asked me the way to the nearest restroom or the price of a hotel or the name of the mayor. There is no reasonable cause for keeping these things secret, and so the other has a reasonable expectation of the truth.

Our examples thus far have covered cases in which the other person asks for information. The situation is different in those circumstances in which I am not asked for information, but volunteer it. In these cases the other has a reasonable expectation of the truth. By volunteering the information, I announce that I intend to communicate and so create a reasonable expectation of the truth. There are exceptions to this when it is clear that I am merely fooling around, telling a tale, or am so biased that you should expect nothing from me. In general, however, volunteering information creates the reasonable expectation.

In this context of voluntary dissemination of information, we note with the National Association of Physician Broadcasters that the health care worker who uses the mass media to spread medical news must be accurate, give full disclosure, and enjoy editorial independence. This independence is necessary to avoid conflicts of interests that might result from dependence on a drug company or censorship by an editor.

Federal antikickback regulations also forbid witholding information about actual or potential conflicts of interest. Thus, patients have a right to know that a pharmacist is being paid to persuade a physician to prescribe a given brand or that physicians earn frequent-flier miles for prescribing a given brand. Such activities might cause the professional health care provider to put financial interest before the interest of the patient. For this reason, concealing such relationships might constitute fraud, that is, deliberate deception of the patient.

Even when I volunteer information, other persons cannot reasonably expect the whole truth unless I tell them that they will get the whole story. Absent such a promise, there is no reason to think I am volunteering the whole truth. In most cases, the whole truth is not particularly useful or even a good thing. Indeed, people who attempt to give the whole truth often bore us to death with irrelevant details or scandalize us with their lack of respect for the reputation of others. There are even cases when giving the whole truth actually leads to deception, since the important truth can be concealed in a pile of irrelevant detail.

The Right to the Truth

More difficult questions arise with regard not to the reasonable expectations of truth, but with the *right* of a person to the truth. As already noted, the patient has a right to the information needed for informed consent because that information is needed to make decisions about treatment. In other cases when there is no question of treatment, the patient may have a right to truthful information because he or she has paid for it. That is, the person may have a right to the truth by purchase. For example, the patient who goes to a genetic counselor for information pertinent not to a treatment but to marriage has a right to the truth. In this setting, it is precisely information that he has paid for.

There is a third set of circumstances in which the patient has a right to information even though there is no informed consent involved and no explicit purchase of information. The patient has a right to the information when he needs it to make important nonmedical decisions or to avoid great evils. Here, as in the case of informed consent, the need of the patient for the information gives birth to the right to the information. The principal example of this is the nonmedical need of the patient to know that he or she is dying. Religious thinkers stress that the dying person needs to make peace with God. There is also the need to set one's financial and personal affairs in order so that survivors may not suffer more than necessary. The personal affairs may involve no more than a goodbye, but they can also call for a reconciliation with enemies or estranged family members. These are not medical issues, but they are important. Even if one tries to deny the patient's strict right to know that he or she is dying, the concealment of this truth denies a person a chance to take care of these duties. The denial treats such important duties as trivial and, in the process, mocks the dignity of the person, whose needs are more than medical.

The Placebo Problem

A placebo (Latin for "I will please") is "a preparation devoid of pharmacological effect given for psychological effect, or as a control in evaluating a medicinal believed to have pharmacological effect" (Blakiston, 1972). In short, it is something that chemically should not have an effect. In more popular terms, it is a sugar pill. Although useful, the definition may be too narrow, since many other things, from the physician's diploma to a nurse's bedside manner, can have therapeutic psychological effects. Indeed, some writers (Carlton, 1978) say that until recent times most medicines were placebos. Furthermore, it can be argued that psychological factors such as the faith of the patient in the physician are still important placebo-like factors. One way or another, placebos are still used not only for research and psychological effect, but for keeping the patient satisfied and off the physician's phone. Sometimes the physician is really using a placebo without knowing it. This happens when the physician believes the treatment helps, even though there is no scientific evidence for it. In view of the above and leaving aside the use of placebos in research, we will redefine the placebo as *anything that is used to effect a therapeutic outcome or anything that does affect the outcome when the entity used is not supposed to have active biological powers.*

The ethical problem is clear. Does the use of the placebo involve unethical deception of the patient?

Before attempting to answer that question, a few remarks are in order. First, even drugs with active pharmacological properties have enhanced effects when the patient believes in them. Second, the Hawthorne effect in industrial psychology shows that merely paying attention to a worker will increase productivity and cooperation. The same certainly holds true in health care. Third, placebos, or at least belief in the placebo, have been shown to affect the immune system and even to produce addiction (Brody, 1987).

All this need not surprise us, since the effects of drugs depend not only on their pharmacological properties, but on attitude, that is, on the mental set of the user and the setting in which the drug is taken. In addition, although many have a tendency to see disease in terms of biological causality, many diseases have psychological dimensions that can be influenced by a placebo. When we are dealing with multicausal systems in which the observer affects the observed and when we expect only probabilities rather than certainty, it is easy to make a place for factors such as placebos, even though they cannot be neatly pinned down.

None of this, however, should be taken to justify using a placebo in place of an effective pharmacological agent, except in highly restricted circumstances. A general idea behind the practice of regular (or scientific) medicine is that a person's belief system does not supplant the structure of nature as uncovered by scientific research. This is part of the reason why, for example, American law does not allow Christian Scientists to forego regular medical care for their children facing life-threatening health conditions. Thus, while the placebo effect may make important contributions to a patient's care, a physician cannot simply rely on that effect. Exceptions to this principle do arise with regard to psychological addictions, but great care must be exercised in these cases to protect the patient from mistakes or prejudices on the part of the health care provider.

In view of all this, whether or not providing a placebo is deceptive depends on the exact way in which it is presented. If the physician says, "I am going to prescribe something that often helps in these cases and has no bad side effects," it is hard to see how he is deceiving the patient. Certainly, he is not lying. In such a presentation, the patient knows what she or he needs to know in order to give informed consent. No untruth is spoken, and no information to which the patient has a right is suppressed. Indeed, the physician is far more likely to deceive with regard to a pharmacologically active drug if he says, "This will make you better." This is promising too much, whether said of a placebo or a test drug.

Where deception is not the ethical issue in the use of the placebo, there are other problems with placebos, such as overpricing or using them in place of accepted treatment. Overpricing can be condemned as a form of theft, and the failure to use accepted treatment when it is called for is simply malpractice.

Summary

It is wrong to tell falsehoods in those situations in which there is a reasonable expectation of the truth. The expectation of the truth varies with the place of the communication, the roles of the communicators, and the nature of the material to be communicated. When we volunteer information, we create a reasonable expectation of the truth, but not necessarily of the whole truth. We have an obligation to communicate only when the other person has a right to the information as a result of contract, relationship, or special need. The use of the placebo is not wrong per se as long as the patient is not told a lie.

CONFIDENTIALITY

All these obligations must be seen not only in the context of truthfulness, but in the context of confidentiality. Indeed, it is only after we have considered confidentiality that we can tackle the difficult and often neglected questions about the health care provider's right or obligation to communicate with families and other third parties about the condition of the patient.

Confidentiality is concerned with keeping secrets. A secret is knowledge that a person has a right or obligation to conceal. In the present section, we shall concentrate on obligatory secrets. The obligation to keep secrets arises from the fact that harm will follow if the particular knowledge is revealed. There are three types of obligatory secrets, which are distinguished by the types of harmful consequences that result from revelation. These are the natural secret, the promised secret, and the professional secret.

The *natural secret* is so named because the information involved is by its nature harmful if revealed. As we saw in chapter 3, we are obliged to avoid harming others unless there is a proportionate reason for risking or permitting the harm. Because the obligation to avoid harm is universal, even a layperson is obliged to keep secret the fact that a friend has AIDS lest the person be shunned and persecuted unjustly. This obligation exists no matter how the information was obtained. Similarly, we are obliged to keep to ourselves information about the private peculiarities of people that might cause them embarrassment if revealed. We might be obliged to keep secret the fact that a person was in the hospital if revelation of the fact would hurt his or her business. Even the patient's name can be confidential if revealing it might cause either inconvenience or embarrassment to the patient. The psychiatrist who sold mailing lists of his patients certainly caused them inconvenience and may have exposed them to serious loss of reputation, even though the only thing revealed was the fact of treatment. Unfortunately, this fact has been known to stigmatize an individual in certain groups.

It should be obvious that sometimes the harm that comes from concealing a natural secret outweighs the harm that is being avoided. In these cases, proportionality can justify revelation and at times make it a duty. If a friend with AIDS attempts to give blood even after you have argued with him, you have a proportionate reason to tell the Red Cross of his condition in order to prevent harm to recipients of his blood. On the other hand, you would not be justified in telling the Red Cross of an AIDS victim who had no intention of attempting to donate blood. In this case, there is no foreseeable harm. You would have a similar justification for telling classmates that one student insisted on attending class even though she had infectious hepatitis. You would have no justification of generally revealing her infection if she stayed away from class.

The *promised secret* is knowledge that we have promised to conceal. Generally, the promise has been exacted because the matter is also a natural secret, in which case the nature of the matter makes the secret stricter. The special evil of revealing promised secrets arises from the harmful effects of breaking promises. Social life depends on people keeping promises, and we depend on social life for nearly all our basic goods. In addition, most of us are wary of the person whom we cannot trust to keep a promise. We leave that sort of person out of many social interchanges.

Here, as in the case of the natural secret, there may be proportionate reasons for revealing the secret. The good to be attained, however, must offset the evil that results from the broken promise, as well as from the nature of the information. One will be justified in revealing the intention of someone to kill, even though one swore an oath to keep it secret. A layperson might, despite promises, be justified in revealing a friend's diabetes to a health care professional if the friend is not following medical advice and so threatening his or her health. Once again, it is a question of proportionality, that is, of the need to justify risking or permitting harm by a proportionate good.

The *professional secret* is knowledge that, if revealed, will harm not only the professional's client, but will do serious harm to the profession and to the society that depends on that profession for important services. In many cases, but not all, this secret is recognized by the law so that a professional would not have to reveal "privileged communication" even in court. This means that a physician *cannot disclose* information learned in confidence from a patient unless the patient gives permission. Clearly, the professional secret is the most serious of all secrets, because its violation can cause the greatest harm.

The importance of the professional secret in health care is best seen by contemplating the consequences if patients lack faith in the confidentiality of their dealings with the health care system. When the law required health care providers to report minors with sexually transmitted diseases to parents (a legal exception to confidentiality), infected teenagers suffered without care and kept on spreading sexually transmitted diseases until the United States had an epidemic. Their distrust of the health care system thus led to a major health problem. A change in the law that restored the principle of confidentiality encouraged young people to go for treatment and cut the incidence of these diseases.

Not only teenagers but all men and women rightfully feel that the condition of their bodies is private and to be shared with those that they choose to help them, but not with anyone else. We do not want to tell our secrets to someone who cannot be trusted to keep a secret. Indeed, with the exceptions noted below, the patient-provider relationship implies a promise of secrecy. For this reason, if for no other, health care providers must observe secrecy to keep their services acceptable to the people who need them.

Society has long recognized the importance of professional secrecy. To protect confidentiality, society has even given physicians statutory immunity from testifying about their diagnosis and treatment of patients. The immunity of other health care professionals differs from state to state. In general, society has, for the reasons given below, expected all health care professionals to maintain confidentiality. Unfortunately, the complications introduced by third-party payers, such as Blue Cross, indicate that there is probably a need for rethinking the whole area of professional privilege (Taranto, 1986). We will say more about this later.

The professional secret, then, must be kept because of the nature of the knowledge, the implied promise, and the good of the profession and the society.

The Patient's Bill of Rights of the American Hospital Association (1992) is quite clear about the obligation of professional secrecy in the hospital setting:

5. The patient has the right to every consideration of his privacy concerning his own medical care program. Case discussion, consultation, examination, and treatment are confidential and should be conducted discreetly. Those not directly involved in his care must have the permission of the patient to be present.
6. The patient has the right to expect that all communications and records pertaining to his care are confidential.

The application of these statements requires some amplification and explanation.

Confidentiality and Consultation

Unless explicitly forbidden by the patient, a health care professional has a right to consult other health care professionals in an effort to help the patient. In cases of doubt, the permission of the patient or surrogate should be obtained. Among other things, the patient who must pay for the consultation should have a right to decide whether he or she can afford it. It is understood that the person consulted is bound by the same secrecy. Providers are not ethically free to discuss patients merely to pass the time of day or in a public place where they may be overheard. The hospital cafeteria is not a suitable room for a consultation, let alone a gossip session. Neither are health care professionals free to satisfy their curiosity about patients who are not in their care. A physician not involved professionally has no right to look at the chart of a friend or neighbor who happens to be in the hospital. The principle of confidentiality operates on a need-to-know basis and that means *a health care need to know.*

Residents, interns, and other students in a teaching hospital are not free to look at charts without the permission of the patient unless they are directly involved in the care of the particular patient. Some justify a general right to inspect records in terms of a general consent signed by the patient or surrogate on entrance to the hospital. This is a dubious justification because the average patient does not read the form and has no idea of what rights he or she has signed away. We argue, then, that more explicit permission is required if residents and interns are to ethically examine the records of patients whom they are not directly involved in treating.

Exceptions Required by Statute Law

The exceptions to confidentiality may be grouped under four headings: (1) exceptions commanded by statute law, (2) exceptions arising from legal precedent, (3) exceptions arising from a peculiar patient-provider relationship, and (4) exceptions due to a proportionate reason.

Exceptions are commanded by many statutes for such things as gunshot or knife wounds, child abuse, certain communicable diseases, acute poisoning, and automobile accidents. Some states demand that public authorities also be informed of illegitimate births, birth defects and deformities, cerebral palsy cases, industrial accidents, and chronic drug addiction (Annas, 1975, pp. 115-116). Since each state has its own laws, local statutes must be consulted. In each case, the law presumes that the public good demands an exception and so outweighs the harm of the revelation. It is also assumed that the patient knows that these cases are not covered by the implied promise of the patient-provider relationship.

Health care professionals often find that the assumptions behind these laws are not warranted in a given case. That is, they see more harm than good occurring if they violate confidentiality.

Child abuse laws in many states make mandatory the reporting of suspected abuse, whether physical or mental, whether arising from omission or commission. The provider can be torn between conscience and the law, since she or he may believe that the reporting will only make things worse for the abused child, or that the local child protective services will not handle the situation properly, or both of the above. There is no easy answer to this problem, and in the last analysis the providers must consider both the danger to themselves and to the suspected victim when making a decision.

Exceptions from Court Decisions

Exceptions arising from legal precedent, that is, from court decisions, are harder to pin down because the courts in one state often differ from those in another and because courts change opinions over time. The famous *Tarasoff* case[4] held that a psychiatrist should have warned a woman that a patient was threatening to kill her. The court argued that the therapist had to take reasonable steps to protect third parties from the patient. It is not at all clear that revealing the homicidal tendencies of the patient in the *Tarasoff* case was necessary or useful. Indeed, two years after the original decision, the same California court that condemned the psychiatrist reworded its ruling so that a professional only had to "exercise reasonable care to protect foreseeable victims." In *Rogers v. South Carolina Department of Health*, the decision went further and said that there was no duty to warn, since the patient had not made threats against a particular person. This is more in line with the general ethical practice. It rightly assumes that even psychiatrists are not very good at determining who will actually commit murder, let alone whom they will murder. Other courts have relied on this same thinking to say that the psychiatrist need not reveal the ravings of his or her patients to those who are mentioned as possible victims. Most patients are probably only blowing off steam, and it is estimated that two out of three times, predictions of violence are wrong. In other words, flipping a coin might have given better results.

Regardless of the merits of the case, many courts have been holding psychiatrists liable if they do not take steps to protect both third parties and the patients themselves. This often leads to health care workers overprotecting themselves by hospitalizing more people than is necessary and by keeping them hospitalized for longer times. Other mental health workers are playing it safe by not taking any patients who show tendencies to violence. All these reactions are not in the interests of either patients or the public. Unfortunately, some courts have used the *Tarasoff* case as a wedge and have decided that the warning and information connected with it are not part of therapy, so the psychiatrist can be forced to reveal it in a criminal proceeding (Leong et al., 1992; Weil, 1993). At least one state court has gone further and created an obligation to warn of a threat to damage property when persons *may be* injured (Helminski, 1993). These are serious breaches of confidentiality.

Unfortunately, some professional organizations are not aware of the dangers, so we get statements like the following from The American Hospital Association's Committee on Biomedical Ethics (1985, p. 24).

> Also subject to state law, confidentiality may be overridden when the life or safety of the patient is endangered such as when knowledgeable intervention can prevent threatened suicide or self-injury. In addition, the moral obligation to prevent substantial and foreseeable harm to an innocent third party usually is greater than the moral obligation to protect confidentiality.

This opinion, like that of many courts, overlooks the fact that professional confidentiality is necessary to protect society's interest in having sick people seek treatment for health. Unfortunately, in a society that sees everything in terms of individual rights, such errors are common. Here as elsewhere a fine balancing of interests is called for.

Exceptions Arising from Unusual Relationships

The exceptions arising from a peculiar provider patient relationship occur with family and military personnel who owe a loyalty to their employer as well as to the patient. As long as the patient understands that he or she is not fully protected by confidentiality, there is no serious ethical problem, unless the company or military provider is the only one available. The Judicial Council of the American Medical Association (1996) draws useful distinctions in the industrial context:

5.09 CONFIDENTIALITY: PHYSICIANS IN INDUSTRY. Where a physician's services are limited to pre-employment physical examinations or examinations to determine if an employee who has been ill or injured is able to return to work, no physician-patient relationship exists between the physician and those individuals. However, a physician is obligated to divulge important health information to the patient which the physician discovers as the result of the examination. Nevertheless, the information obtained by the physician as a result of such examinations is confidential and should not be communicated to a third party without the individual's written prior consent, unless required by law. If the individual authorizes the release of medical information to an employer or potential employer, the physician should release only that information which is reasonably relevant to the employer's decisions regarding that individual's ability to perform the work required for the job. A physician-patient relationship does exist when a physician renders treatment to an employee, even though the physician is paid by the employers. If the employee's illness or injury is work related, the release of medical information may be subject to the provisions of workers' compensation laws. The physician must comply with the requirements of such laws, if applicable. However, the physician may or may not otherwise discuss the employee's health condition with the employers without the employee's consent or, in the event of the employee's incapacity, the family's consent.

Exceptions Due to Proportionality

The exceptions due to proportionality cannot be reduced to a few simple rules. Suffice it to say that a great good and generally a public good must be at stake to justify a revelation that will harm the profession and the society, as well as the patient. Ordinarily, a professional will not be allowed to reveal information merely for the good of a third party, even if that third party happens to be a patient. In general, the physician may not, without the permission of his patient, tell a wife that her husband has syphilis, even though she incurs a danger of infection. Nor should the physician inform the husband that the wife is pregnant or intending an abortion. The good of the third parties involved does not, except in rare cases, justify harm to the patient, to his or her trust in the profession, and ultimately to the society that depends on the profession. In particular, the harm to the patient's confidence in the profession and the patient's resulting hesitancy about seeking advice or treatment make it unethical to make such revelations except in rare cases.

The rare exceptions involve more than the good of isolated individuals. It can be argued rather persuasively that there is a proportionate reason for discreetly revealing to a wife the fact that her husband *certainly has AIDS*. Here we are dealing with a disease that can harm not only the wife, but children yet to be born and, through dramatically increased health costs, society itself. It becomes hard to justify revealing the suspicion that the husband *might have AIDS*. In the first case, we are dealing with the threat of a life-destroying process, in the second with the possibility or some unknown probability of a life-destroying process. As the probability becomes greater, the case for revelation increases in strength. The issue is made more complicated by the fact that warning the wife may be useless and so unjustified, since the warning comes too late.

The American Nurses Association (ANA) (1990) approved of a *limited* ethical privilege to disclose *probable* exposure to the HIV virus when the patient refuses to uphold his or her duty to protect others by preventing transmission of the infection agent. For the exercise of this privilege, the ANA lists five conditions:

1. an identifiable third party at risk;
2. a belief that the risk is significant;
3. a belief that the third party does not know he or she is at risk;
4. the patient being treated refuses to tell the third party or is considered unreliable; and
5. the treated patient is notified and there is a written record.

Although these conditions are no doubt well intentioned, they contain too much "belief" and no reference to the measurement of probability, which we will discuss under the duty of the infected health care provider to disclose her or his condition to patients.

The task of considering all the factors and weighing the relative harms and benefits becomes very complicated in the consideration of exceptions due to proportionality. In practice, the authors believe that the presumption should be in favor of confidentiality unless the case for revelation really shows proportionate goods to outweigh the harm to the profession and the society.

Familial Exceptions

In the past, medical practice has generally assumed that the provider was free to reveal the condition of hospitalized patients to their families whether or not the family was a surrogate. Indeed, at one time the American Medical Association (Annas, 1975, p. 124) stated that "reporting to one spouse information about the medical condition of the other is not a breach of confidentiality." The previous paragraphs have already indicated cases in which such revelation would be neither desirable nor ethical. Ethically, it is better to insist that spouses of competent patients may not be told without the permission of the patient, which is the current position of the AMA (1996, section E-5.05). The patient who reasonably assumes a promise of confidentiality may have many good reasons for keeping the matter secret from a spouse. The disclosure of the disease may cause anxiety in the spouse, promote smothering behavior, or in some cases arouse suspicion of infidelity. Annas (1975) remarks that permitting the physician to tell the spouse often results in the patient not being told, especially when the news is very bad.

On the other side are those who argue that compassion for the spouse and family justifies revelation. Except when dealing with surrogates, the permission of the patient should be obtained since the relationship is with the patient and the first loyalty is owed to the patient. To the extent that the spouse and family are patients because of their suffering, they should be treated with compassion and concern, but such compassion does not warrant breaking confidentiality.

Most of the previous paragraph would have to be rewritten if the professional relationship were with the family and not the individual patient. In England, for example, the reporting of child abuse is not mandatory, and visiting nurses see their relationship as one with the family and not the individual patient. The English visiting nurses often refuse to testify in cases involving child abuse lest they damage their relationship with the family. We cannot condemn that stand as long as the terms of the relationship are clear from the beginning.

Exceptions in the Case of Children and Adolescents

Traditionally, it was assumed that health care providers had not only a right but an obligation to report to parents on the health of their children. However, the law has provided for an increasing number of areas where the health care provider either need not or must not reveal the health problems of the child or adolescent to the parents. We have already noted the case of sexually transmitted diseases. Similar reaffirmations of the right to confidentiality exist in the areas of abortion, substance abuse, and contraception, but not in the area of sterilization. The law varies from place to place in the United States, but the underlying idea is clear. When confidentiality is necessary for the health of the patient, to protect the patient's rights, or to protect the public health, traditional exceptions that permitted or required that parents be informed become questionable. For a full treatment of the law and the provisions in each state, the reader should consult Morrissey, Hoffmann, and Thorpe (1986).

Media Publicity and Confidentiality

In recent years the medical problems of prominent people and the drama of new medical technology have often been media events, complete with press conferences by physicians, briefings by medical spokespersons, and TV reporters giving their spiels against the backdrop of a hospital. Quite aside from the drama of these media events, some hospitals will give brief summaries ("She is critical" or "He is in stable condition") of a patient's condition. Unless the patient or a surrogate has given informed consent to such revelations, the supplying of information and the publicity may easily violate the principle of confidentiality in health care. In some cases, as noted earlier, even the revelation of the fact that a person is a patient may have harmful effects. Here, again, there needs to be a careful balancing of the need of family members to know and the privacy of the patient. Once again, the authors hold that, in case of doubt, the presumption should be in favor of confidentiality.

Some will argue that the public has a right to know about public figures, especially political figures whose health is of true public concern. Even if we grant this claim for the sake of argument, it does not follow that health care providers have as a general rule either an obligation or a right to supply the information without the permission of the patient or the surrogate. If the public has a right to the information, the sick person and not the health care provider has the obligation to provide it.

Hospital Records, Research, and Confidentiality

A stay in the hospital is or should be meticulously documented in both the financial and medical records of the institutions. Diagnosis, treatment, nurses' observations, progress, and discharge are all reported and stored for future use. Implicitly, the patient has given permission for those involved in her or his direct care to see these records. The permission is on a need-to-know basis. Nurses' aides do not need to see the records and so do not have implied permission to read them.

It may also be argued that the patient has given permission to a peer review board or another quality assurance board since these boards provide the patient with additional protection. In practice, the billing office has enough information to allow the curious to make rather accurate deductions about the patient's illness. Aside from these individuals and the third-party payers, treated in the next section, no one else has a right to see the record without the permission of the patient.

Although the records are made primarily for the good of the patient, they also provide a valuable source of information for health care research. The patient, even if care is provided at public expense, retains the right to privacy. The records should not be used without the informed consent of the patient. That is, the patient should know that a bit more of his or her privacy is being surrendered if consent is given. Merely having the patient sign a form on admission is not sufficiently respectful of the patient's right to privacy.

When proper consent has been obtained and research is done on the records, two things should be kept in mind. First, only summary data with no identification should be used in publishing the research. Second, the number of people who see the record itself should be kept to a minimum. Both of these provisions help to protect confidentiality and to remind people of its importance.

Confidentiality and Third-Party Payers

The introduction of third-party payers, whether governmental or private, into the health care system has weakened confidentiality. When we sign into a hospital or have our physician apply for reimbursement through our insurance policy, we give permission for nonprofessional employees to supply the insurance company with information about our diagnosis and treatment. At the insurance company, the information is handled by clerks and fed into a computer. Although in theory the information is still confidential, a large number of people have seen it in transit and, in practice, clever people can access it with considerable ease.

If this health information came into the hands of life insurers or employers, it could have harmful consequences. For example, some companies refuse to hire people who have had a history of cancer on the grounds that they represent a risk of higher health insurance rates for the company. Although this appears to be illegal as discrimination on the basis of an alleged handicap, former patients have been injured in this way. In addition, if the revelation involved treatment for a mental condition, chances for promotion or election to public office might be affected. In short, the computerization of health care information represents a potential for harm to patients.

The dangers to confidentiality impose special obligations not only on health care providers but on health care administrators as well. In the first place, all personnel, clerical and nonprofessional as well as professional staff, should be thoroughly oriented with regard to confidentiality. The penalties for the violation of the rule should be both clear and severe enough to demonstrate the seriousness of the matter. In the second place, systems should be in place to control access to records and to make sure that the need-to-know principle limits even professional access to information to the necessary minimum.

Confidentiality and the Public Good

When no specific piece of legislation commands revelation for the public good, physicians can often find themselves in a dilemma. The patient expects confidentiality, and a violation of confidentiality will certainly hurt society. Yet, keeping the matter secret may also harm society. Nowhere is this clearer than in the case of AIDS. Some health care professionals have called for the right to report the AIDS carrier as well as the AIDS victim to those who might be infected. They want the right to inform other doctors about the condition of the patient even without the patient's permission. Some even demand that the AIDS patient be quarantined if there is no other way to prevent him or her from spreading the disease.

This issue is too grave to be left to individual judgment. Furthermore, as pointed out in chapter 1, the roles of health care providers are determined by society and clients, as well as by members of the profession. Thus society needs to speak through specific legislation that will spell out the exceptions so that both health care providers and patients will know where they stand in the relationship. The legislator must keep in mind that, if the exception to confidentiality and the imposition of quarantine lead to fewer people getting treated, we may only have succeeded in hiding the problem, rather than in solving it. The experience with reporting venereal diseases of minors should be kept in mind in any legislation on AIDS.

Confidentiality and the HIV-Positive Provider

Is a health care provider obliged to inform a potential patient that the provider is HIV-positive? The answer depends on two factors: (1) the effect of secrecy on the effectiveness of the profession as a whole, and (2) the risk of infection to the patient.

Because there is danger to the profession as well as *possible risk* to patients, the American Medical Association takes a nuanced position in answering the question. Relying on the idea that the welfare of the patient is primary, the AMA says that the physician should *err on the side of safety even when there is uncertainty about the physician's infection*. In particular, the AMA *believes* that, if there is an *identifiable risk*, HIV-infected physicians have an ethical obligation either to withdraw from the case or to inform the patient of the condition and get written, informed consent. If there is no identifiable risk, the AMA defends the right of the physician to continue practicing medicine. The American Nurses Association wants nurses who handle bodily fluids to reveal their status if they are HIV-positive. In general, the professional associations have proceeded very slowly and continue to debate the exact shape of the professional obligation.

The recommendations in the previous paragraph, although based on the primacy of the patient, also seem justified by the need to protect the reputation of the profession. Here, as elsewhere in this chapter, the reputation of the profession is important for the functioning of professionals and so for the good of society. If the public is aware of some professionals putting the good of the professional ahead of the patient, the entire profession will be hurt. The suspicion of a few tends to blacken the many. This can lead to patients staying away from the health care system and thus creating additional health problems. The courts and legislatures will undoubtedly decide that in some cases disclosure is mandatory, no matter what the cost to the health care provider. Already one New Jersey case (NJ Stat Ann 10:5-4; Office of the Surgeon General, 1991) upholds the right of hospitals to restrict the surgical privileges of an HIV-infected physician. (For more on the legal and ethical problems of health care institutions in this area, see Barnes, et. al., 1990.)

Although the argument based on the good of the profession could justify the guidelines given by the professional associations, the question of actual risk to patients needs more careful consideration. We must first ask about the chance of the physician's or nurse's vital fluids mixing with those of the patients. Second, we must ask what is the chance of becoming HIV-infected once the fluids have mixed. Third, we want to know the probabilities of HIV infection developing into full-blown AIDS. In short, there is a three-stage calculation of risk prior to imposing a duty on the health care provider.

If there were no risk to an individual, there would be no *obligation* to follow the socially based advice of the professional associations. The *universal precautions* of the Centers for Disease Control, however, do not eliminate all risk and so leave the provider's condition relevant to the provider patient relationship. The crucial question becomes whether *the risk is so high that the advice of the professional associations becomes an ethical duty*. Note that even though AIDS is a terrible syndrome, we are ethically justified in risking even death when the risk is small. For example, we risk death when we cross a busy highway, but granted a good reason for crossing and having taken precautions, we cross ethically since the risk of death is small.

First, what is the risk of a patient becoming HIV-infected as a result of exposure to an HIV infection in a health care professional? This question can hardly be answered on the basis of empirical studies. Only one health care professional, a dentist, appears to have infected patients. Even then the infection may not have been from dentist to patient, but from patient to patient as a result of poorly sterilized instruments. Studies of the patients of HIV-infected physicians have not produced any unambiguous results. The occasional patients with HIV infection belonged to high-risk groups and could have been infected elsewhere (Barnes et. al., 1990).

Some estimate that in surgery there is a one-in-forty incidence of a significant skin puncture with a three-to-ninety chance out of 10,000 cases of HIV infection from the puncture. Thus, no matter what the actual exposure rate to the HIV-infected fluids, the seroconversion rate, that is the actual conversion to the HIV-positive state, is extremely low even if we allow for the effect of repeated acts of exposure.

Finally, we must ask what is the risk of getting AIDS as a result of seroconversion. Whereas it was once assumed that 100 percent of those with the virus would end up with AIDS, we now know that even without treatment some infected patients never progress to that point. Host factors play a major role in seroconversion and the course of HIV disease (Fauci, 1993). Further, important advances have been made with regard to post-exposure prophylaxis, that is, treatment immediately after exposure to reduce the threat of HIV infection or at least to dramatically slow the progress from infection to disease (Centers for Disease Control, 1998).

Because the chances of a particular health care worker's infecting a particular patient are very small and nearly negligible, it seems unfair to burden all HIV-infected health care professionals with the choice of avoiding all contact with bodily fluids, or going into another line of business. The decision should be made on a case-by-case basis. In addition, we agree with the New York State Department of Health, which requires not merely an identifiable risk, but *a significant risk* before a health care professional can be barred from practice (Barnes et al., 1990, pp. 315-316). This position has the advantage of being consistent with the Americans with Disabilities Act, which requires that an employer must first establish a significant risk that cannot be removed by reasonable accommodation (Gostin and Curran, 1990, p. 307). We do not intend to get into this complicated legal argument, but we note that the first courts that ruled on such questions have also affirmed an obligation to reveal a risk that could affect the patient's informed consent. As our knowledge of the actual risks increases, we may see legal obligations applied more widely to health care workers, or perhaps eased if precautions are developed that minimize the risk to the patients.

We note one possible exception to the significant-risk rule. When a patient asks the health care professional whether he or she is HIV-infected or has AIDS, the patient obviously may consider any risk subjectively significant. If a false answer is given to the patient, we are inclined to believe that there is a defective consent and a physician–patient relationship based on deception.

Although this position has a certain plausibility, it involves giving great weight to the subjective and often unfounded fears of the patient. Indeed, one of the great problems in the ethical world of AIDS is precisely the exaggerated fears of infection, leading to both ethical and legal stands that are based on the equivalent of superstition. For this reason, we believe everyone should proceed with caution in this area. Certainly, the final word on this question will be spoken only after years of public debate and the collection of more data bearing on the question.

SUMMARY

Professional secrecy is the most obligatory of all secrets, since the violation of confidentiality damages not only the patient, but also the sacredness of promises and the good of society and the profession. Professional secrets can be shared in legitimate medical consultations and revealed for proportionate reasons or when there are proper statutory or court-imposed exceptions. There is also an exception to confidentiality in special relationships, which are not true provider–patient relationships.

CASES FOR ANALYSIS

1. Mary is in need of a kidney transplant, and her parents and siblings have been tested for compatibility. Her father is afraid of operations and knows that kidney trouble runs in the family. Before the test, Mary's father tells the doctor that he does not want anyone, especially his wife, to know that he is compatible. He explains that if the family knows they will pressure him into being a donor. The father turns out to be the only one who is compatible. Mary asks the doctor, "Are you sure no one in my family is compatible?"

Is the father a patient and protected by confidentiality? Even if he is not a patient, is his explicit request, which was not refused, a protection of his confidentiality? If the matter is confidential, what can the physician ethically say or do to protect the secret?

2. The Smith family is in a car accident, and all five family members are hospitalized as a result. The father is critically injured, and in two days it becomes clear that he is going to die. The wife, although making good progress, is still confined to her room. When she is told of her husband's deteriorating condition, she insists that the physician tell her husband, since he is the sort of man who would want to know. The children, still in the hospital, have not seen their father and keep asking about him. The physician refuses to tell the husband of his condition. He dies a few days later.

Did the physician have an obligation to tell this patient that he was dying, especially since this patient would want to know? Did the physician have a right to tell the wife since the patient was competent and there was no need for a surrogate? What should the children have been told when they asked about their father?

3. Dr. Xavier has been the Loyolas' family doctor for more than twenty years. He is shocked when Mary, the sixteen-year-old daughter, comes to tell him that she is pregnant and wants his help in getting an abortion. Since abortions are against Dr. Xavier's conscience, he refuses. He also informs the parents of Mary's condition and her intentions.

Can the physician justify his action by the use of proportionality between good and evil effects? The good of the profession and the society must be considered in answering the question. Why did a British medical society publicly reprimand this physician?

4. Huntington's chorea is a genetically transmitted disease that affects both males and females. Only one gene from either parent is required to transmit the disease to offspring. If a person knows that the disease runs in his family, there is a 50/50 chance that he will have it. Although some tests have been developed to detect the disease, generally people will not know that they have it until the symptoms appear, generally in midlife. In the United States, one person out of 10,000 has it. Thus, there are over 20,000 active cases in the United States, and there are probably 100,000 people who are uncertain whether they have it.

With Huntington's chorea, there is a continuous and irreversible deterioration of the mental, physical, and motor functions. Clumsiness and forgetfulness are followed by angry outbursts, disorientation, incontinence, loss of speech control, and writhing and twisting of the entire body. Ten or twenty years of suffering lead to death. Victims often commit suicide.

Dr. Calvin discovers that Mary X., age forty, has Huntington's chorea when she comes to ask for help with her memory loss and angry outbursts. He does not tell her the truth, because there are no medical decisions to be made, but most of all because of the horrible death she faces. A few weeks later, when Mary's son, age twenty, comes in for a premarital blood test, Dr. Calvin wonders if he should tell the son that he has a 50 percent chance of having the disease and so should hesitate about having children.

Is the physician ethical in concealing the truth? Does Mary need to know the diagnosis for any possible decisions about herself and her children? What is the significance of the fact that she has paid for the diagnosis? Could the physician's silence be justified by paternalism or therapeutic privilege? What is to be said of the argument that, since there is no treatment, there is no need for informed consent?

5. Doctor Curious has a habit of wandering around the hospital and looking at the records of friends who are in the hospital. The nurses have tried to stop him, but he has retaliated by making their lives miserable and belittling them in public at every opportunity. Nursing administration has been notified but has done nothing, since it wants to avoid rocking the boat.

What are the nurses' ethical obligations after they have done everything mentioned in the text? See chapter 12. Is "not rocking the boat" a sufficient excuse for the administration to do nothing further?

6. Administrators at the Oxcrossing Mental Health Center have decided to cooperate with a project that will centralize all public mental health records for four adjoining states in a central computer for research purposes. The professional staff objects and refuses to go along unless all identifying information is removed. The administration agrees, but is later caught restoring Social Security numbers. The staff retaliates by listing only vague, harmless diagnoses so that the records now reveal little or nothing.

Is the staff ethical in altering the records to protect confidentiality? Note that incomplete or suspect records can endanger third-party reimbursement. Is there any possible reason for identifying the subjects for research purposes? What further steps should be taken to protect confidentiality in the future?

7. Professor Garrett is in the hospital and explicitly forbids social workers and dietitians to see his medical record. "I do not want them involved in my care," he says. The nurses humor him, but allow the social worker and the dietitian to see the records, since that is normal hospital policy.

This case involves the patient's right to control who is consulted about his case. Is there a written hospital policy on this? Should the patient be told of the policy or lack of it upon admittance? Does a patient have to accept all policies of a hospital or should some of them be negotiable?

8. John O. is a school nurse. In the course of talking to a student in his office, he discovers that the youngster is on drugs and even suspects that the student may be peddling them. He reports all this to the principal.

What is the student's understanding of the relationship to the school nurse? Is there an explicit warning that the school nurse may report things to the principal and other authorities? Granted that the previous question is answered with a yes, is the nurse justified in revealing the information to the principal?

9. George has gonorrhea. He does not want to tell his wife, but does want to protect her from the disease. While undergoing treatment, he asks the family physician to test his wife without her knowing it. When the wife comes in with a bad case of bronchitis, the physician tests her, saying, "I just want to run another test on you to rule out a possibility, a mere possibility, you understand." He finds she has been infected and treats her without her knowing the diagnosis. He merely tells her, "I want you to take these antibiotics as a precaution." In this way, he protects the husband.

Is the family physician deceiving the wife by suppressing the information? Is his medical treatment of the wife ethical? Suppose that the disease was AIDS. Does this change the ethics?

10. Dr. Timorous has been requested to examine Mary and Stan Koska to see if there is a danger of them having children with Tay-Sachs disease, a genetic disease leading to a progressive mental and physical deterioration. Over a period of months, a baby with this disease will go blind, and suffer motor paralysis, spasticity, and, finally, rigidity of the muscles. Death usually occurs in the third year of life.

The test indicates that Stan has a recessive Tay-Sachs gene. Dr. Timorous tells him this and suggests that he tell his brothers and urge them to have the test, since they too are thinking of having children. Stan feels contaminated and ashamed and refuses to say anything to his brothers.

Dr. Timorous knows the brothers socially. Although they are not his patients, he has seen one of them professionally in the past. He debates with himself. Should he send carefully worded letters to the brothers urging the screening? Should he just keep it all to himself? What is the ethical thing to do?

Is there any way of getting the brothers screened without breaking confidentiality? If there is no way, would Timorous have a proportionate reason to break confidentiality? Would Timorous be unethical if he remains silent? Here the seriousness of the disease and the odds of it being passed on are very relevant.

11. Dr. Maternus has been the family doctor for the Garrett family for fifteen years. He has delivered all six of the Garrett children and belongs to the same church as the couple. Recently, during a routine checkup on Tom Garrett, age three, he notices suspicious bruises in places that do not fit in with the father's story of the child falling out of bed. Ordinarily, he would report this as suspected child abuse. In this case, he keeps it to himself. It is unthinkable that the Garretts would abuse a child. Why start an investigation that will only cause ill feelings?

Does Maternus know the Garretts so well that he is justified in breaking the law? What danger does he run by not obeying the law? What dangers is he exposing the child to? What harms can come from following the law? Note that the law calls for extreme confidentiality in investigation. In a large percentage of cases, the investigation leads to no action.

NOTES

1. In the appendix to her book *Lying,* Bok (1979) gives long citations from Augustine, Aquinas, Francis Bacon, Sidgwick, Harrod, Grotius, Kant, Bonhoeffer, and Wamock on the morality of lying. These writers present a huge array of opinions and theoretical approaches.

2. This definition differs from that given by Bok (1979, p. 14) in that it attempts to include wording that takes care of the cases in which a falsehood is justified.

3. In natural law, speech against the mind, that is, a lie, would be considered intrinsically evil. For natural law, there are several different types of intrinsic evils; abortion, killing, and lying are some example. For practical wisdom, what is intrinsically evil is harm done to the dignity of the individual. As mentioned in chapter 1, a main cause of the difference is the confidence that underlies the natural law theorist's claim to know nature. The practical wisdom theorist is not so sure.

4. *Tarasoff v. Regents of the University of California*, California Supreme Court (17 California Reports, 3d Series, 425). The case was decided on July 1, 1976.

6

PROFESSIONAL STANDARDS AND INSTITUTIONAL ETHICS

INTRODUCTION

As we saw in chapter 1, it is the traditional understanding of the professions that they were supposed to control entrance into the profession and to police themselves. This obligation is twofold. In the first place, there is the obligation to maintain and improve the quality of health care.[1] In the second place, there is the obligation to police the profession in order to protect the public from dangerous and unqualified practitioners.[2] Furthermore, given contemporary insights into social groups such as the professions and given recent changes in the delivery of health care, it is becoming clear that professional standards and their enforcement are inseparable from the institutional framework within which the profession functions. It has also become clear that these health care institutions themselves have ethical obligations (Reiser, 1994).

In particular, the institutions that deliver health care services have ethical problems with competition and the resulting impacts on quality, safety, and efficiency, the training of workers, and conflicts between hospital policy and the conscience of the workers. Finally, even health care institutions with carefully worked out policies on these and similar issues must face the fact that it is one thing to have an ethical policy and quite another to make sure that it is enforced.

Many of these institutional problems have become more widespread as the health care industry, including the HMOs, attempts to lower costs or at least slow the rate of increase. Economy thus comes to dominate efficiency, safety, and often even the quality of care. As noted in chapter 4, the managed care movement can be seen as the cutting edge of this effort. In some cases, the ethics of the institution involve broad questions involving the very structure of the health care system; in others, they involve internal policies and procedures. We will begin with the problems associated with maintaining quality, then consider policing, and conclude with a discussion of the effects of competition.

JUDGING QUALITY

Although the traditional conception of a profession, supported by contemporary codes of professional ethics, demands that the professions lead the effort to protect quality in the professions, there are difficulties. In the first place, there is no agreement as to the criteria for quality health care. In the second place, even if we had agreement about the criteria, there would still be grave problems in applying the criteria to the complexity of day-to-day practice. With increasing concern for health care that is both high quality and cost efficient, there is currently a great deal of interest in evaluating quality, and advances are being made.

Three broad criteria could be used to measure the quality of health care: (1) inputs, (2) process, and (3) outcomes. The input analysis would look at the preparation of the health care professionals and their credentials, as well as the availability of state-of-the-art equipment and facilities. Process analysis of quality (or practice guidelines) would consider what the health care professionals did or did not do. They would be judged in terms of procedures and protocols that are approved by the appropriate bodies, or at least by an informal consensus of professionals. The third method, outcomes analysis, would look at the results of the health care. It would ask if patients got better and how soon, as well as whether the health care system as a whole lowered mortality rates or the rate of infection. As part of the evaluation of the quality of health care, the rates in one country or part of a country might be compared with the rates somewhere else (Gifford, 1996).

Two of these methods rest on assumptions that are debatable (Jonas et. al., 1981). The input method assumes that the right credentials combined with the right equipment equal high-quality care. The credentials, however, do not tell us if the practitioner graduated at the top or the bottom of the class or is well trained in the use of the latest equipment. The process method may unearth mistakes, but it does not ask whether the approved and accepted methods are themselves sound. In short, it assumes that the accepted methods are normative. The outcome method is actually the basis of all medical research, which seeks to discover if a given treatment or medication helps the patient. The best results seek to control all of the relevant variables. For example, how sick are the patients? Were there complicating factors? In researching medical outcomes, a large number of variables complicates the task. The results are presented in terms of probabilities.

Modern medical education and practice are built on scientific research. Now, although modern medicine has a scientific basis, most health care workers including physicians are not scientists and are often unaware of advances in statistics. These advances can greatly improve outcomes studies, with the occasionally disconcerting effect of identifying common but useless treatments. For example, a few years ago a scientific study showed that Proscar, the then leading drug for treatment of the benign enlargement of the prostate, was absolutely useless. Although alert practitioners had already noted this, many were still prescribing a drug that was essentially a placebo.

The results of a study by the National Research Corporation in the late 1980s indicated that physicians were not far advanced in their thinking about quality evaluation and scientific outcomes studies. The study asked how quality in health care should be measured. The physicians surveyed offered the following answers: (1) by health outcomes (24 percent), (2) by internal physician review (13 percent), (3) by peer review (13 percent), (4) by patient satisfaction (9 percent), and (5) by mortality rates (9 percent). Only numbers 1 and 5 are concerned with what could be objectively measurable outcomes. Numbers 2, 3, and 4 do not tell us how outcomes would be measured, but by whom.

Quality and Measurement

In health outcomes and mortality measurements, there are problems of definition and of the selection of populations for study. The norm for improvement in health is not a simple thing. Whereas one group will define it in terms of mortality and expectancy of disability, another will define it in terms of restoration of full functioning, while still others see health only in terms of being able to function as one pleases. Thus, preference scales must be considered. Clearly, the disagreements about the nature of health taken up in chapter 4 complicate outcomes research. Until society can arrive at a consensus about the matter, outcomes research will have to take one definition at a time and measure outcomes in terms of that. Bit by bit, such work will advance our understanding of outcomes and possibly the goals of medicine.

The mortality criterion poses similar problems. One area may have a higher death rate than another simply because it has a much older population. Merely increasing the amount of medical care may or may not improve health and mortality statistics. Indeed, if health care lowers the mortality rate while leaving us with more suffering old people, it may not have been quality health care at all. Indeed, one may ask if care that decreases human dignity and prolongs human suffering is even worthy of the name health care.

Strangely enough, there is evidence that during strikes of physicians and other health care workers the death rate goes down (Rothman, 1983), only to return to its former level when health care is restored. Although the lowering of the death rate may be due to the postponement of elective surgery, it does point up the fact that health care can be damaging to your health. The writings of Illich (1976) and Robin (1984) on iatrogenic (physician-induced) diseases raise similar interesting questions about the relative value of health care.

In all this it is well to remember that 70 percent of all conditions presented to the primary care physician are self-limiting; that is, they will go away by themselves. Treatment may speed up the healing, but it is not always necessary. In any event, it may be hard to say how much of the "cure" is due to health care and how much to natural causes or the patient's own activities.

The final difficulty involves the fact that improvements in the health of entire populations as well as of individuals are due to factors other than health care. Environmental factors such as clean air and water and safe working conditions are important for health. Genetic endowment also plays a major role in both health and longevity. Finally, cultural and lifestyle factors such as diet, exercise, sleep, the use of tobacco and alcohol, and the safety of one's sexual practices may have more to do with maintaining and improving health than all the health care in the world.

Epidemiological studies can help us to separate the environmental factors from health care effects. This should lead to a greater understanding about where to invest those resources devoted to health. Already we know that the elimination of the use of tobacco products would dramatically reduce the cost of treating the many diseases that are influenced if not caused by tobacco. Advances in genetics will increasingly permit the health care professions to factor out what they cannot change. This, too, should help to focus care more precisely and possibly reduce costs. No matter how great the difficulties, devotion to the scientific method must focus research on outcomes. Without this research, we allow medicine to serve any interest that can take advantage of an illusion.

We are left with the not surprising conclusion that assessing the quality of health care and the contribution of health care to the well-being of society is not an easy task. Yet it is a task that needs to be done. Since the individual practitioner cannot do it, the health care professions and, ultimately, society as a whole have an obligation to research the issue and to make public policy in accord with the results of the research.

THE OBLIGATION TO POLICE

The healing professions, like other full-fledged professions, fulfill needs in society, and in return for this they are given special privileges, such as a monopoly on certain activities. These professions are also charged with policing their own members in order to protect the clients and the public good. Because special knowledge is required to furnish this protection, the society has frequently given the decisions of professional groups the force of law. Thus, to a large extent, the professions are accountable directly to themselves and only indirectly to the government.

In court, where there is accountability to the public, the health care professions often find themselves more severely judged than when only peers are involved. Indeed, it may be argued that the increasing malpractice judgments against health professionals indicate that the professions should be more stringent in their self-policing and should look to the standards of the public as well as to those of the profession. Self-interest as well as professional obligation call for vigorous self-policing if the professions are to keep their privileges.

The policing includes examinations for licensing and in many cases periodic reexamination, peer review by hospital staffs and supervisory personnel, and, increasingly, review by panels appointed to hear complaints about professional misconduct.

Official Policing

In theory, the State Board of Nursing Examiners and the State Medical Board are the official policing agencies for their respective professions. Although generally appointed by the governor, the nominations come from the profession, so these boards can be seen as professional groups backed up with state power. There is, however, debate as to how well the state medical boards do their jobs. According to the Federation of State Medical Boards, the number of physicians against whom actions were taken in 1998 was 3,767, which represents a slight increase over the previous year's total of 3,728 and a dramatic increase over 1991's total of 2,804 (Federation of State Medical Boards, 1999). In 1999, a study of the Federation's figures by Health Research Group of Public Citizen indicated that serious disciplinary actions affected an average of 3.76 out of 1,000 non-federally employed physicians in the U.S. The report questions the adequacy of this number since there were only 2,731 serious disciplinary actions, a number lower than the previous year and 12.6 percent lower than in 1994 (Wolf, 1999). These numbers are important because of estimates that between 150,000 to 300,000 Americans per year are injured or killed by medical negligence. In part, this lack of effective oversight is due to the fact that in many states the boards lack the data, the funding, the staffing, and the statutory support to pursue cases of negligence and incompetence (Wolf, 1999).

In practice, many states have legal impediments that block them from disciplining physicians. The variation in legal impediments and zeal may help to explain why disciplining differs greatly from state to state. In 1998, Missouri disciplined less than three percent of all the physicians in the state. While in 1985, Alaska disciplined none, in 1998 it disciplined nearly fifteen percent of physicians practicing in state. New York, with 54,926 practicing physicians, disciplined 414, that is, a mere .75 percent. A review of figures for the entire country reveals dramatic discrepancies with some states seriously disciplining 15.4 per 1,000 physicians and others as low as less than one of 1,000 physicians. If all states disciplined physicians at the same rate as the top five, the number of disciplinary actions would more than double (Wolff, 1999).

The seeming failure to police vigorously may be a cause of the number of malpractice suits, and the increase in policing may be an attempt to hold down suits by weeding out the bad apples.

The practice acts in the various states generally have provisions about self-policing. The following excerpt from a Pennsylvania law entitled *Impaired Professionals* (63 P.S., 422.4) is an example of the statutory duty to denounce. Note that this act also provides immunity from prosecution for those who blow the whistle in good faith.

> Any hospital or health care facility, peer or colleague who has substantial evidence that a nurse has an active addictive disease for which the professional is not receiving treatment, is diverting a controlled substance, or is mentally or physically incompetent to carry out the duties of his license shall make or cause to be made a report to the Board: Provided that any person or facility who acts in a treatment capacity to impaired nurses in an approved treatment program is exempt from the mandatory reporting requirements of this subsection.

Although the health care professions recognize a duty to denounce, they are not in agreement as to what should be done and on what basis. Different professions have different requirements. Physical therapists require that even *alleged* unethical, incompetent, or illegal acts be reported. The Pennsylvania proposal requires *substantial evidence*. The American Nursing Association requires that the nurses *safeguard* the patient, while the physical therapist is specifically required to report. Even within a profession, there have been substantial shifts in requirements. The 1980 American Medical Association code asks that the physician *strive to expose*, whereas the 1957 version of the American Medical Association Code called for the physician to expose without hesitation. In view of these differences, it is necessary to go back and develop a consistent ethics of self-policing and whistleblowing for the health professions.

The Problem of Secrecy

When there is a problem, the official board responsible generally operates in secrecy, and even when the meetings are open to the public, there can be little or no notification to the public. If we add to this the fact that even malpractice suits are frequently settled out of court, with a proviso that neither side talk about the suit, the public has little chance of finding out who has been in trouble and who has not. While this protects the innocent among the health care professionals and keeps the profession from having a tarnished reputation, it hardly helps patients to avoid those who are guilty of malpractice in a moral and/or legal sense.

This problem is not unique to the health care professions. The clergy and lawyers are equally silent about the transgressions of their members. There may not be an easy solution when the rights of the professional to a presumption of innocence conflict with the need of the public for information about which professionals and institutions are selling as a quality product what may have shoddy material mixed in.

In practice, the shrewd health care consumer will consult with friends who are physicians and nurses to find out who is respected for competence and who is suspect. Unfortunately, the average health care consumer either lacks such contacts or thinks that a professional license is a guarantee of quality for life. Making public the information in the National Practitioner Data Bank will help consumers to protect themselves in this effort.

The Obligation to Denounce

The obligation to denounce can arise from both general ethical principles and from the nature of the health care professions, that is, from the special role that is assigned to the health care provider.

The general obligation to avoid evil unless there is a proportionate reason for permitting or risking it is at the root of the obligation to denounce (see chapter 3). The nature of the health professions adds additional force as well as specification to the general obligation to avoid evil. All the health professions involve a commitment to the health of the patient and to the good of the profession. The public considers the commitment to the health of the patient to be part of the role, as well as part of the contract with the health care professional. Traditionally, physicians have been patient advocates, and professional nurses have adopted the advocacy role as part of their general professional role. The trust in the promise of advocacy and the good will of the professional further increases the obligation to protect the patient. In short, health care practitioners have not only the general obligation to avoid evil, but the specific obligation to prevent evil from happening to patients.

It is not merely an obligation to the individual patient, but to all patients and to the public health that creates the obligation. This is clear from the following positive obligation proposed in the American Nurses Association (1985) code: "The nurse works with members of health professions and other citizens in promoting efforts to meet the health needs of the public."

The good of the profession also demands that the individual practitioner and the profession as a whole work for the elimination of harmful practices and the control or removal of practitioners who engage in them. This comes not only from the commitment of the profession, but from justifiable self-interest. If a profession does not police itself, the public and society will ultimately demand an accounting.

Reporting and the Impaired Professional

The law on impaired professionals cited earlier provides an exception when the health care professional is undergoing rehabilitation. There is great need for such rehabilitation because professionals in health care, physicians in particular, have had higher than average rates of drug dependence, alcoholism, mental problems, and marital troubles. Health care can be dangerous not only to the patients, but also to the providers of care.

This rehabilitation exception is justified as long as patients are in no danger during the rehabilitation period. Indeed, granted the protection of patients, health care professionals ought to strive to get impaired colleagues into treatment. This obligation springs not only from the general duty of beneficence, but from a collegial duty to other professionals and the obligation to protect the profession and the patients. In no case, however, should the effort to help an impaired professional be an excuse for risking harm to patients.

The Means of Protecting the Public

To fulfill the obligation to police their own ranks, the professions have a variety of means available. No one of them will cure the problem, but all of them taken together will have an impact. Some protection can be afforded by demanding proof of continuing education. Not all groups and not all specialties inside groups currently demand such proof. Additional protection can be afforded by the quality assurance programs, professional review boards, and even utilization review boards.

Where there is a chain of command, as in a hospital or other health care facility, dangerous or lax practice should be reported through that chain. If the matter is serious and nothing happens, the health care professional may have to use other methods to remedy the situation.

Public Denunciation or Whistleblowing

Peer review and reporting through the chain of command do not always work. In these cases, public denunciation or whistleblowing must still be part of the armament of professional ethics. The obligation to blow the whistle, when all else has failed, is grounded in two simple ideas: (1) those who remain silent are consenting, and (2) the inaction of good people is the main reason why bad people continue to harm others.

What Should Be Denounced

In general, anything that violates the rights of the patient or threatens the physical, psychological, or medicoeconomic well-being of the patient should be considered for denunciation (Garrett, Klonoski, and Baillie, 1993).

We say that it should be *considered* for denunciation, since it should be obvious that some threats of harm are so trivial and so infrequent that the harm to the morale of the health care team will not justify the small good to be obtained by denouncing them. The morale of the health care team is important and we will return to it later. The obligation to blow the whistle, then, is *limited to events that are, with rare exceptions, repeated and are of such a nature as to seriously harm patients or the profession*. Something should be done about the physician or nurse who seldom practices sterile technique, since sooner or later serious harm will result. Something should be done about the provider who frequently comes to work under the influence of drugs or alcohol. There may be no need to denounce the isolated instance of drunkenness, although the provider should be kept temporarily away from patients.

Repeated violations of the patient's rights, including those in the *Patient's Bill of Rights* of the American Hospital Association, should also be denounced. Not all these rights are equally important, but repeated violations show a contempt for patients that should not be tolerated. Indeed, since perceived contempt for the patient will cause more and more malpractice suits, mere self-interest dictates action in this area.

Problems with Whistleblowing

The legal obstacles to whistleblowing are important if not always clear-cut. While the public might think of a license to practice medicine or nursing as a privilege, this license also represents a valuable property right. As such, it is guarded by the right to due process. As a result, a health care provider who has his or her license taken away by the licensing board can sue for damages, as well as restoration of the license. This has made many boards hesitant to act.

Even if the health care professional whose license has been revoked or suspended does not sue, she or he has the right to have the case reviewed by the courts. This process can drag on for years. The result is time consuming and expensive for all involved. If the board of licensing lacks funds for good lawyers, they may hesitate to get involved in cases that may drag on forever.

In some states, the law does not allow for a gradation of penalties. The licensing board in these states may hesitate to take away the license except in the most serious cases. The result is that there is relatively little policing in these cases. Other states that provide not only for revocation and suspension, but for fines and censures and conditions of rehabilitation, have more flexibility and so are less hesitant to use a lesser penalty that may do the job.

The social obstacles to whistleblowing are known to everyone. Nobody likes to be a snitch. There are three reasons for this. First, we are all aware that we are not perfect and so might be the next victim. Second, we all develop loyalty to our group and fellow workers and may regard whistleblowing as a violation of this loyalty. Third, we know all too well that the whistleblower may suffer retaliation from the organization, as well as from the individual who was denounced.

The awareness of our own imperfection and the fear that we may be next is understandable, but not a valid excuse. If this were an excuse, then we would have an excuse for doing nothing about any evil in the world. A health professional does not have such an excuse when repeated events threaten serious harm to patients. The matter is too serious to permit such general and casual escapes.

Whistleblowing can hurt the credibility and cohesion of the health care team and the health care profession. Loyalty to both makes one hesitate about blowing the whistle. Group and peer loyalty is an important factor, since the good of the patient depends on the smooth functioning of the group, and this depends on trust and even loyalty to the team. The team, however, is not the goal of health care, but only a means, and so the team is subordinated to the good of the patient. To put the team first is to displace goals and to act as if patients existed for the doctors and nurses, and not the other way around.

For all that, loyalty does have its claims. Fellow feeling for those with whom one works and on whom one depends is not only understandable but necessary in health care, as in the rest of life. For this reason, among others, we have insisted that it is only when other means have failed and when there is a repeated threat of serious harm to patients that whistleblowing becomes obligatory. Once again, it is a question of a complicated balancing of factors.

The fear of retaliation is not unfounded. People have been fired for blowing the whistle even when they were justified for doing so. Whistleblowing can also lead to being blackballed or shunned. In some cases, the denunciation provokes countercharges and involves the provider in long and costly litigation. It takes courage to blow the whistle. In line with our general principles, the potential harm to oneself must be part of the calculation of the consequences. The risk to oneself, however, cannot be the sole factor. The good of the profession and the patient and the seriousness of the evil to be avoided have their ethical claims.

In this context, the remarks of Shirley Stroll, a nurse clinician who exposed abuse in a Veterans Administration hospital, are very much to the point. She gives ten rules based on her experience with whistleblowing. Several are particularly chilling: Rule Four: Expect the worst: the loss of your job at least. Rule Six: Know you will be criticized and humiliated. Rule Nine: Do not expect that your life will ever be the same. It will not. The realization of such truths has made even the brave hesitate to blow the whistle, with the result that much evil continues unabated.

All these difficulties provide health care workers with so many potential excuses that there is a danger that the good of patients will not be properly protected unless the health care professions unite to protect their members who fulfill their duties to patients. We will return to this when we consider the obligations of the profession as a whole.

No one is obliged to do the impossible. In some cases the evil is so rooted in the institution that no individual can remove it. When this occurs, there is certainly no obligation to denounce or to do anything except possibly resign when the evil is too monstrous.

Who Should Denounce

Those who are formally charged with preventing the evils have the greatest responsibility in this area. Supervisors, chiefs of staff, and ombudsmen are the clearest examples. Because they are formally charged with preventing the evil, we do not believe that they can be excused merely because they might suffer as a result of doing their duty. The board of directors or the trustees of a health care institution have the ultimate responsibility for everything in their facilities. They have the obligation to make sure that there is no need for denunciation. One can, however, see cases of individual members having to blow the whistle on the entire board. This might occur when an institution continuously covers up the incompetence of employees and physicians who are seriously harming patients.

Not only those formally charged with preventing the evils, but every health care professional, also has the *prima facie* obligation to blow the whistle. This obligation disappears only when the good anticipated is outweighed by the evil. Finally, even nonprofessionals who see the evil have some obligation to prevent it. This group generally has less power, and its obligation arises from the general duty to avoid evil, and not from professional commitment to the patient. Even the nonprofessional cannot merely stand mute in the face of fraud and clear incompetence.

When One Should Blow the Whistle

Denunciation or whistleblowing is a last resort. It should occur only after a whole series of interventions has been attempted. In the first place, the health care professional who witnesses an evil should attempt to intervene personally and discreetly with the person at fault. Unfortunately, it is often clear that this will do no good or will involve disproportionate harm to the whistleblower. When this is true or when the intervention has failed, the person should proceed to report the evil through channels. At times, this is not feasible, since it may be first-line supervisory personnel who are the guilty parties or are protective of the guilty parties. When either of these conditions exists, going over the heads of supervisors is necessary. Only when all these interventions have failed is the witness of the wrongdoing justified in going first to outside supervisory agencies, such as the Board of Medical Examiners, the State Board of Nursing Licensure, or legislative oversight committees. When these groups fail to respond, the desperate and dangerous appeal to the press and the general public is in order, at least when we are dealing with extremely serious matters.

Obligations of the Professions and Institutions

It should be obvious that the professions and health care institutions need to set up mechanisms for receiving complaints and for judging them according to the rules of due process. The boards, however, will lack credibility if they are composed only of members of the profession. There is a need for outside members on the boards for several reasons. In the first place, the outsiders should bring to the board a sensitivity to the views of the general public and a critical point of view that does not simply say, "But that is the way we have always done it." In the second place, the outside members, who are consumers rather than providers of health care, will be less tempted to give too much weight to the good of the profession as opposed to the good of patients and the public. The outside member is also more likely to look critically at the nontechnical aspects of the case, which have much to do with the dignity of the individual. Such critical examination of the human aspects of health care can easily be overlooked by the busy health care professional. In short, outside members should help to reinforce the credibility of the board and, more importantly, should increase protection for the dignity of the patient.

If the boards are to work, people must not fear retaliation if they report wrongdoing. In practice, this means that some professions, such as nursing and physical therapy, must have more power and be ready and willing to defend their members against retribution. This is particularly important because nurses, in particular, are the professionals most likely to observe incompetence and fraud in nurses and in physicians. If the nurse abandons her or his advocacy role because of fear of retribution, the entire health care system suffers.

The last paragraph mentions power, since it is impossible to do good without power, even as power allows some people to continue doing evil. While we insist that might is not right, we also insist that right without might is not practically effective. The problem of power in health care, however, is a subject for another book.

Summary

Health care professionals and institutions have an obligation to improve health care and to report and even denounce those health care professionals who are dangerous to patients. Improving the quality of health care is particularly difficult because we have no easy method of evaluating quality. Eliminating dangerous practitioners is equally difficult. Many of the existing institutions that are supposed to set policies for both quality and the lack of quality are not particularly effective, for a variety of reasons. Loyalty to the patient should, with the rare exceptions of trivial matters, take precedence over all professional loyalties. The various health professions need to organize and demand greater accountability from their members in continuing education and in meeting professional standards.

Those who report failures and those who handle the reports should make sure that due process is followed, evidence gathered, and the accused given a chance to rebut the accusations. Mere rumors should not be the basis of denunciations, although they should sometimes be reported for investigation.

INSTITUTIONAL ETHICS

Promoting Quality

The maintenance and promotion of standards falls within the responsibilities of individual health professionals, but professional groups and health care institutions must all be involved. These groups include a hospital's medical staff committees on credentials, tissues, and medical records and government-mandated professional review organizations (which oversee Medicare and, in some states, Medicaid as well). In theory, peer review by the board that oversees state licensure would also have some weight in promoting quality. In practice, things are not quite so simple.

Hospital utilization review procedures are concerned with the allocation of hospital resources in an effort to provide high-quality care in a cost-effective manner. Their focus is on cost considerations, such as overutilization, underutilization, and inefficient scheduling of resources, rather than directly on the quality of care.

The credentials committee, also called the peer review committee, examines the credentials of those who apply for staff privileges in a hospital. Since such committees are powerful, they have a special obligation to screen carefully in order to protect both hospital and patients. Unfortunately, the peer review committee must worry about interference with interstate commerce when they refuse staff privileges (Wermiel, 1991). In theory, the Health Care Quality Act of 1986 protects such review boards from legal suits when they report incompetent doctors. In practice, they can be sued if they fail to follow due process and had no valid reasons for their judgment.

The hospital's tissue committee examines and evaluates the tissues removed during surgery to see if the surgery was really medically indicated. The medical records committee not only examines records for completeness, but is also to act as a judge of clinical care as this is reflected in the records.

Professional review organizations (PROs), which replaced the professional standard review organization (PSRO), were federally mandated to determine whether the care given to Medicare patients is of sufficient quality and delivered at a reasonable cost. State and Medicaid programs may also use PROs. As with utilization review, the PROs' concern with cost and only subsequent focus on professional standards does not ensure that they are truly determiners of quality, let alone sources of improved quality.

Hospital-based continuing education programs can make some contribution to maintaining quality, in part because they are used to recertify licenses in states that require continuing education. Unfortunately, these are not universal and, like continuing education in general, may be of mediocre quality and lacking in comprehensive treatment of the field. Even when continuing education is required by the state board of nursing or medical licensing, it may mean nothing, since it is enforced only by a rare audit that asks the practitioner to produce proof of his or her continuing education.

In theory, the state boards of licensure and registration as well as the boards for certification in a specialty ought to promote quality. In practice, they do not always succeed.

In general, the boards that control state licensure are largely concerned with entrance into the profession and occasionally with disciplining those who violate standards. The license does not certify the practitioner as an expert, but only says that he or she has met minimum standards of safe practice. Often, in medicine, the license is granted for life without any requirement for reexamination or even continuing education. Some continuing education programs are voluntary. Some require part of the continuing education programs to have accredited sponsorship; others do not. Thus, continuing education in medicine and the other health care professions is hardly a uniform product that protects the patients.

Some state nursing boards require evidence of continuing education for maintaining the status of a registered nurse, but this is not universal. In nursing, as in medicine, continuing education does not attempt to provide for systematic updating of all areas of the profession, but leaves this to the discretion of the practitioner.

Physicians who have had the proper residency and pass an examination administered by one of the specialty boards that have the power to certify the physician in a given area are called board certified. Physicians can practice without certification. For many years, only the family health board required recertification. In recent years, however, seventeen of the twenty-three primary specialty boards have come to require periodic recertification. The most promising programs demand not only continuing education and written reexamination, but a practice-based, oral examination (Kettlekamp and Herndon, 1990) as well as other new methods of performance evaluation (Langsley, 1990). Curiously, some individuals would like to guarantee that failure to pass the reexamination would not result in decertification (Edmonson, 1990). Such ideas seem to defeat the goal of improving medical care through reexamination.

The American Nurses Association (1985) has a program for certification and recertification in various specialties (Fickeissen, 1990). The requirements vary greatly from specialty to specialty. While some require supervised work under a certified nurse, others will accept teaching in place of clinical practice. As a result, the meaning of an individual certification is unclear.

The National Practitioner Data Bank, provided for in the Health Care Quality Improvement Act of 1986, started to operate in the fall of 1990 (Hachney, 1991). The Data Bank records malpractice payments made on behalf of any licensed health care practitioner, sanctions imposed on physicians and dentists by licensing boards, and other adverse reactions of hospital peer reviewers. Hospitals and licensing boards can use these data to make sure that they are not accepting people who have had serious trouble in other jurisdictions. There are complications; for example, lawyers for the plaintiff in a malpractice suit can get information only if they can prove that a hospital did not consider the Data Bank in giving privileges to a specific individual. Unfortunately, the Data Bank is not open to health care consumers, with the result that secrecy still protects professionals and institutions, while relegating patients to second place. But this data bank is a step in the direction of promoting quality by making appropriate information available.

All health care professions have an obligation to strive for the improvement of health care, and the institution of strict recertification programs is a step in the right direction. As yet, although the American College of Physicians has tried, there is no effective way of evaluating and reevaluating those human qualities that are demanded for quality health care. In the absence of such evaluation, health care may become more and more technical and less and less humane.

Due Process in Handling Denunciations

Those who are denounced have a right to due process, that is, to the protection of a fair procedure. While it is not necessary to have the elaborate procedures of a court system, a certain minimum is required. First, the supervisor should make sure that the charge is clear and specific and described in nonevaluative terms. Dates and places and details are important. Vague charges, such as "Everybody knows she is careless," are of little value. In other words, the supervisor should concentrate on what was done or not done, not on what the accuser feels about the event.

Second, the supervisor should demand evidence. Were there other witnesses? What is on the chart? Is the accuser willing to put everything in writing so that there is evidence if the accuser later tries to back out? We note that the need for evidence at this stage pretty well rules out the anonymous whistleblower. Yet even the anonymous charge should be investigated if it is serious enough. The matter should proceed, however, only when real evidence is discovered.

Third, when the investigation reveals evidence, the supervisor or the appropriate board should allow the accused to answer the charge, to face the accuser, and so to defend himself. The meaning of the facts is not always as evident as the facts themselves. The person accused of drunkenness because she was staggering may have been suffering from an inner ear infection. The person accused of striking a patient may have been defending himself. Things are not always what they seem at first glance.

Health care facilities should have due process procedures in place to protect the accused from unjust allegations and to protect accusers from their own enthusiasm and lack of experience.

Individual Conscience and the Institution

Not only are there demands on the individual health care professional to protect the profession, but there may be professional or institutional demands that cause the professional to feel the need to protect himself. Generally, a health care professional is not obligated to provide treatment or care that is contrary to his or her conscience. The basic principles of this exception are discussed in chapter 3, but in an institutional setting it is good to have a specific idea of how this exception is to be invoked. When an employee asks to be removed from a case because treating the particular patient is against his or her values or moral beliefs, the institution needs a policy and a procedure to handle the case with respect for both the conscience of the employee and the needs of the patient. The following suggestions, taken largely from Weber (1995), are a helpful starting point.

First, it is useful to distinguish between cases in which the employee is saying "It is wrong to do this," or "It is wrong for me to do this." The first statement implies that the treatment is not in line with professional and ethical standards. Thus, a nurse might object to being involved in any way with an assisted suicide. A supervisor should not only grant a request for removal from such a case, but should initiate an investigation into the institutional acceptance of this procedure in the interests of ethical patient care. This last point assumes that the institution has a policy and procedures for such an investigation.

On the other hand, saying "This particular act is wrong for me" does not necessarily imply that professional ethical standards are being violated, but that the employee's conscience is. This is a matter of judgment, which can vary among the different individuals involved. For example, a nurse might feel that additional tests are wasteful when performed on a terminal patient. The first concern in such a case would be to ensure that adequate information was available to allow such a judgment to be made. After establishing that there is no misunderstanding, Weber suggests that the following distinctions are important: "First, the refusal is based on conscientious objection to participation in a particular type of treatment or procedure, not a refusal to care for a particular (type of) patient." Thus, the request ought not be based on the fact that the patient has AIDS or is a chronic alcoholic or is black or a Catholic. Such a request would be discriminatory and irrelevant to the health care of the patient.

"Secondly, the request appears to reflect a consistently held value of the employee." For example, an employee cannot use restraints on incompetent patients for a number of years and then decide that he or she does not want to apply them in the case of a particular incompetent. An issue of conscience carries the implication that it is thought-out and long-standing.

"Thirdly, the care responsibility that the employee wants to be excused from is not fundamental to the profession." The issue must not be one that would be an ordinary activity of the practitioner in that profession; if it were, it would raise a more fundamental question of whether the individual could continue to be a member of the profession, not just an employee of the institution.

ETHICS COMMITTEES

Institutional ethics committees, or hospital ethics committees, are multidisciplinary groups drawn from the institution and the local community. We discussed these committees in chapter 2 in connection with the evaluation of surrogate decision making. Although ethics committees originated in the role of consulting in difficult cases, they do have additional opportunities and responsibilities in the institutional setting (although there are concerns about this; see Fetcher and Hoffman, 1994). In particular, they have a responsibility for educating the institutional community and the local community about medical ethics questions, for developing institutional policy, and, more recently, for critiquing the ethics practices of the institution itself.

Public Education

The task of informing the public about health care ethics is a general concern of the profession. As noted in chapter 3, the professions have a responsibility rooted in their expertise to educate the public about what is good and bad in health care. Their record in this area has been spotty at best, but greater efforts are now being made. For example, the American Medical Association has become very vocal about their opposition to physician-assisted suicide and their concern with the related issue of appropriate care of the patient at the end of life (see chapter 7). This activism by the medical profession, whether or not society ends up agreeing with them, is a welcome development in meeting the profession's social obligations.

Ethics committees have proved to be a useful and convenient mechanism for attempting to educate the public. For example, when the federal government passed the Patient Self-determination Act (PSDA), which required health care institutions receiving federal money to ask if the patient had a living will (see chapter 2), hospital ethics committees were at the forefront both of writing policies for hospital implementation of the act and of presenting the idea of a living will to the public. Although anecdotal evidence suggests that these public sessions were well received, more formal studies suggest that few people write living wills until they have to, and the health system itself is still not terribly responsive to such patient requests (SUPPORT, 1995). In short, although ethics committees have been active in public education, it seems prudent not to expect them to have dramatic short-term effects.

Writing Policies

Ethics committees have also had the responsibility of writing policies for their institutions. Examples of these policies have included advanced directive policies, confidentiality policies (see chapter 5), medically futile treatment policies (see chapter 7), and policies on genetic screening (see chapter 11). These policies have an important long-term impact because they define the institution's mission statement and guide daily institutional activities. It is possible that the real educational impact of ethics committees is accomplished indirectly through these policies.

Enforcement of Policies

Writing policies alone does not guarantee that these documents will be effective. They must be enforced and become part of the character of the institution. This is a difficult task that requires leadership from both the administrators and heads of staff, as well as the cooperation of the employees.

For example, as just mentioned, the PSDA demands that hospitals or their delegates ask patients if they have a living will or a durable power of attorney in health matters. A brief survey of former patients indicates that this is often neglected. In some hospitals, as few as four per cent of the patients complete an advanced directive (Berrio and Levesque, 1996).

Even when there is an advanced directive, it may be unknown or not followed. For example, there may be no mechanism for alerting staff of the directive; there may be delays in obtaining the directive from the patient or records office; or there may be no standard procedure to make sure that the physician or social worker has spoken to the patient about the matter or given the patient the literature on the directive. On a deeper level, staff may not be trained until they are emotionally at ease with the directives.

Similar problems can be found in the enforcement of policies on futile treatment, euthanasia (Asch, 1996), or confidentiality on computer systems (Iverson et al., 1995). Some of these concerns may be addressed by good policies, but all depend on education and training, that is, the cooperation of an informed staff.

Ethics Committees as Institutional Watchdogs

It has been suggested (Glaser, 1993) that ethics committees should also watch over the operation of the institution. In part, this is exactly what writing policies involves, but the suggestion is that these committees should also begin to understand themselves as sources of critique and change within institutions. They should do this by focusing on how the institution functions as a system: its decision-making procedures, the flow of institutional power, the effective use of resources, and the correlation between basic values and institutional operation. It has also been suggested that ethics committees should review the impact of health care financing on clinical decisions (Miles, 1992). These tasks might put ethics committees more directly in the line of responsibility for enforcing policies, possibly blurring administrative responsibilities. However, these suggestions are particularly interesting in the context of HMOs and managed care. They may be an element in the development of mechanisms for assuring quality and professional standards in managed care institutions.

COMPETITION AND INSTITUTIONAL ETHICS

Managed Care and the Role of Health Care Professionals

There are so many forms of managed care and health maintenance organizations that it is difficult to give a detailed analysis in this book. In general, however, it may be said that HMOs and managed care aim at reducing costs while maintaining quality. In particular, they strive to keep the use of resources from increasing more than necessary.

To attain reduced costs, HMOs try to shift the pattern of distribution by providing physicians with incentives to limit care (Jenkins, 1996). This represents a significant change in emphasis for the health care provider. In chapters 3 and 4, we discussed the role of health care providers as patient advocates and gatekeepers. Physicians, in particular, have always had a dual role as care providers and as economic agents (e.g., in running their practice), but generally the pressure on them as economic agents was not institutional. With the development of managed care delivery systems, more and more physicians are becoming employees and operating their practices within an institutional framework. Their compensation and even their employment may depend on how they meet institutional demands to control costs. This creates a very different situation for the physician as he or she decides how to care for a patient (Morreim, 1991).

For example, physicians in most managed care arrangements are not permitted to use an expensive brand-name drug if an equivalent generic drug is available. In some cases, when two drugs are identical in their effects, the less-expensive drug is required even though it may have unpleasant and painful side effects (Rundle, 1996). In many cases, the physician can use only drugs included in the group's approved formulary; and the physician often needs permission to refer his or her patient to a specialist. Although the arrangements vary greatly, these few examples will suffice to illustrate the general direction of managed care.

Unfortunately, there have been few broadly based empirical studies of *outcomes* of such arrangements. There are studies of the use of particular drugs or treatments (Calderone et al., 1996), but no studies of the managed care treatment of even such a widespread disease as diabetes (Quickel, 1996). A large number of studies of worker and customer satisfaction have been completed, but these do not answer key questions about actual improvement in health or rate of infections and the like.

A survey of some 30,000 patients' customer satisfaction showed that they were most satisfied with non-for-profit HMOs and PPOs (Liberman, 1996). Evidence also indicates that for-profit health care institutions do not do a superior job of selecting doctors, helping patients pick a doctor, or guaranteeing stability of their doctors. Thus, 15 percent of respondents in the survey said that their doctors had left the health plan during their treatment. This rose to as high as 30 percent in the case of plans that gave little satisfaction to consumers. While useful, customer satisfaction studies do not provide information regarding the all-important medical outcomes.

Careful studies of the actual effects of managed care are necessary before managed care can be either definitively justified or condemned. Such studies are obligatory for health care institutions, for, without them, there is no real quality control. This is a primary institutional obligation.

A further concern is that the protocols and results of these studies be made public. HMOs have been reluctant to release even what data they have. This has been a long-standing problem in the health care field. But one clear advantage to further institutionalizing health care is that now there are good incentives and good opportunities for evaluating the delivery of care. Public pressure has made strides in forcing out this information, and one can hope that this trend will continue (Winslow, 1996b).

Market Competition and HMOs

Managed care and the HMO have brought with them competition, with all its advantages and problems. The advocates of this new health care system tend to focus on the virtues of competition. The advocates of this market approach argue that market competition in health care is efficient and so will produce more or better products at lower cost. Unfortunately, in the area of health care, some of the requirements for true competition are not verified. First, medical knowledge by its very nature is not equally distributed between providers and consumers. The people with more knowledge have the power to exploit those without it. Second, the rush to competition has lead some for-profit health care groups to amass considerable market power, enabling them, at least temporarily to demand concessions from other institutions whose market they threaten to take. For example, a powerful HMO moves into an area, signs up employers with promises of cost reductions, and then forces the local hospital to lower its charges. If this leads to a greater efficiency in the hospital, this is good; if it forces the hospital to lower quality or even to close its doors, this obviously harms the community.

Unfortunately, while much of the increase in efficiency brings lower costs to employers who supply health insurance, from the consumers' point of view, it can result in a lowering of the quality of services. As discussed in chapter 4, this is a problem of distribution. If a for-profit HMO is to lower costs while making a profit for shareholders, something has to give: the scope of services, the staffing patterns, or entry into the HMO.

Those who compete for profit do not like to serve unprofitable markets. Thus, rural areas and inner city ghettos will not be favorite locations for HMOs bent on profit. Also, difficult situations will arise with AIDS patients, cancer patients, or the elderly (Jeffrey, 1996). As noted earlier, the market is often efficient in producing, but is not very fair in distribution.

The ethical institution will be aware that the accessibility of care is as important as the cost of the care.

Also, as institutions compete for patients, there may be wasteful competition in the local area. Does every hospital need the latest computerized axial tomography scan or magnetic resonance imagining equipment, the newest lithotripter for crushing kidney stones, and diaphoresis machines for cleansing the blood? Does every hospital in a small city need a money-losing trauma center? Should extremely expensive neonatal intensive care units be regionalized? In short, should institutional ethics complement a concern for efficiency in a way that demands that the institutions cooperate rather than compete?

In the past, a local health service administration board would decide whether there was a need for the latest machine and decide where it was placed. These boards aimed at reducing unnecessary duplication of equipment and services. This method was first circumvented by local politics and then destroyed by Congress. At this point, many hospitals went on a building spree, thus raising costs for bond payments and creating empty rooms, which obviously brought in no income. Such errors are common in for-profit business and are perhaps a cost of the market economy in which supply and demand equalize only in the long run. All of which leaves us with this question: To what extent should the health care institution be part of the competitive market economy?

Studies by the Pennsylvania Health Care Cost Containment Council indicate that some of these overexpanded hospitals have occupancy rates as low as 49 per cent. Any other industry that operated at such a low rate of use of productive facilities would soon be out of business. At the same time, most of these hospitals are in rural areas that will go unserved if competition destroys all of them. If such areas are not profitable for their present owners, there is no reason to think that they will be profitable under HMOs. The crisis of the rural hospital is not simply a matter of inefficiency, but of a local market that is too small to support the institution without government aid.

All this suggests that regional cooperation rather than competition may be the way to containment without cost shifting and useless duplication. Such cooperation would require federal waivers. This means that institutions dedicated to the well-being of patients, rather than profits, have an obligation to work toward such cooperation and the legal changes necessary to make it possible.

Costs and HMOs

Just as there is little real evidence on the effects of managed care on the health of patients, also, little is known of the actual ability of HMOs to contain rate increases in the long run. In the first place, serious studies are missing. Second, global estimates of decreased costs to companies often neglect to mention that the employees have been forced to assume a larger part of the health care premium. Third, the decreases are due in part to the fact that fewer full-time workers are covered by employer-sponsored plans (Burkins, 1996). Fourth, as might be expected, small businesses have not experienced the same drop in costs. Finally, no plan is immune to the inflationary pressures that work on all health care in the United States.

HMOs and the Quality of Medical Care

The distribution of medical care is an extremely complicated issue involving many different types of problems. Although managed care addresses several important concerns with regard to the cost and quality of acute care, it leaves a number of issues out of the system. For example, basic medical research is likely to receive less funding since HMOs are designed only to *deliver* care, and already research facilties have felt the pinch (Winslow, 1996a). This focus of HMOs will also hurt medical education, since students, residents, and, in general, the resources necessary for medical education are cost-*inefficient* from the perspective of delivery. Certainly, research and education are essential to the long-term interests of the HMOs, so corrections may be made to include funding for these tasks. In the meantime, there are likely to be difficulties and adjustments, and even the long-term resolution of these difficulties depends on the ability of market forces to respond adequately to the health care needs and expectations of the society.

Quality Issues: Staffing

The institutional drive to contain costs most often leads to a reduction in the number of registered nurses (RNs) and other licensed personnel who care for patients. RNs and licensed practical nurses (LPNs) are replaced by clinical or patient care assistants, partners, or technicians, generally grouped under the heading of unlicensed assistive personnel (UAP) (Manuel and Alster, 1994). Many of these were recruited from the ranks of the janitors and cleaning staff. Most of them did not graduate from high school and have a maximum of fifteen days on-the-job training. Yet these unlicensed personnel perform such duties as drawing blood, inserting urine catheters, monitoring vital signs, and even stapling wounds.

The hospitals justify this on the grounds that they supply unlicensed workers to relieve the nurses for their true nursing duties. In this way, it is argued, there is no reduction in the quality of care. Unfortunately this maneuver does not free the nurse so much as turn him or her into a supervisor, a position for which he or she not may have had adequate training.

Since the RN is professionally and legally responsible for the acts of those she supervises, this increases stress even as it decreases time with patients and erodes work satisfaction. This stress shortens the working life of these professional men and women. There are examples of hospitals in which large numbers of nurses have resigned rather than face the extreme difficulties of such added responsibility. We shall return to this problem later when we consider safety issues in the reduced staffing.

There are questions as to whether this issue can be addressed adequately from within the individual institution. As we discussed earlier, denouncing and whistleblowing can lead to dire consequences: the nurse may get fired or simply get the worst shifts and tougher assignments. Many nurses put up with the stress in silence because they need the job.

The American Nurses Association has studied the impact of staffing by RNs on the quality of health care, that is to actual outcomes. Final results were not available at the time of writing, but preliminary results reported at public hearings indicate that, when there is a low ratio of patients to nurses, nursing indicators such as bed sores and hospital-induced infections are significantly lower. This study of outcomes is significant, since merely interviewing staff or asking patients about their satisfaction will tell little unless the interviewer is sworn to confidentiality.

Hospitals have been hesitant to release the figures on which outcomes could be judged. This does not excuse them from studying the matter in-house and changing policy and procedures in response to the facts. This we would hold is a primary institutional obligation.

Safety Issues

Although we have anecdotal evidence of harm to patients in HMOs, there has been little scientific study of this issue. This is due, among other things, to the reluctance of hospitals to release the data on readmission rates, infections, and death rates that would provide the basis for such studies. The Joint Commission on Hospital Accreditation does not appear to have studied this matter scientifically. Even a government-sponsored study by the Institute of Medicine could not get the material from the hospitals. At the same time, there is no evidence that HMO staffing patterns actually reduce costs over all.

When hospitals have "credentialed," unlicensed assistants of one sort or another and have placed their supervision under registered nurses, the hospital and the supervisor are both ethically and legally responsible. The legal dimensions of this fact are still developing and need careful study (Benesch, 1994). In particular, the nurse must ask if she or he is competent to do supervision, has adequate control over the unlicensed, and is able to take the stress. To take on the supervisor's responsibility when the answer to even one question is a "No" would appear to be unethical cooperation in the dubious activity of the institution. As noted elsewhere, only serious reasons can justify such cooperation.

In today's health care environment, the hospital and other health care agencies have an obligation to study the impact of all changes on the safety of patients, as well as on the quality of the care.

SUMMARY

The health care institution has an obligation to study the impacts of cost reduction and changed staffing patterns. These studies should examine outcomes and not simply general impressions. Equally important, the institutions must ensure that policies are backed up with enforcement procedures. Finally, both policies and procedures must be developed to protect both the conscience of the health care workers and the mission of the institution.

CASES FOR ANALYSIS

1. Mrs. Lewis was head nurse on a medical surgical floor in a community hospital of 250 beds. Over the course of six months she noticed that all patients admitted from the Shady Rest Nursing Home had signs of severe injuries other than those connected with the admitting diagnosis. There appeared to be patient abuse in the nursing home. Mrs. Lewis investigated discreetly and found no explanation possible except abuse. In accord with the obligations of the law in her state, she reported the matter to the Department of Welfare Bureau of Inspection.

The Welfare Department investigated immediately, found proof of abuse, and threatened to close down Shady Rest if there were any recurrences. Mrs. Lewis was overjoyed until her hospital administrator, bypassing the director of nursing, called her in and warned her that she would be fired if she reported any other instances of abuse. Shady Rest sent the hospital a lot of business, and good relations had to be maintained.

Mrs. Lewis was even more shocked when she discovered that the administrator was a golf partner of the owner of Shady Rest and was doing an old buddy a favor. Despite fears of retaliation, Mrs. Lewis consulted a lawyer, who threatened the hospital with exposure and with the penalties that would follow if one of its employees failed to follow the reporting provisions of the law on abuse in nursing homes.

Did Mrs. Lewis act correctly? What should she have done if she could not afford to consult a lawyer? In what other ways can whistleblowers protect themselves? Must the art of intimidation be part of the tool chest of health care professionals in order to protect their patients? Is power an appropriate consideration in health care ethics?

2. All the nurses in obstetrics and all the physicians on the obstetrics and gynecological service know that Dr. Borracho is an alcoholic. He frequently appears so intoxicated as to be unable to measure the dilation of the cervix. On one occasion, he examined a woman and told her she had several hours before delivery. The baby's head appeared before he got out of the room. Up to now there have been no serious injuries to mothers or children, because the nurses have been able to stop him from committing really serious mistakes. Of late, however, Dr. Borracho is getting violent when the nurses intercede. The director of nursing has been informed and has done nothing because Borracho has a lot of influence in the hospital and the director does not believe in rocking the boat with physicians.

Have the nurses done enough by reporting the problem? Should they go elsewhere in the hospital, such as to the physicians' peer review group? Should they use groups outside the hospital, such as the media, the State Department of Health, or the State Nurses Association? Should patients be encouraged by the nurses to file official complaints?

3. About half the residents of the small town of Pamplona know that Dr. Cannabis is the equivalent of a drug pusher. He will write anyone a prescription for just about anything at any time or in any place. You do not have to be his patient, and no questions are asked as long as you hand over $10 for the prescription. Repeated denunciations to the State Board of Medical Examiners have done little good. Dr. Cannabis is a member of the board of directors of the hospital, and his group practice is a major supplier of patients to the hospital.

What should be done? If so many know that Dr. Cannabis is pushing drugs, who has failed in his or her obligation to report it? If medical authorities will not cooperate, is there an obligation to go to the police and the district attorney?

4. Ms. Smith, a nurse in the 150-bed community hospital in Ocala (population 50,000), is a shrewd overseer. She has noted that Dr. Coupay does an extraordinary number of hysterectomies on very young women. He does as many as 10 to 15 per week.

While nursing Dr. Coupay's patients, Ms. Smith gets the impression that they were rushed into the operation and did not fully understand what was happening. Through friends in Pathology, she hears a rumor that most of these hysterectomies appear to have been unnecessary, since there were no signs of cancer or fibroid tumors and no signs of damage to the uterus. She mentions this to her supervisor, who tells her that the matter is being investigated. Besides, the hospital census is down and those patients help to keep things going. Six months later, the situation is unchanged.

Ordinarily, the hospital tissue committee would take care of this problem. In the absence of action from the tissue committee, should Mrs. Smith make a formal complaint? If a formal complaint does no good, what should she do?

5. Dr. Furibund carries a large, loaded handgun strapped to his leg at all times, including his long hours in the operating room. Dr. Furibund is an obnoxious person and thoroughly disliked. He justifies carrying the gun on the grounds that people are out to get him. The carrying of the gun violates hospital rules and makes his fellow surgeons and the nurses very anxious, especially when he brandishes it in public. The chief of surgery has witnessed Furibund showing his gun in the physicians' lounge but has done nothing about it.

What should be done inside the hospital? If the hospital will not act, should the police be informed? Should the physician's insurance company be notified?

6. On a July weekend, Mrs. Allesfertig, nursing supervisor of the whole hospital, discovered that the intensive care unit (ICU) was seriously understaffed. She pulled two nurses with previous ICU experience off other floors to bring the unit up to strength in view of the extreme level of acute care needed. On the following Monday, Dr. Bestknabe, with overall responsibility for the ICU, closed the unit to further admissions until the staffing had been worked out on a permanent basis.

Should the new staffing policy give the nurses authority to refuse to admit patients when the staff is not sufficient to handle them? (In some hospitals, nurses have this authority.) Can any policy take precedence over the professional judgement of trained ICU nurses?

7. Mrs. Rousseau, RN, CFNP, MSN, has been assigned to train nonlicensed personnel to assist RNs in drawing blood, inserting catheters, and taking vital signs. She has five hours of lecture and fifteen hours of on-the-job training. Her pupils, most of them from a government poverty program, are a mixed group. Some are bright, dexterous, and quick to learn. Others are slow and awkward. Others, since they cannot multiply, cannot take a pulse for fifteen seconds and multiply by four, but must count through an entire minute. They often get confused about how many beats they have counted. About half the group has trouble hearing even a severe irregularity. One or two do not even notice when a patient is turning blue. This appears to be a matter of attention span, since when not busy they appear to be off in space.

Because by passing them, Rousseau will put them on the floor, she is torn apart. "Some of them just do not have it," she muses to herself.

Should Rousseau approve all of them despite her serious doubts? Which candidates should be rejected out of hand? Should she go with the principle of "Don't rock the boat," and merely suggest a better screening method for future candidates?

NOTES

1. The obligation to maintain and improve the quality of health care is acknowledged in ethical code provisions like the following selections from the American Nurses Association Code for Nurses (1985):

5. The nurse maintains competence in nursing.
7. The nurse participates in activities that contribute to the ongoing development of the profession's body of knowledge.
8. The nurse participates in the profession's efforts to implement and improve standards of nursing.
11. The nurse collaborates with members of the health professions and other citizens in promoting community and national efforts to meet the health needs of the public.

Although it is not as explicit or broad ranging, at least one principle of the American Medical Association (1980) applies here:

V. The physician shall continue to study, apply and advance scientific knowledge, make relevant information available to patients, colleagues and the public, obtain consultation, and use the talents of other health professionals when indicated.

2. The obligation to police, which includes the obligation to blow the whistle, is recognized in varying ways by the following excerpts from the codes of health care providers.

The American Nurses Association (1985):

3. The nurse acts to safeguard the client and the public when health care and safety are affected by the incompetent, unethical or illegal practice of any person.
10. The nurse participates in the profession's effort to protect the public from misinformation and misrepresentation and to maintain the integrity of nursing.

The American Physical Therapy Association (1987):

7.1 Physical therapists are to report any conduct which appears to be unethical, incompetent, or illegal.

The American Medical Association (1980 version):

A physician shall deal honestly with patients and colleagues and shall strive to expose those physicians deficient in character and competence, or who engage in fraud or deceptions.

The American Medical Association (1989) is more explicit:

9.04 DISCIPLINE AND MEDICINE. A physician should expose, without fear or favor, incompetent or corrupt, dishonest or unethical conduct on the part of members of the profession. Questions of such conduct should be considered, first, before proper medical tribunals in executive sessions or by special or duly appointed committees on ethical relations, provided that such a course is possible and provided, also, that the law is not hampered thereby. If doubt should arise as to the legality of the physician's conduct, the situation under investigation may be placed before officers of the law, and the physician-investigators may take the necessary steps to enlist the interest of the proper authority.

7

ETHICAL PROBLEMS OF DEATH AND DYING

Few areas in medical ethics are as difficult as those concerning death and dying. These topics raise questions about the meaning of life, the purpose of medical treatment, and a person's right to determine when medical treatment, and even life, should end.

The first part of this chapter takes up the *ethics of the patient*, and the second is concerned with the *ethics of the care giver in the face of death and dying*. The third and final part is devoted to issues involving surrogates. The ethics of the patient involve the refusal of treatment or the request to discontinue treatment when such acts will lead to, or at least hasten, death. Of necessity, this involves a discussion of the ethics of both passive and active suicide. Once we have discussed the ethics of suicide, we proceed to a consideration of the health care provider's ethical problems in cooperating with the patient's refusal of treatment or even physician-assisted suicide, as well as related questions involving living wills, the patient in a permanent vegetative state, and the quality of life for the individual person.

ETHICS OF THE PATIENT

First, we shall attempt to answer two basic questions: (1) Is refusing treatment suicide? (2) Is suicide always unethical?

Refusal of Treatment and Passive Suicide

In chapter 2, we argued that a patient has a right to refuse treatment. In chapter 3, we developed the idea that the patient needs a proportionate reason for refusing to begin or continue treatment. In short, using the approach of practical wisdom, we argue that it is ethical for the patient to refuse treatment for a proportional reason, *all things considered*. Unfortunately, many people, including many health care providers, want to challenge the right of the patient to refuse treatment when the refusal leads to death or at least a speeding up of the death process. Emotionally, if not intellectually, those who object to the patient's decision argue that such a refusal is suicide and unethical, because all suicide is unethical. The issue becomes more disputed when it is necessary for surrogates to make the decision.

Let us start with a commonsense definition of suicide as *the intentional termination of one's own life*. This definition will include all those cases in which a person wants to kill herself or himself, whether the person does this by omitting something (passive suicide) or by doing something (active suicide).[1] It does not include cases in which the person does not intend to terminate her or his life, but omits an action or performs an action that the person foresees as possibly leading to death. A person who gives up food so that others may live is often not considered to be committing suicide, even though this person may starve to death. Even if one calls this altruistic act suicide, it is still ethical in a consequentialist view, since there is a proportionate reason for risking or permitting death. Similarly, the person who dies because he or she has refused treatment in order to avoid a degrading and painful existence may be said to commit suicide, but this would be a passive suicide. In line with what was said in chapter 3 about the proportional nature of the patient's obligation to care for himself, arguably this is an ethical action. A serious difficulty is identifying when such refusal is not truly a passive acquiescence to the inevitability of a disease, and instead is a disproportionate seeking out of death.

Part of the difficulty is in the meaning of the word *intend*. One can know that death will result from one's actions without *intending* to die (consider the discussion of the principle of double effect in chapter 3, and O'Rourke, 1996). Altruistic acts leading to death are rarely considered suicide because of this distinction. However, particularly in medical ethics, we can be faced with situations in which a patient or the patient's surrogate may intend the patient's death, not because he or she wants to die, but because a medical condition or the treatment for it is intolerable. They intend their deaths only because of the inhumaneness of their circumstances. The real issue (what is intended) is the elimination of suffering, and the means is perhaps discontinuing ventilation. A test for this would be that given a life without this suffering, the patient would prefer to be alive. It is in this sense that we refer to a proportionate reason for refusing treatment and ultimately conclude that not all suicide defined as the intentional killing of oneself is unethical by common-sense or practical wisdom standards.

Why Is Suicide Thought to Be Unethical?

The difficulty of this question centers on the question of what constitutes a proportionate reason. To answer this question, we must first look at the reasons given for condemning active suicide. These arguments make a *prima facie*, or presumptive, case against active suicide, but do not in our opinion prove philosophically that suicide is always and in all circumstances an ethical evil. This is important not only for the ethics of the patient, but in considering the ethicality of a health care provider cooperating in active suicide.

The notion that suicide is wrong has been supported by a number of arguments. The first argument is religious and theological. It holds that our lives belong to God and are merely loaned to us, so we have no right to dispose of our own lives, even though we have the right to use them within limits. In this view, we have no more right to kill ourselves than we would have to wreck a rented car. This is a strong argument for those who believe in the basic premises. Even the proponents of this argument, however, must admit that God might, at least by way of exception, grant a person permission to commit active suicide. While they are very hesitant to admit exceptions in cases of active suicide, they do permit some passive suicide. They admit, for example, that a patient is not required to use extraordinary means to continue existence. As noted in chapter 3, this amounts to saying that in certain circumstances passive suicide can be justified by a proportionate reason. Indeed, these religious writers praise the person who lays down a life for a friend or suffers martyrdom for the sake of religious faith, although they are quite clear that a person ought not to go about looking for martyrdom.

The second argument holds that human life is so precious that to act against it is to act against the greatest of all human goods, or at least against the good on which all other human goods depend. These assertions might appear true in the abstract, as long as one does not specify the specific condition of that life. The abstract consideration overlooks several important truths. In the concrete, life may be experienced as an overwhelming burden, and the word *life* may designate no more than a vegetable existence in a specific case. Furthermore, life can be so painful and so crushing that it renders all other goods impossible. Finally, life can be barely recognizable as human, as in the cases of those who are in a permanent vegetative state. Those who have been in real pain know how pain eats up all other consciousness and abolishes control of much activity, even as it makes us insensitive to the feelings of those who love us. Even though medical science has become adept at controlling pain, it often succeeds at the cost of the patient's consciousness. When the choice becomes overwhelming pain or unconsciousness, it appears that life is no longer the substratum for all other good things. In the concrete, then, life may not be the greatest of all goods or that good upon which all other goods depend. In short, life is not an unambiguous reality such that it is always a good. We shall return to this issue in the second part of this chapter.

Those who hold that life is precious and the basis for all other goods recognize the fact of the vegetative state and of pain. Often, then, they will permit an ethical, passive suicide for a proportionate reason, even though they reject active suicide, that is, the direct killing of oneself.

The matter cannot be settled merely by permitting passive suicide for a proportionate reason. There is need for a longer look at the value of life and the relative importance of the quality of life. We will return to this question after we outline the remaining arguments against suicide.

A third argument, this one consequentialist, condemns suicide because it harms the community. This, too, is a bit oversimplified. As a matter of fact, not all suicides harm the community. Some suicides may be a positive benefit to the community. If Americans over age 70 committed suicide at the first sign of serious illness, there would be tremendous savings in Medicare and Social Security costs. Of course, these financial savings may be offset by the economic productivity or other contributions of people over 70, but the point remains that suicide is not simply harmful to the community.

As noted in chapter 1, the individual person and not the community is the intrinsic good, and the individual should not be automatically or unnecessarily subordinated to the community. Certainly, the individual must consider the impact of his or her actions on the society, but the effects on society are not the decisive factor. In short, the harm to the community must be considered in judging proportionality, but the good of the community is on the level of means and is not the intrinsic good. We shall return to this shortly. Thus, the mere fact that a suicide might hurt the community does not settle the issue.

A fourth argument proposes that suicide is wrong because it has substantially harmful consequences for other individuals. Once again, we agree that these consequences must be considered, but we insist that they are not the only factors to be considered in judging the proportionality of the goods and evils involved. The value of the human person is not solely, or even primarily, dependent on her or his utility for others, either singly or in a group. Thus, the actual and potential harm to the patient can at times be the decisive factor in deciding the balance of good or evil in the suicide situation.

While some writers might theoretically accept the exceptions we have just pointed out, they will argue that, in practice, suicide should be forbidden because of the wedge principle in its logical or empirical form. That is, they argue from the long-term consequences of allowing exceptions. Their arguments, based on each of the principles, deserve study.

The empirical form of the wedge principle, which argues that exceptions will lead to the dramatic spread of suicide, seems to have little foundation. Suicide will never become popular for the simple reason that most people are attached to their lives even when they are very difficult. Admitting reasonable exceptions to the general condemnation of suicide hardly seems likely to change this.

The logical form of the wedge principle, which argues that we should be consistent, hardly seems applicable for the practical wisdom theorist who consistently insists on the need for considering the effect on dignity of all the elements of the situation and refuses to rely on oversimplified analysis. We suspect that an emotional need for clear and certain moral rules, rather than consistency, motivates most objections to exceptions.

This much seems clear: Active suicide, although generally an evil, is not universally evil. All major theories appear to allow room for exceptions. Certainly, the follower of practical wisdom must admit exceptions, because in some cases the person can quite reasonably decide that, all things considered, continued existence is more evil than the termination of existence. When one is already dying and life is a ball of pain, the value of biological existence may, in the view of some patients, evaporate into nonsense and at the very least becomes a serious moral question for loved ones.

Summary: Suicide and the Ethics of the Patient

The distinction between passive and active suicide remains important for this discussion. Both the arguments above and the treatment of beneficence from the patient's point of view (chapter 3) make it clear that the refusal of treatment, even considered as passive suicide, is ethical given a proportionate reason, all things considered. The present chapter also points to the argument that even active suicide can be ethical for the patient, granted proportionality of all things considered.

To say that it is ethical for a patient to commit active suicide in certain circumstances is not, however, to say that patients have a right to do so. To put it another way, the ethical correctness of active suicide does not necessarily imply a right not to be interfered with (a liberty right), let alone a right to have others help them (substantive right). For example, this point by itself does not answer the question of the ethical correctness of physician-assisted suicide. It is necessary, then, to consider first the health care provider's ethics of active suicide prevention and then the ethics of cooperating with a suicide. After this, we will return to the simpler case of the health care provider cooperating with passive suicide.

An Alternative View

This review of arguments against suicide reveals a common thread in the suggestion that the life of the individual is an element of a larger picture that morally limits the individual's actions. This establishes a tension between the individual's autonomy and the moral limits on the exercise of that autonomy (see the following discussion of physician assisted suicide). Becker describes a different view held by Japanese Buddhism, where "the acceptability of suicide, even in the early Buddhist community, depended not on terminal illness alone, but upon the state of selfless equanimity with which one was able to pass away" (Becker, 1990, p. 619). The central concern is not one of power (who has the authority to do what) or the nature of the action itself, but of the state of one's consciousness. If one is angry or fearful, one is not ready for death no matter how it comes. This position is connected with a strong belief in an afterlife and rebirth. For the Buddhist it matters how one dies, for this influences what happens to the soul in the next world.

HEALTH CARE PROVIDERS AND THE ETHICS OF SUICIDE PREVENTION

In chapters 1 and 2, we stressed the fact that private individuals, including health care providers, do not have a right to interfere with the activities of others unless authorized to do so by society. In addition, we stressed the fact that, in general, even society is justified in interfering and authorizing others to interfere only for overriding social interests.

In the present context of suicide prevention in the United States, several points seem clear. First, society has a clear interest in the preservation of life itself. As we have seen, life has a fundamental value, and an important advantage to living in society is the protection social life affords to life itself. Second, although the value of the individual is not purely and simply his or her value to society, most individuals are valuable to society, and society has a legitimate interest in preserving most of its citizens. At times, there may even be a very strong overriding social interest, since the individual in question may be particularly valuable to society. Society could, then, legitimately forbid suicide or cooperation with suicide on the grounds that the suicide robbed society of someone valuable. In addition, societies recognize that suicides do affect the rights of others. Spouses and children, in particular, have important legal and moral claims on a would-be suicide. For example, if a child's claims to such things as food and shelter are not met because of a suicide, society will be burdened with the child's support. For these reasons, many societies have made suicide a crime, that is, an offense against the society. Finally, the society may conclude that groups, such as the health care professions, need to be insulated from the active suicide to protect the functioning of the profession.

In the United States, most states make cooperating with suicide a crime, although suicide itself is not. This acknowledges that, even though a person may be free to commit suicide, the society does not want to encourage it and definitely does not want others helping, since that help can easily turn into homicide. Yet, as we shall see, there are cases in which society might well authorize controlled cooperation with suicide.

Even though it does not make suicide a crime, American society authorizes medical and police personnel to frustrate and restrain attempted suicides and to initiate a due process that can lead to involuntary commitment to a mental institution for those who are judged to be a danger to themselves or others. It should be noted, however, that in some states, such as New York, suicide refers only to self-inflicted harm *and not to a decision to refuse life-sustaining treatment* (New York State Task Force on Life and the Law, 1986).

When danger is limited to the patient, that is, when there is no damage to society or spouses and children, this societal practice raises serious questions. Szasz (1977) and other libertarians (those who believe in the maximum freedom compatible with the rights of others) object strenuously. Szasz writes:

> The individualistic position on suicide might be put thus: A person's life belongs to himself. Hence, he has a right to take his own life, that is, to commit suicide. To be sure this view recognizes that a person may also have a moral responsibility to his family and others and that, by killing himself, he reneges on those responsibilities. But those are moral wrongs that society, in its corporate capacity as the state, cannot properly punish. Hence the state must eschew attempts to regulate such behavior by means of formal sanctions, such as criminal or mental hygiene laws (p. 76).

The Szasz position ignores the fact that society might still have a legitimate interest in coercing a person into fulfilling her or his responsibility to family and others, as well as in preventing harm to other individuals or groups. Laws authorizing the prevention of suicide can have legitimate social purposes. There may also be room for a legitimate form of the weak paternalism discussed in chapter 2.

This weak paternalism is found in the position of Greenberg (1974), who insists that many who attempt suicide do not really want to die and that efforts to save them are justified. Greenberg, however, notes that a suicide prevention policy should interfere as little as possible with those who, after due consideration, still want to commit suicide. Thus, the prevention would be temporary, with the purpose of ensuring the patient's autonomy. This position, however, recognizes that in general the state should not interfere unless for an overriding state interest or the protection of the rights of others.

In this context, it needs to be stressed that the prevention of suicide by involuntary commitment requires legal procedures and is not simply a medical question. These legal procedures have been made increasingly strict in recent times, since in the past the power of commitment was often abused. This was particularly true when a simple physician with no psychiatric training had sufficient authority in court to assure the commitment.

The laws on active suicide and involuntary commitment of those who are suicidal are not without their problems. Sometimes the law and its application seems more paternalistic than guided by an interest in protecting society. In some cases, the law can be questioned with regard to the lack of full due process or clear norms for commitment. Whether we approve of these laws or not, they are there, and the reasons for their existence must enter into the decisions of health care providers.

HEALTH CARE PROVIDERS AND THE ETHICS OF THE DEATH OF A PATIENT

It is time now to return to one of our basic questions: Is it ethical for the health care provider to cooperate when a competent patient refuses treatment? Further, may a health care provider cooperate with a patient's active suicide? In using the word *cooperation*, we mean to stress that the competent patient has asked for or consented to the cooperation. When there is an incompetent or doubtfully competent patient or only surrogate consent, we are dealing with an even more delicate problem that we will discuss separately.

Cooperation with a Patient Who Refuses Treatment

Let us now turn to a health care professional's cooperation with the patient's refusal of treatment or the demand that life-sustaining treatment be withdrawn. The laws that forbid cooperation with active suicide do not forbid cooperating with such a refusal. Increasingly, court decisions affirm the right of the patient to refuse treatment, including nutrition and hydration. As noted in chapter 2, such a person cannot be treated against his or her wishes without a court order. Such orders are not automatically granted. Indeed, the right to refuse treatment and to refuse nutrition and hydration has been recognized not only in the case of terminal patients, but in the case of competent nonterminal patients, as well as being recognized in surrogates for such patients.[2] However, the question is far more complex than the mere legal aspects, and we must now consider the ethical complexities.

In these cases of passive suicide, the patient or surrogate exercises the right to refuse treatment or demands the discontinuance of treatment in order to avoid suffering or to avoid the difficulties of continued treatment; generally this also implies that discontinuing treatment will speed up dying. (In no case does discontinuing treatment imply discontinuing care.) As we saw in chapter 2, the competent patient has the right to refuse or discontinue treatment. Yet a variety of court cases on the subject indicate that there are more complicated emotional and ethical problems for health care providers and for society. In a sense, there is a landscape in which such refusal can be more or less acceptable, depending on whether the patient is terminal with death imminent; merely terminal; terminal and in a permanent vegetable state; nonterminal and in a permanent vegetable state; nonterminal, noncomatose, and incompetent; nonterminal, noncomatose, and competent, but with difficult life prospects; or even nonterminal, noncomatose, competent, and without difficult life prospects. These considerations are particularly important for surrogate decisions.

When the patient is terminal and death is imminent, no treatment is medically indicated (see chapter 3), and the competent patient's rightful refusal of treatment does not conflict with the health provider's form of beneficence. There may be an emotional problem in admitting defeat, but there should be no ethical problem. We note that, although the patient may not be competent at the end, refusal of treatment may be accomplished through a living will or a surrogate, especially through a surrogate who has durable power of attorney for health matters. We will return to the objections against the living will later.

When the patient is terminal but death is not imminent, for example when the disease or injury progresses slowly, and granted the consent of the patient or surrogate, it appears ethical to omit *treatment* on the ground that nothing can be accomplished in thwarting the progress of the disease. But it is not ethical to omit *care*, since human dignity is to be respected (see below).

The AMA Council on Ethical and Judicial Affairs (1996) takes a clear stand on the issue:

> E-2.20 Even if the patient is not terminally ill or permanently unconscious, it is not unethical to discontinue all means of life-sustaining medical treatment in accordance with a proper substituted judgment or best interests analysis.

The treatments include artificially supplied respiration, nutrition, or hydration. In its recent opposition to physician-assisted suicide, the AMA has strongly endorsed a program to educate physicians to the appropriateness of switching from therapeutic treatment to palliative care. The group has gone from a tentative, negative position ("not unethical") to a much stronger positive stand (AMA, 1996). We shall return to the special problems of nutrition and hydration later in this chapter.

As we shall see later, this position on discontinuing treatment is reinforced by the law in those states that recognize living wills and durable powers of attorney. These legal instruments will be discussed later in this chapter.

Discontinuing Treatment

Let us look at the reasoning behind the ethical correctness of not beginning or of stopping treatment in the case of the consenting patient who is terminally ill. First, the health care provider has no obligation to prolong dying merely for the sake of prolonging it. That is, it makes no sense to prolong life when the true result is the prolongation of the dying process. Furthermore, when treatment is only prolonging the agony of the patient, its continuation is unethical as an insult to human dignity (Cahill, 1977). In such cases, the health care provider would be ethically justified in discontinuing treatment *except when the patient insists on treatment*. Even in this case, however, there can be exceptions. When there is a severe shortage of medical resources, the physician might be justified in stopping nonindicated treatment even over the protests of the patient. We say "might be justified," since justification would depend, among other things, on a new social consensus about the duties of health care professionals and on a reasonable certainty that a shortage exists. There are also problems in discontinuing treatment when the patient's surrogate(s) objects. We shall return to these questions later.

It should be noted that cessation of life-sustaining treatment does not always bring about a swift and painless death, even though it may speed up the process of dying. For example, if kidney dialysis is discontinued, the person remains conscious and suffers vomiting, internal hemorrhage, and convulsions. The removal of a respirator does not lead to death immediately, and the patient suffers the pain and panic of suffocation. The obligation to care for the patient demands that every ethical effort be made to alleviate these sufferings with drugs and other methods that will not prolong life. Much recent research suggests that physicians are particularly deficient in their willingness and ability to provide adequate pain palliation for dying patients (SUPPORT, 1995; American Medical Association, 1995). This could be one of the main concerns that drive the interest in physician-assisted suicide. Beyond this, when such pain relief is not possible for the patient, or when the harm is not the pain, but the insult to dignity, there arises the difficult problem of actively cooperating in the suicide of the patient.

Feeding and Hydration

In our treatment of the health care provider's formulation of the principle of beneficence in chapter 3 we touched on the problem of feeding and hydration in the context of the final Baby Doe rule. We now return to the question of whether nutrition and hydration are medically indicated for terminal patients.

Before answering this question, it is necessary to show that the nutrition and hydration in question are generally not matters of sipping liquids or spooning in chicken soup, but of serious, uncomfortable, and occasionally painful medical procedures. A brief look at the methods will show their medical nature.

There are several methods of intravenous nutrition and hydration. Nearly everyone is familiar with intravenous, or IV, feeding, in which a tiny tube is inserted into a vein in the arm or hand. This method is only temporarily useful for improving hydration and electrolyte concentrations. Often the patient has to be restrained from tearing out the tube. Another IV method involves inserting a catheter (small tube) into a major vein in the chest. This is a more costly method that increases the risk of infection and again often leads to restraint of the patient.

There are also two methods of feeding and hydration by inserting tubes into the intestinal tract. The first method involves inserting a tube into the person's nose and down the throat and then into the digestive tract. This method is very annoying to both patients and families and, although inexpensive, often leads to pneumonia. The second method involves cutting an opening in the abdomen and inserting a tube directly into the stomach. The hole is then closed surgically.

We are dealing with medical procedures, not with simple tasks of everyday living. The question, then, is whether these procedures are medically indicated. That is, do they do more harm than good for the patient? In treating a terminally ill or irreversibly comatose patient, the physician should determine whether the benefits of treatment outweigh its burdens. At all times, the dignity of the patient should be maintained. The AMA Council on Ethical and Judicial Affairs quoted earlier expressed the emerging consensus that it is not wrong to withdraw these treatments under appropriate circumstances.

The appropriate circumstances might be found in the following types of cases: (1) the procedures are futile, since the procedures are unlikely to achieve their purpose; (2) the procedures would be no help to the patient even if successful; (3) the burdens outweigh the benefits (Lynn and Childress, 1983).

The following are examples of futile treatments (taken from Lynn and Childress, 1983): (1) the patient has a severe clotting deficiency and has a near-total body burn; (2) the patient has severe congestive heart failure with cancer of the stomach, which delivers food to the colon without passing through the intestine and being absorbed. In this case the fluids introduced by hydration will kill by acting on the congestive heart failure when not much of the food is absorbed in any event.

In a second class of cases, there is *no possibility of benefit* to the patient who has permanently lost consciousness, as in patients with anencephaly, persistent vegetative state, and preterminal coma. In these cases, feeding is sometimes done for the sake of the family, but it is not medically indicated. Finally, there are cases in which feeding and hydration impose a *disproportionate burden*: (1) the patient's need for nutrition arises only near death, a point at which hydration causes terminal pulmonary edema, nausea, and mental confusion; (2) patients who, although they might benefit in one way, have fairly severe dementia, such that restraints are needed, with the result that the patient suffers constant fear and discomfort as he or she struggles to be free. Life is prolonged, but in a captive state.

All this may be summarized by saying that, when hydration and nutrition become medical procedures, the ethics of their omission is based on the ethics of medical indications and not on common-sense notions. Some will argue that life is to be preserved at all costs, but as we saw earlier in this chapter, most ethics theories allow that the value of life has limits for the individual and for society.

A word of caution is appropriate here. When a competent patient is sedated to control pain, his resulting incompetence is due to the sedation. Hydration and nutrition probably cannot be withdrawn at that time, if his incompetence (or unconsciousness) is cited as part of the justification for the withdrawal. The physician cannot create an adverse condition and then use that as justification for ceasing treatment.

In some cases nutrition and hydration are indicated on the compassionate ground that such a death is sometimes more painful than death from the particular disease. The patient may be faced with the choice between a slow death from cancer with adequate pain control or a slightly more rapid and more painful death from dehydration and starvation. In such a case, the omission of feeding and hydration would be cruel. Health care professionals involved in hospice work have observed that, although deprivation of nutrition and hydration is painful in healthy people, they do not as a rule produce pain and suffering in the terminally ill (Cox, 1987). One cannot, then, simply assume that starvation or dehydration is always painful, or for that matter that it is never painful. Each case must be evaluated individually, and ultimately the choice of the manner of death belongs to the competent patient.

The complexities arising from statute law and court decisions are enormous (Meisel, supp. 1991, pp. 191-193). Thus, although some states have an outright prohibition of a living will ordering the discontinuance of hydration and nutrition, most require nutrition and hydration *only if necessary for the comfort of the patient.* Still others concern themselves only with simple spoon feeding and permit the withdrawal of artificial medical forms of feeding. In short, the health care professional must be aware of the law in his or her state, as well as of the ethical principles.

Antibiotic: Omission or Withdrawal

Before discussing the ethics of omitting or stopping treatment with antibiotics, it is important to recall that the medical indications principle requires that the *patient as a person* gain more than she or he loses from the medical treatment. It may not be the case that the treatment of a particular disease or condition is of benefit to the patient if the patient has other problems. Thus, if antibiotic treatment cures pneumonia only to prolong the slow death of a terminal cancer patient, it is not medically indicated, since the cure of the pneumonia leads to a medical net loss for the patient. Indeed, it is very much like the cruelty of prolonging the life of a condemned man so that he will be alive for his hanging. On the other hand, if the pneumonia is adding to the cancer patient's discomfort, antibiotic treatment is medically indicated, since the patient will enjoy a net gain as a result of the treatment. Despite the language of some living will legislation, we believe that this principle holds whether or not the patient is technically terminal.

Here, as elsewhere in this chapter, the warnings about patient or surrogate consent should be kept in mind. Medical indications alone do not give the final ethical answer.

First, let us treat the use of antibiotics in terminal cases. It makes no sense to treat the pneumonia of a terminal cancer patient with antibiotics, since this will merely prolong his or her dying and so the pain. On the other hand, it makes sense to treat the decubitus ulcers of the terminal cancer patient, since the ulcers are painful to the patient and treating them will not prolong his or her life. To put it another way, it makes sense not to prolong life for the terminal cancer patient, but it does not make sense to increase the pain. The good of the patient in all its complexity must be considered.

With the general principle clear, we may now consider a series of cases in which (1) the patient may or may not be terminal, that is, in the end stages of a terminal disease other than that which is being considered for treatment; (2) the patient is in a persistent vegetative state; and (3) where the patient is considered severely and irreversibly demented.

In case 1, antibiotics seem to be medically indicated, although the patient and her or his surrogate have a right to refuse them. In case 2, the antibiotics do not appear to be medically indicated although some families and health care workers may comfort themselves with hope for a miracle. In case 3, the severely and irreversibly demented patient can still profit from the antibiotics, although on a minimal level. Granted surrogate consent, antibiotics should be administered to this patient.

Although many physicians do not consult patients in these cases, they have an ethical obligation to explain the medical indications and obtain a consent or refusal of consent from a competent patient or a competent surrogate. When there is no surrogate, no competent patient, and no advanced directive, the physician must fall back on the medical indications principle alone and omit the antibiotic when no net gain for the patient is anticipated.

Cooperation with the Refusal of Treatment by a Nonterminal Patient

The most emotionally difficult cases arise when the patient refusing treatment is not terminal, but will become so when the respirator is unplugged or the treatment is not started or is stopped. This can occur when the patient judges that it is not worthwhile living on a respirator forever or being fed artificially for years. It occurs when the patient chooses not to live at a level below his or her ideal. In all these cases, the treatment is medically indicated from the health care provider's point of view, but does not produce a proportionate good from the patient's point of view. Regardless of the emotional turmoil suffered by the provider, here (as in chapter 3) the patient retains the right to refuse treatment. Only a court order or a court-appointed guardian has the right to overrule the patient in these cases. The justice of even such court rulings is not beyond question if the death will not injure society or third parties.

What, however, is to be said of the case in which the nonterminal patient not only refuses medically indicated treatment, but asks the health care provider to keep her comfortable while she dies? This was one issue in the Bouvia case (see case 2 at the end of this chapter). In this case, the patient refused food and drink, but asked to be made comfortable in the hospital while she starved to death.

The health care provider can ethically refuse to cooperate in such situations, not only on the ground of individual conscience, if that is the case, but also because the health care professions should not be involved in helping nonterminal patients to shorten their lives significantly. We note, however, the complicated result that, in the long run the California courts ordered the hospital to comply with Ms. Bouvia, but she did not carry out her plans. Granted that health care providers have no right to force treatment on patients, it seems clear that healthy or mildly ill patients do not have the right to force physicians or hospitals to provide positive support for their attempts at self-destruction. As noted in chapter 3, health care providers who refuse to cooperate with a patient already in their care must provide for continuity of care, such as involving another physician, lest they be guilty of abandonment. But cases in which there is a reasonable disagreement on the meaning of the prospects of the patient must be decided on a case-by-case basis, recognizing the concerns of both parties.

PHYSICIAN INITIATIVES

Under certain circumstances, it may be appropriate for a physician to take the initiative in discussing termination of care for the patient. The physician is obligated to inform the patient clearly and completely about his condition in order to obtain consent for treatment. This should include an accurate description of the burdens and benefits of continued treatment and the odds of success. At times, this means the physician must tell the patient when it is likely that the patient will die no matter what is done. Also, the physician is obligated to provide treatment that does not harm the patient. Treatment that is not reasonably likely to work should not be provided; it misleads the patient and it wastes resources. These considerations lead to the issues of Do Not Resuscitate Orders (DNRs) and medical futility.

The No-Code Order

A no-code order is a written order to do nothing if certain situations arise. Most commonly, it is a do-not-resuscitate order (DNR), that is, a written order not to attempt resuscitation in cases of cardiac arrest (Standards and Guidelines, 1986). A slow code, also called a show code or merely a walk slowly code, involves a verbal order to the staff to respond slowly when the patient has a cardiac arrest. Winslade and Ross (1986) note that this is often used to give the appearance of resuscitating, especially to the family. There are also partial codes, which limit the resuscitation efforts. Each of these codes needs separate consideration.

The Joint Commission on Hospital Accreditation requires every hospital to have a no-code policy. While hospital policies should be consulted, a no-code order may be ethically issued when the treatment in question or resuscitation is not medically indicated. In other words, a no-code order is correct when, from a medical point of view, more harm than good will be done to the patient by treatment or resuscitation. This is usually the case when there is no further therapy for the underlying disease process for a terminally ill patient. The order is also justified by the patient's express wish that resuscitation not be attempted. It should be noted that this is a written order for which the physician accepts public responsibility and that should be medically justified on the chart. Granted these conditions and consent, except in the limited circumstances indicated previously, the no-code order is ethical.

The slow code is used to give families the impression that everything is being done for the patient in situations in which most of the time a no-code order would be medically and ethically justified. The temptation to issue such an order can be great when a family insists against all reason that a patient be kept alive, even when the patient is brain dead. Nevertheless, the deception involved should be condemned as unethical. The fact that there is no written order and so a refusal to take public responsibility for the decision is also reprehensible.

We note again that the family may have nonmedical reasons for prolonging the life, even the vegetative life, for a while longer. They may want time for one last relative to arrive to enter into the farewells and the grieving process. There may be legal complications involving the moment of death. When respecting such reasons does not cause the patient additional pain and suffering, the reasons should be given some weight. Certainly, they should not be ignored and the family deceived about what is going on.

The partial code is a written order to omit some medical interventions, but to employ others. There may be sound medical reasons to attempt chest compression and electrical defibrillation or to omit intubation. The reasons for these specific orders and omissions should be entered on the chart. Indeed, to avoid any ambiguity, all no-code orders should specify what is not to be done with respect to each illness. Such specification will clarify thinking and accountability and help reduce the risk of carelessness.

Medical Futility

The situations discussed in this chapter raise the issue of when medical care might be considered futile, that is, when the continuation of a particular treatment might have the anticipated medical effect and yet not be beneficial to the patient. An example of this would be the continued ventilation of a ventilator-dependent, permanently comatose, terminally ill patient (a prominent example of this is the case of Helga Wanglie; see Cranford, 1991). Ordinarily, the patient's surrogates in consultation with the patient's physicians would decide whether to continue or to discontinue treatment. The question of medical futility arises when the patient's physicians disagree with the surrogate's decision to continue treatment. Can the expertise of the physician be used to justify discontinuing treatment in the face of surrogate disagreement? This is a situation different from the one mentioned above in which the society decides not to pay for treatment. Here we have the expertise of the physician facing off with the autonomy of the patient. Can the patient or surrogate demand treatment contrary to expert advice?

The abstract answer to this last question must of course be "No" or else the claims to expertise that ground the profession are pointless (Tomlinson,

1995). This answer is the justification for hospital futility policies and in general justifies various forms of weak paternalism. But it is an answer with serious limitations (Truog, 1992). First, it does not justify the arbitrary imposition of the physician's preferences on the patient. Any determinations of futility must be rooted in expertise; hence, they must be public and subject to confirmation. Second, such determinations involve value judgments, since they involve the physician's evaluation of what is beneficial (Ackerman, 1991). This pits the patient's values against those of the physician, and may ask the physician to decide issues (such as predicting the occurrence of functional or cognitive decline) that are simply not possible to determine (Drickamer, 1997). By virtue of our concern with autonomy, the patient wins such conflicts when they involve refusing recommended treatment. When the issue involves patient or surrogate demands for continued treatment, the principle of autonomy should continue to prevail. The problems of insensitivity or the abuse of power are great enough in these situations that, until a more clear public understanding of physician expertise is developed, caution should favor the patient. (For a clear example of physician and hospital insensitivity, see *Rideout v. Hershey Medical Center, 1995.*)

COOPERATION WITH ACTIVE SUICIDE AND EUTHANASIA

Physician-Assisted Suicide

We return now to the problem of a patient's active suicide in the health care context, usually with the intervention of the health care provider; in other words, physician-assisted suicide. When the patient asks the health care provider for the means to kill himself or even for the administration of the means, the prevailing health care ethics are clear, even if we admit the patient's competence and right to commit suicide. Traditionally, the health care provider has had a *prima facie*, that is, a presumptive, duty not to cooperate for two reasons. First, despite doubts about the complete justice of the law forbidding help to people attempting suicide, it is a crime to help a person commit suicide by supplying the means. Second and more important from an ethical perspective, by the nature of the profession the health care provider should be devoted to healing. *Active* cooperation in suicide is incompatible with a professional obligation to heal. This is the traditional position regarding the health professions, and it is the position taken recently by the AMA (1994a,b, 1996b).

Although there is ethically a presumptive obligation against cooperating in an active suicide by supplying the means of death, it is important to recognize that there are cases in which neither healing nor comforting is possible. In these cases, the refusal to actively participate may be equivalent to dooming the patient to senseless agony. While Quill argues that pain is a major reason for justifying assisted suicide (Quill, 1991), the AMA argues that advances in pain control have been so successful that virtually all pain can be controlled (AMA, 1996a). Furthermore, a number of studies suggest that the main reason for patient interest in suicide is not pain relief (Emanuel et. al., 1996). Clinical depression and a concern for future loss of control and dignity are cited as frequent causes of this interest.

Although depression may often be treatable and loss of control can in some ways be addressed, the problem of the patient's dignity transcends these problems. Dr. Jack Kevorkian has received great notoriety in the United States for his support of physician-assisted suicide. However questionable some of his actions have been (he is currently serving a sentence for manslaughter, after administering a lethal injection to a patient while being videotaped), he initially raised a challenging issue. His first assisted suicide was a woman, Janet Adkins, suffering from Alzheimer's disease. Her choice of suicide was rooted in a concern with the effects of the disease on her family and on her dignity. Pain palliation did not address her concerns. Even with good medical care and counseling for her family, her concerns for her dignity remained.

Since the health care professions should comfort when no healing is possible, investigation must continue in two areas: pain control for all patients, but especially those dying (see discussion later in this chapter), and our understanding of the physical, emotional, and social aspects of the dying process. A terminally ill patient's fear of abandonment and of the loss of dignity must be accepted as a reality for the healing professions and dealt with just as a viral illness would be. Too few physicians are equipped to care for their patients' emotional and social well-being in the last months of their lives. Dr. Kevorkian has indeed forced the health professions to address this aspect of patient care, and it will remain a difficult issue. Physicians in particular need to be prepared to help their patients and this will require substantial efforts at education. Persistent efforts to legalize physician-assisted suicide will also force consideration of exceptions to existing legal practice so that in extreme cases there may be active intervention and cooperation in the suicide of at least competent terminal patients who are in great agony. Physician-assisted suicide, when it aims to protect human dignity and when it is done with informed consent, may not be traditional, but it does appear to further compassionate care of the dignity of the human person. In other words, the professional obligation to heal always functions within the larger question of human dignity (Miller and Brody, 1995) and may do so in ways we do not yet fully understand.

Any exceptions to the law made for the sake of recognizing that human dignity and autonomy include more than mere life will have to be hedged with protections against abuse and provide a conscience clause protecting the health care professional. If the health care provider's conscience prohibits suicide unconditionally, the provider must have appropriate legal protection. The safeguards will be similar to those we will discuss in conjunction with the living will.

On the other hand, it is particularly necessary to investigate the concern that the possibility of physician-assisted suicide will break the bonds of trust between the physician and patient. Will the approach of the physician bring help or death to the patient? This dramatic question is to suggest that such uncertainties inevitably accompany the possibility of physician-assisted suicide (Kass, 1991). A major problem with the argument is that the support for physician-assisted suicide is coming from patients seeking out Dr. Kevorkian or voting for state referendums legalizing the action. If the trust relationship would be harmed to the ultimate detriment of the patient, it is surprising to find so many patients supporting it.

Societal Experiments with Physician-Assisted Suicide

The longest continuing experience with physician-assisted suicide is in the Netherlands (Kuhse, 1986). In 1972 a Dutch court refused to penalize a physician who had put her mother to death at her mother's explicit request. The reasoning of the court may be summarized as follows: Physicians have a conflict of obligations. On the one hand, they have a duty to obey the law and, on the other, a duty to look out for the best interests of the patient. They cannot be held criminally responsible for following their duty as doctors by acting in the patient's best interests. The practice became more widespread until in 1993 the government passed a law that gave conditions under which physicians could assist in the suicide or euthanasia of a terminally ill patient. These conditions include 1) the patient must initiate the request; 2) the patient must be experiencing intolerable suffering; 3) all alternative treatments must be exhausted; 4) the patient must be fully informed; and 5) a physician experienced in assisted suicide or euthanasia must concur with the request. There are reports of problems with this, particularly concerns that the option of assisted suicide is used to coerce or shame patients into suicide or that the practice has blurred the distinction between suicide and euthanasia, particularly in questionably competent patients (AMA, 1994b). A report in 1990 (van der Maas, 1991) concluded that about 2 per cent of the total deaths in the Netherlands were due to assisted suicide or euthanasia, and a subsequent report suggests that 78 per cent of the population remains in support of the practice.

The key question is this: If it is permissible to *allow* some patients die, why is it not permissible to *help* the patient to die? These questions were put to the United States Supreme Court in 1997 in two cases, *Compassion in Dying* and *Quill v. Vacco*. The *Compassion in Dying* case hinged on the question of whether the constitutional right to privacy included a right to determine the timing and nature of one's death. The *Quill v. Vacco* case suggested that it would be unjust discrimination to allow a patient to *refuse* life-sustaining treatment and not allow another patient to *request* life-ending medication, since the differences between the patients' conditions were not chosen by the patients. The Supreme Court, however, chose to say only that the constitution did not speak to the issue, and that the states would have to work out a socially acceptable, political solution.

An example of such a political solution has occurred in the state of Oregon. Passed by a slim margin in 1994, Oregon's Death with Dignity Act legalized physician assisted suicide in the state. It was not implemented because of court appeals, and was ultimately put back on a ballot for a possible repeal. The repeal measure was rejected by 60 per cent of the voters in 1997. After more political maneuvering, the act become law in Oregon in 1998, and in March of 1998 the first two patients died by means of physician-assisted suicide (Hoover and Kinsey, 1998). The Act remains controversial and quite complicated. It raises questions about the professional obligations of physicians, of course, but also hospice, insurers, nurses, pharmacists, and health care facilities (Woolfrey, 1998).

Two Other Scenarios

When a health care provider deliberately omits a medically indicated treatment for which the patient has given informed consent, this is unethical and possibly homicidal. There is a positive obligation to do what is medically indicated when informed consent has been given. This does not hold when nothing is medically indicated.

The death of the patient resulting from the fact that the provider never proposed the medically indicated treatment for consent is unethical and possibly homicidal, because once again there is a positive obligation to present the medically indicated treatment.

Care for the Dying and Pain Control

The use of such terminology as DNR, no code, or slow code, all of which stress omitting a treatment, might lead to the impression that there is no need to care for the dying. This is an impression often reinforced by the physician's declaration, "There is no more that we can do." On the contrary, as death approaches and the technical devices of medically intensive care become useless, there is need for humanly intensive care. The dying patient needs the support and comfort of staff, family, and friends. Limits on visits should be removed. After proper preparation, even children should be allowed to visit (Jordan, 1987). Long-absent relatives should be encouraged to come so that reconciliations may be made or memories shared. All this should be provided for in a care for the dying policy that recognizes that death is natural and is, indeed, the last great human experience in this world.

Pain control, especially in the dying patient, has been a neglected area in American medical education (AMA, 1995). As mentioned earlier, this is one of the reasons given for the interest in physician-assisted suicide, but studies suggest that patients in pain want pain relief, not death (Colburn, 1996). One of the central problems in pain control is the issue of who decides when the patient is in pain. Many health care providers refuse to accept the patient's own statements, preferring to wait for physical expressions like grimacing, flinching, or grabbing the bed rails. The claim is that one should wait for these "objective" expressions of pain because pain medication is too attractive to the patient. Fear of the patient getting high or becoming an addict blinds the care giver to the reality of the patient's suffering. Generally, when the patient says he is in pain, his judgment should be the one that matters (Henkelman, 1994). Many studies have shown that even powerful narcotics like morphine are not addictive when used properly to treat pain, and a dying patient's dependence upon pain relief is due to the persistence of the pain, not to addiction. There is little reason a dying patient should not be kept comfortable, particularly when that is her request (Catholic Health Association, 1993).

Hospice is an underutilized form of care for the dying patient in the United States. But the average patient's length of stay in a hospice setting in short, which suggests that physicians or patients and their families are reluctant to accept a determination that the patient is terminal. This is certainly understandable, especially with the patient or her family, but it suggests that many patients continue to receive aggressive medical care beyond the end of a reasonable hope of improvement. This harms the patient, and may in fact shorten the patient's life (Foster and Lynn, 1988) and it wastes resources.

SURROGATES AND THE TERMINATION OF TREATMENT

Up to this point, we have limited ourselves to the case of competent patients who refuse treatment or ask to have treatment discontinued. As a matter of fact, the patient is often incompetent. In these cases, the health care team needs to consult the surrogates about discontinuing treatment for the terminal patient. By *terminal patient*, we mean one whose condition will lead to death within a year, or who is irreversibly comatose, or when there is a medical judgment that efforts, including resuscitation, would only prolong the dying process. In all these cases, nothing appears to be medically indicated; that is, intervention will not produce more medical benefits than burdens. Ethically, as noted in chapter 3 and discussed above under "Medical Futility," the health care professional generally has no obligation to do what is not medically indicated. The exceptions arise when the patient or the surrogate has nonmedical reasons for continuing treatment. Ethically, however, there is always the obligation not to inflict unnecessary pain on the patient.

The Living Will and Durable Power of Attorney

The living will is a document signed and witnessed at a time when the patient is clearly competent. It is a patient's written directive to continue or to withhold treatment or to administer pain killing drugs if the person has an incurable injury, disease, illness, or condition from which the patient has become incompetent and can no longer speak for himself or herself. In short, it is a written determination of treatment for certain limited situations. In practice, it is most frequently used to discontinue treatment.

The laws that add legal approval to the ethical force of such declarations provide for various safeguards against abuse, in particular, the abuse of ignoring the directive. *The Uniform Rights of the Terminally Ill Act* (Uniform Law Commissioners, 1989), for example, requires that the physician who has been provided a patient's living will must make it part of the medical record. It also demands that the physician who is unwilling to comply with the wishes of the patient promptly inform the patient and take all reasonable steps to transfer the patient to another physician or health care provider. The act goes so far as to cover the cases of pregnant women when by stating as follows:

> Unless the declaration [living will] provides otherwise, the declaration of a qualified patient known to the attendant physician to be pregnant must not be given effect as long as it is probable that the fetus could develop to the point of a live birth with continued application of life-sustaining treatment.

Thus, although it recognizes the right of the woman to control her own body, it also recognizes the right of the fetus in cases where the dying mother has not made a decision about this particular issue.

The Uniform Rights of the Terminally Ill Act makes a revocation of the will possible at any time and in any manner without regard to the patient's mental or physical condition. This means that there will be no quibbling about whether the patient is competent to revoke the living will.

Depending on the law of a particular state, the living will legislation may contain other provisions designed to prevent abuse. Thus, some provide that the patient must have been judged terminal by two physicians and the will witnessed by people who are not health care providers or beneficiaries of the person's last will and testament. In short, the legislation passed in many states seeks to prevent the more obvious conflicts of interests and dangers to the patient. The same may be said of the durable power of attorney for health care.

Some states that do not recognize the living will do give legal force to the durable (or permanent) power of attorney in health matters. This power of attorney appoints a surrogate for health affairs and gives general direction to that surrogate. It is more flexible than the living will in that powers of the surrogate or agent are not limited to desires concerning life-prolonging treatment. It differs from ordinary powers of attorney in that it is durable; that is, it continues even when the person who made it becomes incompetent.

About forty states have health care power of attorney statutes. Some states also have statutes designating a surrogate if the patient has not done so through the power of attorney. Both the *Uniform Rights of the Terminally Ill Act* (Uniform Law Commissioners, 1989) and the *Uniform Model Health Care Consent Act* (Uniform Law Commissioners, 1988) have similar if not identical provisions for a surrogate (Meisel, supp. 1991, pp. 169-170).

Both the living will and the durable power of attorney in health matters are useful because they provide clear indications of the will of a competent person and help to avoid conflicts among surrogates as well as debates as to which surrogate has the authority to consent or the correct interpretation of the wishes of the patient.

Studies show that the lack of physician initiative was the greatest perceived barrier to planning directives (Emanuel et. al., 1991; SUPPORT, 1995). Another study of conformity with advanced directives in nursing homes showed that in a quarter of the cases the use of the directives was limited by inattention to them or by giving priority to considerations other than patient autonomy (Danis et. al., 1991).

The federal *Patient Self-Determination Act of 1990* (Omnibus Budget Reconciliation Act, 1990) imposes a duty on health care agencies that receive Medicare or Medicaid money to inform patients of the existence of the living will and the durable power of attorney and related matters. Advanced directives signed by patients must be made part of the hospital or nursing home record. In the Cruzan case the Supreme Court speaks not only of the right to refuse treatment but of the importance of expressing that right in a written advanced directive to take effect if the patient is incompetent when a decision must be made. In short, society recognizes these legal instruments as important means of protecting patient autonomy.

In view of the *Patient Self-Determination Act*, all states will have living will and related legislation in a short time. Fortunately, the Conference of Commissioners on Uniform State Laws has passed and updated *The Uniform Rights of the Terminally Ill Act* (National Conference of the Commissioners on Uniform State Laws, 1989, section 10), and the American Bar Association approved it in 1990. There are, then, excellent models to follow.

Although neglect of patient autonomy will never be abolished so long as the absent-minded and arrogant are involved in health care, the 1989 revision of the *Uniform Rights of the Terminally Ill Act* provides for penalties that may improve memories and temper arrogance with fear. Coupled with the *Patient Self-Determination Act*, this revision will likely encourage this carefully crafted approach to the problem of advanced directives.

The most difficult cases occur when the wishes of the now-incompetent patient are unknown, the surrogates insist on aggressive treatment to assuage their own guilt, and the physician regards the treatment as prolonging the agony of a dying patient. The law is not clear, and the physician who discontinues treatment in these cases fears being sued for negligence. Ethically, however, the obligation is to the patient and not to the family. The answer seems clear, but the anguish remains.

The health care team may sometimes ethically continue treatment if the patient or the surrogates insist that they seek some legitimate nonmedical good for the patient, but the health care team may also refuse to treat by then handing the case over to someone else. In at least one court case, the judge ruled that the hospital could overrule the decision of the surrogates when treatment was futile. Here there was no need to hand the case over to someone else.

Despite the media dramatization of these cases, it is routine to have hospitals discontinue treatment for terminal incompetent patients and to a lesser extent for permanently comatose patients with the permission of the surrogate. This is as it should be, except in those cases in which the hospital staff has evidence that the surrogate is acting against the desires and best interests of the patient. As we shall see later, the use of advanced directives such as living wills and durable power of attorney can further clarify the proper course of action.

Letting the Patient Die without Consent

In some cases, the health care provider might let the terminal patient die even without consent from the patient or a surrogate. With the terminal patient, there is nothing medically indicated except such activities as will preserve dignity and keep the patient comfortable. From a medical point of view, the physician is not obliged to do what will produce more harm than good. Indeed, if treatment, especially aggressive treatment, is producing more harm than good, we may even argue that the physician has an obligation to cease treatment. In practice, however, the health care team needs a consent, except in rare cases, which will be discussed later.

The New York State Task Force (1986), in speaking of orders not to resuscitate, said that such orders should be issued without consent only if (1) two physicians judge that resuscitation would be futile, or (2) there is a judicial finding that a do-not-resuscitate order (DNR) would be consistent with the patient's known wishes or, in the absence of information about those wishes, that the order would be in the patient's best interests. This is a strict standard and makes good sense where there is no consent.

The authors are inclined to think that, when treating a terminal patient deprives other patients of medically indicated treatments under clear conditions of serious scarcity, a weighing of the consequences seems to create a clear obligation to stop treating the terminal patient and devote the resources to areas where they are medically indicated. This, however, might be abandonment in the present system of roles that makes the patient–physician relationship personal and independent of outside factors, such as the needs of others or of society; but it would be consistent with the health care professional's obligation to society (see chapter 1). In time, society may change the definition of roles and grant health care professionals a carefully controlled right to terminate treatment of the terminal patient when other and viable patients are being deprived of resources. We must stress, however, that the termination of treatment is not the same as the termination of care. More will be said about this under the heading of care for the dying.

The Good of the Patient versus the Good of Third Parties

The previous section presents the case of a terminally ill patient by which the interests of a third party seem, at first glance, to be ethically decisive; but, on reflection, these interests are of ambiguous value. The case raises worrisome questions about the danger of making these decisions not for the good of the patient, but for the good of society, the good of the family, or even the good of the hospital or the health care provider.

Although the courts and writers on ethics have rather consistently ruled that patients are not to be allowed to die because they are or will be a burden to the society or the hospital, the economics of health care is creating pressures to deny treatment in such cases, or at least to deny payment by society for such treatment. In short, the ethics of distribution rears its head. The following facts need to be considered carefully.

A number of years ago, one-quarter of the $75 billion spent on Medicare was used to maintain the elderly in the last year of life, and most of that was spent during the last month of their lives (Kieiman, 1985). In the case of William Bartling (Gallagher, 1985), the Glendale Adventist Hospital spent more than half a million dollars on seven months of care for one patient. Under the diagnostic-related group (DRG) system, Medicare paid less than $50,000 of that total. With the frequency of such cases growing, even the richest hospital in the richest country will have to give more attention to the right of providers to terminate the treatment of the terminally ill.

Although we may not wish to terminate treatment for the good of society, our principles in chapter 4 indicate that society may reasonably decide not to pay for treatments that do no more than prolong biological life. We expect that insurance companies and business firms that pay for health insurance will move in the same direction. Although the authors are aware of the alleged danger of homicide, sound public policy and legal safeguards should be able to deal with the wasteful prolongation of biological life and the danger of homicide.

Cost and the ability to pay would not be ethically relevant in an ideal world, but in the world of scarce resources the economic side becomes a clearly relevant factor, even if it should not be decisive.

The Place of Ethics Committees

Many hospitals have formed ethics committees to help with the ethical problems of the termination of treatment and related issues. These committees have several missions. First, they are supposed to educate the hospital and its employees, as well as the other constituencies of the hospitals. Second, they are to develop policies with regard to the problem areas, especially the problems of death and dying. Third, they are to act as advisory consultants to health care providers and possibly families. In this last role, as consultants, some worry that the committee's decisions might be taken *de facto* as binding, rather than advisory, and so usurp the role and rights of patients and families, as well as of health care providers (Levine, 1984). On the other hand, this third function can be looked at as a support mechanism for decision-makers, both lay and professional. This, too, may create problems if the committee ends up supporting the institution or the dominant figures in the institution, rather than looking carefully at the ethics. Finally, no matter what the intentions of the ethics committee are, there is no doubt that the courts have and will make them part of the decision-making process in particular cases. This is a good if it gives decisions a broader base, but it is not an unqualified good if it undermines the rights of patients, families, and professionals. Others (McCormick, 1984) raise issues like the following. Committees can end up diffusing responsibility (Meisel, 1989, p. 473). When committees seek consensus, they can easily end up avoiding the real point at issue and issuing carefully worded opinions that avoid the problem.

There are also questions about how privacy and confidentiality are maintained, as well as about the committee's immunity from civil and criminal liability. The committee, insofar as it has members who are representatives of the general public and such non-health-care personnel as ethicists, are not covered by the normal professional secrecy. In any event, one cannot assume that patients and families consented to having the most intimate details of their lives discussed by a committee.

At the same time, because ethical decisions in health care ethics involve more than health, life, and death, they require more than medical or nursing expertise. The exercise of the practical wisdom that is at the heart of our approach calls for the wisdom of a larger group that looks at more than medical and nursing indications. As we note in our treatment of the institutional review boards in chapter 16, it is not always easy to get a representative group whose opinions will approach disinterested practical wisdom. At this stage, then, we think it best to consider the ethics committee as a very worthwhile experiment, with all the results not yet in.

Once again, we warn (Meisel, 1989) that there is no legal duty to follow the recommendations of an ethics committee. They are not a substitute for judicial review. There may also be legal liabilities for the members (Meisel, 1989, p. 480).

The Place of the Family in Death and Dying

Although the health care provider is to make decisions not to initiate or to terminate treatment in terms of medical indications, the patient, if competent, and otherwise the surrogates should be consulted, since their feelings, rights, and obligations are involved. The surrogates, moreover, may know of factors that would call for the prolongation of even a vegetative life. There are cases in which a woman has been kept in a vegetative state so that the child she was carrying might be delivered. In addition, questions of inheritance and even the need of absent family members to say farewell enter in. For these and similar reasons, the family should be involved even when, in the absence of the family, the provider would be ethically justified in not initiating or terminating treatment as not medically indicated.

At a certain point in the dying process, the family members become secondary patients in need of information about the state of affairs and emotional support. Too often, families are neglected and left to fend for themselves. Yet, insofar as health care professionals are dedicated to relieving suffering, the duty of compassion is in the role of all care givers. The duty to relieve suffering demands concern for the well and the living, as well as for the ill and dying. Families as well as those who are patients in a legal sense have needs that should be respected.

Some hospitals have formed bioethics teams to provide support to families and to aid them in making difficult decisions about terminating or continuing treatment. The team is comprised of a physician, a nurse, a social worker, and a member of the clergy. Anyone who notices a family or a surrogate in anguish may call for the services of one of these teams. The teams do not make decisions or issue formal opinions. In no case does the team attempt to impose a decision on the family. Team members offer moral support to the family, explain the medical options in clear language, and point out to the families the range of ethical decisions that could be made. When the family does make a decision, the team supports the decision in an effort to reduce continued anguish. Interestingly, not even the attending physician is allowed to block the intervention of these action teams that are devoted to the family as well as the patient.

The Value and Quality of Life for the Individual Person

In agreeing that the health care provider may ethically withdraw some treatments from the person in the persistent vegetative state, we have at least implicitly agreed that such a state has little value for the patient. We have, moreover, permitted the health care provider to make a quality of life decision on a medical indications basis. This forces us to face these questions: What are the minimum factors that give life a value to the patient? What is the threshold of meaningfulness of human life to the possessor of human life?

Biological human life has value as a means, a precondition for specifically human activities of a human person. This makes us face the crucial question of what activities are specifically human, such that lacking these or a reasonable hope of getting them back makes biological human life cease to have value for anyone.

Most will agree that life in a permanent vegetative state has no value for the person because there are no recognizable human activities and, indeed, there is a lack of even basic animal activities such as sensation. Having said that, we face vast disagreements. Some demand a maximum, some a minimum of human activity in order for life to be valuable to the person.

Some demand a maximum. They see the person as having value only when the powers of intellect and creativity and the strength of the body are at their perfection. To be less than perfect is to be valueless for those who want the maximum. From a philosophic point of view, the perfection of human life does demand all these things. Unfortunately, none of us will ever have all these characteristics in their fullness. It seems ridiculous, then, to demand what is impossible.

Some settle for a minimum in the form of the ability to interact with other human beings (McCormick, 1981). That is all that infants can do, and we find them charming and lovable and rejoice in their pleasure. The retarded and the senile can still interact with others, albeit on an unsophisticated level. We may not want to be like them, but their lives still have some value to them. The same can be true for the terminally ill who can still interact with their loved ones.

On reflection, we may realize that perhaps even our simplest interactions with others are the most important and rewarding part of our lives. Perhaps loving or snuggling with another person is the best thing in life. Emotional and loving contact on even a simple level gives life value to its possessor. The authors refuse to downgrade those who will settle for that as giving meaning to life. We are not wise enough to make the judgment that more is required, nor are we sure that more is really better.

Most of us probably fall somewhere in between these two extremes in our judgments. We will settle for less than perfection, but we want more of life than the ability to interact with other human persons on the simplest level. Most of us want or even demand some level of comfort or at least freedom from pain. We are the people who sign living wills and request that treatment be discontinued and no resuscitation be attempted when we are terminally ill and in great pain. Yet, we can no more prove that this middle ground is correct than we can canonize either the minimalist or maximalist position as universal principles for all humankind. None of us is wise enough to arrive at objective answers to subjective questions.

Although the American College of Physicians (1984) believes that physicians must make judgments about the quality of life, their code stresses the subjective nature of the decision. The following statement in the *Ethics Manual* deserves careful consideration:

> Assessment by a physician of a patient's quality of life can feature promi-
> nently in making clinical decisions. It is wise for physicians to be aware of the
> personal and subjective values that may contribute to such evaluations. Thus,
> the assessment may vary according to physician's age, present health, history
> of personal illness, cultural background, and long-standing knowledge of the
> patient as a person. Clinical decisions that hinge on assessing quality of life
> should be undertaken with great care and full cognizance of the subjectivity
> of the assessment, with full patient participation, or, if that is not possible,
> with participation of knowledgeable and concerned relatives or guardian.
> Under ordinary circumstances, a physician's judgment about quality of life
> should not be unilateral.

We stress that, in practice, when the desires of the patient are not known, the minimalist position of the value of life should prevail in the physician's decisions.

SUMMARY

The main issue is that patients may ethically refuse treatment for proportionate reasons, and health care professionals may cooperate with those
patients' requests. The easiest examples of solid, proportionate reason
include a terminal diagnosis, with death imminent, and a request from a
competent patient. As these conditions are altered, the justification of a
refusal of life-sustaining treatment becomes more doubtful. But in all
cases, the central issue remains caring for the dignity of the patient, which
involves respecting the patient's wishes, protecting the integrity of the

profession, and sparing the patient life under conditions which are generally understood to be extremely burdensome, either because of pain, suffering, or degradation.

CASES FOR ANALYSIS

1. Joe contracts bilateral pneumonia. He is treated with antibiotics and put on a mechanical respirator. After a few weeks, the pneumonia improves and the physician starts to wean Joe from the respirator. Even with a gradual approach, the weaning fails and Joe demands to be put back on the respirator when he becomes terrified at being short of breath. The physician feels that the ultimate chances of weaning Joe are now no more than 20 percent.

Joe, eighty years old and accustomed to being in control, becomes discouraged and increasingly unable to bear the painful medical procedures (constant intravenous feedings, frequent needle punctures for arterial blood gases, suctioning, etc. After three weeks of unsuccessful attempts, Joe refuses to cooperate. He asks that the respirator be disconnected. "I want to die," he states.

Despite the pain, Joe is alert and aware and is, in the opinion of the staff, fully competent. His wife and one son keep begging the physicians and the nurses to do something to help Joe to recover fully.

Does Joe have a right to refuse treatment on the respirator? Do the physician and the nurses have a right or duty to help Joe psychologically and pharmacologically to overcome his anxiety when taken off the respirator? Do the wishes of the family have ethical or legal weight in such cases? Physicians are often sued for keeping a person on a respirator. There is only one case where the doctor was charged for removal from the respirator and it was thrown out of court. Is the mere fact that the family may sue a justification for not following the expressed wishes of a competent person?

2. Elizabeth Bouvia was diagnosed as having cerebral palsy at the age of six months. At age 10 she was placed in an orthopedic hospital, where she remained for seven years.

She earned a B.S. degree in social work, married, and for a year attempted unsuccessfully to have a child. Her husband, whom she had met as a pen pal while he was serving a sentence in jail, has left her. Elizabeth drops out of graduate school because of difficulties in finding a clinical placement required for her program. As a result of this, the state threatens to take away her assistance for transportation.

At this time, Elizabeth Bouvia admits herself voluntarily to the hospital on the grounds that she is suicidal, a quadraplegic victim of cerebral palsy, and confined to a wheelchair. She has limited control of her right hand and needs to be fed. She also has severe progressive arthritis that causes constant pain. Her condition is in no way life-threatening, and she has a life expectancy of 15 to 20 years.

She seems to have plans to starve herself to death in the hospital, away from friends and relatives. She refuses to eat solid food. The physician threatens to have her certified as mentally ill so that he can force-feed her. The hospital also threatens to put her out on the sidewalk. The hospital does seek to transfer her to another facility, but is unsuccessful. In the meantime, the hospital force-feeds Elizabeth. She repeatedly tears the nasogastric tubes from her nose. The tube is forcibly reinserted each time she removes it.

Elizabeth seeks legal assistance. The American Civil Liberties Union enters the case and applies for a court order restraining the hospital from discharging her or force-feeding her. Bouvia testifies that she is no longer willing to live, since she found it disgusting and humiliating to live so dependent a life. She wants to starve to death while nurses give her painkillers and keep her clean and comfortable. She has a metabolic condition that causes her blood to become excessively acidic without food. One internist treating her estimates that she could be dead within five days because of the condition.

The first court decided that Bouvia had a legal right to starve herself to death at home, but not to demand that a health care facility help her while she did this. Another court finally decided that she had a right to hospital care while starving herself to death. Many years later, Bouvia was still alive. This might justify a health care provider who said that Bouvia was only seeking attention and knew how to work the system.

Will any of the theories of suicide permit Bouvia to deliberately starve herself to death? Is Bouvia competent? Would the hospital be ethical in getting a guardian *ad litem* who could then consent to a feeding tube? Would it be ethical for health care providers to cooperate with someone who is not terminally ill and still has the minimum quality of life, that is, is able to interact with others?

3. Hector was admitted to the hospital in acute respiratory distress; he is anxious and gasping for help. Sixty-eight, he has had chronic pulmonary disease for the last ten years. He is also a diabetic, who has lost both legs due to complications from his diabetes. During the last five years the effects of both diseases have left him increasingly debilitated, and for the last year he has been in a nursing home. His wife and daughter visit him regularly in the nursing home, and are present for his admission to the hospital. His diagnosis was bilateral pneumonia. He was put on a mechanical respirator and given antibiotics. Within two weeks the pneumonia was cleared up, but attempts to wean him from the respirator proved unsuccessful, possibly due to damage to his lungs, weakened respiratory muscles, or even fear of breathing on his own. Also, his insulin levels have become increasing difficult to control, and during one attempt to wean him from the respirator Hector went into a stress-induced insulin shock. Since then Hector has refused to cooperate with further attempts to wean him from the respirator. He says he wants the respirator turned off, a step vigorously opposed by his wife. You are the doctor. What do you do?

4. Susie, a fourteen-year-old, was riding her bike home from a friend's when she was hit by a truck. Taken immediately to a hospital emergency room, she was put on life-support and treated aggressively for a severe head trauma. The neurologist called in to assist said she would have been killed instantly except for the helmet she was wearing. Three months later, Susie is in a deep coma, with a minimal response to sharp and intense pain. She is still in the hospital and there is no immediate prospect of transferring her to a skilled, long-term care facility. Her neurological prognosis is grave. She is on a ventilator and is receiving artificial nutrition and hydration. In spite of a maintenance dose of antibiotics, she shows the signs of pneumonia. Susie's mother has gone through a severe psychological reaction to the accident. After Susie stabilized in a deep coma, her mother wanted treatment discontinued. Now she no longer comes to the hospital and refuses to talk with anyone about Susie. Susie's father insists on treatment, arguing that her use of the bicycle helmet, purchased the night before the accident, was a sign that she was meant to survive the accident. The neurologist recommends not treating the pneumonia and suggests taking her off artificial nutrition and hydration; in his judgment continued medical treatment is futile. You are the attending physician. What do you do?

5. You diagnose a patient as being in the early stages of Alzheimers. The patient is a sixty-one-year-old male, a professor of music, very active both as a teacher and a performer, with high visibility in the community. He has a wife, who is an architect, and two children, both in their thirties with successful careers out of state. The patient is shocked by the diagnosis, but is not completely surprised; he had been forgetful lately, as well as becoming disoriented while playing familiar pieces and having increasing difficulty learning new ones. He is vain about his abilities and very much in control of all he does. His loss of control disturbs him, and as he gets over his shock he becomes determined to fight the disease. You are able to arrange for him to be tested for a new research project involving a proposed treatment to slow down the progress of Alzheimers when it is detected early enough. When the tests come back (the entire process has taken about three months), your diagnosis is confirmed but your patient is denied participation in the research project because (unexpectedly) the disease is too advanced. This disappointment coupled with increasing incidences of disorientation while performing music (there has been little substantial effect on his day-to-day functioning) has deeply discouraged your patient. Two weeks later, your patient returns and asks you to provide him with enough medication so that when he decides that the disease has taken too much of him he can die. He says he has thought deeply and hard about this. He does not want to end up a burden to his family and friends. He is a skilled teacher and does not want to end up unable even to communicate with others. But most of all he does not want to live without his ability to perform and enjoy his music. As a physician, what do you do?

NOTES

1. There is a dispute as to whether the difference between active and passive killing is of any ethical significance in the context of euthanasia. (See Rachels, 1975, p. 78, and Sullivan, 1977, pp. 40-46.) This dispute has become an important issue in the legal discussion of physician-assisted suicide (see later in this chapter and, for a more recent example, Dixon, 1998). The terms are, at least, descriptively useful, and since society still accepts the distinction as having some ethical utility, it is disregarded at one's risk. At least one of the present authors agrees with Rachels that active euthanasia ought, with suitable safeguards, to be made legal.

2. See *BioLaw: A Legal and Ethical Reporter on Medicine, Health Care and Bioengineering* (1986) and supplements for up-to-date analysis of court decisions with regard to the right of nonterminal patients or their surrogates to refuse treatment or demand the withdrawal of treatment, including the withdrawal of nutrition and hydration.

8

ABORTION AND MATERNAL–FETAL CONFLICT

INTRODUCTION

There is probably no more disputed and emotional issue in medical ethics than abortion. As often presented in the United States, the question of abortion appears to pit the interests of the fetus against those of the pregnant woman. Some describe this as a conflict between innocent life and selfishness, while others view it as a conflict between a person's right and ability to control her body and the surrender of that control to an alien invader.

The scope of this conflict between woman and fetus has increased as our knowledge of the complex and sophisticated relationship between the mother and the developing fetus has grown. The health habits of the mother during pregnancy can have a dramatic effect on the health of the child. Is the mother obligated to alter her behavior to maximize the health of her fetus? For example, should she not smoke, not drink alcoholic beverages, obtain prenatal care, and maintain emotional calm? If she does not, should the health care profession or the society intervene for the sake of the fetus?

Additional problems arise with new medical knowledge that enables physicians to treat fetuses *in utero*. Unique in medical practice, physicians must go through the mother to treat the fetus; in other words, they cannot medically treat the fetus without medically intruding on the mother. Thus, for the physician to treat her fetus, the mother must give informed consent to a procedure that does not benefit her. She must take on the risks and burdens of surgery with no direct personal medical benefit.

Put in the terms of a conflict of rights, the abortion question seems to have no resolution short of capitulation by one side or the other. As suggested in chapter 1, often in philosophical ethics the either/or approach is futile and obscures both the complexity of the problem and the fact that, in human life, right and wrong are not always clear. Indeed, while the biological basis for tension between the fetus and the pregnant woman is obvious, many aspects of the opposition between the interests of the fetus and those of the woman are social in origin. This suggests that more care must be taken in formulating the issues at stake, particularly the role of society. Finally, in some situations no analysis may show us a clear way out; in particular, maternal-fetal conflict brings us face to face with the tragic in human life.

Ethics and Religion

The abortion issue has drawn religious groups into the public controversy. As mentioned in chapter 1, religious groups generally rest their case on scripture or some other source of divine revelation, such as church tradition, but will also use philosophical arguments, that is, arguments drawn from reflection on human experience. As this book is a philosophical treatment and does not treat theologies based on divine revelation or church tradition, we will limit our discussion to the philosophical arguments.

Law and Ethics

Not everything that is unethical is a suitable object of law. In the first place, law ought to be concerned primarily and directly with the public good. It should seek to regulate the behavior of people only when that is necessary or highly useful for the public good or when it is necessary to protect the rights of the individual in the society. In the second place law should not get too far ahead of the public conscience, since this will make it largely unenforceable and it will encourage contempt for the law. The American experience with Prohibition in the 1920s illustrates this last point.

Granted these limits, law is extremely useful and even necessary for defining and specifying ambiguous moral and social problems. These specifications should be congruent with basic ethical principles and the consensus of the society.

DOES THE FETUS HAVE RIGHTS? U.S. LAW

Of necessity, any consideration of abortion in the United States must consider the questions of whether the fetus has rights and whether these rights should be protected by law. Even if the fetus has rights, doubt still remains regarding the prudence of laws on the subject, considering their difficult enforceability and the unsettled state of the public conscience. It is possible to conclude that abortion is unethical and immoral and still hold that it may not be prudent to legislate on the matter, although most groups on both sides of the issue favor legal intervention to support their position.

The Supreme Court Decisions

In *Roe v. Wade*, the U.S. Supreme Court answered, in a manner that has been surprisingly enduring, certain constitutional and legal questions about the legality of abortion in the United States. It clearly declared itself incapable of deciding the ethical issue.

In the first place, the Supreme Court decided that the fetus does not have rights in the sense of the Fourteenth Amendment; that is, it does not have a right to the protection of due process of law. Moreover, the Court did not attempt to settle the question of whether the fetus has ethical and moral rights. In the second place, the Court acknowledged the relative right of the pregnant woman to privacy, that is, a right not to be interfered with. This right in these cases is relative and not absolute, because there can be important state interests involving the protection of health and medical standards, as well as the issue of the protection of prenatal life in the third trimester. Indeed, the Court said that states may prohibit abortion of viable fetuses except when abortion is necessary for the preservation of the life and health of the mother.

In the 1989 *Webster v. Reproductive Health Services* case, the Supreme Court modified its position in *Roe v. Wade* by suggesting that the trimester system was unsound and unworkable and that the state's interest in the fetus could not be limited to viability. It also allowed that the individual states would be responsible for providing the guidelines that would replace those based on *Roe v. Wade's* trimester system. The central result of this decision is to move the basis of abortion law from the courts to the state legislatures and thus to a closer approximation of a social consensus.

This move was confirmed in the *Planned Parenthood v. Casey* decision in 1992. Here the court reaffirmed the basic principles of the *Roe v. Wade* decision, while arguing that not enough attention had been paid to the state's interests in the situation.[1] A state would be free to regulate abortion as long as it did not place an *undue burden* on the woman's right to an abortion. Under this principle, the court affirmed several types of restrictions on access to abortion services.

We do not intend to argue the Supreme Court decisions and their consequences, but we note that they do raise two crucial issues. First, the *Roe v. Wade* decision is put in terms of the status of the fetus relative to the right of the mother to noninterference by the state. In our treatment of the ethics of maternal–fetal conflict and of a health care provider's responsibility in this situation, we too, must ask two questions: (1) What is the ethical status of the fetus? This may be interpreted as asking whether the fetus has rights or has such a connection with the dignity of the human person that we ought to attribute rights to it. (2) If the fetus has any rights, on what ethical basis are disputes between the rights of the fetus and the rights of the pregnant woman to be settled?

Consistent with the American tradition, these questions have been framed in terms of rights, and the underlying question is always one of the dignity of the person and the necessity of protecting that dignity. Indeed, the final question may be, whether the dignity of the human demands that the fetus be respected, even if the fetus itself is not a person.

A second point to be noted about the Supreme Court decisions is that the law must be responsive to and reflective of the social conscience. Some had hoped that the Supreme Court had settled the issue and specified the rights of pregnant woman and fetus with the *Roe v. Wade* decision. The political agitation that continues seems to indicate that society has not said its last word on the subject. Indeed, although general questions on polls indicate that the vast majority of Americans favor the woman's right to privacy in this area, more specific questions bring out the fact that about half of the respondents want to limit abortions to such cases as a serious threat to the mother's health, incest, or rape. In short, the social debate continues, and the issues need to be addressed over and over.

Finally, we must remember that no matter what the health care professional's personal stand on abortion may be, there remain questions of health care ethics, such as the relation of abortion to health or the possibility of coercion in performing or refusing to perform abortions. These questions will occupy the final section of this chapter.

THE DEFINITION AND TYPES OF ABORTION

To understand the ethical problems of abortion, it is first necessary to define abortion, classify the various types of abortions, and specify the range of goods (motives) that are alleged as justifying abortions. This will show that the term abortion does not designate a single reality.

Abortion has been traditionally defined as the expulsion or removal of a nonviable fetus, that is, a fetus that cannot live outside the uterus at that time. The definition is relative because the viability of a fetus depends on where and when the expulsion occurs. A fetus delivered in a neonatal intensive care unit is viable far earlier than one that comes into the world in a shack hundreds of miles from any health care professional. But, as implied by the *Roe v. Wade* discussion, a third-trimester fetus, which is generally viable, is also the possible object of an abortion, so the definition must be expanded to include the expulsion or removal of any fetus where death is the intended outcome. We must include this last point about intention to distinguish an abortion from a cesarean section, in which a viable fetus is removed precisely to save it.

In biology, the term *fetus* is applied at the beginning of the ninth week of pregnancy, well into the second trimester. This name change, however, is not of moral significance, and even expulsions early in the first trimester are still referred to as abortions. There is debate as to when the human conceptus is to be considered a fetus in a moral sense and not merely in a biological sense. Only after we have determined the moral status of the fetus will we be able to say whether the expulsion of the conceptus, the embryo, or the biological fetus is ethically significant.

An abortion can be spontaneous (a miscarriage) or the result of human intervention. Many spontaneous abortions occur during the first trimester of pregnancy. Estimates are that from 15 to 50 percent of all conceptions spontaneously abort. There is really no way of telling the exact percentage, since spontaneous abortions often occur without the pregnant woman being aware of it. In the second trimester, spontaneous abortions are somewhat more common than natural death among viable fetuses. Even if abortion is an evil, spontaneous abortions in general are not considered moral problems. A spontaneous abortion might be a moral problem if it could have been prevented by reasonable behavior or by medically indicated treatment in situations in which there was no proportionate reason for permitting or risking the spontaneous abortion.

Abortions that occur because of human intervention may be classified as direct or indirect. This is a distinction that is particularly important in the use of the principle of double effect in natural law ethics, but it is also important for any discussion of proportionality (see chapter 3). The indirect abortion is an unintended side effect that is either risked or permitted when certain things are done. For example, an indirect abortion might result from a medicine taken to cure a disease, from anesthesia, or from an unrelated surgical procedure. Even if abortion is an evil, the morality of the indirect abortion is the morality of proportionality. It is a question of whether the evil of the risked or permitted abortion is offset by the good resulting from taking the medicine or undergoing the surgery.

In direct abortion, the abortion is the intended consequence. The fetus is to be deliberately destroyed. If the fetus has innate or attributed rights, this is an attack on these rights. If the fetus is a person, this is a direct assault on an individual person who is, as we saw in chapter 1, an intrinsic good in terms of which all consequences are to be measured. Thus, the ethical or moral status of the fetus becomes the issue.

THE MORAL STATUS OF THE FETUS

Part of the reason for the moral dilemma of abortion is that it is not clear whether the biological fetus is a person or has rights. Simple biological existence does not entail moral status. If it did, all living things might be persons. Although something like this position has been proposed, it has not been generally accepted in the American tradition. The moral status of the fetus has been treated repeatedly and in great detail over the least two decades.[2] With Wikler (Shaw and Doudera, 1983), we suspect that there is no completely satisfactory intellectual solution to the problem of the status of the fetus. In the first place, ethical principles involve emotions as well as intellect, so that purely intellectual solutions are not always compelling. Second, and even more to the point, given the conflicts involved in the question, we are likely in an area of opacity, that is, an area where it is impossible to answer the question directly on the basis of human experience (see chapter 1). Yet the question is crucial, since the problem of the moral status of the fetus involves the basic question of the moral status of human beings and persons in general.

The Limits of Rational Argument

Endless arguments can be made about what constitutes a person.[3] One method often used to clarify this problem (particularly useful for a natural law position) is to identify when the fetus becomes a moral person by reference to some physical event, such as conception or the development of a functioning brain, or to some physical characteristic, such as the fetus's type of DNA or the nature of its parents.

In other words, some argue that a fetus is a person from the moment of conception on the ground that the fetus is a human being and all human beings are persons. This stipulation begs the question and is not particularly convincing. Others argue that there is no person before the development of a functioning brain. Even if one agrees with that, it does not follow that there is a person present after the development of a functioning brain; other considerations ranging from viability to self-awareness might be necessary. As suggested here, numerous difficulties with each of the efforts raise doubts about the ability of any to succeed.

The basic difficulty is that the choice of such events or characteristics is apparently arbitrary and leads to inconsistencies in the treatment of other groups affected by the definition. For example, if a fetus becomes a fully moral person at conception because it has a full complement of human DNA, what is the moral status of other cells that also have a full complement of human DNA? If self-consciousness is the characteristic identifying a moral person, then infants, the permanently unconscious, and those suffering from severe dementia or Alzheimer's disease are also not persons.

Even if we focus on the fetus alone, it is not clear whether there are any sharp divisions in the fetus's development. This is the point that the Supreme Court's *Webster* decision raises about the trimester system central to the *Roe v. Wade* decision. However important "quickening" and "viability" have been historically, today it is clearly understood that the development of the fetus is a continuum unmarked by clearly separate stages.

More importantly, what is it about human DNA or self-consciousness that indicates the presence of a moral person? This question forces us to the heart of the matter, which is the definition of a human being. Numerous attempts have been made to define a human being, and the quality of the definitions and the thinkers making them have not protected them from dispute. Thus, we can claim neither a clear biological marker nor an accepted definition of a person to begin our discussion of the moral status of the fetus.

Consequently, our discussion of the moral status of the fetus must begin from a different perspective. As we argued in chapter 1, we must begin any ethical discussion, including this one, from our society's practice regarding the dignity of the human person. The moral status of the fetus is an ethical issue that, like all ethical issues, has its roots in the dignity of the human person and its expression in the social understanding of that dignity. Thus, the moral status of the fetus will reflect not only the moral status we grant to the retarded, the senile, and children, but the degree to which we want to protect persons by forbidding exceptions that might threaten them.

The willingness of a society to attribute or grant moral status and rights to the fetus depends first on whom we already acknowledge as having moral status and rights. The moral status granted the fetus depends on where the whole of society wants to place the outer defenses of the rights already assumed as existing.

The Demands of Defending the Marginalized

We suggest that, in practice and because of the opacity of the problem, the wedge principle must be invoked to arrive at a position. In other words, rights are attributed even to the fetus as part of a web of protection including all to whom we grant rights. This approach protects the dignity of the human being by attributing the rights that flow from that dignity to others who are not clearly and unequivocally persons. Thus, it is argued that, if we do not grant a serious right to life to all beings that are biologically human, we logically open ourselves up to permitting the killing of seriously retarded infants, the senile, and the permanently insane. Indeed, it may be argued that if we restrict the serious right to those who are, in some higher sense, clearly persons, it would be right to kill small children who as yet have shown no signs of personhood. It may even be argued that, when you weaken respect for human life on this simplest of levels, you have created a situation that might lead to killing the retarded, the senile, and the insane. The logic is correct and, we think, dangerous.

For this reason, the authors think that the wedge principle is the principle that best protects human dignity. That is, the wedge principle gives the largest outer defense to those to whom we currently accord the right to life. While the authors have not seen convincing proof that the empirical form of the wedge principle is verified by cases of historical atrocities, it seems clear that moving away from the biological criteria provides at least a temptation to go all the way and to act as if the retarded, the senile, and the insane have less of a right to life and to health care. In the past, those who weakened the defenses of human dignity went on to negate moral status for women, Jews, gypsies, blacks, and indeed anyone who was not a member of their group.

The respect for human life is, however, lowered by many factors other than deliberate choice. Famine, which creates a competition for survival, lowers the respect for the lives of the weak, that is, those who have the least chance for survival. Indeed, it would seem that scarcity, which makes it more difficult to express the respect for life, lowers that respect as it lowers the expression of the respect. In hard times, when basic resources are particularly scarce, there is a tendency to consider certain kinds of people a burden to be dispensed with. This tendency is particularly strong when we cannot see the face of the other or when we see the person as different from us and so less than human. This tendency enters not only into the abortion debate, but into a person's attitude toward killing the enemy in war. All this is tragic, and we strive to avoid the situation that creates the tragedy, but the fact remains that we scale down our values when our backs are against the wall.

The lines are drawn in accord with what the writer wants to or has decided to protect. This depends not merely on subjective whim, but on the world view that forms a person's basic moral outlook. We shall return to the concept of world view later in the chapter.

The authors believe that life has value even for those who can only interact humanly on a very basic level (see chapter 7). This belief appears to be the dominant belief in American society. Although not always successful, our society attempts to care for the severely retarded, as well as those who have serious mental illnesses. Although they contribute nothing to society and can enjoy little of what most of us aspire to, they still have that minimum capacity for simple human interaction. In all honesty, we must admit that none of these positions can be proved or has intuitive validity. However, it is possible to set the criteria of personhood so high that very few can live up to them. In short, if we demand too much, we will deny serious rights to most existing human beings and set the stage for justified slavery. In world history, we have seen many cases of Jews, Gypsies, African Americans, women, crippled infants, the aged and infirm, as well the merely weak, being exploited and killed because, against all reason, they were labeled as less than human or at least as lesser human beings and so without rights. The fear of that happening again makes the authors move cautiously with regard to any definition of a human being or person that tends to eliminate groups of people whom American society has traditionally and reasonably defended as having serious rights to life. Such a tradition should be guarded and modified only after the most penetrating analysis of all the factors involved.

Summary

The position we have described here rests on the wedge argument, that is, a refusal to make exceptions lest the door be opened to abuses. This method of argumentation leads to the conclusion that, when there is doubt, we should expand the area of rights to protect the value of human life and the rights of persons. The constant use of the wedge principle amounts to building a high and strong wall around the acknowledged rights.

The argument does not, however, settle the issue of who has rights by their very nature. We have, then, a powerful practical argument, rather than a carefully established theoretical basis for an absolute opposition to abortion. This is in line with our general approach of practical wisdom, which looks at all implications of an activity in the light of human dignity.

This position, resting on the wedge principle, leads the writers to hold that a fetus has a serious, although not absolute,[4] right to life. Logically, these two principles lead us to say that the right exists nearly from the moment of conception. We hedge regarding the moment of conception, because it is not clear that the wedge principle needs to be invoked to cover the period between conception and implantation. It may be possible to allow a few days leeway without undermining respect for persons. As we have discussed, the attempt to fix a precise moment when the fetus has rights or certain types of rights seldom leads to convincing answers (Bayles, 1984). The effort may be admirable, but it seeks a clarity that is not available. There will always be some arbitrariness, because we must draw the line not only in terms of (inconclusive) objective criteria, but in terms of our subjective need for certitude and our desire to build a wall around the rights of those we want to protect. On the other hand, in view of our long tradition of respect for the dignity of the severely handicapped and for all groups, the stand is not unreasonable in our society. Tradition itself has an objectivity in the form of the culture and the values of the entire society.

The conclusion that the fetus has a serious, although not absolute, right to life and logically has it from the moment of conception is not to deny that the pregnant woman, too, has serious, although not absolute, rights over her body. Indeed, the conflict between the serious rights of the fetus and the serious rights of the pregnant woman is a crucial area in the abortion debate. A fair discussion must take both sides into account.

THE AUTONOMY OF THE PREGNANT WOMAN

The basic expression of the dignity of the human being is her autonomy, as we discussed in chapter 2. This idea, and that of informed consent, protects any person in her self-governance and in her ability to refuse any unwanted touches. The question of abortion raises a fundamental question about the scope of a woman's autonomy: how much can it be limited by the good of another?

In United States law, the Supreme Court decision in *Roe v. Wade* affirmed the right of privacy, that is something very much like autonomy. It also stated that the right to privacy was not absolute, but could be limited by the interests of the state in the health of the mother or the interest of the state in the potential life that is present during the third trimester. There has been much disagreement over the right to privacy. While the majority opinion in *Roe v. Wade* cited precedent, the dissenting opinion claimed that this right was simply fabricated and had no genuine constitutional foundation.

Since we cannot resolve this legal debate, the authors wish to draw attention to a fundamental moral issue at stake: where does the autonomy or privacy of the pregnant woman give way to other concerns?

This discussion of the rights of the pregnant woman is complicated by the presence of two types of problems. In abortion, the issue is the woman's right to act to terminate the pregnancy and the extent to which that right is limited by the dignity (or rights) of the fetus and the interests of the state. As we will see, a woman's reasons for this action can be varied, and at times may involve medical benefits and burdens for which the idea of informed consent would apply. Yet other motives for an abortion do not fit this patient model of the expression of autonomy in informed consent. In these cases, does the autonomy of the woman justify demanding an abortion (as opposed to consenting to the medical benefit of one)?

In conflicts over the treatment of the fetus, the issue is the right of the woman to give or withhold consent to medical procedures that are not for her benefit and that may involve substantial risks for her. Although an obstetrician may view the fetus as her patient (*Williams Obstetrics*, 1996), there is no access to that patient except through the mother, a separate patient. Can one patient's (the mother's) refusal of consent be overridden for the good of another patient (the fetus)? On what authority should such overriding be based: the dignity of the fetus, the beneficence of the profession, or the interests of society?

Given our starting point in autonomy as a fundamental expression of human dignity, unless there are serious overriding social interests, the decision to have or not to have an abortion is to be made by the pregnant woman or, if necessary, a proper surrogate. Like all ethical decisions, it is to be made in the context of the demands of human dignity as understood and supported by the society. The woman decides under the difficult obligation to consider all relevant ethical considerations, but it remains her decision.[5] Following our earlier discussion of the limits of beneficence and justice, her autonomy may be overridden only in cases in which she is incompetent, or in which there are clear and significant goods for the profession or for society that require these limits. The same concerns we mentioned earlier regarding protecting the marginalized apply to the pregnant woman as well. When autonomy is denied, dignity is also denied.

The importance accorded to the woman's right to decide gives added strength to informed consent with respect to obstetric treatment of the fetus. In other words, not only is there the tradition of informed consent, rooted in the woman's autonomy, which would control the procedures that can be done on the woman, but there is also a tradition of privacy, that is, legal space in which the woman may make a decision even involving the future health of her fetus. The unique relationship of mother and fetus draws together these two theoretical issues into one practical problem.

The Pregnant Woman and Abortion

Although dignity entails the woman's autonomy, the question still remains regarding when that autonomy must give way to other concerns. This would include events when the woman herself must be persuaded not only that is it her right to decide but also that it is her obligation to make a good decision. To aid in this decision, we must be clear on the conflicting issues. First, there is the conflict between the serious, but not absolute, rights of the fetus to life, and the serious but not absolute rights of the woman to life and protection of her health. Second, there are conflicts between the serious, but not absolute, right of the fetus to life and the often far from serious and not absolute right of a woman to a wide variety of interests, ranging from the good of the woman's family to the goods of a certain career timetable or a child of a certain sex. The conflicts cannot be settled on a simple individual rights basis, and the impact of such decisions on the respect for human dignity in general must be a continuous concern.

In an ethic based on practical wisdom, which makes the individual human person the intrinsic good, the conflicts between these rights must be judged in terms of the following factors. There is the question of whether abortion goes against the intrinsic good or the dignity of the individual human, or if it threatens the rights and development of the person and thus the dignity of all persons. Thus far, we have only established that the fetus has a serious, but not absolute, right to life, and certainly we have not established that the fetus is an individual person and so an intrinsic good. Indeed, we have argued for the serious right of the fetus in terms of maintaining limits that protect the rights of other persons when there is a conflict of rights involving more or less important means to the intrinsic good of human dignity. It must be asked if the proposed good consequences for the woman justify the bad consequences for the fetus and for others who have a serious right to life. Furthermore, this analysis must be undertaken in light of the larger concerns of society's understanding of the value and nature of human life.

It is necessary, then, to consider the various goods used to justify an abortion. Sometimes this involves looking at the medical and nonmedical indications for an abortion. Within an ethic of practical wisdom, we are looking at the effect of an abortion on the dignity of the persons and society involved. It is not simply an assertion of some persons' rights, nor is it just a more complicated conflict between the rights of the fetus and the rights of the pregnant woman.

The Motives for Abortion

The motives for abortion indicate the range of proposed goods that people seek to obtain by abortion. These goods can be classified under six main headings:

1. Abortions that are therapeutic from the woman's point of view, whether necessary (a) to save the mother's life or (b) on the basis of other medical indications.
2.. Abortions that are eugenic for the fetus, that is, the view that a particular fetus is better off dead.
3. Abortions that are eugenic from the social point of view, which may include socioeconomic as well as sociomedical reasons and, indeed, might be part of a population policy. In this point of view, society is considered to be better off without this particular fetus being born.
4. Abortions for juridical reasons, such as rape or incest, although obviously other factors such as maternal mental health are involved.
5. Abortions centered on family goods, for example, cases in which the family would suffer psychologically or economically from the birth of another child or a severely ill child.
6. Abortions for the sake of miscellaneous goods from the woman's point of view, which include everything from lifestyle and career patterns to the desired sex of the baby.

Therapeutic Abortion

Only the first category contains therapeutic abortions, those connected with curing the pregnant woman or saving her life. Some cases in the fourth class, abortions for juridical reasons, may be included here if they also involve threats to the mother's physical or psychological health.

Examples of therapeutic abortions include the case of a woman with certain kidney problems, such that pregnancy could lead to death from uremic poisoning. An abortion for this woman could be seen as therapeutic, with one life pitted against another. In other cases, the pregnancy might not lead to death, but could threaten serious and permanent impairment of the woman's health. Thus, a woman with diabetes might lose her sight if she carries the fetus to term. We would see the life of this fetus as confronting serious health problems for the woman. Finally, there are cases in which carrying the fetus to term is considered a danger to the psychological health of the woman. The psychological harm might range from mild upset to psychosis.

Those who do not grant the fetus a serious, although relative, right to life have no interest in the nature of the reasons given for *therapeutic* abortion since, for them there is no conflict between the right of the mother and the less significant right of the fetus. Those who recognize the fetus as having a serious right to life must face and resolve not only the conflict of rights, but the emotional turmoil and anguish of being in what is often a no-win situation. When we face the dilemma of *the relative right to life versus the relative right to life*, we are indeed involved in a tragedy in which our principles do not give us a way out. If one grants a serious right to the fetus, ethical theory does not give us a clear way of resolving either the ethical conflict or the emotional turmoil. No matter what choice is made, great evil follows. In these situations, ethics fails us and we are left with the necessity of choosing in sorrow, knowing that either choice is wrong from one point of view and right from another, equally convincing, point of view. This seems to be part and parcel of the human condition. In such cases, one must decide and act on the basis of her understanding of human dignity. Regardless of what decision has been made, she ought to act with sorrow, knowing that a real good has been sacrificed.

When something less than the woman's life is at stake, it seems simple to resolve the conflict, since a serious right to life ought to take precedence over a right to some lesser good, such as one's eyesight or one's sanity. This may be true in many cases, but in other cases such an analysis is simplistic in that it excludes the consideration of goods that are not clearly the object of rights. Consistent with the demands of practical wisdom, the woman must consider the good of the family who might have a blind or a psychotic mother if the fetus is carried to term, just as she must consider what it means to her to possibly suffer that fate. There are important moral consequences no matter what the decision, and there is no easy settlement on the basis of theory. Indeed, this broader consideration of the problems involved forces us once again into the tragic dimension, similar to the life-versus-life dilemma, in that no matter what one does a great evil will result.

Actions suggested by practical wisdom can only reflect the particular conditions of human life. Practical wisdom cannot always give answers that avoid the tragic. Even absolutist theological positions cannot take away the human condition and remove the emotional conflict that should accompany such important decisions.

Nontherapeutic Abortions

The nontherapeutic abortion causes no personal ethical problems for those who do not grant the fetus a serious right to life. It does create problems not only for those who grant the right but, as we shall see later, for health care professionals who are dedicated to life and health.

The first of the nontherapeutic abortions, supposed to be eugenic from the point of view of the child, is generally characterized by the feeling that *this fetus would be better off dead.* This is alleged to be the case when the fetus has been diagnosed as having a serious genetic defect, or a chance of being born retarded, or the like. The abortion is for the good of the child.

This class of cases brings us directly back to the problems of the quality of life and of the right of another, even a mother or father, to make those judgments for a person or for a being with a serious right to life (see chapter 7). What makes life meaningful for one individual can range from the simple ability to interact with other human beings to the highest development of the loftiest human potentials. None of us seems wise enough to judge the limits of life for another, and the implications of the wedge principle urge us to approach this question with great caution.

Abortions that are supposed to be eugenic from the social point of view are based on the idea that this fetus, if allowed birth, would be a burden on society. In short, *it would be better for society if the fetus were not born.* The reasons given in these cases embrace not only the chance of serious birth defects, but the fact that those defects will cost society a great deal of money. Sometimes it is simply alleged that society has too many people and too few resources to support them. This has been the central issue in the well-publicized use of abortion as a means of population control in China, where famine and poverty have been persistent concerns until very recently (Qui, 1989). This has led to a variety of social policies designed to limit each family to one child. Because of tradition-based concerns to have a male heir who will continue the family name, parents have selectively aborted girls. In addition to this sexism, social eugenicism often includes racism of the worst sort, both historically and currently. The Nazi efforts at eliminating handicapped persons, as well as Jews, Gypsies, and other non-Aryan nationalities are well known. But in the United States, for example, there have been cases of government employees illegally forcing abortions on American Indian and African American women in the name of welfare reform.

Several serious arguments question the social eugenic approach. First, and most basic, is the fact that society exists for the individual and not the other way around. This limits what society can do even to protect itself. Second, even when, as in chapter 4, we grant society rights in this area, society itself and not individuals ought to make the decision as to when it is necessary to neglect an individual in the name of the public or common good. Third, the long-term and not merely the short-term effects of such thinking should be carefully weighed.

Pregnancies resulting from rape and incest, our fourth category, are often put forward as prime candidates for abortion. Sympathy for the victims makes the case particularly emotional. We can all understand why a woman would not want to bear a child that resulted not from an act of love or even passion, but from cruel and deliberate degradation. Certainly, the effects of both the rape and the pregnancy on the mental health of the individual victim need to be given serious consideration. Perhaps they may even create the equivalent of a life-versus-life situation.

Our abhorrence of incest creates a similar sympathy coupled with concern about the possibly defective genetic endowment of the fetus and the destructive psychological effects on the victim. Once again, the actual consequences need to be considered, and they may or may not create the equivalent of a life-versus-life situation.

At the same time, abortion will not undo all the effects of rape and incest and may only create new problems. Most important of all is the question of whether making exceptions for these cases opens up the way for abuses. Once again, we are back to the wedge principle. There are dangers in denying the fetus's serious right to life on the grounds that his or her father was a criminal or that the child might be less than perfect or might be a burden to the mother or to society. In addition, the extent of the trauma to the woman is very much influenced by the degree of society's intelligent and sympathetic assistance and by whether the alternatives of adoption, foster care, and institutionalization are viable. In short, there are many factors to consider even when dealing with the result of rape and incest.

Our fifth class of indications comprises the familial consequences—social, psychological, and economic—of the birth and development of a particular fetus. Let us take the mother of five who has just gotten off welfare and discovers that her fourteen-year-old daughter is pregnant. She sees her daughter reentering the ranks of the poor plus spending years raising the child. Adoption may offer an alternative, but adoption is not always possible. The mother feels trapped and once again faces the agony of living on welfare and the difficulties of a fourteen-year-old too young to raise a child.

Consider also the case of the parents who already have a child with Down's syndrome and are told that they are about to have another. Not only financially, but emotionally, their backs are against the wall. They foresee mental collapse for themselves and severe neglect of the handicapped child that they already have. Adoption is not generally a feasible alternative when dealing with a retarded child, and they shudder at the thought of putting the child into a substandard public facility. People who consider abortion in such situations settle for what they judge to be the choice that is the lesser evil.

Ideally, these conflicts could be removed by superior public care and changed attitudes toward the adoption of the handicapped. In practice, the competition for scarce resources often leaves the handicapped neglected and their parents in the dilemmas we have described. While the authors are inclined to side with the fetus in these cases, they fully sympathize with parents who seek to protect their family and children.

The miscellaneous category includes a wide variety of reasons for an abortion. These include fear of changes in lifestyle that come about with a pregnancy and the entrance of the child into the family. Or perhaps the pregnancy will ruin a career or affect material comfort. The authors doubt that the fetus's serious right to life should yield to such minor goods.

Social Support and the Abortion Problem

Many of the cases mentioned in the previous pages indicate that society's willingness or lack of willingness to help with health care or social services enters into the abortion decisions that women and families make. For a detailed discussion of this point with specific respect to the role of law, see Glendon (1987). Simpler adoption laws might make a decision for life easier. Better law enforcement might decrease the cases of rape and incest. A willingness to supply better care and auxiliary services for the handicapped might make families less afraid of bringing a child into the world. All these good things, however, involve the distribution of scarce resources and all the problems that we discussed in chapter 4. Even the richest society in the world cannot escape the human condition.

Ethics and Tragedy

The approach of practical wisdom taken in this book demands proportionality between the good effects intended and the bad effects risked or permitted and sometimes even intended. In view of this, it should be clear that there is no neat set of answers to the question of a woman's substantive right to an abortion. Nor are there neat answers to the exact extent of the fetus's serious right to life. The life-versus-life case, however, points up the tragedy at the root of so many cases involving debate about the ethics of abortion.

In the life-versus-life cases, theory does not permit us to give primacy to the woman or to the fetus. Two equal goods are in conflict. Although some argue that the woman is a person with full rights and the fetus has only diminished rights, they offer a dangerous distinction, and the wedge principle, as elaborated earlier, should make us hesitate about adopting it.

THE ETHICS OF ABORTION AS A SOCIAL PHENOMENON

The social phenomenon of abortion involves a broad variety of social issues in the United States, ranging from religious faith to political party, from issues of truth to authority, civility to tolerance. Conflict or agreement in the discussion of abortion rests far more on one's position with regard to these questions than it does on one's analysis of the moral status of the fetus. Given the complexity of these issues, an adequate discussion of abortion becomes a discussion of an individual's and a society's world view, including theories of justice, public policy, and public discourse.

A major issue is whether abortion is a question of public policy at all, which is to suggest on one level that the issue is to be resolved privately by a woman and her doctor. To ask this question is to answer it by favoring the woman's right to choose. The apparent attraction of privatizing the decision is, at best, a resignation in the face of the ideological nature of the discussion and, at worse, a surreptitious abandonment of social accountability for the fetus.

It has long been noted that the private discussion of this issue is more nuanced and open than the public discussion (Callahan and Callahan, 1984). This is in part due to the absence of social pressure, the lowered stakes of private discussion, and the opportunity for leisurely and thoughtful exploration. Some put the issue in the context of bringing the characteristics of private conversation into the public realm. But this falsely and naively tries to solve the problem by pretending that the conditions of a private discussion may be made those of a public one. The civility made possible by friendship, the nuance made possible by time spent together, and the open-mindedness of shared concerns are all elements of private conversations that are not directly translatable into public discourse.

A more honest and demanding question is whether there can be a public discussion over such a contentious issue. The private debate will have to lead the way. Individuals must first privately develop a nuanced position, and the individual's conviction must then be able to rise to support an emerging public position, expressed and refined at increasingly higher levels of social organization and finally taken up by a fortunate politician who will be saying nothing new.

Unfortunately, such a development of public opinion is idealistic and not under our control. But it is possible for concerned professionals to do two things, at least, to promote this task. As Arendt (1958) pointed out, we need to establish and maintain public spaces in which discussions that are more than private, but less than fully public, may be encouraged. This is particularly true of the abortion discussion.

Second, we need to attend to the philosophical and theological assumptions that have brought us to this difficulty. In any tradition there arise moments of crisis that challenge the coherence of the tradition's obvious premises (MacIntyre, 1988). So too, may we be looking at the limits of our traditional position on rights. The talk of rights does indeed have an important function in certain practical and historical contexts; but this importance must not blind us to searching out thoughtful alternatives, especially when we are at a difficult impasse.

For example, the study of the philosophy of technology may be able to shed light on the assumptions that we make about medical practice, particularly on our assumptions about the ease and perfectibility of life. These assumptions are often at the heart of the more contested cases of abortion or abortion requests. The problem of abortion may be better solved by examining what leads to it, rather than simply focusing on the problem as presented.

An Alternative View

There are significantly different ways of approaching the issue. For example, LaFleur, in discussing the morality of abortion in Japan, points out that

> one privately will often be told that in Japan the availability of abortion is in fact *protective of family values* to the degree that it makes unnecesaary the birthing of unwanted children. Then, because it is assumed, first, that unwanted children are both pitiable and more prone to become problematic for society itself and second, that family strength and well-being are maximized when it can be assumed that all persons within it are *wanted* and valued, logic seems to compel the conclusion that abortion is needed as a necessary "safety value" to ensure familial, societal and national strength (LaFleur, 1990, p. 538).

The central issue in this depiction of the Japanese is the question of family and social order. Thus the issue of rights is submerged in the larger question of social good. Just as informed consent owes its primacy in American medical ethics to our understanding of dignity as basically individualistic, so too the flavor of the American debate over abortion is rooted in the rights that derive from that individualism. The Japanese traditional emphasis on community places the individual in a social context that identifies and limits that individuality. The priority of the community thus presents a way of resolving disputes. The American alternatives of either "Pro-Life" or "Pro-Choice" both appeal to the rights possessed by individuals as the source of meaning for their position. Lacking a common ground for discussion, there is no way to bring them together; the exercise of one set of rights is the denial of the other. While the Buddhists in Japan have reinforced the concern with family and community, religious groups in the United States have embraced the individualism inherent in the rights debate and generally are part of the standoff.

ABORTION AND THE HEALTH CARE PROVIDER

The health care provider must face three sets of problems. The first concerns her or his *personal* stand on the morality of abortion and the maternal–fetal conflict. The second involves health care *institutional policies* on personnel. The third set concerns questions of *professional ethics*, which exist even for those who have no personal ethical problem with either issue. This third set of problems involves such matters as forced abortions, forced medical treatment, and professional involvement in nontherapeutic abortions.

Abortion and Personal Ethics

The health care provider who follows the approach given in this chapter must decide whether a particular abortion is ethical and, in the process, decide whether she or he will cooperate with the woman who wants an abortion. When the provider has decided that the particular abortion is unethical, she or he should ordinarily withdraw from the case. At times, however, the matter of cooperation is not that simple. Must a nurse withdraw who occasionally tends women in the recovery room after an abortion? Can a physician continue to practice in a hospital that performs many abortions that the physician considers unethical? The classical principles on cooperation can be applied in situations like these.[6] Thus, although a provider should not perform or directly participate in an abortion that she or he considers unethical, there may be proportionate reasons for taking care of patients under treatment as a result of an abortion. The most obvious reason is to prevent further harm to the patient. There are even proportionate reasons for continuing to work in a hospital that performs a large number of abortions that the health care professional judges to be unethical. Thus, granted that continued association with the hospital is not taken as approval of unethical conduct, the needs of the profession and of patients in the area can often supply the justification for continued association with the group.

Those who see no problems with abortion will have no problems of conscience in this area. Those who see all abortions as murder will feel compelled to fight against abortion in any circumstances. Holders of both positions must, however, face the problem of institutional policy and its relation to the conscience of those who disagree with it.

Abortion and Institutional Policy

The strong feelings associated with the abortion question can push individuals to promote institutional policies that ban those who disagree with them. Catholic hospitals, for example, might be tempted to ban not only physicians who perform abortions, but those who do not publicly condemn abortion. Hospital boards, which see the provision of abortions as a mandatory service to women who desire them, may be tempted to deny privileges or employment to health care professionals who are either against abortion or who see the need for deciding each case on its own merit. In short, all sorts of providers may be excluded by health care institutions that believe that they have excellent reasons for their policies.

The authors grant that, as individuals, members of institutional boards must follow their consciences. As members of the board, however, they need to consider four points. First, the institution should have a written public policy. In short, there should be no secret blackballing of potential employees and physicians who desire staff privileges. Second, the policy should be rooted in the publicly stated and carefully articulated philosophy of the institution. In other words, the policy should be relevant to the stated purposes of the institution. Third, the policy should, insofar as consistent with the philosophy of the institution, respect the consciences of the health care providers that it employs. Fourth, the policy should also be in accord with state laws that protect the conscience of health care professionals. In a pluralistic society, at least, it requires a strong justification to exclude those who are against abortion if they will never be involved with abortions. An equally strong justification is required to exclude those who are in favor of abortions if they will never be involved in abortions.

The Nontherapeutic Abortion

Even if the health care provider's personal ethics permits abortion, the health care professional and the institution must still ask whether the abortion is medically indicated and therefore within the ethics of healing. In short, there is a question as to whether a nontherapeutic abortion is a suitable activity for a physician or a nurse or for a hospital or other health care agency.

Therapeutic abortions, those concerned with preserving the life and physical health of the woman, are within the purview of health care providers. If an abortion is medically indicated, the physician or nurse whose conscience otherwise permits abortion may participate. When the abortion is not medically indicated, as with abortions done for social reasons, for eugenic reasons, or for the convenience of the woman, the participation of a health care provider is ethically questionable. Health care providers are supposed to be healing, not passing judgment on the quality of life or the good of society, much less facilitating the nonmedical goals of some patients. Traditionally and, we believe, correctly, the professional health care provider is committed to health and not to supplying what the customer wants and will pay for regardless of need. Just as physicians have refused to act as executioners in those states that mandate death by lethal injections, which only physicians may prescribe, so should they refuse to blur their professional role by participating in nontherapeutic abortions. The tradition, however, seems to have weakened, and the mores of contemporary American society appear bent on making the health care professional a huckster who can do nearly anything a patient will pay for. The authors believe that this can only weaken the health care professions and ultimately harm society.

In practice, there is much dispute as to what constitutes a therapeutic abortion. Some physicians argue that an abortion is therapeutic if it prevents or alleviates a serious physical or mental illness, or even if it alleviates temporary emotional upsets. In short, the health of the pregnant woman is given such a broad definition that a very large number of abortions can be classified as therapeutic. Even with this broad definition of health and therapeutic abortion, many abortions are still nontherapeutic. Abortions to preserve lifestyle or career plans are hardly therapeutic or medically indicated. Eugenic abortions of either type are also not therapeutic.

The abortion problem is just one example of an area in which there is need for serious consideration of the role of the health care professional in a society that often acts as if it had a right to purchase every convenience. Is it right to perform plastic surgery on people who will not benefit from it? Is it right to patch up athletes and send them back into the game, thus risking their health and possibly their lives? Is it right for a health care professional to abort a fetus for the convenience of a healthy pregnant woman? In short, is it right to use professional expertise for nonhealing purposes?

The authors believe that the answer to all these questions is a clear "No". In our opinion, the health care professional loses professional status and turns into a mere tradesperson when medical indications are banished and patient convenience or provider profits are made the dominant criteria of practice. Thus, nontherapeutic abortions remain an ethical problem even for health professionals whose purely personal ethics do not condemn such abortions. Perhaps there is a need for a separate group of health professionals who make no pretense at healing, but handle nontherapeutic abortions, executions, and other services for which the public is willing to pay. Such a separation would not solve the abortion problem, but it would make clear that health care professionals are dedicated to healing and not to death or mere money making.

Coercion and Abortion

The principles of informed consent apply in abortion as in all medical procedures. Indeed, they should probably apply more stringently, not only because such high goods are at stake, but because there are so many temptations to abuse the freedom of the pregnant woman. Indeed, the situations are such that both the Pro-Choice and the Pro-Life groups are concerned about them. The two situations that call for special consideration are (1) cases in which parents are pressuring the young woman to have or not have an abortion and (2) cases in which government employees deceive or even blackmail poor women into having abortions.

Parental pressure is understandable in many cases. The family is often in a highly emotional state, since it sees disgrace, expense, and the frustration of dreams if the child has a child before she is able to care for it and before she has grown up. At the same time, the child often realizes the consequences in only a vague way. The family feelings may be similar even when the case involves not a child but a young adult. The family's feelings can lead to intense pressure for an abortion. The young person is threatened with loss of love and banishment from the family if an abortion is refused. The pressures can become so great that we are probably dealing with coercion when the competence of the young woman to choose becomes doubtful. The health care professional should be very careful to make sure that informed consent is truly given.

Those families who oppose abortion absolutely and who see abortion as murder can create equally great pressures against an abortion. When these families threaten banishment and loss of love if there is an abortion, we are once again in the area of coercion. We are faced, then, with a class of cases in which all too often, neither the client nor the surrogates are particularly competent. The case is even more complicated in that outsiders are often biased in favor of birth or abortion, so there is no easy and satisfactory appeal to counselors or courts.

In this sort of case, the health care provider whose conscience permits abortion in the case at hand should attempt to reduce the pressure and to have the decision made at a time when feelings have settled down. When there is relative calm, the patient should be honestly informed about the procedures, her alternatives, her risks, and the costs. If the provider attempts to do much more than calm and inform the patient, the health care provider may become yet another force that reduces freedom.

Those whose conscience forbids cooperation in the abortion in question must withdraw from the case if the patient chooses abortion. Before the patient has made a decision, they, too, should attempt to increase the competence of the patient and to give the proper medical information required for informed consent. As long as they avoid coercive behavior, the providers may, in accord with their consciences, explain their moral position on the procedure. Those who cannot refrain from coercive behavior should not be professionally involved in such cases at all.

The second class of cases involving fraud and even blackmail on the part of government employees and health care providers demands vigorous action. In the past, welfare workers and workers in the Indian Service have told clients that their government support would be cut off if they did not have an abortion and consent to sterilization. Since the clients were generally Native Americans or blacks, the deception and blackmail look alarmingly like genocide. No matter what stand one takes on abortion or sterilization, such conduct is a blatant violation of autonomy and deserves outright condemnation, even if some sort of "good intention" is present. Certainly, health care providers should be on their guard and report any such incidents.

MATERNAL–FETAL CONFLICT

When the mother seems likely to bring the fetus to term, we enter into our second set of problems: the conflict between the fetus's claim to health and the woman's autonomy. There are three types of difficulties here: The first involves the woman's behavior during pregnancy; the second her obligations if her fetus is diagnosed as requiring medical treatment; and third, the health care professional's obligations to mother and fetus.

It is important to note that some argue that by speaking of a conflict between mother and fetus we are begging important questions. The use of technology, such as ultrasonography and electronic monitoring, has created two patients out of one, not just by making the fetus visible but by making the mother transparent. This has dramatically changed how we think about pregnancy without changing the reality of pregnancy (Mattingly, 1992). We must be careful about what we have lost in this transition (such as presumed significance of the mother and the importance of the mother's emotional attachment to her pregnancy) as well as what we have gained (Hornstra, 1998).

Limits on a Mother's Behavior

In the first case, the issue involves various types of behavior that the mother may pursue to the possible detriment of the fetus. Smoking, drinking alcohol, and using any of a wide variety of drugs are examples of maternal behavior that can have a lifelong and substantial impact on the health of the fetus. Is the mother obligated to change her behavior to protect her fetus?

We must grant that in most cases the concern of the mother for her child will lead her to curtail most behaviors known to be hazardous. The most interesting ethics cases are the unusual ones, yet that should not blind us to the basic fact that most people have goodwill. Respect for the dignity and worth of the developing child, coupled with the family's self-interest in having a healthy child, is generally adequate incentive for a mother to care for her fetus in accordance with the best available medical advice.

But there are cases in which, for a variety of reasons, a mother-to-be does not act in the best interests of her child. Ignorance or bad medical advice is an unavoidable aspect of human life. Smoking, drinking alcohol, and recreational drug use are somewhat more under the control of the mother. We choose to do these actions. Yet, a woman who has been smoking for ten years may find it very difficult to give up smoking, particularly in the face of the tensions and difficulties of pregnancy. Another difficult issue concerns whether a woman is an alcoholic, a problem now generally considered a disease, to what extent is she responsible for harm to her fetus (Terry, 1996)?

The health care professional does not have power over the behavior of a patient for the sake of medical care or, especially, out of concern for hypothetical outcomes. Just as a cardiologist cannot require a patient to stop smoking (although he or she can refuse to continue to treat the patient if another physician can be found), so, too, an obstetrician cannot force a pregnant woman to cease behavior that threatens her child (although he or she, too, can decline to continue to treat the patient).

It may, however, be in the interests of the state to intervene and override a refusal of consent, if that state interest is an expression of a clear ethical consensus from society. Infants born impaired represent a huge demand on the resources of the society and can challenge some fundamental accomplishments or goals of the society (note, for example, the effect of crack cocaine babies on a city's educational system). Given an effect that is significant for the infant and for the society, state intervention may be appropriate. Such intervention would require special legislation, the establishment of an enforcement mechanism, and the imposition of penalties. All these steps involve problems both for the state and for health care professionals. Questions like the following have to be answered: Does an offending mother have a right to due process? Can you stop her dangerous behavior without sending her to jail? Would the relationship between the health care professional and the patient be seriously endangered by the obligation to report suspected abuses to the authorities?

A word of caution is necessary. The demands of establishing a significant effect or of creating an effective response are daunting. For example, years of study have not made precise the correlation between alcohol consumption and its effect on the fetus; some fetuses are affected dramatically by only a little alcohol, and others seem unaffected by massive quantities (Abel, 1990). Many experts argue that there is not enough information to justify any claim even to a correlation. Much more study is necessary to understand fetal alcohol syndrome, and this is only one of several possible problem areas. The basis for the state's interest must be clearly established before such intrusion on patient autonomy can be justified.

Additionally, some of the behaviors under discussion, such as drug abuse, are already illegal. There seems to be little advantage to expanding state intervention in areas in which the basic behavior is already prohibited, with debatable success. As we mentioned before, the law represents only one small part of a society's influence on an individual's behavior.

When a Mother Refuses Consent

When the mother refuses consent to a medical procedure intended to aid the fetus, a different type of problem exists. The physician has a diagnosis of a patient (the fetus) and a proposed treatment. Unlike the hypothetical concerns regarding the mother's behavior during pregnancy, the mother and the physician are confronted with a definite problem and a greater medical probability of treatment.

Our previous comments above about the presumption of maternal goodwill still apply in this situation. The American tradition has been, and seems to remain, based on the idea that primary responsibility for the care of children rests on the parents. A parental decision, coupled with the autonomy of the mother as a patient inextricably bound to the treatment, is compelling unless there is a clearly established overriding state interest. Although there is no doubt that parents do make poor decisions, that it can be difficult for the mother to separate her concern for her child from her concern or fears for herself as a patient, and that parents may act according to controversial religious views, no other person or group is likely to make better decisions for a child than the child's parents.

Maternal Fetal Conflicts and Professional Obligations

Recent authors (Chervenak and McCullough, 1985) have suggested "vigorously attempting to persuade the woman to accept the required restrictions or treatment," or, if that fails, "a more coercive approach, e.g., threatening to seek or seeking a court order, may sometimes be morally justifiable." They suggest this because they understand the profession to have beneficence-based obligations toward the fetus that in extreme cases can override the autonomy of the mother and the status of parents as surrogates.

Although this situation can be particularly difficult for a physician whose training is directed to action, it is still the case that the interests of the profession are never adequate to override the autonomy of a patient (unless covered by one of the exceptions mentioned in chapter 2). The profession's respect for the patient must remain at the heart of its ethics, even in the face of a conflict between the needs of two patients. As suggested by the American College of Obstetricians and Gynecologists, physicians are "almost never" justified in going to court to compel treatment of a pregnant woman (Gianelli, 1987). Unless there is a clear ethical consensus from society, such as a law, the profession cannot override a refusal of consent.

It is important to remember the limits of the competence of the health care professional. The values of the parents are often outside the ambit of medical values. Often, the parents may belong to a different cultural group or social class that does not share the physician's concerns (the source of the autonomy-beneficence conflict in the first place). In short, medical values may not be central to the situation unless society has given them a special legal status. Furthermore, we must remember that medical judgments regarding outcomes are not infallible and often vary widely in their probability. Thus, society and the profession must be careful about imposing them on parents.

State Interests and Fetal Treatment

On the legal side, state interference with the right of the mother-patient to refuse treatment for herself and the fetus should be sought only when there are both overriding state interests and a very probable medical judgment that the damage risked is great and the treatment effective. This is a very difficult standard to meet, a point that led the Court of Appeals for the District of Columbia to note [in *Re A.C. (573 A.2nd 1253 {D.C. 1990})*] that in virtually all cases the decision of the woman would prevail (see also Neale, 1990).

Indeed, with Field (1989) we note that the state interests are greater in cases of maternal drug abuse and heavy drinking than with abortion itself. When a child is born with defects resulting from drug or alcohol use, the state faces enormous medical bills. The Institute for Medicine estimates that fetal alcohol syndrome alone involves annual medical costs of $276,826,000 (Abel, 1990, p. 104). There are similar costs for babies born addicted to crack cocaine. But these are consequences of what are often already illegal actions. Again, this is an indication of the limits that the law has in controlling our behavior.

It is worth noting that these problems are often rooted in the social conditions under which people live. There is a strong correlation between poverty and such problems as a lack of prenatal care, drug and alcohol abuse, and poor nutrition. Although there *may* be criminal abuse when the fetus is hurt as a result of freely adopted maternal behavior that has been proved to have serious effects on the child (Popovits, 1991), poverty and its related problems force the society to share responsibility with the parent for the problems of the child.

SUMMARY

Even if the fetus is not a human being with all the rights of a person, it can be argued that the fetus has a serious right to life. This argument rests ultimately on the use of the wedge principle in protecting the rights of persons and those we already acknowledge as having a serious right to life. Neither the rights of the fetus nor the rights of the pregnant woman are absolute. When the rights of these parties are in conflict, a settlement is to be sought in weighing the goods and evils to discover who has a superior claim. Often, no clear decision is possible, and the moral person is faced with a tragedy in which ordinary moral categories may no longer apply.

Ultimately, views on the ethics of abortion and other maternal fetal conflicts depend on the world view of the actors in the drama. Unfortunately, our pluralistic society does not have a universally accepted world view, with the result that the conflicts in this area will continue.

CASES FOR ANALYSIS

1. Jean has her first child at age fourteen. By the time she is thirty, she has five children ranging in age from five to sixteen years old. Married and divorced twice, she has spent eleven years living on Aid for Dependent Children. During the past five years, however, she has been working in a rehabilitation center, taking courses, and advancing on the job, even though she has no degree. In the process of all this, Jean discovers that she is intelligent and capable of controlling her own life. She is also aware of her mistakes and is determined to prevent her children from making the same mistakes she has made. When she notices her sixteen-year-old becoming overly interested in boys, she enrolls her in a state-supported boarding school for poor families. Despite this, the daughter becomes pregnant. Jean foresees another child at home, a daughter without education and work, and the start of another cycle of Aid for Dependent Children. Moreover, tests reveal that the child will have cystic fibrosis and will pose additional burdens on the family. Certainly, such a child will have no chance of adoption. Jean's dream of self-sufficiency appears doomed. She brings all this up at the physician's office while she has a bad case of the flu.

The patient is asking for both medical and moral advice. What can the physician say? Who is responsible for answering the moral questions? Should the presence of cystic fibrosis affect the decision?

2. Ivan and Elena have three children with Down's syndrome. Despite their efforts at birth control, Elena is pregnant again. Tests reveal that the fourth child will also have Down's syndrome. Ivan works on the janitorial staff at the local general hospital and earns just a little over the minimum wage, not enough to put the family over the poverty line. His employer provides family health coverage. With food stamps and occasional help from their families, they barely get by. Elena cannot work because the children require constant supervision and care. In any event, she is unskilled and could not get a well-paying job.

Ivan and Elena are loving parents and do not want to put their children into an institution. They doubt whether they can handle a fourth handicapped child. It is not merely a question of the money, but of stamina. The previous winter, when Elena came down with the flu for a week, the household almost came apart at the seams. Ivan was even tempted to beat the children when they kept whining for attention.

The couple asks one of physicians at the hospital to perform an abortion.

Is the abortion medically indicated? If it is not, can the health care professionals ethically perform it, even if they see nothing wrong with abortion?

Is it ethically significant that this is an intact two-parent family? Should its financial condition affect your analysis? How? If there are signs of disintegration, what is their significance? Are the desires of Ivan and Elena ethically relevant to the decision?

3. Ms. Q. is a thirty-year-old woman who is pregnant for the first time, having spent several years in a local infertility program. She has been treated previously with clomiphene citrate, a fertility drug that increases the incidence of multiple births among those who subsequently become pregnant from 1 percent to 8 percent. You, the physician who prescribed the drug, indicated to the patient that its use involved "some risk of multiple gestation."

At nine weeks gestation, ultrasound reveals the presence of triplets. After discussion, with her husband, Ms. Q. asks you to terminate two of the fetuses. She says she really wants to have a child and "be a good mother," but doesn't feel capable of caring for more than one child at a time. Even though all three fetuses appear healthy, her preference is to abort two rather than have triplets.

A technique similar to amniocentesis (in which the uterine cavity is entered) has been used to selectively terminate a defective fetus, when a serious fetal anomaly, such as a trisomy disorder, occurs in multiple gestations. This technique could be used to terminate two of the triplets, but it entails an incremental risk of miscarriage. What do you do?

4. Theodora and Ambrose have been living together for three years. They plan to marry in another six months, when Theodora finishes college and is no longer dependent on her parents for tuition. When she tells Ambrose that she is pregnant, he explodes and says, "Well, you may as well know that I have AIDS. I discovered it just last week. Now I suppose the baby will have it, too. Let's call everything off. I just can't take any more." He stalks out of the house. She has not heard from him in two weeks. She decides to have an abortion and approaches you for help.

How certain is it that the baby will have AIDS (at least will be HIV-positive)? Is it important to know if Theodora is HIV-positive? This case is deliberately lacking in details since this is closer to real life; do not introduce new facts, but struggle with the uncertainty in trying to make a decision.

5. Jerry and Thomasina, married with no children, live the good life. Jerry, an architect, and Thomasina, a senior systems analyst for a major corporation, have combined incomes that put them in the upper 3 percent of all family units in the United States. They have a condominium in New York City, a second home in the Pocono Mountains, and spend two weeks in the Caribbean every winter. They are on the upward slope, and things can only get better. In three years they plan to have one male child to carry on the family name. If the conceptus is female, they intend to abort it. Thomasina gets pregnant three years ahead of schedule. They decide to abort, since taking a leave would block her from promotion to a position that will open up in six months. They come to you for help with the abortion.

How weighty is their motive for an abortion? Since they are successful, should society intervene in their private choices? Should the possibility of adoption be a factor in the decision?

6. Laudator and Desiree have been married for five years. Laudator works as a janitor at the local public school, and Desiree has a part-time job in a dress factory. They have no family and few friends. Each is the other's whole life. Because Desiree is a juvenile diabetic, they have practiced birth control lest a pregnancy cause serious harm. In addition, since Desiree's life expectancy is short, they do not want to adopt, since the child might soon have no mother. Now they discover that Desiree is pregnant. The physician tells them that Desiree will almost certainly lose her sight permanently in the course of the pregnancy. She may also die if her kidneys, which have already weakened, give out. The nurse-midwife advises an abortion. Laudator, faced with the loss of Desiree, wants an abortion. Desiree secretly wants the baby so that when she is dead Laudator will have someone to love. She thinks that the loss of her sight would be a small price to pay for the child.

Is an abortion in this case medically indicated? Is the ethicalness of an abortion complicated by the motives and the situations of the two people? Will Laudator be able to care for a blind wife or to run the family if Desiree dies? Has the midwife allowed nonmedical factors to influence her advice? Is her nursing advice based on her nursing education and experience?

NOTES

1. State court decisions have added to the state's interest in the fetus, regardless of viability. In a number of cases, damages have been awarded for wrongful-death claims when the issue was responsibility for the death of a nonviable fetus (McMorris, 1996).

2 There is voluminous literature on the subject of abortion. One comprehensive anthology is Louis Pojman's *The Abortion Controversy* (New York: Prentice-Hall, 1999).

3. One way to divide the philosophic discussion is between its classical arguments and its modern arguments. In general, the classical argument attempts to delineate the personhood of the fetus by operating within the assumptions of classical metaphysics, while the modern versions begin with some version of Cartesian subjectivism.

For example, this line of argument includes, among many philosophers such as Baruch Brody (1975), the National Institutes of Health, Human Embryo Research Panel (1994), which argued that, because a person is a thinking being and thinking requires neurological activity, the fetus acquires personhood during fetal development specifically with the development of the primitive streak.

The general difficulty with such claims is their arbitrariness on both issues of a definition of person and of a physical marker. Why rationality rather than freedom, for example, and why the primitive streak when there seem to be problems both of a continuity of physical development and other specific opportunities for identifying a break in the continuity?

The "modern form" of this attempt includes the well-known argument by Michael Tooley (1972) that the fetus is not a person because the fetus does not and cannot have a concept of self. Similarly, Mary Ann Warren (1973) rejects the personhood of the fetus because it lacks consciousness, reasoning, self-motivated activity, the capacity to communicate, and self-awareness, all of which define a person. By contrast, a more recent argument by Marquis (1989) concludes that the fetus is indeed a person, because it has a future, which, even if currently unformed, will nevertheless be the future of a self-aware and self-creating being.

All these arguments are about attempts to fuse rationality and freedom as criteria of personhood and can be seen as attempts to go beyond the classical dichotomies. Philosophically, they are very interesting. However, they all very clearly do not lend themselves to identifying any physical markers to aid agents in identifying which being is and which is not a person. This creates challenging problems particularly in dealing with fetuses and with handicapped or incompetent patients. How are we to find the presence or absence, the possibility or the impossibility, of self-motivated activity or of a future self-consciousness? Whatever the philosophic interest in such concepts may be, they are quite opaque to the practicing physician.

4. The fetus does not have an absolute right to life because no one has such a right. One being's rights limit those of another being, and we have social arrangements to resolve conflicts between these rights. When the conflicts are irresolvable, we are faced with the tragic in human existence.

5. The classic versions of defense of the woman's right to decide emphasize the rights of the woman to such values as life, autonomy or bodily integrity. Arguments such as those of Judith Jarvis Thomson (1971), that we must consent to the use of our body to keep others alive, have remained for twenty-five years the centerpiece of a woman's general right to an abortion. From this supposed bedrock of autonomy and bodily integrity, others have outlined mechanisms to limit access to abortion by balancing autonomy with other social considerations, such as the viability of the fetus or the need to protect the medical profession.

On the more limited question of an indirect abortion, the traditional Catholic position is that of double effect; if efforts to save the life of the woman are foreseen to likely or certainly destroy the fetus, those efforts are licit as long as the death of the fetus is not directly intended. The proportionate significance of a woman's right to life is at the core of such justification.

Adding to the discussion, many argue that the woman has moral concerns beyond either her autonomy or the personhood of the fetus that may or may not oblige her to carry the fetus to term. Some contemporary feminists, such as Celia Wolf-Devine (1989), argue that the feminist criticism of male violence demands that a woman not resort to the violent destruction of the fetus, finding alternatives in an ethic of care. Others, such as Sally Markowitz (1990), argue that in a sexist society, where the sexual activity of women is controlled by men, abortion is necessary even if regrettable.

In short, *part* of the problem involves establishing how powerful is the woman's (or any individual's) autonomy.

6. The classical principles vary for consequentialists and deontologists. A consequentialist, in line with the principle of proportionality given in chapter 3, would permit cooperation in evil to prevent a greater evil, provided that one is not acting directly against the intrinsic good, that is, the individual person. A formulation of the classical principle from a deontological point of view is found in Ashley and O'Rourke (1978, pp. 197-199).

9

NEW METHODS
OF REPRODUCTION

INTRODUCTION

Starting with the introduction of artificial insemination and ending with
the use of frozen embryos, the human race has introduced important modi-
fications into the reproductive process. Undoubtedly, additional methods
will be implemented in the future. Although these methods have brought
blessings to childless couples and to those who want children without the
inconvenience of pregnancy, they have also created ethical problems, or at
least questions about the ethics of the procedures. Some people are against
all the new methods on the grounds that they are either unnatural or
unsuitable for humans beings. More specific allegations of ethical problems
range from the charge that artificial insemination is unethical, since the
donor masturbates in collecting the sperm, to questions about whether a
frozen embryo has a right to be born. Nearly all the new methods of reproduction create social problems, since society must be able to identify the
parents if it is to ensure both that the offspring are cared for and that they
do not end up as public charges. These questions are accompanied by others about the ethics of those health care professionals who are not engaged
in healing, but in facilitating the questionable interests of healthy people
who are capable of having children in the traditional way or who are
beyond ordinary childbearing age.

In the pages that follow, we will discuss selected methods of reproduction in some detail and indicate when they appear medically indicated, what ethical problems are raised by the methods, and, in particular, what social dimensions need particular attention. At the end of the chapter, we will discuss the more general charge that these procedures are unnatural, that is, artificial, and therefore unethical.

ARTIFICIAL INSEMINATION AND THE GENERAL PROBLEMS OF ASSISTED REPRODUCTION

The oldest of the new methods of reproduction is artificial insemination (AI). This involves harvesting sperm and inserting it into the woman's vagina by means of a syringe. The sperm may originate from the woman's husband (called homologous AI) or from a donor (heterologous AI).

Three objections are raised against this procedure from a natural law perspective. First, it generally involves masturbation on the part of the man, and second in heterologous AI it seems to involve adultery, since the woman and the donor are having a sort of intercourse without being married to one another. The third objection is to the artificiality of the procedure, that is, to the intrusion of human artifice in a natural process. From a natural law perspective, the ordinary natural process, or those processes that express the proper development and activity of a natural being, should be respected. AI, and in general all forms of assisted reproduction, are unethical, since it involves technologically altering how human sexual reproduction occurs.

For example, the Roman Catholic Church has objected to AI on these grounds, which they tie to the right of the child to be born as the result of a choice to complete a marriage through procreation and raising children (Congregation for the Doctrine of the Faith, 1987). This focus on what is the natural origin and development of a human individual and a human family explains their objection to AI on the grounds of masturbation and possible adultery. Finally, the Catholic concern with artificiality leads to an objection even to artificial insemination by the woman's husband when the semen has been obtained aside from actual intercourse between the spouses.

From either a consequentialist or practical wisdom point of view, the first two objections are pointless. In the first place, there is no evidence that masturbation has any harmful consequences and absent other problems it seems not to degrade the individual. Second, if the husband agrees to the procedure and the couple is prepared for the emotional stress of the procedure, the harmful effects of adultery will not occur. Adultery from a consequentialist point of view is condemned because it leads to one or all of the following evils: (1) weakening of the marriage, (2) violence by the injured spouse, and (3) doubt about parentage of the offspring and so problems about the inheritance of property and the obligation to support the child. In the case of homologous AI, none of these consequences is likely to occur. Heterologous AI is more complicated because of the emotional tensions that may occur when raising a child with a different genetic background than the parents. Human society has a long tradition of dealing with this situation in the form of adoption, so this potentially troublesome emotional issue can certainly be handled by parents and a society prepared for it.

There may also be unwarranted harmful difficulties in the following situations: (1) when the woman is not married, (2) when the donors are not screened, (3) when the donor's identity is concealed, (4) when one donor is used frequently in a given area, and (5) when banks for frozen sperm and ova are used.

Artificial Insemination by Donor and the Unmarried Mother

When the mother in question is not married, there can be questions as to whether it is good to deliberately bring a child into a one-parent family or into a family that has a role model for only one gender. Although adoptions by single parents have become more common and can be justified by the fact that an orphan is better off with one parent than with none, the significance of the one-parent and one-gender family continues to receive close social consideration as a problem of artificiality. In addition to the general question about deliberate formation of such families, one needs to ask the following questions about each particular case. Is this woman capable of supporting the child without public assistance? Is she mature enough and emotionally stable enough to provide a healthy home environment? In short, one ought to ask all the questions social workers consider when investigating candidates for adoption. Indeed, these are the questions that everyone ought to ask before they proceed to have children. It appears clear that legal regulation is required if the interests of children are to be protected.

Artificial Insemination by Donor and Screening

Unlike marriage, where pride and passion blind the partners to important health considerations, there is no reason why donor insemination should not be done in such a way as to avoid the production of seriously handicapped offspring. Furthermore, given the significant numbers of people infected with HIV, the health history of the donor should be an important part of the health history of the child. The American Medical Association (1996) has taken a very clear stand on this:

E-2.05. Thorough medical histories must be taken of all candidates for anonymous semen donation. All potential donors must also be screened for infectious or inheritable diseases which could adversely affect the recipient or the resultant child. Frozen semen should be used for artificial insemination because it enables the donor to be tested for HIV infection at the time of the donation, and again after an interval before the original semen is used, thus increasing the likelihood that the semen is free of HIV infection.

With the advent of AIDS, the use of fresh sperm should be and is forbidden, not only by the AMA, but also by groups such as the American Association of Tissue Banks and the American Fertility Society. The American Fertility Society has voluntary guidelines for sperm storage, lab procedures, and disease testing, including a six-month waiting period to allow for follow-up AIDS testing. A reputable laboratory is the best bet for preserving the patient's safety. These better labs will reject up to 90 percent of the sperm presented for sale and will also take careful health histories, screen for lifestyle dangers, administer physical examinations, and perform standard tests for sexually transmitted diseases (Carey, 1991). Obviously, these precautions apply to nearly all the new methods of reproduction.

Concealing the Donors

In addition, physicians using donors often mix the sperm of several donors together and keep no records in order to avoid the possibility of the donor being sued for support. Although this may be understandable from a legal point of view, it creates some health care problems. Without some knowledge of the parentage and genetic heritage of the child, future health care providers will have to operate without important data. For this reason, there should be a single donor, and the health history of the donor should be available. The original fears that motivated concealing the donor have been removed in many areas. Some governments have provided that when the husband agrees to the donor insemination there can be no paternity suit against the donor. In addition, these laws assume that the husband gave consent unless the contrary can be established. The laws on the subject frequently provide that the children of the insemination can be told the identity of the donor when they reach age 18.

Artificial Insemination by Donor and the Danger of Incest

When the sperm of a particular donor is used frequently in the same geographic area, particularly a small area, a danger of incest with attendant genetic problems is created. For this reason, the American Medical Association (1996, section E-2.05) correctly rules that physicians must takes steps "limiting the number of pregnancies resulting from a single donor source so as to avoid future consanguineous marriages or reproduction."

In this context, it should also be noted that the frequent use of medical students as donors can be seen as a sort of genetic imperialism in which physicians seek to reproduce their own kind at the expense of other groups in society. Quite aside from this, medical students may not be of the best genetic stock, no matter how rigid the screening for training as a physician.

IN VITRO FERTILIZATION

In vitro fertilization, or test tube fertilization, is used when for one reason or another the ovum of the woman cannot descend through the oviduct in order to be fertilized. It involves treating the woman with hormones to stimulate the production of ova, taking ova from the woman by a surgical procedure and taking sperm from the husband or donor, and bringing them together in a Petri dish. After conception has taken place and cell division has begun, the *conceptus* is mechanically introduced into the woman's uterus in the hope that it will nest and grow to maturity.

In addition to the problem of artificiality, there are several other specific objections to *in vitro* fertilization. The procedures are expensive and not covered by insurance, so only those with some wealth can attempt this method. In addition, most attempts do not succeed, so they need to be repeated. Added complications are introduced if the woman is not married, or if the sperm comes from a donor, or if the fertilized egg is not reintroduced into the woman but put into a second woman who will act as a surrogate mother. We will discuss the problems of the surrogate mother later. Here we will consider only the basic problems of the simpler case.

The Discard Problem

The *discard problem* arises from the fact that, at least in the pioneering days of the procedure, fertilized eggs that were not introduced into the woman were either discarded or used for experimental purposes. If the conceptus has a serious right to life, the discard would involve abortion and the experimentation would be human experimentation on an unwilling subject. We shall return to the ethics of experimentation in chapter 12.

The discard problem has been minimized because of improvement in techniques, which now use fewer eggs and increase the chances of nesting and a baby being born by introducing several fertilized eggs into the woman's vagina. The optimum number appears to be four fertilized eggs. The additional fertilized eggs are then frozen to provide material for additional attempts if the first implantation does not succeed. This has the added advantage of reducing the number of surgical procedures necessary to obtain eggs, but the freezing of eggs creates additional problems (discussed later in this chapter). Even by minimizing the number of eggs fertilized, this remains a serious problem, with the accumulation of thousands of frozen embryos over time.[1]

Rates of Success

There is wide variation in the success rate of *in vitro* fertilization. The couple has a right to accurate information about the success rate of the institution and physicians with whom they are dealing. Exact figures, rather than vague generalizations, are required if there is to be informed consent. A Centers for Disease Control (1997) study determined that approximately 24 percent of women treated for infertility got pregnant and 78 percent of these pregnancies resulted in live births. Individual clinics had success rates of from 7 percent to 35 percent. In addition, the couple should be informed of factors particular to their attempt that may affect the outcome. For example, endometrial receptivity (i.e., the sensitivity of the lining of the uterus) is reduced in stimulated cycles and is the biggest obstacle to the fertilized egg taking hold when implanted. Patients should be informed of this if such stimulation is to be used (Paulson and Sauer, 1990). This obligation to reveal the odds is all the more serious in that research has shown that failure tends to increase anxiety and depression in both husband and wife and create stress in the marriage (Shannon, 1990).

A new version of this occurs when a donor supplies the eggs (oocytes), which are fertilized *in vitro* and then implanted in the wife of the sperm donor. This has been done with postmenopausal women after proper preparation of the endometrium and has resulted in live births (Sauer, Paulson, and Long, 1990). In some cases the eggs were purchased from young women who answered an advertisement in the newspaper.

In all cases the attempts cost $10,000 and up, with three or four attempts often needed before an implantation, which, of course, does not guarantee a live birth. These cases raise questions about the proper use of health care resources, the sale of eggs, and the dangers of the procedure to the children of postmenopausal women.

Frozen Embryos, Sperm Banks, and Social Issues

Embryos are frequently frozen at the time of *in vitro* fertilization in case the embryos implanted first in the woman do not nest and reach birth; this is what gives rise to the discard problem. The frozen embryos are a reserve that can be used to avoid subjecting a woman to another operation to obtain ova. This technique could be used by people who wish to postpone reproduction for some time, but worry that their semen or ova may not be suitable at a later date. In these cases, the stored frozen embryo is introduced into the vagina of the biological mother or a surrogate at a future date when a child is desired.

Both the Rios case and the Davis case have shown that serious problems can result when there are no legal provisions to cover such problems as the right of the frozen embryo to be born and, in case the parents die, the rights of someone other than the parents to adopt the embryo and inherit from its estate (Ozar, 1985). In 1981, the Rioses, a very wealthy couple, had one fertilized egg implanted in the wife, and two were frozen. The implanted embryo spontaneously aborted, but Mrs. Rios was not ready for another implantation. Some time later the Rioses adopted a child. The husband, wife, and adopted child were all killed in an airplane crash in 1983.

According to the law of both Australia, where the conception took place, and the United States, where the Rioses were citizens, if the conceptus were born alive it could inherit the parents' wealth. It is not clear, however, whether, in the absence of a will, the child would be the child of the woman who bears it or the woman who supplied the egg. Similarly, is the child the child of the sperm donor or of some other father? If the donors, in the Rios case the married couple, are dead, who makes the decision as to whether the child will be born and as to who will have custody when born?

Laws on *in vitro* fertilization and related matters such as frozen embryos enacted by the Province of Victoria in Australia, the site of much research in this area, are informative (Singer, 1985). The law provides that only parents who are married may be treated and then only as a last resort and after at least a year of other treatments. The use of donated sperm, eggs, or embryos is also to be a last resort, either when there is no reasonable hope of a pregnancy or when, without the donation, the woman would risk having a child with a hereditary disorder. No payment may be made for sperm, eggs, or embryos, although related expenses can be covered.

In the case of frozen embryos, the law provides that, if the woman who donates the egg is incapable of receiving the embryo, she and the sperm donor may consent to the embryo being given to another woman. If that consent cannot be given because the donors are dead or untraceable, the minister of health may order the hospital to make the embryo available as a gift.

In the Davis case, a couple in Tennessee went to an *in vitro* fertilization clinic for assistance in becoming pregnant. The first attempt failed to produce a pregnancy, and before a second attempt could be made, the couple's marriage fell apart. In the divorce proceedings, a major issue was who would get control of the frozen embryos. Mrs. Davis wanted them so that she might bring them to term, while Mr. Davis, who wanted no part of future child support payments, wanted control so that he could have them destroyed. The court had to decide whether the embryos were persons or property, since each would be handled differently under Tennessee divorce law. The court judge decided that the embryos were more like persons, but he was overruled by the Tennessee Supreme Court, which called the embryos an "interim category," neither persons nor property. The Supreme Court was concerned that if the embryos were considered persons, the designation would interfere with the right to privacy of the woman.[2]

Although these legal provisions specify certain things and avoid others, they bypass serious philosophical and ethical issues. Is the frozen embryo a person and does it have a serious right to life? If it does, who has the obligation of fulfilling that right, especially when the "parents" are dead or no longer together? On the other hand, do even married couples have a right to have children by any means? These are questions that should be answered before more comprehensive laws on the subject are passed. In the meantime, it seems best to delay further implementation of the techniques that cause more problems for society than they solve.

Risks to the Mother and Child

The risks to the woman can be calculated, but the risks to the potential offspring are largely unknown. The risks to the woman include the risk of treatment with hormones, the risks of the operation (laparoscopy) and the anesthesia, the risk of damage to the uterus at the time of insertion, and the risks of ectopic gestation (a pregnancy outside the reproductive system) and of amniocentesis (discussed in chapter 10, in our consideration of ethics of testing and screening). Of particular importance is the fact that the hormones used to stimulate ovulation can dramatically increase the chance of ovarian cancer (Roloff, 1993).

One serious nonmedical risk associated with *in vitro* fertilization is the possibility of switching embryos and gametes (Robertson, 1996). There are several examples of this in recent years, the most dramatic being a Dutch woman who gave birth to fraternal twins, one white, one black, after a technician used an improperly cleaned pipette. Embryos have also been inadvertently lost or discarded. Given the dignity and serious right to life of the embryos, such carelessness is serious and harmful.

The largely unknown risks to the fetus complicate ethical judgments in this area. We do know that there is an increasing number of healthy children born as a result of *in vitro* fertilization and that many childless couples are willing to undergo the risks and the expenses associated with it. Although it would appear that the risks in general are not as great as some originally feared, there are risks, such as those associated with multiple births. Furthermore, there are always risks in any individual case and, as with all medical procedures, risk remains a relevant ethical factor, especially in an elective procedure (Cohen, 1996).

SURROGATE MOTHERS

Some fertile women cannot bear children because of some other defect in their reproductive system. In these cases it is possible to do an *in vitro* fertilization and then implant the fertilized egg in the uterus of another woman, who will deliver the baby and allow the baby to be adopted by the couple who supplied the egg and the sperm. In this case, the woman who adopts the child is actually the biological (or genetic) mother of the child, while the woman who carries the child to term is simply the gestational mother.

Another type of problem occurs when the woman has no fertile eggs. In these cases, the woman's husband artificially inseminates the surrogate, who agrees to let the initiating couple adopt. These surrogates may be recruited by newspaper advertisements, lawyers, or various profit and nonprofit groups interested in promoting surrogate motherhood. In practice, the surrogate mother has her health care expenses covered and is paid a fee. These fees, plus the uncertainty of who is responsible for the child and worries about coercion, raise serious ethical and legal objections to the use of surrogate mothers. Other objections of less importance are discussed by Robertson (1983) and Krimmel (1983).

In 1983, the American College of Obstetricians and Gynecologists issued a nonbinding set of guidelines entitled "Ethical Issues in Surrogate Motherhood" (Robertson, 1983). The guidelines note that the surrogate faces all the physical risks of pregnancy and its long-term health effects and even the remote possibility of death. There is also a danger of psychological harm when the surrogate is separated from the child. A consideration of all these risks must be part of the decision to participate. In addition, it is not at all clear whether the surrogate mother alone or the surrogate plus the adoptive parents should make decisions about the fetus. Included are decisions about smoking and alcohol use during pregnancy. There may be particular problems if the surrogate decides to abort the fetus over the objection of the adopting parents. The American College of Obstetricians and Gynecologists also raised questions about the dedication of couples to parenthood when they wish surrogate motherhood only as a convenience rather than for medical reasons. The guidelines particularly warn physicians against accepting payment for recruiting or referring potential surrogate mothers.

Although the fee may be viewed as compensating the surrogate for the inconvenience and risk of being pregnant, it is in fact a payment for the purchase of a baby. Robertson (1983) says that it is quibbling to question whether the couple is purchasing a service or buying a baby and holds that they are really buying the right to rear a child. No matter what may be said of that, most states have laws against selling babies, and others make adoptions illegal if money is paid for anything other than legitimate expenses. The commercial nature of the transaction appears in typical contracts (Krimmel, 1983), which provide genetic tests of the fetus and state that the surrogate must have an abortion if the child is defective, or keep the child herself. In the famous Baby M. case (see case 5 at the end of this chapter), the contract also provided that the surrogate took all risks, including the risk of death, and that she would be paid nothing if she miscarried before the fourth month and only $1,000 after the fourth month, even if the child was stillborn. If the surrogate handed over a live, healthy baby, she would be paid $10,000. The surrogate abdicated her legal right to abort unless the physician said it was necessary for her health. The surrogate also agreed not to smoke cigarettes, drink alcoholic beverages, or take medications without written consent from her physician.

Such provisions indicate that the fee is a payment for a healthy child and not for the rental of a uterus. In short, payment is rendered only for a satisfactory product. One can easily imagine a contract that had the same provisions about sex and eye color. No matter what one thinks is quibbling, it all looks too much like buying and selling a product and so treating a human being as a commodity, an object of commerce. Although the motive for all this may be a desire to share one's love with a child, the fact remains that the presence of fees—often large fees—makes the transaction very dubious despite some court decisions that have upheld the surrogate contract.

Because this is a gray area and best not left to the courts, legislation permitting and prohibiting or otherwise regulating surrogate motherhood has been introduced in many states. Among other proposed regulations are those that permit the surrogate a cooling-off period during which she can rescind the contract and requirements for counseling before the contract is signed. Between legislative battles and conflicting court decisions, we can expect a decade or more of struggle to resolve the problems posed by surrogate motherhood.

When the surrogate donates her services, as one sister might do for another, the problem of buying and selling babies is obviously not present, although the far more serious problem of responsibility for the child remains.

Responsibility for the Child

The ethical problem connected with responsibility for raising the child is well illustrated by the following case. Mr. and Mrs. Smith contract with Mrs. Jones to bear a child that will result from artificial insemination by Mr. Smith's sperm. Mrs. Jones delivers the baby, who turns out to be seriously retarded. The Smiths pay Mrs. Jones's delivery expenses but refuse to adopt the baby. Since the contract between Mrs. Jones and the Smiths is not enforceable in the particular state, the Jones are left with a baby that they do not want and who has some serious handicaps. The Jones then sue Mr. Smith for child support on the ground that he is the genetic father. A DNA test reveals that Mr. Smith could not have been the father and that Mr. Jones is the father. Presumably, Mr. Jones had intercourse with his wife at the time of the artificial insemination. The Smiths sue to get back the money they spent on Mrs. Jones's medical care.

In this case, no one wanted the child and it was not immediately clear who the father was. As a result, the responsibility for raising the child was blurred and settled only after medical testing and legal proceedings. It should be noted that another set of complications would have occurred if Mr. and Mrs. Jones did not want to give up the child. In this case, Mr. Smith could have sued for custody.

Some people argue in favor of surrogate motherhood on the grounds that it is just another form of adoption. Indeed, since one or both of the adopting parents might be a genetic parent of the child, it is argued that it is a very suitable form of adoption. This is simply not true in the absence of clear regulation. Davis (1985), writing in a British context, raises important points that are equally applicable in the United States. First, there is no careful screening of the suitability of the commissioning couple that wants to adopt the child of the surrogate mother. Not everyone should be allowed to adopt or to use the surrogate mother route. Second, there is no careful screening of the surrogate mother, thus increasing the chances that there may be unnecessary births of defective children. The mere fact that a surrogate is willing to carry the child does not mean that she is a suitable biological and gestational mother. The surrogate may have both genetic problems and habits that threaten the health of the fetus. Until such problems are solved by legal measures, the adoption analogy is unjustified.

All these difficulties could be mitigated if not solved by clarifications of the law. Indeed, nearly all the new methods of reproduction require such clarification. The specification of responsibility should not be left simply to contractual agreements, since society has an interest in deciding who is responsible for what. The task may not be simple, because there are fifty sets of state laws covering the problems. In 1986, Annas reported on Kentucky court decisions that approved baby sales if the price was agreed on *before conception* and gave the surrogate mother the right to cancel her contract up to the point where she gave up her parental rights. Further complications were introduced when the court decided that the donor of the egg would be the natural and so the legal mother and the sperm donor the natural father if (1) the surrogate had contracted to have the baby by *in vitro* fertilization, and (2) tissue typing confirmed the genetic links between the child and the gamete donors. It is not at all clear whether the rights of the child are really protected or even considered.

Rights of the Surrogate

Although the good of the child and, in particular, the protection of the child's future is the main concern, consideration must be given to the surrogate or gestational mother. Although the surrogate may agree to give up the child for adoption, she may form such an attachment to the child that she decides to keep it. At this point, she may be coerced into giving up the child by the threat of an expensive lawsuit or other harassment. While the law generally favors the gestational mother, the surrogate may not be able to afford a lawyer, and so the surrogate may be effectively blackmailed. Ethics obviously forbids this, but we need laws to protect the surrogate.

Taub (1985) believes that the surrogate is most likely to suffer psychologically when the child is given up. Indeed, the psychological dangers are such that an institutional review board (see chapter 12 on research ethics) would probably not permit surrogate motherhood if it was being carried out as a research project. This aspect of the problem certainly requires more careful study.

We must also face the fact that the presence of payment may tempt financially distressed women to agree to surrogate contracts against their best interests. Winslade (1981) discovered that 40 percent of the volunteer surrogate mothers were unemployed or on welfare. This is an additional reason why ethics would seem to forbid the payment of money other than for reasonable expenses.

Cohen (1984) suggests that the surrogate mother could be better protected if the states passed laws permitting revocable birth agreements, just as they now permit revocable adoption agreements. Such a law would forbid payment for anything but expenses and would leave the child with the gestational mother pending the settlements of any disputes.

The Uniform Status of Children of Assisted Conception Act (National Conference, 1988) is child-oriented, but does not take a definitive stand. The act offers the state two alternatives. Alternative A provides, among other things, for procedures like those used by well-run adoption agencies and an agreement that is void if not approved by a court. Alternative B makes all surrogacy agreements invalid. Neither alternative solves all problems. Those interested in the problems and legal intricacies should consult Yoon (1990).

THE CHARGE OF ARTIFICIALITY

Those who condemn the new reproduction methods as artificial do so because the artificial is inherently evil, because it risks harmful consequences, or because it involves venturing into the unknown.

The approach of practical wisdom used in this book emphasizes the consideration of all aspects of the experience and balancing the burdens and benefits in the light of human dignity. In the context of the new modes of reproduction, we can anticipate some problems because we know something about the problems involved in adoptions. Similarly, because people do not want just a child, but a certain type of child, we can anticipate trouble with surrogate mothering when the "right" type of child is not produced (Krimmel, 1983). Unfortunately, more often than not, we lack even analogical evidence about both the presence and the absence of risk. In these cases we are not dealing with the probability of an evil, but with fear of the unknown and *all the evils that could be there*.

The fear of the unknown is widespread, but it is not a justification for doing nothing. If humankind had refused to venture into the unknown because of what could happen, we would have made no progress and would still be living a very primitive existence. We are ethically justified in venturing into the unknown to obtain real goods. Indeed, granted the nature of human curiosity, we are probably justified in venturing into the unknown just because it is unknown.

If we take the artificiality objection to be a deontologically based argument, we are then faced with the need to distinguish between what is ethically and what is unethically artificial. Nearly all modern medicine, with its elaborate testing, complicated transplant surgery, and synthetically produced medications, is certainly artificial. Nature did not provide these directly to us. Yet, few would argue that the testing, surgery, and medications are unethical. Humans beings have merely used their natural talents to produce things that, while not found in nature, do come from our nature as thinking, problem-solving beings. Unethical artificiality must be something more than merely the synthetically produced.

If the objection to the concept of artificiality is made on a teleological basis (as in natural law), then the problem is not just one of identifying those human accomplishments that are supportive of, for example, human flourishing, and those that are not, but also one of clearly identifying what is human flourishing. Does assisted reproduction replace a fundamental human act (such as human sexuality), or does it augment a fundamental human act (the family) (Kass and Wilson, 1998)? This issue is particularly important as assisted reproduction blends with our developing abilities in genetic manipulation, such as cloning.

Which still leaves open an interesting and challenging problem for all ethics theories: are there any limits, natural or otherwise, to human efforts to alter the conditions of their existence? Assisted reproduction may or may not transgress these limits (if they are there), but this is only the first topic that raises the problem. Transplanted organs, xenographs, mechanical organs, genetic therapy, and genetic enhancements are all current or foreseeable medical interventions that may be unethically artificial. Many of the current "hot issues" in health care ethics rest on this disputed question of limits to our ability to change our existence. As has been clear throughout this chapter, these questions of limits cannot be answered by more medicine or more scientific research; rather they must be answered by society's ethics discussion.

Artificiality and the Family

Some of the thinkers who object to nearly all the new forms of reproduction do so on the basis of a required unity between love and procreation, that is, between the unitive and procreative function of sexual intercourse (Congregation for the Doctrine of the Faith, 1987; Kass and Wilson, 1998). This objection raises questions about what exactly is, or ought to be, a family.

One of the classic studies of the family as a social structure demonstrated that there are several different forms of the family, and that a majority of societies are polygamous (Murdock, 1949). The nuclear family (of mother, father and children) has been of necessity the biological building block of any familial structure, but social family structures have taken several forms, such as the corporate family and the extended family, as well as the nuclear family and modern forms as the *kibbutz* or the single parent family. Changes in the social family structure have been driven by changes in the economic system. In particular, the effect of industrialization has been to encourage the nuclear family because of the economic advantages of mobility and focused responsibilities, and the role the family plays as a consumer rather than a producer of goods and services. In the modern economy, the work of socialization of children has been shifted from the family to public schools and day care; even health care has been taken out of the family, as pediatricians have replaced grandparents as a source of experienced advice in caring for children.

Given the historical variety of types of family, and the contemporary changes in the family, those who insist that there is a most natural form and function to the family have a tough argument to make. As mentioned above, some argue that there should be a union of love and procreation in establishing a family and raising children. But, while this is undoubtedly a romantic ideal, it is not always possible, as in, for example, the case of infertile couples. More basically, this view of the relation between social and natural function is neither as traditional nor as universal as might be thought.

Thus, the idea of the family is of more limited use in establishing claims of artificiality than it appears at first. Faced with a (conceptually) modest problem of a couple's infertility, the question then becomes the force of our ethical position in the face of a medically correctable condition. A young, married couple who wish to have children seem to be ideal candidates for assisted reproduction. The natural desire is present, the social structure is present, and the only element missing is a medically correctable condition. But how far do we go in giving people control over their biological nature? Even more problematic is the situation in which individuals want to control procreation using medical tools, for example, post-menopausal women who wish to have children. This aspect of the problem of artificiality is found not only in new methods of reproduction, but also in genetic research, transplants, and even cosmetic surgery. This question of limits goes well beyond the ordinary ground of health care ethics, and takes us into areas of ontology and metaphysics that are the focal points for the deepest struggles of the contemporary age. We cannot solve these issues here, but it is clear that we will all live out the solutions we as a society devise.

THE ETHICS OF THE HEALTH CARE PROVIDER

The health care provider is supposed to do what is medically indicated, given the informed consent of the patient. The first question, then, is whether the new reproductive modes are medically indicated. This involves asking whether they are aimed at making up for a defect in the reproductive organs of the people involved or are merely ways for healthy people to avoid some of the inconveniences of reproduction. When the new reproductive mode makes up for a defect in the human reproductive system, we are dealing with a medical problem and the question becomes one of proportionality; that is, whether more good than harm will be done from a medical point of view.

There will be particular doubts about medical indications if the treatment includes provision for the abortion of fetuses found to be probably, or possibly, or definitely defective in the course of the pregnancy. Indeed, if abortion is unethical except when some serious right of the mother is threatened, such eugenic abortion and its inclusion in the surrogate mother or *in vitro* fertilization agreements should be condemned.

If the new reproductive mode is merely a way for healthy people to avoid the inconveniences of reproduction, we are not dealing with a medical problem at all, but with the sale of a service to whomever is willing to pay for it. This would occur in the case of the single man or woman who wants a baby without having what they consider the emotional involvement of intercourse or the difficulties of pregnancy. The woman wants donor insemination and the man wants to hire a surrogate mother. A woman might also want a surrogate mother when she wants a child, but views a pregnancy as interfering with her career. The case is similar with parents who want to store a frozen embryo as a safeguard against a future loss of fertility. In all these cases, convenience rather than medical indication is at the root of the request. For this reason, the involvement of health care professionals is at least inappropriate. It can easily be unethical, because some of the procedures involve risks that are unnecessary for healthy people. Performing an operation to procure eggs for in vitro fertilization when no health problem exists does not meet the requirements of proportionality for a health care provider.

The problem is more serious than merely a question of medical indication versus convenience. There is also a question of whether a health care provider should cooperate in activities that, if not illegal, are socially problematic and possibly unethical. As noted earlier, single-parent families are considered less than ideal. It is questionable whether health care providers should help in creating more single-parent families.

Serious problems arise when the husband has not consented to donor insemination, since the evils of adultery reappear. It is not ethical for health care providers to facilitate adultery. Furthermore, when the husband has not consented, legal problems arise about who is responsible for the child, since in this case it is easy for the husband to disavow the child and to prove that he is not the father (Annas, 1984). To create such a situation hardly accords with the most basic of obligations to do good and avoid evil.

Since the use of surrogate mothers generally involves payments that might violate the slavery laws or others laws involving adoption, the health care professional should be particularly careful. Such procedures would appear to call for health care professionals to have their own legal counsel in these matters. More importantly, the provider should beware of involvement in situations in which the offspring may be the victim, since the assignment of legal responsibility is not always clear. In short, the risks involved are such that it would take a very serious reason to justify cooperation, even when the reproductive procedure might seem medically indicated. In other words, the presence of medical indications in the adult patients does not mean that the provider can disregard the good of the offspring and of society.

Although medicine and the health care professions have generally and correctly concentrated on the good of the patient, the good of society needs particular consideration in the case of the new modes of reproduction. A defective child is generally a burden on society, as well as on the parents. The health care providers should certainly do all they ethically can to avoid the conception of such children. The physician has an obligation to screen donors of semen for genetic defects and other disorders that affect the fetus. Other disorders might include drug addiction, alcoholism, AIDS, and herpes. It seems clear that surrogate mothers and host mothers who hold embryo transfers in the intermediate stage should also be screened, on the grounds that there is no justification for exposing the offspring and society to unnecessary problems. Once again, legal provisions for screening would seem to be in order.

We will go a step farther and say that the health care provider would be unethical if he or she aided the reproductive activities of people who are obviously unfit to be parents or when there might be special problems for the children. For example, drug addicts, alcoholics, child abusers, and a whole array of emotionally unstable individuals are obviously unfit to be parents. In cases of doubtful competence in parenting, we need more information about consequences before we can give either definitive approval or definitive condemnation to either a class of new reproductive methods or an individual case of a new mode of reproduction.

A QUESTION OF DISTRIBUTIVE JUSTICE

The new modes of reproduction involve more than risks to children and society. They cost money and they use scarce health care resources. Those that involve *in vitro* fertilization and surrogate mothers generally involve a great deal of money and large amounts of medical resources. Since these are not covered by health insurance, let alone Medicaid, use of the new modes of reproduction will be the privilege of those who are comfortable economically. This raises the question of social or distributive justice. The conclusions of chapter 4 are applicable here. First, the central task of health care is to meet the needs of human dignity, such as maintaining and restoring health and alleviating pain. Second, society has a duty to provide its members with access to an adequate level of health care that fulfills basic needs. Third, in the interests of social contributions, society must permit individuals to purchase more than the care adequate for basic needs. Ideally, the additional care should be purchased only when the basic needs of all have been met.

In view of these conclusions, the authors argue that *ideally* no resources should be diverted to the new modes of reproduction until the basic health care needs of all have been satisfied. In practice, this is not possible, given the rights of individuals to dispose of their own resources.

In any event, we argue that the new modes of reproduction cannot be considered necessary for basic health care needs. For this reason, there should be no direct government support or insurance coverage for the new modes of reproduction, particularly when the new mode is used only for the convenience of the patient and not to remedy or bypass a physical defect. In these cases, the services do not constitute health care or any essential good. It would be foolish to spend public monies to gratify an individual's or couple's desire for convenience.

The use of public monies or insurance to pay for even "medically indicated" services does not appear to be part of what constitutes adequate health care. In the first place, the services do not remedy the defect in the person, but merely bypass it. The defect, moreover, is a problem only when the person wants children. The defect does not lead to sickness or death or serious impairment of day-to-day functioning. It does not seem right to devote public funds or insurance funds to the treatment of such a defect while there are far more serious problems that call for resources.

We do not think that there is any injustice in society deciding that people do not have a right to these particular services. Indeed, the new modes of reproduction raise the question of the justification of all sorts of health provider activities that may be profitable, but do not make good sense either in terms of the healing function of the professions or the shortage of resources.

SUMMARY

The new methods of reproduction currently available for patients stretch the meaning of the social institution of the family and raise a wide variety of ethical problems. But given the desire of most people to have children, these medical advances are likely to stay with us. While natural law positions remain skeptical of the ethical appropriateness of the interventions in the natural process of reproduction, most other positions have less sweeping but still serious objections.

Many of the basic problems arise with artificial insemination and focus on the stability and usefulness of marriage as a focus for child-rearing. The potential for injuring one of the spouses or for neglecting the children conceived through AI is troublesome. Health problems may arise when the donor's identity and health history is concealed or never known. These problems exist when either donated sperm or donated eggs are used. *In vitro* fertilization leads to the difficulties involved with the use of frozen embryos and to concerns with genetic screening and genetic manipulation of the embryos. Surrogate motherhood, by separating the genetic and gestational roles of the mother, adds additional confusion to questions of economic and social responsibility for the child, especially if the child suffers a congenital problem.

At the heart of the problem is the society's changing understanding of what constitutes a family, and with that the question of what is unacceptably artificial in generating a family. The notion of what a family is changes with historical, particularly economic, developments and there is room in that history for further development. Clarifying these questions about assisted reproduction will undoubtedly add to that history.

A final concern is the question of distribution. As these new reproductive technologies are produced, the importance of these new abilities must be balanced against the obligation to provide a basic minimum for health care for everyone. In this task, the desire to have children must be weighed against the problems of sickness or death suffered by others, and resources must be distributed accordingly.

CASES FOR ANALYSIS

1. Mr. and Mrs. Baldinucci, citizens of the United States, are in their thirties and have been married for ten years. Mrs. Baldinucci has a congenital defect that prevents her from having children. The Baldinuccis are well-educated professionals, easy in their relationship, and respected in their community. They have tried to adopt a child, but have grown impatient with the delays. At this point, they approach an agency that offers to find an English surrogate mother for a fee of $9,000.

Mr. Baldinucci goes to England to give sperm. The surrogate mother is inseminated by a nurse. In a recorded interview, the surrogate claims that she conceived with the second insemination attempt. She voluntarily gives up her parental rights for a fee, leaves the hospital some hours after the birth of the child, and has not seen the child since. The Baldinuccis then apply for guardianship of the child. The court, considering only the interests of the child, grants them custody on condition that they return to Britain if the court should so order. There is no way to enforce this condition since the couple have no property in England. The couple then return to the United States with the child in their custody, but not legally adopted.

There are doubts as to the citizenship of the child and her rights to inherit. She is at best the illegitimate daughter of Mr. Baldinucci, the natural father, and has no legal claims on Mrs. Baldinucci.

The gestational mother receives the sum of $30,000 for her story from a magazine, which runs the story without her name but with a picture. The agency that had arranged the agreement refuses to pay the surrogate her fee, since she has made so much from the story.

The basic question is whether the good of the child has been adequately protected. What more should be done to protect the child? Is an American adoption by Mrs. Baldinucci in order? Was the gestational mother risking harm to the child by publishing her story and picture? Was the agency ethical when it refused to pay the surrogate because she made money from the story?

2. A couple has three children, aged seventeen, fourteen, and twelve. The seventeen-year-old has leukemia that has resisted all attempts at a cure. As a last resort, the oncologist recommends a bone marrow transplant. Unfortunately, the patient has a rare tissue type and no appropriate donor can be found. The parents recognize that if they had another child, this new child might have the same tissue type as their oldest (the fourteen- and twelve-year olds do not have it). If so, this child could then be the needed bone marrow donor. They are referred to a fertility specialist for help in becoming pregnant (they are in their mid-forties and need *in vitro* fertilization due to an earlier tubal ligation) and for any help that can be given in having a child with the "right" tissue type. A new technique that has been developed which allows the physician to genetically screen embryos. After *in vitro* fertilization a cell is removed from each embryo and tested to see if it is the genetic match the couple is looking for. If it is, that embryo will be used for an attempt at implantation. If it is not, it is destroyed. Is this an appropriate reason to become pregnant? Is the attempt to select a compatible embryo ethically appropriate?

3. Jessie and James married young and had hopes to quickly start a family. Unfortunately, Jessie is discovered to have endometriosis, and her physician thinks she has little chance of conceiving, although she does have healthy ovaries. Jessie's mother, an active woman in her early forties, volunteers to be a gestational mother for a child conceived with Jessie's ovum and James sperm.

Is it ethically important that the gestational mother is the child's natural grandmother? How would that affect the emotional relationships in the family? Is it possible to talk about what is best for the child in this situation?

4. John and Mary, a childless couple, feel that only a child can save their marriage. They do not, however, want to interrupt their careers with a pregnancy. They start thinking that the use of a surrogate mother might be a solution to their problem. The marriage counselor tries to convince them that their marriage has basic problems and a child will only make the marriage more difficult. Indeed, the counselor argues that it would be very unfair to bring a child into a family that is bordering on breakdown. Despite this advice, John and Mary go to a lawyer and pay for a surrogate mother, whom they have not met.

Rosha, the surrogate mother, age thirty-four, has recently been discharged from a state mental hospital and has a long history of alcoholism and drug addiction. Both of Rosha's parents were diabetics, and one of her brothers has mild Down's syndrome. The surrogate contract calls for her to refrain from smoking and drinking and taking drugs during the pregnancy, but her previous history gives little assurance that she will abide by these provisions. Her husband reluctantly agrees to the surrogate contract.

What are the appropriate social controls for surrogate motherhood? Should there be standards of qualification for surrogate mothers, enforced by a certified social agency? Would qualifications that limit access to this economic activity be discriminatory? Considering the particular surrogate mother in this case and the problems of the adopting couple, are John and Mary ethical in signing the contract?

5. In what came to be known as the Baby M. case, Mary Beth Whitehead, married to Richard Whitehead at age sixteen, agrees to be a surrogate mother. The contract specifies that the wife of the adopting couple is infertile and provides for the payment of $10,000 for a healthy child. Mary Beth already has two children of her own, but is inspired by the infertility of her sister, whom she hoped would conceive if she herself became pregnant.

In accord with the agreement, Mrs. Whitehead is artificially inseminated with the sperm of William Stern, married to Elizabeth Stern. When the child is born, Mrs. Whitehead does not want to give up the child; she refuses to sign the adoption papers and flees to her parents' home in Holiday, Florida. She keeps the child there for four months until the court gives temporary custody to the Sterns. Mrs. Whitehead says that at the end, something took over and overpowered her so that she could not give up the child. Her obstetrician says that during her three days in the hospital she was distraught and cried constantly.

The Sterns sue in New Jersey to enforce the agreement, to strip Mary Beth of all parental rights, to win custody, and to prevent Mary Beth from having any visitation rights.

Mr. Whitehead has served thirteen months of active duty in Vietnam. On discharge he became a truck driver for construction and sanitation companies. He was injured in an accident and blinded in the left eye. In December 1973 he married Mary Beth, eight years his junior. The following year they had their first child, Ryan, a boy. In January 1976, they had a daughter. In 1978, Richard fell asleep at the wheel after drinking and hit three poles. He lost his driver's license and truck driver's job. He entered Alcoholics Anonymous. At this time, Mary Beth took a job as a dancer and bartender in her sister Beverly's bar for a few months. Over the course of their marriage, she had also earned money cleaning houses, running coat-check counters, and selling ski equipment in department stores at Christmas. The couple separated for six months at one time. During at least part of this period, Mr. Whitehead was working for the sanitation department at an annual salary of $28,500. They were still in financial trouble and failed to make a lump sum payment on a house they had bought in 1986 from the sister, who then sued to foreclose.

Witnesses testify that Mrs. Whitehead is an excellent mother, and no one even remotely suggests that she neglects or abuses her children. Proof of such would be necessary to declare her an unfit mother.

One mental health expert testifying on behalf of the Sterns diagnoses Mrs. Whitehead as having "mixed personality disorder." Another does not confirm this, but describes her as impulsive, overly dramatic, self-centered, and in need of psychotherapy.

The Sterns put education and careers ahead of marriage and children. They had dated for five years before marrying in July 1974. They were in their late twenties at the time of their marriage. Mr. Stern had a doctorate in chemistry and she had one in human genetics. Right after the marriage, Mrs. Stern began medical studies and decided to put off pregnancy until she finished her residency, at which time she would be thirty-six. By the time she had finished her residency, the couple had rejected the idea of having their own children. During the previous years, Mrs. Stern had suffered several symptoms of multiple sclerosis, such as brief numbness in her toes and legs and blurred vision. She diagnosed herself as having multiple sclerosis. The Sterns saw pregnancy as a risk of aggravating the symptoms. The condition was not independently diagnosed until they were in the middle of the custody battle, and the doctors considered the symptoms mild. Some neurologists would urge a woman with Mrs. Stern's symptoms to have a child if she so desired.

Mr. Stern feels a great need for a child and says he loved this child more than he loves his wife. The depth of the need seems to spring from the fact that he lost all his relatives except his parents in the Nazi camps in World War II. He has a need, according to one doctor, to show love to someone to whom he is biologically related.

Is there evidence that either couple would be adequate parents? Do the motives of the two couples have any ethical significance? Were the best interests of the child protected at all times? What are the interests of the society?

NOTES

1. As an example, review the controversy in England in the summer of 1996 over the first effects of a law mandating that frozen embryos were not be kept longer than five years. Several thousand embryos were to be destroyed, and there was a great outcry over this "carnage," as well as great confusion over how to avoid it.

2. For a discussion of the Davis case, see *Biolaw*, Vol. 2, pp. U2415-2419.

10

THE ETHICS
OF TRANSPLANTS

INTRODUCTION

The problems connected with organ transplants are material for the drama of life and death and the romance of new technology. The problems also involve ethical decisions for donors and recipients, as well as for members of the health care team and ultimately for society as a whole. The answers to some of the ethical questions shift with changes in the state of the art and the changing level of risk involved. The answers may also change as the availability of organs increases or decreases or as society is more or less able or willing to pay for transplants. The underlying problems remain the same. When is it ethical to donate an organ? When is it obligatory to donate an organ? Is it always ethical for the patient to accept an organ? What are the medical criteria for the allocation of organs? What should society pay for in the area of transplants? These are the principal concerns of the present chapter.

Many transplant procedures also pose questions about the ethics of experimentation. Finally, there are questions of informed consent involving patients and donors or the surrogates of the deceased in the case of cadaver transplants. The question of informed consent in experimental procedures will be treated in chapter 12.

In the pages that follow we will first consider the ethical problems of the donor and the recipient and then move on to the more complicated problems of the health care team and of the entire health care system.

THE ETHICS OF ORGAN DONATION

The Ethics of the Living Donor

The ethics of the living human donor are strongly influenced by the question of whether the donation involves a renewable resource, such as blood or bone marrow, or paired nonrenewable organs, such as the corneas or the kidneys, or nonpaired nonrenewable organs, such as the heart or the liver.

Today there are few ethical problems with the donation of a renewable resource such as blood, since there are no real dangers to the donor and few to the recipient if the blood has been properly screened for such things as AIDS. On the other hand, bone marrow transplants involve risk and some pain to the donor. These facts, plus the varying rates of success, make the calculation of proportionality a little more complex than in the case of blood donation.

The donation of a nonpaired, nonrenewable organ such as the heart or the liver from a living donor spells death for the donor. The donation of such an organ *inter vivos* (between living persons) would be unethical except in rare cases, unless one approves of altruistic suicide. The rare exception arises when a living donor gives his or her heart as the donor is simultaneously about to receive a heart and lungs from a third party. The exception arises because in this case the donation of the heart does not entail death.

All this presupposes that the donor gives informed consent. A special problem arises when the living donor is a child, even a child conceived to provide compatible bone marrow for a sibling. The surrogates who must give permission for such a transplant must operate in the best interests of the donor and have no right to subordinate the good of one child for the benefit of another. Indeed, to conceive a child as a source of a transplant seems to reduce the child to the level of a mere instrument. For these reasons, the authors seriously question the ethics of such transplants. Possible exceptions are treated in chapter 12.

The Living Donor of Nonrenewable Paired Organs

The only nonrenewable paired organs that can be donated are our corneas, lungs, and kidneys. The donation of these is not unethical per se, although attended by risks that need to be justified by proportionality. As we saw in chapter 3, there can be no proportional reason for risking harm if a harm-free or less risky alternative is available. In the case of transplants, the less risky alternative of cadaver donations can raise ethical questions about donations *inter vivos*. That is, the alternatives remain a part of the consideration of the proportionality needed to justify taking risks. Whether the cadaver donation is a true alternative depends on such factors as availability and the success rate of cadaver transplants in a given institution.

The exact nature of the alternative changes with the state of the art and is sometimes hotly debated among experts. Today the alternatives are such that there would seem to be few if any cases when it would make sense for a living person to donate a cornea. The supply of cadaver corneas has increased to the point where the need for a living donor is rare.

The case of kidney donation is more complicated because cadaver kidneys are in short supply and because the success rate with cadaver donations is not, at this writing, equal to the success rate of *inter vivos* donations between matched relatives. This advantage, however, will be lost as immunosuppressant drugs and better matching take away the advantage of having a donation from a living relative.

Proportionality in Transplants

For the sake of exploring the ethics of the living donor of a matched nonrenewable organ, let us assume that a kidney donation *inter vivos* offers the best hope in a given case. What are the factors that must enter into the ethical calculation of proportionality? Since the transplantation of the kidney involves an operation with general anesthesia, there is risk of death and of blood clots that can do serious damage (Starzl, 1985). The donor, having given his or her backup kidney, has increased the risks if anything should happen to the remaining kidney. These risks might be significant if the donor is a relative. In those cases, family history often indicates that the donor, too, is at risk. Other abilities or disabilities of the particular donor will also enter into the calculation. For example, a hemophiliac (a bleeder) risks more than a healthy person when there is a question of a major operation. A single person has less at stake than a married person with ten children. A donor who can afford excellent medical care if anything goes wrong is in a different position than the person who has no way of getting adequate care. All this becomes part of the equation.

The size and nature of the risk versus the possible good to the recipient are crucial factors. If the potential donor comes from a family with a history of kidney problems and the transplant has a low chance of success, the ethical balance changes. The living donor must consider these medical burdens and benefits. In addition to the medical factors, the donor must also consider all obligations to family, friends, society, and self in deciding whether potential goods to the recipient outweigh the potential harms to all the other people who will be affected. The donor,

like patients in general, must consider the proportionality of the consequences, *all things considered*.

For both the donor and the health care professional, their decisions
are further complicated by medical controversy regarding the use of the
immunosuppressant cyclosporine versus careful matching with traditional
immunosuppressants (Department of Health and Human Services, 1986).
There are also problems with patients who have had or rejected a previous
transplant or who have been exposed to foreign HLA antigens through
blood transfusions. Patients who have been sensitized to these antigens are
difficult and at times impossible to match. The National Task Force
(Department of Health and Human Services, 1986) noted that half of all
those awaiting cadaveric kidney transplants in the United States were
already sensitized. Only greater organ sharing with groups that have par-
ticipated in serum-sharing programs can hope to meet the needs of many
of these sensitized patients. This is not the place to discuss such technical
matters in detail, since research may alter the debate from day to day. It
should be clear that the state of the art in such areas dictates the medical
feasibility and so the ethics of many transplantations.

The Living but Terminal Donor

The possibility of transplanting from terminal patients and, in particular, from anencephalic infants raises numerous of questions (Capron,
1987). The basic question, however, is simply whether it is ethical to terminate the life of the donor to supply an organ or tissue to a patient. The
answer would appear to be a clear no. The fact that the anencephalic
infant[1] is going to die in a short time does not mean that it is already dead
or without dignity and rights. Treatment may be ethically terminated and
the dying process shortened for the sake of the infant, but the actual killing
of the child in order to get its tissues is impossible to distinguish from murder no matter how noble the intent. Thus, neither the patient nor the surrogate has a right to consent to such a transplant.

Transplanting Fetal Tissue

Animal experimentation with the transplantation of fetal tissue has
created the possibility of new treatments for diseases due to brain deterioration. While we will return to the issue of fetal experimentation in the
chapter on the ethics of research, a few remarks are in order with regard
to the use of tissue from live fetuses (Mahowald, Silver, and Ratcheson,
1987).

This is a complex issue and would require a chapter of its own for adequate treatment. We confine ourselves to two remarks and a brief comment

on the use of brain tissue from anencephalic fetuses. First, in line with what has been said in chapters 8 and 9 great care is necessary in any area in which widespread adoption of a practice can lead to disrespect for human dignity and human life. Second, in the present case, even if the tissue is from a dead fetus, the informed consent of parents should be required, lest fetal tissue be treated as so much throwaway material that has no dignity. This is no more than an extension of our culture's centuries-long insistence on decent burial and other signs of respect for the dead. In the authors' opinion, even such small protections of human dignity should not be disregarded.

Since the first edition of this book, there has been increasing pressure to take organs from anencephalic fetuses. Such fetuses lack a brain except for rudimentary brain stem tissue. This condition, which is generally diagnosed *in utero*, is such that even if a child is born it will not live for very long. Because the brain stem deteriorates in time, anencephalic infants or fetuses that are to be used for transplants would have to be respirated and kept alive until the moment of transplant. This poses its own ethical problem (Berger, 1989).

Perhaps because the condition is hopeless, many parents of such fetuses wish to donate the organs for use in other children. Although we see no difficulty with such donation after the child dies, we cannot approve the killing of the fetus for transplants. Such killing comes too close to infanticide and the treatment of living human tissue as a mere means. We are, of course, against raising fetuses for the mere purpose of creating transplant tissue.

For a rather conservative but still useful consideration of these problems, see Berger (1989).

Selling Organs

Some people are morally repelled by the idea of selling blood or organs. They see it as degrading to make even a part of a person an object of commerce. The National Organ Transplant Act of 1984 (Public Law 98-507) goes so far as to forbid the sale of organs in interstate commerce, and some states ban payment for specific organs. The usual arguments in favor of the law may be summarized as follows. First, selling organs will make it harder for the poor to get expensive organs and so make equality of access to treatment more difficult. Second, the poor will be tempted to sell their organs in time of great need and will be exploited. Third, organs should be looked on as a national resource. Another argument (Murray, 1987), while not condemning sale outright, sees donation of organs as such a strong bonding agent in society that the sale of organs should be strongly discouraged. These arguments demand some comment.

Viewing organs as a national resource is dangerous if it implies that the organs belong to the society rather than the individual. Since it seems clear that the organ belongs to the individual, it follows that *prima facie*, that is, presumptively, it is ethical to sell the organ whenever it is ethical to donate the organ. At the same time, the social bonding function of donation points up goods such as dignity and self-respect that are obtained by donation and not by sale. Since the social bonding, that is, the increase in felt community union, is particularly beneficial, the balance of good would generally favor donation over sale. A consideration of additional problems with sale reinforces this general conclusion.

The first problem that might result from widespread sale of organs involves the exploitation of the poor. The second involves a distribution of organs in accord with the ability to pay, rather than on the basis of need.

The problem of exploitation of the poor arises from the fact that those in need may be tempted to sell organs without consideration of the alternatives and without concern for the long-range health consequences. The problem exists even in the sale of blood, but this problem is not as serious, since blood is a renewable resource. Organs, however, do not renew themselves, with the result that a donation is a serious matter. The temptation can be very great when an advertisement in the newspaper offers huge sums for a kidney. This is particularly true when the organs are to be imported from poor nations in which even modest sums by American standards may seem enormous to the donor. At the same time, paternalistic protection of those who are allegedly exploited poses its own ethical problems. From the poor seller's point of view, being "exploited" may be a lesser evil than seeing his children suffer from malnutrition or go without proper shelter.

Granted that, all things considered, selling the organ might be the greater good for the impoverished organ seller, it is still based on an exploitation of the seller's extreme need and so should not be encouraged. It is not, however, the selling itself that is wrong, but the exploitation. Insofar as this exploitation results from conditions supported by society, society should change the conditions or at least regulate the sale of organs to prevent exploitation through coercion or price gouging. The right of the seller, however, should not be completely denied when lesser measures will provide protection.

If the selling of organs spreads, a strong market for organs may develop, the price may soar, and the distribution of organs would be based on the ability of the few to pay the high prices rather than on medical need. Assuming that organ transplants are socially defined as part of adequate care, this adds to the complications of the humane distribution of organs, which will be discussed later. It is obvious that the health care system already works to favor those with more resources. This is true even in England and other countries that have systems of socialized medicine. As noted in chapter 4, this is not necessarily unethical if the system provides adequate, but not necessarily maximum, care for all.

With Andrews (1986), we note that the dangers that might occur from selling organs can be controlled by laws that prohibit brokering organs and make sure that the sale was truly voluntary.

The social bonding argument, which stresses important human and community benefits that arise from the donation of blood and organs, rests on and seeks to promote a series of important values. First, it sees the body as belonging to that class of things that are sacred and so not really suitable for trade or ordinary barter. Second, it stresses the noncontractual bonds that arise from gift giving and serve to create healthy noncontractual obligations between families and whole societies. Third, both these values are valuable counterbalances to commercialized and bureaucratic life, which can break down the sense of both individual worth and communal solidarity.

We believe that all these points argue against the sale of organs, but not to the extent that makes sales, *per se*, unethical. The social bonding arguments do, however, give us an ideal to strive for. We conclude that, although the sale of organs cannot be considered necessarily unethical, caution is in order.

The Ethics of Cadaver Organ Donation

The ethics of organ donation after the donor is dead are obviously much simpler than the ethics of donation *inter vivos*. There are, however, legal and ethical problems.

Some Background: Brain Death

The development of our ability to transplant organs has challenged our ability to understand the precise nature of death. When dealing with a cadaver donation, it is important to harvest and transplant the organ as quickly as possible. This puts great importance on the ability of the physician to determine as precisely as possible the moment of death of the patient. This raises concerns about the philosophical ambiguity regarding the nature of death (as well as the beginning of life, see chapter 8), and has created a debate over the criteria for death. The philosophical and even theological ambiguity about the nature of death is clearly seen in the disputes about whether death is the end of all existence, a reentry into another life on earth, or the passage to an eternity of happiness or punishment. Even a generalized definition, such as death as a complete change in the status of the living being characterized by the irreversible loss of those functions essentially significant to it or death as the irreversible loss of capacity for social interaction (Veatch, 1987), does not solve the problem. We still need social agreement as to which characteristics are essentially significant and what level of social interaction is sufficient.

Although legal definition is accepted by all the states, the Uniform Determination of Death Act (UDDA) has been adopted by many and provides as follows:

An individual who has sustained either (1) irreversible cessation of circulatory and respiratory functions or (2) irreversible cessation of *all functions of the entire brain including the brain stem* is dead. A determination of death must be made in accordance with accepted medical standards (italics added).

The Harvard criterion of irreversible coma (Beauchamp and Perlin, 1978) is an example of one set of medical standards. These criteria call first for the elimination of the possibility of hypothermia and coma induced by barbiturates and then the application of the following four tests: (1) unreceptivity and unresponsivity even to intensely painful stimuli, (2) no movement or breathing during an hour-long period of observation, (3) no reflexes, and (4) a flat electroencephalogram. All these tests are to be repeated twenty-four hours later. Other tests are suggested by various groups (Beauchamp and Perlin, 1978). The point to be stressed is that the process of deciding that someone is brain dead is not a matter of a single, simple criterion.

Where this statute on the rights of the terminally ill is in force, society accepts the irreversible cessation of all brain functions according to accepted medical criteria as the death of the person. The person should be pronounced dead, and there is no need for the permission of the surrogates to cease treatment, but there are still questions about consent for donation. Cranford (1988) notes that delicacy requires one to discuss the pronouncement with the family so that they will understand.

Problems with Donation

The Uniform Anatomical Gift Act makes it legal for a person to will his or her body or body parts for medical research or for transplants. Legally, the valid consent of the donor gives the person authorized to receive the gift the right to possess the organ for the uses specified by the donor. Peters (1986, p. 248) holds that this right of the person authorized to receive the gift is "paramount to the rights of others and is preempted only by the rights of coroners, medical examiners, and physicians to conduct autopsies under conditions described in the state's death laws. . . ."

Cadaver donations include not only kidneys, but such single organs as heart, liver, lung, pancreas, and spleen. The list will undoubtedly grow as medical techniques advance.

In general, there is no dispute about the ethical correctness of a person donating organs for use after death. Indeed, such a donation is not ethically neutral, but praiseworthy as a service to one's fellow human beings with no risk of danger to oneself. None of the major religious groups forbids cadaver organ transplants as long as due respect is shown to the body of the deceased. There are problems, however, if a person's religious or philosophical position considers such donation as involving unwarranted mutilation of the body and so disrespect for the dignity of the human body. Such beliefs bind the donor and, as we shall see later, challenge laws that would provide for automatic harvesting of organs without the permission of the dead person or the surrogates.

Is There an Obligation to Donate?

Here, as elsewhere in this chapter, a distinction must be made between an obligation to make a donation between two living persons (*inter vivos*) and an obligation to will all or part of one's body for the help of others, whether that be by way of transplant, blood transfusion, or a harvesting of chemicals in the body.

Although risking one's life, even laying it down for another, may be an altruistic ideal, it is not an obligation. There is no natural or legal obligation, contractual or otherwise, to sacrifice an organ for the good of another person even when the principle of proportionality is satisfied. One individual is not subordinated to another individual even in the areas of life and death. Yet, when the risk to the donor is minimal and the potential benefit to the recipient is great, the person who refuses to help when asked is hardly worthy of praise. This minimal risk is the case with regard to blood transfusions, but certainly not the case with respect to kidney donations.

Granted that a donation *inter vivos* is not obligatory, we may ask if a person is obliged to donate a cadaver or parts of it. At first glance, there appears to be an obligation to donate the cadaver or cadaver part, since the donation can do a great deal of good with no possible harm to the donor. Not to donate would appear to be a form of indifference to the welfare of other human beings. It might even be taken as denying the dignity of the other.

In practice, the complexities of human feeling make this prima facie, or presumptive, obligation problematic. Supported by some religions, individuals can have strong feelings about mutilation and so would oppose donation. In particular, the sensibilities of the survivors may make the would-be donor hesitant to sign over her or his body. Others may feel that the whole process of transplantation is unnatural and should be discouraged. In short, the symbolic meanings of the body and of organ transplantation are factors that prevent us from arguing conclusively to an obligation to donate. These same factors must be considered when we return to the question of whether society ought to abolish the requirement that informed consent be obtained for even cadaver organ donations.

THE ETHICS OF THE RECIPIENT

The would-be recipient of an organ transplant is most often in a desperate condition. No matter how serious the condition, ethical demands are still made on the recipient. Obviously, the recipient must consider whether the transplant will produce more harm than good, all things considered. Once the recipient has been properly informed by the health care team, the effects of the transplant on the recipient's quality of life and on family and society must be taken into consideration. The expense of the transplant and the equally expensive aftercare, often not covered by insurance, are very relevant factors. Unfortunately, the financial effects on others are also ethically relevant. This is particularly true if the transplant promises no more than a few months of tortured life, but guarantees agony and poverty for the survivors. At the same time, it could make good ethical sense if the transplant is funded and will produce useful knowledge for other victims of the disease. That is, the patient can ethically volunteer to be a subject in an experiment as long as undue burdens are not placed on survivors. Indeed, without such unselfish volunteers, medical science could not advance.

If the recipient has a proportionate good to gain, the recipient and his or her family and physicians must respect the autonomy of the potential donors. Families, in particular, can bring such pressure to bear that donors can be blackmailed into the procedure against their wills. This might well be the case of siblings or parents who do not want to donate for fear of damage to their own health, but are given no peace until they have given consent. While such pressure is humanly understandable, it is unethical, and health care providers should guard against it.

Even in life or death situations, it is still unethical for would-be recipients to bribe physicians or for hospitals to give them a privileged position on the waiting list. There have been rumors of rich families buying their way to the top of the list with enormous donations to hospitals licensed to do transplants. While money may talk loudly in such situations, it also eats away at the integrity of the health care profession and destroys any reasonable ethical basis for the allocation of very scarce resources.

THE ETHICS OF THE HEALTH CARE TEAM

The following statements of the AMA Council on Ethical and Judicial Affairs (1996a) present the principal ethical concerns of the physician and the health care team:

> (4) Full discussion of the proposed procedure with the donor and the recipient or their responsible relatives or representatives is mandatory. The physician

should be objective in discussing the procedure, in disclosing known risks and possible hazards, and in advising of the alternative procedures available. *The physician should not encourage expectations beyond those which the circumstances justify.* The physician's interest in advancing scientific knowledge must always be secondary to his primary concern for his patient (italics added).

(5) The transplant procedures of body organs should be undertaken (a) only by physicians who possess special medical knowledge and technical competence developed through special training, study and laboratory experience and practice, and (b) in medical institutions with facilities adequate to protect the health and well-being of the parties to the procedure.

(6) Transplantation of body organs should be undertaken only after careful evaluation of the availability and effectiveness of other possible therapy.

A few comments on each of these provisions will help to clarify the issues involved.

The first concern involves informed consent in an emotional situation in which the wishful thinking of both patient and family, as well as the enthusiasm of health care professionals, could easily lead to misunderstanding. The guidelines insist that the patient comes first, even in research situations, and that informed consent must be respected. This is not always as simple as it seems. In the Baby Fae case, in which a baboon's heart was transplanted into a child, it appears that the parents were not told of the source of the organ. This was a relevant, if emotion-laden, fact and could have affected the parents' decision. It was also a relevant fact from a medical point of view, since the fact that the organ came from another species increased the chances of rejection.

The necessity of proposing alternatives and their chances of success is particularly important in transplant cases, since they generally involve serious decisions in areas where little scientifically established certitude exists. It is not always clear that a kidney transplant will be more helpful than the continuance of dialysis or that a heart transplant will increase the quality of life for all recipients, even though it may increase life expectancy. Christopherson (1982) and Caplan (1985) note that the scientific basis for transplanting a baboon heart into a child was suspect because peers were not given a chance to evaluate all the factors. In any event, the AMA guidelines see a transplant as the last option. The patient needs to know the facts even if they are grim. The physician needs to face the facts even if they run counter to the interests of his or her research.

When a cadaver transplant from a presently living patient is anticipated, the physician should continue to give the donor the same care as usual. This warning is issued lest the health care team be tempted to speed the death in order to get the organs as early as possible or in time for a particular transplant. In addition, the donor must be declared dead by at least one physician other than the physician of the recipient. This is in order to avoid both the reality and the appearance of a conflict of loyalties.

The stress on competence, training, and adequate facilities might seem obvious. It exists because there are ambitious men and women who, in their eagerness to make medical history, might overlook these basic protections for the donor and the patient.

All this says nothing of the crucial ethics of the proper distribution of health care in this area. We shall return to the ethical obligations with regard to the allocation of organs and transplant operations later in this chapter.

Relationships with Surrogates and Families

There are additional problems when the would-be donor is brain dead and is kept breathing so that the organs can be harvested while fresh. It is the opinion of the authors that this sort of cadaver maintenance can be ethical if done for only a short period of time and if families of the dead person and the third-party payers are not billed for the extra time in the hospital. If the breathing is to be prolonged for a longer time, thus increasing the bill and prolonging the agony of survivors, we believe that explicit permission of the survivors is required, as well as explicit and legal arrangements obligating the researchers or recipients to pay for the continued care of the cadaver until the transplant is performed. Without such agreements, the transplant team might end up stealing money from the family and the insurance company, neither of which should be unknowingly forced to pay for keeping a cadaver in good shape for a transplant. Already, one New York court decision[2] has held that a health care provider need not be paid when medical services were rendered over the objection of the patient. We can easily imagine the courts denying payment when there was no consent or benefit to the patient.

The health care team also has ethical and legal obligations with regard to the way in which they approach, or do not approach, the family for permission to take the cadaver organs for transplant. On the one hand, the health care professional, aware of the good that may be accomplished with a transplant, may disregard the feelings and needs of the anguished and grieving family. On the other hand, ignorance of the law and oversensitivity to the feelings of families may cause the health care professional to violate the will of the donor and the requirements of the law. We will examine first the problem of required requests for organs and, second, the case in which the donor card is disregarded.

Some states have laws requiring that the family be asked for a donation. These laws put the provider in a position in which it is impossible to utilize real judgment as to what should be done in a given case. While the laws are well intentioned in trying to increase the supply of organs, they may not promote professional sensitivity and ethical conduct. The feelings of the family may be morally decisive only if the deceased has not made her or his will clear. When the patient has made her or his desires clear, they must be respected. More will be said of this when we treat other efforts to increase the supply of organs.

When there is a valid donor card, there is legally no obligation to ask the permission of the family. If there is a card forbidding donation, an attempt to get the family to overrule the negative decision of the deceased is reprehensible. The will of the patient should rule. Many hospitals, unfortunately, have a policy requiring the permission of the family, even when there is a valid donor card. This practice gives the family the false impression that they have a right to overrule the deceased's organ donation or refusal of a donation. In practice, it may lead to the actual voiding of the donation and a decrease in the number of organs available.

At the same time, there is still the need to be sensitive to the feelings of the family. Peters (1986, p. 260) suggests the following political compromise:

> The family of the medically acceptable declared donor should be informed that the hospital is about to take the necessary steps to give effect to the decedent-authorized donation. The family is not asked to consent to this activity since such a request is both unnecessary and inappropriate. The family is simply informed, as a matter of courtesy, about standard hospital procedure.

The questions of the family should be answered. If the family still objects to the donation, Peters suggests that it should be asked to sign a written declaration of dissent, which will request the recipient to decline the gift. The declaration should give the reasons for the family's objection. In these circumstances, Peters feels the waiver of the recipient should be automatic.

The authors believe that Peters's attempt at a political middle ground may unduly complicate the whole process. Indeed, it appears to put the family through even more agony. Granted that the family should always be told, we do not see why the intended recipient should be informed of the family's wishes and respect the wishes of the family, rather than those of the deceased donor. The body belonged to the donor, not to the family.

When the organs, fluids, or body parts are taken for experimentation or for research, there are additional problems with regard to consent and payment for the commercially valuable results of the research (Andrews, 1986). In this context, we merely note that researchers cannot presume to use even cells or fluids, let alone whole organs, merely because that patient has signed a general consent for treatment on admission to a hospital. As with all truly ethical consent procedures, specific information is required. In the present case, this would include a separate form giving specific information about the experiment or research and the ownership of valuable results.

Increasing the Supply of Organs:
Ethical Problems

In the face of the shortage of organs and the urgency of many situations, there are proposals to increase the supply of organs by improving the recruitment of volunteers and by changing the legal requirements for surrogate consent. The methods proposed pose their own ethical problems.

We have already mentioned the problems caused by laws or hospital policies that require nurses and physicians to seek family permission for the donation of cadaver organs. Others suggest that hospitals should be required to ask about consent to organ donation at the time of admission. Such inquiry would hardly be comforting to the patient, who would rather not think of being a cadaver at that particular moment. Moreover, the patient and his or her family have enough decisions to make regarding treatment or cessation of treatment without being involved in another emotional situation. Again, delicacy and a respect for the freedom of the patient and family seem to dictate at least a reasonable hesitation about such a request at the time of admission.

The supply could be increased if the hospitals obeyed the law and accepted the donor card provided for in the Uniform Anatomical Gift Act as proof of desire to donate. Unfortunately, many facilities do not act on the basis of the donor card, but require the consent of the family. Whether this is because of the fear of lawsuits or respect for the feelings of the family, such facilities not only reduce the supply of organs available, but override the will of the patient, which they are legally entitled to respect.

Since the volunteer method is not sufficiently successful, various laws have been passed to facilitate the harvesting of organs for transplant or other purposes by modifying the need for consent.

A 1968 Virginia law (Lombardo, 1981) provided the medical examiner the right to hand over unclaimed or unidentified bodies to a transplanting physician who has requested them in a case in which the patient was in immediate need of an internal organ transplant. Others wish to pass laws permitting health care groups to harvest organs from cadavers as long as neither the person nor the surrogates have rejected such use of the body. Some would add that the consent should not be presumed when the patient belongs to a religious group known to object to mutilation of the corpse. This proposal is based on a notion of presumed consent, since studies show that the vast majority of people are in favor of organ transplants, even though very few sign organ donor cards.

Such proposals are a strong departure from the American tradition and need to be examined for their long-range consequences, as well as their nature. First, the assent is not truly presumed. The presumed consent is too much like the negative option used by book and record clubs. If you don't reject the selection of the club, you get the book or record and the bill. The system depends on the fact that people in general are too lazy or lackadaisical to reject the offer. There is no true presumption of consent, but an exploitation of human weakness. The same is true of the negative option contained in the presumed consent theory as applied to cadaver organ donations. Once again, human weakness is exploited. In addition, the presumption in organ donations may also exploit human ignorance. If people are not clear that they can say no, they will not say no. Indeed, rather than providing for an informed consent, the "presumed consent" to organ donation is an uninformed and exploitative nonconsent.

More serious yet is the implication in the law of presumed consent that society has the right to control the disposal of bodies not only for the public health, that is, for sanitary reasons, but for therapeutic reasons, that is, for curing particular individuals. The present writers are wary of such an extension of political power, especially when it is being handed over to individuals and institutions in the private sector. Our experience with the donation of whole blood indicates that, over time, education and social bonding will increase the supply of organs. Whereas, at one time, much of the blood used in the United States was purchased, by 1982 only 3 to 4 percent came from paid donors. Indeed, 70 percent was provided on a purely voluntary basis with no strings attached. Perhaps 25 percent was given through blood-credit programs; that is, it was donated for special uses or specific people. Education, good organization, and widespread altruism explain the dramatic change.

Research has shown that organ donation can be increased dramatically if organ banks are given early notice of a possible donor so that a coordinator from the organ bank might approach the family. Streamlined procedures for declaring a patient brain dead and the education of hospital personnel as to which patients were potential donors also increased the supply of organs (McCartney, 1994).

Informed Consent

The transplant team needs the informed consent of the recipient and the donor or, in the absence of an advance directive, of a surrogate when the donor is incompetent. In obtaining these consents, the chances for either short- or long-term improvements should not be exaggerated. Although survival rates for liver transplants continue to improve, frequently a second transplant is necessary (Leventhal et. al., 1990) and the results are poor. Heart-lung transplants and liver transplants often fail and require second and even third transplants with decreasing chances of survival (Busuttil et al., 1991). In addition, the donor and recipient should be told that such procedures as bone marrow transplant involve real pain and not merely discomfort. In short, extreme honesty is called for lest the desire to live and surgical optimism overwhelm the question of whether life is worth living at the cost of great pain or for only a short time.

THE HEALTH CARE PROVIDER'S ETHICS
OF DISTRIBUTION

In the present section we will first study and comment on the ethics of the actual means of distributing organs in the United States and then proceed to a discussion of public policy and the obligations of society. Health care professionals, because of their expertise, are involved in distribution and should be involved in the formulation of public policy.

The pages that follow illustrate the technical complexity that dictates certain aspects of distribution, as well as the conflicting social values that must be reconciled or at least prioritized in developing an ethic and a public policy on the distribution of organs. In particular, we will see the strains between equity, need, efficiency, and the limits of resources.

The Actual Distribution of Organs

In practice, the actual distribution of organs from cadavers and from living donors has often been governed by publicity, that is, by the ability of patients or surrogates to recruit donors or, as one might suspect in a market economy, by the ability to pay.

Distribution by media occurs when some person, generally a child, manages to get such publicity that he or she obtains an organ without going through channels. Media people are aware that, in choosing to publicize the need of one child rather than another, they often "decide" who will live and who will die. This decision is made without any knowledge of who has the greatest need or the greatest chance of profiting from the transplant.

In time, as the organization of organ donation and transplants increases, distribution by publicity should, as a general rule, be eliminated as much as possible in a free society. Yet, although distribution by publicity is not desirable, it may be tolerated at this stage of medical history. First, the publicity raises the public's awareness of the need for transplants and so, in the long run, should increase the supply of donated organs. Second, frequently the media plea brings in more volunteers than those required for the case being publicized.

Like it or not, the ability to pay for at least the cost of the transplant has been a factor in the distribution of transplants. Caplan (1985) has noted that at one large medical center you could not even get on the waiting list unless you had $100,000 to $150,000 in advance. In such a situation, neither need nor equality of opportunity is the primary guide to distribution of donated organs. Such a norm of distribution has nothing to recommend it, although, as we have seen and shall see again, the possibility of reimbursement is still a factor in the allocation of health care.

Location, too, can become a basis for distribution. Because local health care facilities are established to fill local needs, many institutions give priority to those who are part of the area that they serve.

No one of these methods of allocation is ideal, yet we cannot label as unethical either the recipients or the health care providers who benefit from the existing situation. The patient has a primary obligation to self. Similarly, the health care provider has a primary obligation to the particular patient (American Medical Association, 1996). Even granted these primary obligations, there can be unethical methods of getting organs.

At times, physicians, in their zeal for their patients, have surreptitiously conducted unethical searches of existing data banks whose contents were supposed to be confidential. This violation of confidentiality gave the physician's patient a clearly unfair advantage over others who needed a transplant.

From the point of view of the health care system and of society, distribution by publicity and personal privilege does not maximize the good. Those in charge of tissue banks in particular have had to think through the question of priorities. As we saw in chapter 4, the problem is not simple.

Medical Criteria for Microallocation

Some would argue that organs should be distributed on the following basis. The first priority might be given to those who are hospitalized and critically ill, with a lower priority given to those who are stable and at home. The hospitalized and critically ill, however, are not necessarily those who will receive the greatest long-term benefit from a transplant. If the transplant grants only a few years of very reduced quality of life accompanied by great mental depression, it may be a very inefficient use of resources. Indeed, one may ask if it is even medically indicated.

The American Medical Association (1996c), speaking of the allocation of health resources in general, states, "Decisions regarding the allocation of limited medical resources among patients should consider only ethically appropriate criteria relating to medical need. These criteria include likelihood of benefit, urgency of need, change in quality of life, duration of benefit, and, in some cases, the amount of resources required for successful treatment." The Massachusetts Task Force on Organ Transplantation (1984) takes a similar position when it proposes that the first screening of candidates be on the basis of *clinical suitability with reference to the benefits to the patient in terms of life-style and rehabilitation rather than simple survival.* Clinical suitability or the medical indications in terms of these benefits then becomes a crucial element in the distribution of organs.

Criteria of medical or clinical suitability have looked to such items as the absence of other life-threatening diseases, age, and the absence of severe emotional and psychological difficulties. Before discussing these and other proposed criteria of clinical suitability, it will be useful to note technical factors that influence both clinical judgments and priorities.

Technical Factors

Priority according to need plus hope of rehabilitation often has to yield to the limits imposed by time, compatibility of tissue, and the availability of the right personnel and facilities.

In the first place, tissue compatibility is important for the success of the transplant, although new immunosuppressants have made compatibility less crucial. Many centers make the issue of compatibility primary. In the second place, although kidneys can be stored for several days, hearts and livers must often be used within hours. In the case of hearts and livers, then, the ability to harvest and implant the organs rapidly becomes an important factor in distributing the organs. Because the liver and heart must be used so rapidly, there is no time for tissue typing and matching. In practice, it is necessary to know the recipient before these organs are removed. Finally, not all hospitals have the same record of success in using organs, with the result that the skills of the transplant team become a relevant factor in setting priorities for allocation. It does not make much sense to allocate a kidney to a very sick person if the surgeon available has a poor track record.

A little reflection on the facts given in the last paragraph indicates that even rational allocation must deal with random factors, such as the time and place of death and the location of the person needing the transplant. These random factors are in large part not under the control of any human agents, with the result that the ethics often involves simply doing the best you can, all things considered. Allocation also has to deal with both objective and subjective judgments about the relative skills of surgeons and hospitals, as well as the needs of patients. Such judgments, because they cannot be neatly justified, further complicate the already complicated ethics of distribution.

Criteria of Clinical Suitability

While a transplant procedure is in the experimental stage, additional criteria may be necessary to control the experiment and to maximize the chance of success. Originally, to be considered for a heart transplant at many centers, the patient had to meet the following criteria (Christopherson, 1982):

(1) The patient had to be in a physical state where he led "a bed-to-chair existence" and had an estimated life expectancy of less than six months.
(2) Other major organ systems had to be free of disease.

(3) There had to be strong family support.

(4) The patient had to have a history of following medical orders.

(5) There had to be no history of psychiatric illness or substance abuse.

(6) The patient had to be under age 50.

(7) The patient had to be capable of real informed consent.

(8) The patient, his family, or his community had to be capable of paying for such expenses as travel, living away from home, and the like.

This last criterion points up the fact that geography and the ability to overcome its limits is another random factor that affects the distribution of health care. Several of these criteria need comment, since there have been ethical disputes about them.

The Criterion of Family Support

If ultimate rehabilitation is a key part of the screening process, the appropriateness of strong family support as a subcriterion for selection is well illustrated by the Baby Fae case (Caplan, 1986). Baby Fae was at first denied a transplant because the parents did not appear capable of caring for her during the long recuperation period that would follow the operation. Since good care during that period is essential if the procedure is to be worthwhile, the surgeons correctly did not wish to add to the risk factors and turned down the application for a transplant. After much public outcry, more capable guardians were found and the transplant operation was performed. The principle behind all this is clear: Physicians should not allocate scarce resources to those who seem unlikely to benefit from them when they have other patients who have a chance or a better chance to benefit.

When we are dealing with scarce resources and granting the attainment of the basic health care demanded by human dignity, the outcomes should be maximized as much as possible. Although the principle is reasonable, there is and should be debate as to whether the support of parents is the crucial element in maximizing the results. Parents, after all, are part of the natural lottery. Yet the support of the family is often crucial to the recovery of the patient and so becomes part of the medical decision-making process, even though it grants an advantage to those with supportive families. Such inequalities are like those introduced by the presence of genetic inequality. They are facts that cannot be done away with and, *when relevant to outcomes in the use of scarce resources*, they should be given weight.

Loyalty to a Patient and Allocation Decisions

The question remains, however, as to whether a physician has to give priority to a person who is not her or his patient. After all, the physician is responsible to *her* patient, not to another person. Once again, the ethics based on loyalty to the patient comes into conflict with maximizing the results of procedures using scarce resources. The American Medical Association (1996) holds clearly for the physician's patient, and locates the physician's responsibility for allocation decisions in discussions of how the society should establish allocation guidelines and procedures.

> E-2.03 Allocation Of Limited Medical Resources. A physician has a duty to do all that he or she can for the benefit of his individual patient. Policies for allocating limited resources have the potential to limit the ability of physicians to fulfill this obligation to patients. Physicians have a responsibility to participate and to contribute their professional expertise in order to safeguard the interests of patients in decisions made at the societal level regarding the allocation or rationing of health resources.

Although we cannot disagree with the AMA, we find the statement lacking in its appreciation of the complexity of the situation. The statement does not recognize the fact that there is a team involved in transplants, and various agents in the process are not directly responsible for the physician's patient. For this reason and in view of scarcity, social policy, hospital policy, or organ center policy may make the maximization an obligation, even though the ethics of the health care provider in the one-on-one relationship does not, with rare exceptions, look to anything but the maximization of the good of the patient under the physician's care. To the extent that the treatment is paid for by the society, the society may impose reasonable conditions on the distribution of resources in this area, as in so many others.

THE SOCIETY'S ETHICS OF DISTRIBUTION

There are a variety of areas where social attitudes as well as social policy can dramatically affect who receives a transplant and why.

Ageism

As the procedure becomes less and less experimental, questions are being raised about the use of any age as a cutoff for suitability regarding not only receiving a transplant but also donating an organ. By the mid-1980s Thomas Starzl of the Presbyterian-University Hospital in Pittsburgh had already accepted twenty candidates for the operation who were over sixty. He and the ethics advisory committee at Presbyterian-University Hospital distinguish between age and general health on the ground that age does not stand for specific medical criteria. Some people are poor candidates at thirty; others are good candidates at seventy or older. This approach has proven successful, and it has been extended to include the possibility of organ donation by older individuals (Bia, 1999). The consideration of medical criteria is what is relevant; the consideration of age alone is proving to be no more than ageism.

Ability to Pay

The ability and willingness of the patient, family, or community to pay is hardly a part of a medical indications policy. It is, however, a reasonable criterion for the health care institution and the health care providers. These institutions and individuals cannot exist without income. If the individual or the family cannot pay, it becomes a question of whether society will pay. This, in turn, is a question of the way in which a society prioritizes certain values in formulating public policy.

Whether the community is both able and willing to pay is, as pointed out in chapter 4, a function of all the needs of society and individuals, and not merely a question of the need for health care, let alone the need of this particular individual for a transplant. A transplant may or may not be considered part of adequate and humane treatment to which everyone has a right and that society must fulfill.

Although questions can be raised about the appropriateness of some of the criteria, they illustrate the complexity of the problems that must be examined in allocating experimental transplant procedures. At this stage in both medicine and medical ethics, we are far from having definitive answers. As we have said, considering the nature of the problem, it is not likely that there are definitive answers.

Economic Costs and the Distribution of Transplants

Various task forces have attempted to formulate foundations for public policy for the distribution of organs and transplants. The differences between the National Task Force on Organ Transplantation and the Massachusetts Task Force on Transplantation are illustrative of the issues that have not as yet been resolved.

The National Task Force on Organ Transplantation (Department of Health and Human Services, 1986, p. 11) writes as follows:

> In order to insure that patients in need of an extrarenal organ transplant can obtain procedures regardless of ability to pay, the Task Force recommends that private and public health benefit programs, including Medicare and Medicaid, should cover heart and liver transplants, including outpatient immunosuppressive therapy that is an essential part of post-transplant care.

A public program should be set up to cover the costs of people who are medically eligible for organ transplants but who are not covered by private insurance, Medicare, or Medicaid and who are unable to obtain an organ transplant due to lack of funds.

These recommendations involve mandating private health insurers to include more in their policies, as well as extending financial aid to everyone who is not covered by some program. The report unfortunately does not provide careful study of the costs of such recommendations.

Transplants are so expensive that few individuals can pay for them. A single liver transplant might cost as much as $250,000. The follow-up costs of counseling and other psychiatric care plus the continued use of immunosuppressant drugs often cannot be estimated. Both the high costs of transplants and the unknown follow-up costs have rightfully made insurance companies and the government reluctant to pay, lest the cost of health care increase even more. The experience with the enormous costs of government-funded dialysis is used to back up this hesitation. The dialysis program, which originally was to cost only $400,000 a year, ended up costing $2 billion a year as early as 1982. In subsequent years the costs continued to skyrocket.

As long as resources are limited, not everything can be authorized. This is particularly true when it is not clear that the transplant produces medically justifiable results. The mere fact that a transplant extends life does not justify it. As we saw in chapter 6, mere vegetable existence is hardly desirable. When we are not dealing with basic health care, the costs too are factors that must be considered by society in deciding who shall receive and who shall do without. As long as resources are scarce, society must, in accord with the system of priorities described in chapter 4, ration its direct support of health care services that are not at this stage part of basic health care.

The following facts drawn from a University of Nebraska Medical School study in the early 1990s will illustrate the problem (Winslow, 1991, p. 134) and promote understanding of the position of the Massachusetts Task Force. Liver transplant costs for high-risk patients were four times as high as for low-risk patients. Among other things, the high-risk patients averaged fifty-four days in intensive care, while the low-risk patients averaged only five days in intensive care. Furthermore, 71 percent of the high-risk patients were dead within a year, whereas only 6 percent of the low-risk patients died within a year. In short, the low-risk patients were most able to profit from the transplant and at a considerably lower cost.

In view of facts such as these, the Massachusetts Task Force on Organ Transplantation (1984) adopted a less idealistic and more realistic approach. A few of the key recommendations from the Massachusetts report illustrate the differences (pp. 10-11).

> 2. The decision of when extreme and expensive medical technologies, like heart and liver transplants, should be generally available should be made

only after the clinical, social and economic consequences of introducing the procedure, including cost effectiveness, ethical implications and long term effects on society, are studied and reviewed by a publicly accountable body. . . .

5. Patient selection criteria should be public, fair and equitable. Primary screening should be based on medical suitability criteria made available to the public which are designed to offer transplantation to those who can benefit the most from it in terms of the probability of living for a significant period of time with a reasonable prospect for rehabilitation. If there are insufficient resources to transplant all who can so benefit, selection made from the medically suitable group should be based primarily on a first-come, first-served basis.

This approach stresses efficiency and a balancing of costs against social and economic consequences, as well as against clinical benefits. It does not leap to the conclusion that, because transplants can do a great deal of good, everyone has a claim to one regardless of the level of benefits to be obtained or costs to be incurred. The authors favor this approach because it is both realistic and recognizes that more is involved than mere medical indications.

Transplants and Nonimmigrant Aliens

The status of nonimmigrant aliens further complicates the problems. What priority should be given to citizens of another nation who come to the United States for a transplant? The question is particularly poignant because thousands of Americans are awaiting transplants, some of whom will die before an organ becomes available. Some professional groups want to provide a quota for such nonimmigrant aliens; others do not.

The National Task Force on Organ Transplantation (Department of Health and Human Services, 1986, p. 95) recommends that

non-immigrant aliens not comprise more than 10 percent of the total number of kidney transplant recipients at each transplant center, until the Organ Procurement and Transplantation Network has had an opportunity to review the issue. In addition, extrarenal organs should not be offered for transplantation to a nonimmigrant alien unless it has been determined that no other suitable recipient can be found.

Eight members of the Task Force objected to allowing even the 10 percent quota for nonimmigrant aliens in the case of kidney transplants. They argued that the organs come from United States residents and that kidney transplants are paid for by the taxpayers so Americans can reasonably expect to be given priority.

This argument is not unreasonable, and American society may decide that it will not pay even indirectly for noncitizens or nonresidents. This decision would be all the more justified if the society also decided that such transplants are not even part of basic health care. At the same time, such social decisions would leave many of us morally uneasy, since their basis is nationalistic, rather than humane or even utilitarian. The recommendation that allows for the 10 percent quota at least admits that nationality or resident status is not the dominant moral consideration.

One's exact legal status is not a medically relevant factor, but membership may be a relevant factor in the social distribution of goods. At present, there seems to be no easy answer to the ethical importance of legal status.

SUMMARY

Careful distinctions must be made between the donation of renewable and nonrenewable parts, as well as between those that come in pairs and those that do not. The living donor may not donate a nonrenewable, nonpaired part since, except in rare cases, this is equivalent to unjustified suicide. Other donations may be made for a proportionate reason. There is no obligation to donate organs *inter vivos*, but cadaver donation should be seen as an ideal to be encouraged. It is desirable that organs be donated rather than sold, but selling cannot be condemned out of hand.

Would-be recipients of organs should be on their guard against blackmailing or coercing donors. The recipient should look at all the factors when deciding whether to ask for or consent to a transplant.

Proper consent that respects the will of the donor and the feelings of families is essential even in cadaver organ donations. Legal schemes for increasing the supply of organs that disregard the feelings of families or are disguised forms of manipulation should be avoided.

Distribution by publicity may be tolerated because it provides some overall educational benefits for society, as well as individuals. In the long run, a medical indications policy needs to be developed and enforced within the limits of the rights of citizens. Until society specifies that transplants are part of the minimum human and adequate medical treatment to which all have a right, economic factors must still be considered. Membership factors may also be valid factors in distribution.

CASES FOR ANALYSIS

1. Peter, a widowed and childless college professor, age forty, had coronary bypass surgery ten years ago. He made a fine recovery and returned to work with a very high level of involvement in both college and community affairs. In the last year his health has deteriorated badly. He has developed congestive heart failure, which does not respond well to medication. His physician and consulting cardiologist feel that another bypass operation will not restore him to the level of functioning that he desires. The physicians recommend a heart transplant and have Peter placed on a waiting list at a medical center. Peter has a family history of clogged arteries and veins so that the transplant, even if successful, does not guarantee more than a few years of life. If he has to wait a long time for a transplant, it may be necessary to put him on an artificial heart to keep him alive. This artificial heart causes additional psychological and physical problems.

Could the professor refuse the transplant or artificial heart? Is a transplant medically indicated? Does his family history affect the medical indications? Does society have an interest in either encouraging or discouraging Peter to pursue the transplant?

2. Robert, age twenty-five, has lost 50 percent of his kidney function due to diabetes, which has also left him blind and with severe neuropathy in his legs and feet. His general condition is deteriorating so rapidly that he probably has no more than a year to live. Robert's father wants to donate his kidney, if he is compatible. Dialysis is no option in the mind of the father, since he feels that Robert could not take it psychologically. The family has a history of both diabetes and liver problems. The transplant will help with the kidney problem, but will not reverse or stop the progression of the other effects of the diabetes.

Is either dialysis or a transplant medically indicated? Is the father's *belief* about his son's ability to endure dialysis relevant? Should Robert be consulted? Is the father ethical in donating his kidney in view of his family history? Do the ethics of allocation favor or militate against a transplant in this case?

3. Entrepreneurial Hospital, Inc., located in a medium-sized city, has been preparing for its first heart transplants. The team is not yet fully trained, but the chief surgeon, Dr. Hartz, had a great deal of experience at a major medical center before coming to Entrepreneurial. St. Isadore's Hospital, some thirty miles away in a large metropolitan area, has had two years of experience with heart transplants and a fully trained team.

John, a local patient, has been awaiting a transplant at St. Isadore's for over three months when a heart becomes available locally. His physician, with the informed consent of John, asks Dr. Hartz to do a transplantation.

How do the risks to the patient compare with the social advantage of starting up Dr. Hartz's team? Studies show that the success rate is greater with experienced teams that do a large number of these operations. Was the physician looking out for the best interests of his patient? Would it be better to take a chance and wait for St. Isadore's to do the operation?

4. Mrs. Simpatico, a registered nurse, had cared for Joseph for three weeks and had become attached to him and his devoted family. Joseph, who was only thirty, died. The hospital has a policy requiring nurses to ask the families of all dead patients for organ donations. Both she and the family are very upset about the death. Joseph's young wife and three children need comfort and not decisions at this moment. Mrs. Simpatico does not ask for the organ donation, even though the hospital has a long waiting list. When the nursing supervisor discovers this omission, she reprimands Mrs. Simpatico and puts a warning in her personnel file. "One more incident like that," says the supervisor, "and you will be fired. A policy is a policy and it is not up to you to make exceptions."

To whom is Mrs. Simpatico obligated? Does the hospital policy put Mrs. Simpatico in a conflict of interests? Is the supervisor's idea that "a policy is a policy" sound ethics? Legally, nurses are independent practioners even when they are employees. In view of this, can nurses and physical therapists make exceptions to policies when the good of the patient calls for it? Should Mrs. Simpatico allow her feelings to enter into the decision?

5. Two men on the same service are awaiting a keratoplasty (cornea transplant) because of chemical burns on their eyes. One is an alcoholic street person with other serious health problems. The other is a prominent lawyer with a wife and three children. A donor's eye becomes available, and by coincidence both men's circular segments of the cornea match the donor's. The physician makes his decision on the basis of first-come, first-served and transplants the cornea to the alcoholic.

Is it ethical to use the procedural rule first-come, first-served when one patient promises to have better medical results than the other? (The alcoholic has more serious health problems.) Is there a relevance to the patients' social positions?

6. Mary, age four months, has been diagnosed as having liver pathology and other congenital defects. The liver pathology will threaten her life within a very short time unless she receives a liver transplant. Her father, owner of the local TV station, is able to get national media attention, and a donor is discovered within two weeks. John, also age four months, has the same liver condition, but is otherwise in good health. Friends rally around the family and raise the funds for a transplant, but no donor is found. John dies in six months.

In the interests of equality, should we have a law to prevent one person from having greater access to transplants than another? Would such a law be enforceable? What could such a law do about the random factors that influence distribution? Would the parents have been ethical if they had just let the system go on and made no special efforts for their child?

7. Anissa is seventeen years old when it is discovered that she has leukemia. Her primary hope for survival rests on a bone marrow transplant, but there are no likely donors for her unusual genetic characteristics. Her parents, both in their forties, decide to have another child in the hope that the infant will provide a tissue match for Anissa (a 25 percent chance).

Is it ethically right to conceive a child for the purpose of generating an organ for transplantation? There is a 75 percent chance that the infant will not be a tissue match; does this affect the evaluation of the idea? If the infant is a tissue match, can the parents function ethically as surrogates for the infant (can they decide in the interests of the infant that the transplant operation is permissible)?

NOTES

1. The anencephalic infant is born without all or most of the cerebral hemispheres. It is a fatal neurological defect, and most afflicted infants will not survive more than a week. The condition is sometimes misdiagnosed because it sometimes overlaps with other conditions, such as the affliction of hydranencephalics, who survive somewhat longer because their skulls are intact.

2. Elbaum v. Great Neck Plaza [148 A.D. 2nd 244, 544 NYS 2nd 840 (1989)].

11

THE ETHICS OF TESTING AND SCREENING

INTRODUCTION

The present chapter is concerned with the often overlooked ethical problems of tests used in diagnosing the complaints of patients and in screening symptomless populations for the presence of a defect or illness. Although the same techniques may be used in both testing and screening, we distinguish the two by saying that testing is for the diagnosis of an individual with symptoms, while screening is for case-finding in a population without symptoms.

The ethical problems of testing involve not only charges of overtesting, but problems of accuracy. These problems are, in turn, connected with the problem of informed consent in testing and in particular with the question of whether there is an obligation to tell the patient of the limits of the test and its utility, as well as about its risks, if any.

While the problems of testing carry over into the area of screening, that is, case-finding, there are additional ethical problems when the screening is for the purpose of public health or employability, rather than for the good of the individual. These additional problems involve the confidentiality of test results, the risk of the loss of a job, the denial of insurance, or even prosecution for a crime. Second, mass screening may stigmatize an entire population, as was allegedly the case with the testing of African Americans for sickle-cell anemia. Finally, from the society's point of view, there are questions of the cost-benefit ratio of case-finding by screening. In short, are the benefits of screening sufficiently great to justify the cost of finding a case? This problem is especially acute when health care resources are scarce.

TESTING

The Central Question

Although problems with cost-benefit ratios and stigmatization of groups are extremely important, the central question from the patient's point of view is the following: *Will this test and the subsequent treatment lead to more good than harm, all things considered*? From the view of the health care professional, the central question is similar, but not identical. *Will this test lead to treatment that, from a medical point of view, will benefit the patient enough to justify the costs and risks of both the test and the treatment?* This is the medical indications principle developed in chapter 3.

To answer the central question given above, both the patient and the health care professional must ask the following questions: First, how accurate is this test? Second, what are the risks of this test relative to the severity of the illness? Third, is there a treatment for the disease so that it is possible to improve life?

The third question is particularly important. If there is no possible treatment and no possible improvement of life, there is no justification for the cost and risks of the test. The mere desire to confirm the diagnosis is not a justification for the test. In other words, even an accurate test is not automatically justified by the fact that it improves diagnosis. *In health care practice, as opposed to research, the question must always be whether the test can lead to benefiting the patient.*

The Accuracy of Tests

In view of all the above, the first thing to be determined is whether we are dealing with an accurate test. Since it is impossible to discuss all tests and since new tests are constantly being developed, we will confine ourselves to the general nature of the problems and illustrate these with historical examples.

The widely used tests for serum cholesterol provide a clear example of the problem of accuracy (Medical Letter on Drugs and Therapeutics, 1987). Different laboratories testing the same sample often come up with quite different test results. This is partly because different laboratories use different methods. Even when the same method is used, however, the results can vary significantly. One survey, for example, indicated that for all laboratories and all instruments using enzymatic methods the results for a single sample varied from 197 to 397 mg/dl. The correct result was supposed to be 262.6 mg/dl (*Medical Letter on Drugs and Therapeutics*, 1987).

These differences have consequences. According to the National Institutes of Health Consensus Conference Guidelines for the interpretation of the results, one of the lower readings given above would call for no treatment, a higher reading would call for treatment with diet alone, and a yet higher reading for treatment with both diet and drugs (National Institutes for Health, 1995). Some of the treatments with drugs have unfortunate side effects. Unfortunately, the health care professional does not know what the readings mean unless they can be related to the method on which the Consensus Guidelines were based. As a result of inaccurate testing, treatment may be omitted where required or the wrong treatment given.

Studies of medical and even university laboratories indicate that such problems may be widespread. Mendelsohn (1981) noted that Centers for Disease Control studies of even the better laboratories are not encouraging. Between 10 and 40 percent of the laboratory bacteriological testing was unsatisfactory; 12 to 18 percent made mistakes in blood grouping and typing. Hansen, Caudill, and Boone (1985) found that less than 10 percent of the laboratories had acceptable performance for testing barbiturates, amphetamines, cocaine, or morphine. They found error rates as high as 100 percent for other drugs analyzed. The results are all the more surprising in that many of the samples were mailed from drug treatment centers, so the labs should have been alerted to the nature of the samples. The failures may be due to various causes, such as laboratory perceptions of what results are expected, costs, carelessness, personnel problems, methodological design, poor specimens, and even reimbursement patterns (Ingelfinger et al., 1981). The point to be made is clear: Errors in testing are frequent, and many of the errors occur because of negligence or even culpable ignorance. The situation is serious because such errors can lead to unnecessary and even dangerous treatment or to the omission of necessary treatment. Not only those who perform the tests but those who use the results have a serious ethical obligation to make sure that they are dealing with accurate results.

False Positives and False Negatives

Many tests, like those for serum cholesterol, look for the relative amount of a substance in the blood. Other tests, like those mentioned in the previous paragraph, look for the presence or absence of a chemical or an antibody. Tests of this second type should be both sensitive and specific.

Sensitivity is the ability of a test to detect infection when it is present (to return a positive result when the sample is positive). *The specificity* of the test is the ability of a test to detect the absence of infection when the sample is uninfected (that is, the ability to return a negative result when the sample is negative) (George, 1994). Thus, a test is sensitive if it yields few or no false negatives. It is specific if it yields few or no false positives.

A false positive is a result that says that the condition is present when it is actually absent. For example, the test might indicate that the patient has AIDS when, as a matter of fact, he does not. Early tests for Lyme disease yielded false positives in 50 percent of all cases. On the other hand, a false negative says that the patient is free of the condition, when in point of fact the condition is present.

The consequences of either false positives or false negatives can be extremely serious. The false negative gives a false sense of security and leaves the illness untreated. The false positive can torture patients and expose them to unnecessary and even dangerous treatments. Sometimes, as in the case of AIDS, the false positive is an apparent death sentence that can lead to both despair and suicide. If the test results are not kept confidential, they could also lead to isolation and loss of employment and insurance. Both types of error can also expose the health care professional to malpractice suits.

The issue of false positives is particularly acute in testing for HIV (AIDS) infections (Mayer and Pauker, 1987). In the mid-1980s, testing started with an enzyme immunoassay. This assay, called the ELISA, when used in the general population, yields many more false positives than false negatives. Since this test had a relatively high rate of false positives, good procedure called for it to be done several times. If there were repeated positive results on the enzyme immunoassay, more complicated and expensive tests were needed to confirm the diagnosis.

The Western blot test was one of the more common confirmatory tests and was, indeed, the standard against which new techniques were evaluated. Unfortunately, the testing methods had not been standardized, inter-laboratory variations had not been carefully studied, and the criteria for interpretation varied from laboratory to laboratory and even from month to month (Mayer and Pauker, 1987). In some studies of healthy adults, these factors led to a high rate of false positives at several large commercial testing firms. When the Western blot test is ambiguous, the immunofluorescence assay is sometimes used. This test can yield positive, negative, or indeterminate results (George, 1994). The confirmatory test, then, is not perfectly specific when used with low-risk populations. This will have important consequences for the ethics of screening.

In view of the problems, we agree with Field (1989) that no one should be told that he or she has AIDS or the antibodies to the AIDS virus until the false positive rate has been reduced as much as possible. This may be expensive, but in view of the often devastating psychological and social effects of a false positive, expense hardly seems to be the decisive factor.

And because of the long latency period (up to thirty-six months) during which AIDS or the antivirus cannot be detected, it appears to be unethical to tell people that they are AIDS-free without a warning about the latency period.

The problem of false negatives is illustrated by a test that accurately indicates the presence of a disease but not the absence of the same disease. Thus, a brain biopsy for herpes simplex encephalitis (see chapter 12) is valid when positive, but tells us nothing when negative, since it may have missed the focal point of the infection and so detected nothing.

Problems with both false positives and false negatives arise from such usual procedures as tonometry to test for glaucoma (Fortess and Kapp, 1985). Writers like Robin (1984) question the value of the test, since they claim that early treatment has not been proven to stop the advance of the disease and allege that treatment with conventional drugs produces no clear-cut improvement. In the case of such a test with a high percentage of false positives and no clear-cut treatment, the authors consider the test unethical, quite aside from the unnecessary anguish it causes.

The Interpretation of Tests

Test results generally require interpretation in terms of the health care professional's experience and the history and symptoms of the patient. These interpretations are not a question of scientific fact, but the results of more or less probable deductions and of the interpreter's "feel" for the tests. There is room, then, for error.

Even as common a procedure as an X-ray requires interpretation, and experts can and do disagree about the meaning of the same X-ray plate. In one case, an internist saw a broken femur in the X-ray, while the orthopedic surgeon saw no fracture when the plate was placed properly on the screen. Such fallibility of interpretation is a major reason for second opinions in serious cases.

The cervical Pap smear, a commonly used method of detecting the earliest possible stage of cancer of the uterus, requires interpretation, and various doctors examining the same specimen can disagree. One study showed disagreement in as many as 40 percent of the cases (Robin, 1984, p. 180). This obviously leads to a large number of false positives and false negatives. The false positives have often been confirmed by examination of the uterus after it has been surgically removed, at which point the truth is of little help to the patient. While the Pap smear is credited with saving the lives of countless women, it is not an infallible test.

Surprisingly enough, the interpretation of a test also involves disputes about the assumptions behind testing and about the way their results can be summarized (Hlatky, 1986). The clinical presentation of the test, the age and sex of the patient, the presence of more than one disease, and the interaction of the disease with the test all cause complications in interpretation.

The variation in interpretation points up the fact that medicine is an art as well as a science. The art side can be highly subjective and loaded with the values of the interpreter. Thus, the interpreter may be disposed to accept any positive test results as a mandate for treatment, regardless of the rate of false positives or the risk of misinterpretation.

The Risks of Testing

The risks associated with a given test must enter into both the patient's and the health care professional's judgment of proportionality. This judgment of proportionality includes a consideration of the alternatives available.

The issues are well illustrated by the methods of prenatal testing. Although these tests have been discussed frequently and heatedly because of their connection with abortion, they can pose ethical problems in and of themselves. There are three principal techniques: ultrasound, amniocentesis, and chorionic villi biopsy.

Ultrasound is a noninvasive technique in which sound waves are bounced off the uterus and, with the aid of a computer, produce a picture of the woman's uterus and its contents. This appears to be the safest technique, and up to now there is no evidence that it is dangerous to the fetus. Until research shows the nature of any possible effects, the test needs more justification than mere curiosity. In time, it may prove so safe that it can be done routinely.

Amniocentesis is a surgical technique that involves penetrating the abdomen and uterus of the pregnant woman with a hollow needle in order to take a sample of amniotic fluid from the amniotic sac. Ultrasound is generally used to guide the needle. The fluid obtained is cultured and then examined. It should be noted that in 10 percent of the cases no fluid is obtained and that 10 percent of the time, the fluid does not yield a culture.

Amniocentesis has risks for the woman. There are cases of death and complications, such as vaginal bleeding or puncture of the bladder. The rate of complications varies greatly from hospital to hospital and physician to physician. Indeed, there are extreme variations in all effects depending on the way in which the ultrasound is used to guide the needle (Katayama and Roesler, 1986). The same is true of risk to the fetus. A spontaneous abortion may result from the procedure. If part of the fetus is touched by the needle, the fetus necroses (dies). Rh immunization may also occur if the mother is Rh-negative and the fetus Rh-positive. Once again, the test needs to be justified by a proportionate reason and should not be performed routinely.

The age of the pregnant woman is often taken as a sufficient medical indication for this test. Age, however, needs to be combined with other factors that would indicate high risk, since it can be argued that age alone is too crude an indicator of the risk for a particular woman or fetus. Let us illustrate. Studies indicate that the risk of having a Down's syndrome baby increases with age. The statistics in that study included healthy women and women in poor health, as well as women with a history of such births or with relatives who have the disease. The risk for a particular woman to be tested depends on all these factors and not on age alone. Age alone, then, may not be a sufficient indicator of a need for the test. The indicators to be used are debated in medical circles, and when combined with the risks of the test, indicate caution is appropriate. An article and a series of letters to *The Lancet* (CEMAT, 1998), for example, illustrates a considerable range of opinions among physicians. In any event, both the medical and ethical evaluation of the test needs continual monitoring. In time, the risks may even be so reduced that routine use could be justified.

The third technique, chorionic villi biopsy, does not involve surgical penetration of the abdomen and uterus and so is seemingly much safer than amniocentesis. In this technique, the entrance is made by way of the vagina, and a sample is taken from the chorion, which has the same cellular material as the fetus. At this stage of its development, the test cannot detect everything that is detectable by amniocentesis. On the other hand, it can be done earlier and the results are obtained faster.

As with amniocentesis, samples are not obtained in every case. Even though this test might appear to be safer than amniocentesis, there is a worldwide fetal loss rate of 4 percent even when the procedure is performed by experienced obstetricians (McGovern, Goldberg, and Desnick, 1986; Wass, 1986). In addition, research indicates that the children born after this test was performed have a higher rate of deformed fingers and toes, (Fackelmann, 1994). Certainly, at this stage it is not for routine use. Obviously patients should be informed of all these risks.

In many cases in which these three prenatal tests can detect a defect or disease with some accuracy, they cannot detect the severity of the disease. Thus, it is possible to detect neural tube defects, including spina bifida, but it is anyone's guess as to how serious the condition is in any particular fetus (Kolata, 1980). Similarly, amniocentesis can detect Down's syndrome, but it cannot tell us whether the retardation will be mild or severe. This is an important point, since in many cases the diagnosis of Down's syndrome leads to the recommendation for an abortion.

The danger of the tests or of the treatments based on tests that have false positives or false negatives means that many of the tests should not be used routinely. When they are used, they need to be justified by a proportionate benefit to the patient. The patient must have the information needed to judge whether there is a proportionate benefit, all things considered.

The Cost of Tests

For some time, health insurance and third-party payment have pushed cost into the background, so the patient does not often ask about cost, and the health care provider does not mention it. Lately, the rising costs of health care have made it important to think about the costs of tests. Certainly, such measures as diagnostic related groups (DRGs) have made providers and health care administrators much more sensitive to the issue. After all, if you are not going to get paid for every test you make and if you risk losing money if you make too many, caution is in order. Patients will become equally sensitive if higher deductibles have to be paid out of their own pockets. In any event, the era in which cost was no object in health care seems to be drawing to an end.

Here, as earlier in the book, we wish to stress that not merely financial cost, but physical, psychic, and social costs must be justified. The anxiety caused by testing, especially by false positives, must not be overlooked in making the ethical judgment about a particular test. In addition, the fact that some tests carry risks means that these costs, too, need to be justified.

In health, as in every other aspect of life, we must carefully consider our economic resources. We must ask whether the money expended on health produces results proportionate to the expenditure. This question of proportionality between cost and benefit becomes particularly acute when we are dealing not with tests done for diagnostic purposes, but with those done *routinely* as part of the examination of a *healthy person*. This would be the case in the annual physical. In 1980 the American Medical Association abandoned its long support of the routine annual physical (Mendelsohn, 1981). Many hospitals have long ceased demanding routine chest X-rays on admission. This tells us that the medical profession has rethought at least some routine testing in terms of cost-benefit. As we noted in chapter 4, patients who are forced to pay larger and larger sums for testing may also begin to reevaluate their willingness to pay and therefore reevaluate the value of the tests to them, no matter what their value to the health care provider.

The Charge of Overtesting

Physicians have been accused of overtesting, that is, using more tests than are necessary for the good of the patient. This may be due to their desire to know as much as possible about a given case, whether or not the additional data will help the patient. As we have already noted in the consideration of costs, therapeutic rather than merely diagnostic accuracy is needed to justify the tests. Critics in the popular press claim that overtesting is due to the health care providers' efforts to protect themselves against malpractice suits. The professionals are alleged to feel safer if they can prove that they did *everything possible* and not merely everything necessary.

Although this fear of malpractice due to a failure to test appears relatively groundless (Fortess and Kapp, 1985), the fear is still operative. Overtesting exists and can become so extreme that either the hospital or the physician's colleagues in a group practice have been known to bring great pressure to bear on the offender. That is, there are cases of collective judgment by qualified peers that a physician is overtesting. Short of such a collective judgment, it can be difficult to decide when a physician is guilty of overtesting.

Robin (1984) asks whether even the collective judgment is valid, since he believes that overuse is not merely a problem of individual abuse, but a built-in fault of the entire health care system. While he makes a very strong case for this, and despite the various review procedures mentioned in chapter 6, we are still left with only the collective professional judgment as even a rough norm for overtesting in most cases.

There are, however, exceptions. For example, some hospitals still demand a chest X-ray before any surgical procedure, even noninvasive procedures such as lithotripsy. In some cases this unnecessary test continues even after medical staffs have urged its elimination. In health care facilities, as elsewhere in human life, inertia remains a powerful obstacle to paring costs.

We must consider that there is room for wide variation in the use of tests, both by medical specialty and by individual physicians. Internists, by the nature of their work, use more tests than surgeons. A consulting specialist who deals with difficult cases may use many more tests than a primary care physician. A naturally timid or cautious physician may also tend to use more tests. Thus, there is no sharp line to mark off overtesting from prudent testing. The collective judgment norm given above is broad, possibly biased, and, according to Robin, not easy to apply, but it is the best we have.

In closing, we wish to repeat the principles from the beginning of this chapter. A test is useless unless there is some hope of its benefiting the patient, that is, unless it can lead to treatment whose benefits to the patient will outweigh the costs and the risks of both the tests and the treatment. In short, tests are not justified simply to satisfy the curiosity of the health care professional.

Testing and Informed Consent

Tests can sometimes involve more than minimal risks, and even routine tests cost money and require time from the patient. At least some of the elements of informed consent may enter into testing. The patient should be told the purpose of the test and the benefits, if any, to be gained by it, as well as the side effects and the risks, if any, beyond the minimum risks of everyday life. The authors have found that some physicians and nurses are evasive when asked what is to be gained from the test. Indeed, sometimes explanations of even a rudimentary sort are forthcoming only when the patient says, "Well, let's skip the test."

The patient should also be told the costs and the amount of time the test may require. One should not assume that every patient is willing to pay any amount or put up with any inconvenience for a marginal increase in the accuracy of diagnosis. When inefficient laboratories are involved, the patient may waste valuable hours waiting. Indeed, the time may be more valuable to the patient than any benefit the health care provider can bestow.

The fact of costs should not be overlooked just because the patient has insurance that will pay for the test. Indeed, one way to determine the necessity of the test may be to ask if it would be done if there were no insurance and the person could not pay for it. This fits in with our idea in chapter 4 that heightened cost consciousness is necessary if we are to miti-gate, if not solve, the problem of health care allocation.

Even when a health care professional sees benefits from a test, the patient may not agree. For example, a patient may refuse a diagnostic pro-cedure such as cardiac catheterization on the grounds not only of cost, pain, and danger, but also because she or he will not consent to any further treatment regardless of the test result. There comes a point at which some patients just say "enough is enough" and refuse treatment and tests that might lead to treatment. This may seem puzzling to some health care providers, but there are, as we pointed out in chapters 2 and 3, more than medical factors involved in making reasonable patient decisions.

The variability of interpretation and the heavy subjective component in this decision making also raise a question as to whether ethics demands that patients be told the chance of testing errors and not be allowed to believe that they are dealing with certitudes. For example, since the pres-ence of exposure to AIDS is not detectable for a number of months after exposure, a negative test result may give an unjustified sense of security.

When it is not merely a question of the limits of a test, but of the falli-bility of interpretation, should the patient be told and encouraged to get a second opinion? To put it another way, does respect for the dignity of the patient demand more disclosure than currently demanded by the principle of informed consent?

Although revealing such chances of error will undoubtedly make the health care provider's job more difficult, it might also serve to demystify the whole process of health care. Neither of these effects is particularly harmful. Indeed, as we suggested in chapter 4, stripping health care of its cloak of scientific omniscience may help in reducing health care costs. In addition, patients who know that they are dealing with less than scientific certitude will be psychologically freer to exercise more autonomy and exact a greater degree of accountability from health care providers.

ETHICAL PROBLEMS OF MASS SCREENING

The previous section concentrated on the problems that arise from the use of tests not only in diagnosis, but in routine screening of individuals. In this section, we consider related and additional problems that arise when tests are used for mass screening. In mass screening, large numbers of apparently healthy people are tested in order to detect the few people who have what is sometimes a relatively rare condition. Everyone has encountered mass screening during so-called health fairs conducted at shopping malls or by hospitals. At these, everyone is invited to have their blood pressure taken. Sometimes there are instant-detection blood tests for diabetes, and in the past there were chest X-rays for tuberculosis detection.

Two sets of problems are connected with mass screening. The first set is an extension of the problems of routine testing. The second set concerns stigmatization of certain populations, special problems of confidentiality, and the constantly recurring question of the proper distribution of health care resources.

False Positives in Mass Screening

The first set of problems arises from two facts. First, mass screenings with symptomless populations often produce higher rates of false positives. Second, when there is no truly effective treatment for the condition detected, the tests are medically useless.

The example of AIDS testing illustrates both points. Suppose that both tests mentioned in the first part of this chapter have been used to detect and "confirm" the presence of AIDS. If the joint false positive rate were 0.1 percent when symptomless women were tested, ten women without the disease would be falsely identified for each one that was correctly identified (Mayer and Pauker, 1987). If there were only a single-stage testing program, for example, using equipment in a physician's office, the joint false positive rate has been known to go as high as 0.5 percent and to stigmatize fifty disease-free women for each true case actually detected.

The fact that AIDS is a stigmatizing disease for which there is no cure means that the mass screening cannot be justified on the basis of patient benefit. Indeed, a false positive rate that puts many people in a state of unnecessary agony raises further questions about the legitimacy of the screening. Finally, as we will see later, even screening for the protection of others may not be easy to justify.

Robin (1984) raised the same problem of false positives with regard to testing for pancreatic cancer. Similar questions can be asked about other forms of cancer screening, such as using mammography followed by various forms of chemotherapy and surgery (*Lancet*, 1984). Even the optimistic studies (Rodes et al., 1986) say only that their results *suggest* that improved survival in breast cancer screening programs is in *large measure* due to the ability to detect lesions before they become palpable. This study detected only 167 malignant lesions in the 10,187 asymptomatic patients tested. Again, the success rate of such screening raises disturbing questions about its appropriateness, even before we look at the cost factors.

Cost per Case Detected

In mass screening programs, cost can be a particularly relevant factor. In mass screenings, there is a question not only of the cost of the individual test, but of the cost of each case detected. Thus, although an individual test might cost only $3, it might cost $10,000 for each case detected. At the height of the agitation over drug testing in government and business, the Department of Defense spent $52 million dollars on two sets of tests on 3.6 million employees. Since only about 92,000 users were alleged to have been detected, it cost $500 to detect each alleged user. We stress that these were alleged users since, as noted, the tests are not always perfect. There are then cost–benefit problems as well as questions about the distribution of health care resources.

The cost–benefit analysis might favor the drug tests in question if the end result were proven improvement in health or efficiency or security. If there were no such improvements, the tests would have to be judged unfavorably even aside from the issue of stigmatization and civil rights, which we will discuss shortly.

In one instance, 21,071 people were screened for Tay-Sachs disease, and 24 *at-risk* couples were discovered; three pregnancies were monitored and one fetus was aborted. "At risk" refers to the possibility of these couples having a child with Tay-Sachs disease and not to the fact that the couples could get the disease.

The program, which used less expensive batch methods of analyzing blood samples, cost $100,000, not counting the time of volunteers (Goodman and Goodman, 1982). If other methods of analysis had been used, the out-of-pocket costs could have run to $250,000, or $10,400 for each at-risk couple discovered.

Although Tay-Sachs is a particularly horrible fate for a child and its parents, there is still a question of whether, from society's point of view, the money could have been used to better advantage. It could have been used for other ends, for example, to provide basic health care to a large number of others, or it could have been used more efficiently; for example, the government-financed screening program could have used the more economical method of limiting testing to high-risk pregnant women and then testing the husbands only if the woman was positive.

Something similar can be said of the mass screening involved in premarital blood tests for syphilis (Polonoff and Garland, 1979). Since the laws requiring these tests were passed, the use of antibiotics has radically reduced the rate of syphilis in the population. Less than 1 percent of all cases of syphilis were detected by premarital blood tests. In 1978, when only 123 cases were discovered by this method, an estimated $80 million was spent on the tests. Thus, each case detected cost $650,000. Once again, we ask if there are not better uses or at least more efficient uses of public funds.

Similar problems of cost per case detected arise with routine mass screening for AIDS, that is, for exposure to the AIDS virus. While there is a wide variation in estimates for the cost of cases detected by tests on a marriage application, they run from $18,000 to $110,000 per case. The costs of counseling and follow-up are not included in these figures. Further, this type of mass screening would likely not detect many cases, and experience suggests people would go to great lengths to avoid the tests (ACLU, 1998).

The monetary costs of testing plus the debates about the utility of the testing pose serious questions about the ethics of allocation. We will return to this later in this chapter.

Stigmatization

The second set of problems connected with mass screenings involves stigmatization. Stigmatization refers to placing a mark of infamy, disgrace, or reproach on a person or a group. Goffman (1963) refers to a stigma as the situation of a person who is disqualified from full social acceptance. He also refers to a stigma as an attribute, or undesired differentness, which is deeply discrediting. He also gives three classes of stigma, all of which can enter into health care: First, there are the abominations of the body—the various physical deformities. Next there are blemishes of individual character perceived as weak will, domineering or unnatural passions, treacherous and rigid beliefs, and dishonesty. Finally, there are the tribal stigma of race, nation, and religion, these being stigma that can be transmitted through lineages and equally contaminate all members of the family (p. 4).

The process of stigmatizing a person or group often involves emotion, taboos, and social prejudice, rather than reason. Thus, it can occur regardless of how good the intentions of those doing the screening are. So serious are the felt effects of stigmatization that those at risk may prefer ignorance to knowledge, when knowledge can lead to them being outcast. Indeed, so serious are the effects of the stigma when known that most make a serious effort to conceal it.

In the health care context, this effort to ignore or conceal can be particularly strong and very reasonable when there is no effective treatment for the condition that is the object of the screening. Confidentiality becomes increasingly important in these cases. We shall return to this problem shortly.

At the start of the AIDS epidemic, the fear of the disease was enormous and in direct proportion to the ignorance about it. Those who had the disease or who had even been exposed to it were often shunned, even by physicians and nurses in the hospital. They had been stigmatized. An attempt at mass screening for the disease, even in populations at high risk, would have carried the risk of stigmatization and isolation even while there was no hope of a cure. No wonder the gay community, a high-risk group, fought mass screening.

When awareness of a condition detected by mass screening may lead not only to stigmatization, but to the subsequent loss of a job, refusal of health or life insurance, or, in the case of drug screening, trouble with the police, the objections to it become even stronger. Compulsory testing for drug use certainly falls into this category. Here is an invasion of the privacy of the body plus stigmatization that requires the gravest justifications for testing. For this reason, health care providers should be wary of involvement in such testing. We will attempt to draw more careful distinctions later when we discuss confidentiality.

Stigmatization and Genetic Screening

Sometimes, as in the case of Tay-Sachs disease, the screening is not a therapeutic but a preventive health measure designed to obtain information useful in genetic counseling, that is, for advising people about the chance that they will produce defective offspring. Those who object to abortion will naturally object to screening that leads to abortion as a method of avoiding the defective child. Even when abortion is not anticipated, the health care provider should weigh the stigmatizing effect of an unfavorable test on both individuals and groups. The woman who learns that she has an incurable defect such that reproduction is not advisable may feel degraded. If the defect becomes known, the woman with the defect may be left out of the marriage market and become a second-class member of her group. Finally, when the screening involves ethnic or racial groups who are at high risk, there is danger of the entire group being stigmatized. This appears to be the case with screening for sickle-cell anemia among African Americans and Tay-Sachs disease among Eastern European Jews. The most devastating case of all occurs when there is no cure for the disease, as is the case with Huntington's chorea (Rosenfeld, 1984; see the case on this disease in chapter 5).

In the case of Tay-Sachs disease, Goodman and Goodman (1982) note that there was a special problem with the "apparent scientific confirmation of age-old prejudices about racial debility, clannishness and the like." In addition, the stigma discouraged marriage and reproduction between Eastern European Jews at a time when fertility is below replacement and the outmarriage rate is approaching 40 percent.

The problems of mass screening can only increase in the future as science discovers markers for patterns of genes associated with such diseases as heart attacks, emphysema, Alzheimer's disease, diabetes, and certain cancers. If tests for such markers are made standard procedures before life and health insurance can be issued, those stigmatized by the marker may find themselves uninsurable or insurable only at a very high cost. This is particularly serious in the case of health insurance; a person might end up with no insurance and possibly no health care because of a marker for a disease that may never appear or may appear only 20 or 30 years later.

Confidentiality in Screening

The principles developed in chapter 5 obviously apply here. There are, however, special problems when the screening is not for the benefit of the patient, but for the benefit of the insurance company or, allegedly, for public health and safety. We will return to the public health and safety issue shortly.

We stress confidentiality as particularly important to protect the results from insurance companies, which may deny coverage or raise premiums for those who have genetic problems (Frieden, 1991). Since businesses will often, sometimes illegally, turn down applicants with known health problems, breaches of confidentiality in this area can have especially far-reaching consequences.

Even in these cases, the ethical problems are not major if the patient voluntarily consents to the screening and has been informed of the following: (1) the specific persons to whom the results will be revealed, (2) the actual risks of false positives, (3) the potentially harmful consequences, such as loss of a job, denial of entry into the country, or refusal of insurance. Finally, in the event that a test is positive, the person should have the right to be retested by an independent laboratory. This seems particularly important when even top-rated laboratories such as the Civil Aeromedical Laboratory of the Department of Transportation have been known to be sloppy in their procedures and even fraudulent in their results.[1]

While it is difficult to imagine many cases of a truly voluntary consent when there are such serious harmful consequences, we must allow for the possibility. But the health care professional should be on guard against involuntary screening *disguised as voluntary*. The more serious problems arise with involuntary testing and the cooperation of health professionals in such screening.

Health care professionals should not take part in involuntary screening except when it is legally and ethically justified. It takes extremely serious reasons to justify even unwilling cooperation with unjustified involuntary testing.

We must ask, however, when involuntary testing or involuntary testing disguised as routine testing would be ethical and legal. We will divide our discussion into testing that is involuntary because it is mandated by law and that which is involuntary because some private group, such as a corporation, has the power to force the test on employees or prospective employees.

Involuntary Testing and the Public Good

Granted the protection of confidentiality, involuntary testing mandated by law would be legal and ethical only when necessary for the public health and legally enacted. Granted enactment of the law, the screening could be necessary for the public good if it could detect a serious threat to public health and *lead to effective preventive measures*. If no treatment is available for the disease or if there is no legal way to prevent the spread of the disease, the testing can hardly be called useful, let alone necessary for the public good. As the AIDS problem has demonstrated, it is one thing to detect a carrier of AIDS and another to convince the victim to avoid infecting others. Third, proposals to stop the spread of disease by quarantine need to be scrutinized carefully, since the most serious questions of civil rights are involved. A person cannot be deprived of his or her privacy, livelihood, and freedom to travel without due process of law, even when the public good is at stake. Indeed, since it is hard to keep the results confidential, useless tests expose people to the danger of stigmatization on the basis of tests that may have false positives. The danger of stigmatization needs to enter into the justification of even necessary tests.

Despite the potentially paternalistic nature of the law, we see no problem with legally mandated testing of newborns for conditions that should be detected and treated early. Such testing and treatment leads not only to the improvement of the quality of life, but to enormous savings to families and to society.

Compulsory Testing for Private Purposes

The ethics of compulsory testing of employees and prospective employees depend in the first place on whether the condition being detected is relevant to the business. Thus, drug and alcohol abuse by employees can be relevant not only to safety and efficiency, but to the ability to resist temptation in handling drugs and large sums of money. On the other hand, it is not immediately obvious that AIDS is relevant to the functioning of a business, except indirectly through its impact on health insurance premiums. Indeed, a case can be made that testing for AIDS and eliminating those who test positive is discrimination on the basis of handicap, rather than on the basis of job-related factors.

The ethical health care professional will carefully study the relevance of testing before deciding to cooperate with a company that requires tests. When the tests are subject to a large number of false positives, which can have serious negative effects on the worker, the health care professional must see to it that the testing program is scientifically sound so that no unnecessary harm is done.

Testing Patients and Health Professionals

The Centers for Disease Control (CDC) tested the political waters on the question of testing patients in the fall of 1991. While not calling for mandatory testing of all patients, it proposed that hospital patients be *urged* to undergo AIDS testing (Ruffenbach, 1991). There are several strong objections to this. Since this is broad-range screening rather than screening of target groups, there will be a high level of false positives that should then require expensive follow-up tests. The cost, which will be considered later, would be high, and it is not at all clear who would pay for these tests. Obviously, such testing might also provide health care workers with a false sense of security, since the incubation period of the HIV virus is so long that a single test cannot guarantee that the person does not have the virus. In short, there is an inherent risk of a false negative.

In the summer of 1991, the secretary of health and human services, while not calling for mandatory testing of health care professionals, *urged* all those who do exposure procedures to undergo AIDS testing (Ruffenbach, 1991). An exposure procedure is one in which there is risk of a cut and exposure to blood or other fluids that might transmit the HIV virus. Such testing might, as in the case of patients, provide a false sense of security. Repeated tests would be necessary and therefore testing would be expensive. For all that, if a health care worker suspects that he or she has been exposed to the HIV virus, such individuals would be obligated to themselves as well as to patients to undergo testing. The consequences of not testing in these conditions are, first, risk to both parties. The mere desire of health care workers not to know cannot justify foregoing testing that is medically indicated. As noted earlier, a founded fear of a breach of confidentiality would alter the ethics by introducing other possible consequences, such as stigmatization and loss of income. Here, as elsewhere, the debate should continue in an attempt to balance all the interests involved.

Testing and the Ethics of Allocation

The cost of tests on the basis of cases detected and the relationship of cases detected to cases successfully treated raises the problem of social allocation. When the tests are basically useless, since they do not lead to effective treatment or prevention, they are clearly wasteful and should not be paid for out of public funds. Indeed, the government might well spend money educating the public to the sham of such screenings. In other cases, the screening, although expensive on a case-detected basis, can lead to real good for a few individuals. The question then becomes whether such screening is part of the basic health care to which every individual is entitled. Or, to put it another way, is our human dignity disregarded if we are not screened for potential diseases or for diseases that we might transmit to our children? Put this way, the question calls for a negative answer. Our dignity does not demand every possible health service. At the same time, and in line with our principles in chapter 4, the society may decide that such screening is part of the basic health package to which every person is entitled. At the present time, cost consciousness about health care seems to militate against this, but the possibility remains. Public education regarding the dangers and limits of testing and screening should make the society and individual health care consumers less anxious to submit to or pay for tests and screening. In short, future decisions in this area should be based on increased awareness of what testing and health care can and cannot accomplish.

SUMMARY

In treatment situations, tests are ethically justified only if they can lead to an improvement in the patient's quality of life. The accuracy and interpretation of the tests, their tendency to give false positives and false negatives, and the availability of effective treatments enter into the justification of tests. Some tests are dangerous and need to be justified by proportionate benefits to the patient. The costs of tests must also enter into the decision if health costs are to be constrained. Overtesting by individual health care professionals is difficult to establish, although there is a suspicion that the entire system may lead to wasteful testing. The nature of tests raises questions about the duty to give patients more information about tests so that they can accept or reject them in terms of the patient's priorities and values.

Voluntary screening may be ethical if the subject is told who will have access to the results and what harmful consequences may result. Involuntary screening by government needs justification in terms of the public good. Involuntary screening by private groups needs justification in terms of relevance to goals of the particular organization. In all screening, the danger of stigmatization, the high cost of cases detected, and the dangers to confidentiality need special consideration. The cost factors of mass screening often pose problems in the fair allocation of health resources.

CASES FOR ANALYSIS

1. Maggie, a nursing student, is taking part in a health fair at the Uptown Mall. She takes blood pressures with a cuff that has not been calibrated in a long time. Despite this, she suggests that those with borderline and high readings visit their personal physicians. She also does simple checks for blood sugar and makes referrals where indicated. She has no idea whether the machine has been calibrated and what its margin of error is. She has no idea whether any of people she refers will go for help, whether she has needlessly alarmed them, or whether she is wasting her Saturday afternoon at the mall.

What is the health care professional's duty with regard to the calibration of instruments? Is it ethical to use a cuff that has not been calibrated for a long time? What harms can follow from inaccurate test results? What are the professional's responsibilities to individuals during such screenings?

2. Dr. Wilson, a country physician, has invested in office blood-testing equipment and a stress test machine, which he wants to pay off in a hurry. He uses the equipment routinely, since many of his patients have never had a full checkup. He does not worry about the accuracy of the machine, although there have been articles about the need to calibrate them. He does not worry about overuse, since Blue Cross, Blue Shield, and Medicare will simply refuse to pay him if he overuses the tests.

His early experience has been that the tests generate additional income because they unearth problems requiring additional treatment. Besides, the patients appreciate the convenience of taking the test locally, rather than traveling thirty miles to the nearest city to a regular laboratory.

What is to be said for the physician's routine use of these tests? If the insurance companies charge that he is overtesting are they correct? Does the physician have a legitimate economic interest in using the equipment as often as possible? Is he endangering his patients?

3. Mary works as a medical technologist in a large commercial laboratory that has just started to do drug testing for the Azziz Manufacturing Company, the major employer in Mary's small town. She is very aware that some of the tests used to detect drug use are insensitive; that is, they give false positives. Urine tests used to detect marijuana use will give positive results if the person has used ibuprofen, which is found in such over-the-counter drugs as Advil and Nuprin. Some cold remedies, such as Contac, will also cause the subject of the test to show as an amphetamine user. Good procedure would call for expensive additional tests to discover what people have actually taken.

The owners of the laboratory have told Azziz of the limits of the tests, but follow-up tests are not done. Quite a few people are fired after the first tests are reported to the company. Now Mary comes across a positive test for her boyfriend, although she knows he never takes anything stronger than a cold remedy or an antibiotic prescribed by his physician. She falsifies his test result.

Was Mary ethical in falsifying the results of her friend's test? Are there any cases for which Mary would be justified in telling her friend that he had tested positive and should push for a second and more accurate test? Is Mary ethical in working for a company that lets workers lose their jobs without sufficient reason?

4. A for-profit hospital that has just moved into the area wants to demonstrate community awareness and attract business. It decides to sponsor colorectal cancer screening or, more accurately, the free use of hematocrit kits. These detect the presence of rectal bleeding that is not visible to the naked eye and indicate the need for additional examination for possible cancer of the colon.

Although the cost of the individual test is small, the cost of mass screening may be high in terms of the number of cases detected and successfully treated. There is, then, a question of whether the screening really makes good sense. In 1978 the Consensus Development Conference on Mass Screening for Colorectal Cancer concluded that there were insufficient data to prove that the test reduced mortality in a screened population. The report also indicated that the benefit-cost risk indexes could not be calculated and recommended that the uncontrolled use of the method outside of special evaluation studies may not be of benefit to patients. Robin (1984) notes that nothing has changed since that time.

Despite this, the marketing department pushes the tests, even though some of the medical staff object that the campaign may deceive the public. Others on the medical staff disagree.

Is it ethical to "waste" medical resources on sales promotions and marketing? This raises questions about the ethics of the sales promotion of all drugs. What is the real value of advertising, since without some marketing the drug would never get to the patient or get there slowly?

5. Curative therapies for prostate cancer (the most common cancer in North American men) are limited to the early stage. In 1993 the American Cancer Society recommended that all men over fifty submit to an annual PSA (prostate specific antigen) blood test to detect an enlarged prostate and danger of prostate cancer.

The test costs between $30 and $70 and has associated costs for biopsies, ultrasound, and problems related to treatment. It is estimated that the recommended mass screening in the United States would cost $28 billion a year. Fortunately, about 25 percent of the men who test positively turn out to have only noncancerous enlargement of the prostate. On the other hand, some contend that about 40 percent of those who get negative results actually have treatable prostate cancer. Others, who claim that the test is highly accurate as a presecreening test, note that only one out of four selected by PSA for ultrasound and even more expensive tests turn out to have prostate cancer. The problem is complicated by the fact that some with prostate cancer suffer no harm from it. There is no way, however, of telling who these individuals are. Finally, some experts charge that there are no data to show that the PSA test has reduced mortality due to prostate cancer.

Is it ethical to advocate the PSA test in mass screening? Does the cost raise questions about the ethics of health care distribution? Given that 1 percent of patients die from prostate cancer surgery, would it be ethical to operate on the basis of a positive result on this test alone?

NOTES

1. The scandal connected with this laboratory is described by Walt Bogdanich, "Testing Debacle: Federal Lab Studying Train, Airline Crashes Fabricated Its Findings," *Wall Street Journal*, July 31, 1987, pp. 1, 16. It appears that some of the technicians did not even know how to use the sophisticated equipment.

12

THE ETHICS OF BIOMEDICAL RESEARCH

INTRODUCTION

Biomedical research involves both human and animal subjects. We are concerned only with research that utilizes humans including the fetus, as subjects.

The ethical problems with research using human subjects involve not only the research proper, but the use made of the research. We will, then, examine the ethics of both the researcher and the consumer of research. By the consumer, we mean the health care provider who reads the research and must make a decision as to whether the research may be applied in practice.

It is also useful to draw distinctions between validated clinical practice and experimental clinical practice. A practice is clinically validated when it has been scientifically studied in clinical trials and the results of the study indicate that it meets the criteria for validation. Other clinical practices, whether accepted in practice or not, are considered as nonvalidated.

Experimental practice may be of two sorts. First, it may involve the trial-and-error method of determining what will work for *a particular patient* when validated or accepted practices have failed. This sort of experimentation is a part of normal medical practice. In a second sense, the treatment may be experimental practice in that it seeks to find out if this treatment will help *patients in general*. When the treatment is being used to discover generalizable knowledge, we are in the realm of scientific research, where tests should involve a carefully drawn hypothesis in an attempt to draw general conclusions. This type of experimental research is the principal concern of the present chapter.

At the very start, it should be clear that human experimentation is necessary for medical progress. Animal testing is useful, but it cannot provide the final word on either safety or efficacy. At the same time, humans are not mere objects that can be used as the experimenter desires. In the first place, informed consent is even more necessary here than in the case of treatment. This is particularly true when we are dealing with nontherapeutic research, that is, with research that will not directly benefit the subjects. Since research, unlike validated treatment, ventures into the unknown, the risks are greater and harder to estimate, with the result that the calculation of a proportionate reason for the risk becomes very difficult.

THE ETHICS OF THE RESEARCHER

Both governments and professional societies have devoted much attention to the ethics of research. The Nuremberg Code (1948-9), dating from the trials of the Nazi war criminals, and the Declaration of the World Medical Association of Helsinki (1964, and revised in 1975) are further explicated by the Department of Health, Education and Welfare's (now Health and Human Services) *Belmont Report* (1978a). Professional associations, such as the American Psychological Association (1982) and the American Medical Association (1996), spell out the obligations of members in conducting both academic and clinical investigations. One provision of the AMA statement is central to all that follows:

> 2.07 (2) In conducting clinical investigation, the investigator should demonstrate the same concern and caution for the welfare, safety, and comfort of the person involved as required of a physician who is furnishing medical care to a patient independent of any clinical investigation.

More than that is required, however. Research on human subjects is not justified unless the benefits to be derived outweigh the risks taken. The mere increase of human knowledge is not a sufficient justification when there are risks involved. We must agree with Robin (1984) that some research is trivial, done more to satisfy some need of the researcher than to bring any real benefit to the human population. The benefits of even important research must, however, be balanced against the human and economic costs. The memory of Nazi atrocities in medical research made this all too clear and led to the following sample provisions in the Nuremberg Code.

> 2. The experiment should be such as to yield fruitful results for the good of society, unprocurable by other methods or means of study, and not random and unnecessary in nature.

4. The experiment should be so conducted as to avoid all unnecessary physical and mental suffering and injury.
5. No experiment shall be conducted where there is an *a priori* reason to believe that death or a disabling injury will occur, except, perhaps, in those experiments where the experimental physicians also serve as the subjects.
6. The degree of risk should never exceed that determined by the humanitarian importance of the problem to be solved by the experiment.

In our society, the federal government requires that institutions involved in research have institutional review boards (IRBs) to oversee this aspect of research. The main obligation remains with the researcher. The basic principle is clear: Granted informed consent and granted that there is no other way to get the knowledge, the degree of risk to the subjects is to be minimized. Any risk, however, still needs to justified by the humanitarian goods to be obtained from the research. These humanitarian goods are those that directly promote the welfare and dignity of the person. It is humanitarian goods, and not scientific knowledge, that supply the justification for the risks. In human research, knowledge is not self-justifying, and nothing can justify research that disregards the dignity of the human subjects.

Even granted agreement about these points, three different emphases or points of view emerge when actual judgments are to be made (Veatch, 1987). The first point of view stresses protecting the subject from harm, the second emphasizes social concerns, and the third focuses on freedom of choice.

Those who stress protecting the subject from harm use the following rule of thumb: "When in doubt, do what is safest for the subject." This is in line with the very traditional medical dictum: *primum est non nocere* ("the first thing is not to injure"). The second point of view recognizes that the humanitarian good involves society and patients who are not in the research study. It sees marginal risks justified by the good to this broader group. The freedom of choice approach holds that, granted informed consent, the subject should be able to choose what is most convenient even if it involves risks that a prudent person might not want to take. Each of these competing emphases has merit, and in practice all three points of view need to be considered. For this reason, the decision on the ethical correctness of a given piece of research cannot always be delineated with absolute clarity.

The problem is actually even more complicated than this. Sometimes the risks, such as that of radiation, are a matter of public debate and therefore politically and socially controversial (Veatch, 1987). The issue cannot be settled merely on the basis of scientific facts or scientific norms. Society itself must have its say about the ethics of an experiment involving such radiation. In addition, radiation may involve risk to parties not directly involved in the research: offspring, family members, and people who just happen to be in the neighborhood. The authors' practical wisdom approach would call for the consideration of these risks as well as the risks to the subject of the research.

Informed Consent: Information

When we are dealing with therapeutic research, that is, research that may directly benefit the subject, everything required for informed consent in chapter 2 should be revealed to the subject or his or her surrogate. In both therapeutic and nontherapeutic research, the subject should also be told the purpose of the research and whether random assignment will be used. That is, the subject must be informed that he or she may end up in a control group with no treatment, with a placebo, or with an alternative treatment. The subjects should also be informed of prior animal research and their results, with appropriate warnings about overextending the results to human beings. The subject should be told the *possible* therapeutic benefits to himself or others, but should not be given more hope than is justified, especially in desperate situations in which a subject is likely to agree to anything. The Belmont Report (1978a) correctly insists that the subject should be informed that it is possible to withdraw from the experiment at any time. The surrogates, moreover, should have a chance to observe the research and to withdraw the subject as the research proceeds.

No fact should be concealed that might cause the particular patient or a reasonably prudent person to refuse participation in the study. For example, if the experiment involves the injection of dead cancer cells, the subject should be told this, even if the dead cancer cells are harmless. Physicians who failed to give just this sort of information have lost their licenses in the past.

We have serious reservations about *Current Opinions of the Council on Ethical and Judicial Affairs of the American Medical Association* (AMA, 1996) on therapeutic research, which states the following:

> 2.07,(3), B.i. In exceptional circumstances, where the experimental treatment is the only potential treatment for the patient and full disclosure of information concerning the nature of the drug or experimental procedure and risks would pose such a serious psychological threat of detriment to the patient as to be medically contraindicated, such information may be withheld from the patient. In these circumstances, such information shall be disclosed to a responsible relative or friend of the patient where possible.

This statement, which invokes therapeutic privilege in an experimental situation, suffers from all the defects of therapeutic privilege discussed in chapter 2. The unfortunate history of medical researchers abusing patients for the sake of research simply reinforces concerns about the abuse of therapeutic privilege. Any effort to invoke this permission to circumvent informed consent must be done in the clear recognition of the priority of patient care over research, and must be treated with suspicion.

Nondisclosure for Scientific Reasons

Just as physicians sometimes attempt to justify nondisclosure for therapeutic reasons, scientists are tempted to conceal important information for scientific reasons. In particular, they argue that (1) disclosure would invalidate the research, (2) intentional deception is necessary for the research, and (3) disclosure would cause people to refuse their consent.

Before considering each of these points individually, it should be stated categorically and without any ifs, ands, or buts that the pursuit of scientific knowledge never justifies violating the rights of people. Knowledge is never superior to the dignity of the individual human being. The needs of the scientist do not and cannot take precedence over the dignity of the individual.

While the pursuit of scientific knowledge does not justify hiding substantial items of information, it is not necessary to disclose every detail. General rather than particular disclosure is sufficient and ethical for an informed consent and need not invalidate the research. Thus, when *particular disclosure*, for example, the disclosure of who would be and who would not be in the control group, would invalidate the experiment, a *general disclosure*, that is, the revelation that there will be random assignment to a control group, does not invalidate the experiment. A general disclosure of this sort of information is also ethical and suffices for informed consent.

The argument that intentional deception is necessary for the success of the experiment casts doubt on the ethical correctness of the experiment not only because of the deception, but because of the possible motives for the deception. If the subject is being deceived, lest she or he refuse consent, the experiment is clearly reprehensible.

Although the authors of the Belmont Report are not quite so strict, they add important considerations, and their opinion demands great respect:

> A special problem of consent arises where informing subjects of some pertinent aspect of the research is likely to impair the validity of the research. In many cases, it is sufficient to indicate to subjects that they are being invited to participate in research of which some features may not be revealed until the research is concluded. In all cases of research involving incomplete disclosure, such research is justified only if it is clear that (1) incomplete disclosure is truly necessary to accomplish the goals of the research, (2) there are no undisclosed risks to subjects that are more than minimal, and (3) there is an adequate plan for debriefing subjects, when appropriate and for dissemination of research results to them. Information about risks should never be withheld for the purpose of eliciting the cooperation of subjects, and truthful answers should always be given to direct questions about the research. Care should be taken to distinguish the cases in which disclosure would destroy or invalidate the research from cases in which disclosure would simply inconvenience the investigator (p. 12).

Who Pays for Bad Results?

The subject should also be informed of who pays for unforeseen bad results, such as a crippling or debilitating side effect of the treatment. It is not merely a question of who pays for the treatment of the side effect, but of who pays for the loss of income and enjoyment of life. Although it may be argued that, at least in therapeutic research, the risks are the price the patient pays for the hope of a cure, such is not the case in nontherapeutic research. In any event, if the subject and the subject's insurance carrier will bear all the costs, this should be stated and a written agreement obtained at the time that the consent is being obtained.

Informed Consent: Competence and Surrogates

All the factors considered in chapter 1 enter into the consideration of the competence of research subjects to give informed consent. In the research context, however, particular attention must be paid to surrogate consent and to the situation of institutionalized subjects.

There are no special problems with surrogate consent to experimentation that is therapeutic. In therapeutic research, the patient can hope to benefit directly from the experiment, and so the surrogate may judge that the experiment is for the good of the subject. There may, however, be problems with surrogate consent to nontherapeutic research since, by definition, the patient will receive no direct benefit from this. The problems have their roots in the various principles that the surrogate may use.

As discussed in chapter 3, the surrogate may use one of three principles: (1) the substituted judgment principle, (2) the best interests principle, or (3) the rational choice principle.

There is no problem if the substituted judgment principle is used, since in this case the surrogate is doing what he or she knows the subject wants or would want in the situation. If the subject would consent to the research, the surrogate can certainly do so.

If the rational choice principle is used, there are no additional problems aside from those connected with the principle itself. The rational choice principle, you will recall, includes consideration of the good and evil consequences for others as well as for the patient. The American Medical Association (1996), which invokes the rational choice principle for the surrogate, is useful in this context:

2.07, (4), Minors or mentally incompetent persons may be used as subjects in clinical investigation only if:
  i. The nature of the investigation is such that mentally competent adults would not be suitable subjects.
  ii. Consent, in writing, is given by a legally authorized representative for the subject under circumstances in which informed and prudent adults would reasonably be expected to volunteer themselves or their children as subjects.

There are problems, however, if the best interest principle is applied, since in nontherapeutic research the subject is not going to benefit directly. In this case, participation can hardly be said to be in the interest of the subject, let alone in his or her best interests.

Even when the best interest principle seems to forbid surrogate consent, the following points should be considered. When there is no risk or minimum risk to the subject and considerable good to be obtained from the research, it seems petty to forbid consent. Since minimal risk involves no more than the risk of a routine physical examination or the risks of everyday living, there is no real ethical problem with surrogate consent in this sort of research. If there is more than minimal risk, the best interest principle cannot justify surrogate consent. However, the substituted judgment principle and the rational choice principle may still permit consent.

Consent and the Special Classes of Subjects

The case of institutionalized subjects raises special problems for informed consent. It is argued that the institutionalized live in an inherently coercive environment such that there is always undue influence on their consent. This argument is especially plausible when it is a question of prisoners who will get extra privileges and who know that participation may help their cases for parole. At the same time, there may be a question of paternalism that rushes in to protect everyone, whether they need the protection or not. Certainly, the experimenter should be particularly cautious in getting consent from such subjects, but, absent legal restrictions, the institutionalized subject need not be universally ruled out of consideration.

Something similar may be said of the objections against research on older people. The mere fact that a person is old does not make that person incapable of informed consent. If all older people were considered incompetent, then there could be no therapeutic research for the group that most needs medical care. Such paternalism would be insulting and physically injurious to the older citizen. The experimenter should be extra cautious in dealing with the older subject, especially the institutionalized older person, but there can still be ethical experimentation in these areas.

Justice and the Distribution of Research Risks

It has been argued that the overuse of institutionalized persons and the poor constitutes an unjust distribution of research risks. Overuse, or use out of proportion to their distribution in the population as a whole, does not necessarily constitute an injustice. There is injustice *only if justice demands that the risks be distributed equally.* As we saw in chapter 4, equality of distribution of health care is not required for justice, and so risk need not be equally distributed.

Risk and burden can never be distributed equally in a society that believes in free choice and protects the right to refuse to contribute, except when overriding social interests require it by law. In such a society, only two groups of people are likely to accept the burden of being research subjects. The first and smaller group is comprised of extremely altruistic and generous people. The second and considerably larger group is comprised of those who are so deprived that there is some financial or social reward for their participation. As noted, the prisoner participates in the interest of better living conditions and an improved chance of parole. The poor may participate in exchange for medical care or a fee. Although this may not be an ideal situation, it is a situation that must be accepted and worked with under current economic circumstances.

A wider distribution of research risks will come about only if people come to believe that medical research is so important to them and to their society that they feel an obligation to participate and so require it legally. The fact that the general population does not feel as strongly about this as the research establishment is not to condemn the priorities of the general population. After all, there are other goods besides the health care system.

Although there is no overall solution even for a society of good will, certain warnings of the Belmont Report (1978a) are still very applicable to justice on the individual level. The report notes that the poor, the institutionalized, and certain minorities should be protected from being used "solely for administrative convenience or because they are easy to manipulate as a result of their illness or socioeconomic condition." In addition, it would be clearly unfair to offer beneficial research to those whom the researcher likes and to select only "undesirable" persons for risky research.

Conflicts of Interest

Since humans are involved, medical research, like every other area of human life, involves both actual and potential conflicts of interest. An actual conflict of interest exists when the researcher subordinates the good of patients or the public good to his or her own interests. Thus, a physician engaged in research financed by a drug company *in which he owns stock* would be guilty of a conflict of interest if, to increase stock dividends from the drug company, he fudged the data or reported favorable results not justified by the reactions of his patient. In such a case, quite aside from the deception and lying, the physician has put his own financial gain above the long-term good of patients and so ahead of the public good.

A potential conflict of interest exists when the health care researcher is in a position in which many individuals would be strongly tempted to subordinate the public or the patient's good to their own interests. The potential conflict of interest is then a temptation that would cause others to suspect the ethics of the researcher. The good of the health care professions demands that even the appearance of a potential conflict be avoided. As we have stressed in many instances, the good name of the profession is an important good for the effective function of health care professionals. Thus there is a serious obligation to protect this reputation in research as in practice.

We feel that the good of the profession and the reputation of medical researchers demand that even potential conflicts of interest be avoided. Indeed, research universities and hospitals where the researchers work should have written conflict of interest policies and disclosure statements of stock ownership in sponsoring groups. Such a policy, like those in business, would set limits to the ownership of stock in sponsoring companies whether by the physician or the immediate family. (For a discussion of such policies and disclosure rules see Garrett and Klonoski, 1986.)

Ethical Problems of Research Methodology

In general, poorly designed research is both unscientific and unethical, because it wastes resources. When it is poorly designed, medical research also tends to expose subjects to unnecessary risks. Since no good can come of poorly designed research, no proportionate reason will ever justify the risks and the waste of resources. Finally, as we will stress in the section on the consumption of research, poorly designed research that gets published creates ethical problems for health care providers who may hurt patients by using poor research in their decision making.

A brief look at some of the basics of well-designed scientific clinical research will give some idea of what is involved.

In general, if the results of scientific research are to be generalizable, the subjects should be drawn from the population appropriate to the study. Furthermore, even given the proper population, the sampling would still have to be random to remove bias. A random sample is one in which every member of the population being studied has an equal chance of being studied. This condition would not obtain if researchers gave preference to their own patients who belong to the population being studied. Randomness of selection would also be destroyed if selection from the population were made on the basis of the ability to pay, or the willingness to be a subject for pay, or even on the basis of mere availability. Many studies have been known to violate these basic norms. More often than not, only a subset of the population will be selected, and that on the basis of medical criteria. When we are dealing with drug experimentation for such deadly diseases as AIDS, the question of how these subjects are picked becomes crucial. As Macklin and Friedland (1986) suggest, medical criteria may not be value-free. Thus, for example, there might be a temptation to eliminate intravenous drug abusers from a trial for an AIDS drug on the ground that they are less healthy than gay men. This would not only narrow the value of the results, but also discriminate against a whole class of persons in need.

To ensure scientific rigor, medical research needs a baseline, generally supplied by a control group, to use as a basis for comparison with the experimental group. The control group gets the standard treatment, no treatment, or a placebo. The experimental group gets the treatment being studied. To eliminate bias on the part of the subjects and the researchers, subjects are assigned to each group randomly, that is, by a procedure imitating chance. Just as the entire sample was selected randomly from the population to be studied, the sample is then divided and assigned by a second randomization. This is part of the effort to make sure that the two groups are similar and so truly comparable. They would not be comparable if such factors as social status, influence with the researcher, or place of residence influenced assignment.

To further eliminate bias, the experiment should be double-blind; that is, neither the subjects nor the experimenters should know who is in which group. In this way, the patients will not feel better because they have been noticed or just because they have received something new, and the researchers will not be tempted to imagine improvements where there are none.

These basic methods give rise to some very basic ethical questions quite aside from the problem of informed consent.

Discrimination against Women and Minorities

Although unnoticed for a long time, medical researchers often discriminated against women and minorities by simply not including them or not including them in sufficient numbers to get valid results. This discrimination has potentially serious effects if women are treated when no treatment is needed or untreated when treatment is called for.

Minorities have suffered similar neglect, even though we know that there are differences in the effects of some drugs on Asiatics and Caucasians. In view of these problems, we are inclined to suggest that the following measures should be taken. When necessary, they should be backed up by law. First, efforts should be made to ensure that women and minorities are not *underrepresented* in the sample. Second, enough women and minorities should be included in large-scale studies so that it is possible to decide if there are different effects in the different populations. Third, the cost–benefit ratio of the first two suggestions should be carefully analyzed.

These obvious suggestions must, however, face objections about the costs of such procedures and the possibility of stereotyping women and minorities. The regulations issued by the National Institute of Health in 1994 require representative samples of women and minorities only in Phase Three during trials, that is, in the large-scale trials that occur only after the drug has been found safe for humans. The regulations give exemptions even in Phase Three trials. Thus if prior studies have given no evidence of differences, it is not necessary to study differences. This may beg the question, since prior studies may have made no effort to study differences.

Ethics of Randomized Trials

Although the use of randomized trials (studies in which the patient is randomly assigned to either the experimental or control group) is scientifically necessary when there is no baseline, it poses ethical problems when the *a priori* odds (the odds before the experiment starts) are not approximately equal for both the control and the experimental groups. Let us envision a case as follows: Historically, there has been no effective treatment for disease Z. With rare exceptions, those who contract Z die. This is a historical baseline. A drug, Beta, has been found effective in animals, safe in human beings, and effective against diseases similar to Z. Thus, there is some probability that it will work in patients with disease Z. The tests of its efficacy in humans are about to begin. Those assigned to the control group will have no chance of recovery, since there is no effective treatment and the disease in generally fatal. Those assigned to the experimental group may have some small hope, since Beta worked with similar diseases.

Is it ethical to use a control group? As indicated earlier, the answer is "No," since the best interests of those in the control group are disregarded. That is, the control group is not given a chance of the slight hope that Z will help. In addition, the control group serves no scientific purpose in this case, since a historical baseline already exists.

Something similar occurred in the Tuskegee Syphilis Study, in which the Public Health Service used African Americans with untreated syphilis as a control group despite the availability of effective treatments. The supposed purpose was to examine the course of the diease, but the disease was already well known. As effective treatments became available, particularly penicillin, the subjects were neither told of the treatment nor provided it. Thus, there were a variety of failures of research ethics in this study, including a lack of informed consent and a lack of respect for the patient. The racist selection of patients completed the moral nightmare of this case, and has led to concern that minorities are refusing to become research subjects out of distrust (King, 1992).

Let us change the examples. In disease Y, there is a standard treatment, and the research involves a new drug that may or may not be an improvement over the standard treatment. In this research, the control group gets the standard treatment, while the experimental group gets the new drug, Beta. Suppose that halfway through the experiment it *appears* that drug Beta is vastly superior to the standard treatment. Is it ethical to continue the experiment, or should the test be stopped and all patients given drug Beta?

The answer is not as simple as it seems. If the experiment is not completed, we do not know whether the scientific requirements of proof have been met. That is, there is no validation of the drug. There may be an increase in false positives, that is, of cases in which a cure is seen when there is none. There are cases in which the favorable results were due to a poorly designed experiment. Equally serious is the fact that premature termination of the experiment may fail to reveal harmful long-term effects, as well as long-term benefits.

It is our best but by no means unshakable opinion that the experiment should be discontinued in the face of early favorable results under two conditions: First, the good results are certain, statistically significant, or with a high degree of probability due to the treatment, and the discontinuance has been scientifically planned. It is for these reasons that we speak of the *a priori* odds and not of the interim results as posing the ethical problem. Second, the control group being given a placebo or a standard treatment is suffering from a fatal or seriously crippling disease such that there is no proportionality between their suffering and the information to be gained.

Discontinuance in these cases is warranted by immediate beneficence, but leaves us without scientific validation and with all the problems mentioned earlier. In case of doubt, however, the health care professional's first duty is not to science and the future, but to the patient who is present here and now.

There is, in many cases, another solution to the problem of the ethics of random selection. If a crossover study is employed, the odds of both the experimental and control groups profiting are equalized. In the crossover design, there is a set point at which the experimental group is changed from the experimental drug to the other treatment or no treatment, while the control group is now given the experimental treatment. Such a methodology may be a viable alternative in some circumstances and so offer an ethical solution to the problem of random assignment.

Problem of the Double-Blind

The fact that the experiment is to be double-blind (neither the experimenter nor the patient knows who is getting which treatment) raises problems with regard to the deception of subjects and the suppression of the truth in the informed consent procedure. Even when the subjects know that they will be randomly distributed between the control and the experimental group, there can be ethical problems. In the interests of eliminating bias, the double-blind also reduces the ability of health care professionals to respond rapidly to the changing condition of the subject. The subjects cannot be given the best health care in such situations. This aspect should be part of the informed consent process; that is, subjects should be told that they may not get the best medical care in some situations.

Institutional Review Boards

Federal law requires an institutional review board (IRB) in hospitals and educational and research institutions that receive federal research funds. Not all federally funded research must be reviewed by these boards, since exceptions are made for ordinary tests given in educational settings, research involving surveys, interviews, or data collection, or the observation of public behavior. The law does not even require informed consent in these exempt areas.

The composition of these boards is to be structured to prevent conflicts of interest resulting from a narrow approach to their work. The regulations provide that not all members may be of the same sex or from the institution or from the same professional group. In addition, no one may be a member if a conflict of interest would result. Although these specifications of membership may be well-intentioned, they pose problems that will be discussed in a moment.

The IRB reviews and approves or disapproves of the proposed research in its institutions in terms of risk benefit analysis. In addition, the board is to make sure that there is written informed consent that contains the necessary information. Without this approval, the research cannot be funded or permitted to begin. While these boards are not infallible or always effective, they are an attempt to provide some ethical safeguards in research.

Veatch (1987) raises interesting questions about the boards' effectiveness in terms of their composition. Boards that are dominated by professional and institutional members and chosen by the institution may have a systematic bias that causes them to overlook factors of importance to the normal prudent person. On the other hand, the jury model of the board, which is composed of nonprofessionals and so is more representative of the community, is a more powerful representative of the ordinary person and the conscience of the community. A fully representative and randomly chosen board is not really applicable here, since an IRB needs at least some members who understand the complexities of research. The representative model of the IRB contains both experts and representatives of the public. Ideally, such a group would represent all the ethical, moral, and legal interests of society, as well as scientific expertise.

Even given a representative IRB, problems may arise from the method of selection, the method of voting, and the balance between institutional and noninstitutional members. If the institution controls the selection of members, it can easily and even unintentionally stack the committee to favor one rather than another perspective. Perhaps outside groups need a right to appoint representatives with specific points of view.

If voting on the committee is by majority, indeed, if anything less than unanimity is required, a significant point of view may be left out of the decision. Thus, a psychologist who votes against a physiological research project because of anticipated psychological problems in the subjects may be a minority of one, but she or he still represents a valid and important point of view. The same may be said of the layperson who represents the community point of view and is unimpressed by the scientific justifications of acts that are repugnant to the average person. Once again, a majority vote could disregard this crucial aspect of the ethics of research.

Veatch (1987) argues that the number of noninstitutional members on the board should be increased so that the number of perspectives is enlarged. Even though institutional members might represent a large number of disciplines, their membership in the institution may have narrowed their perspective—thus the need for an increased number of public members.

Those interested in more details on the nature, structure, and functions of the IRB should consult the Code of Federal Regulations 45 CFR 46: Protection of Human Rights, as well as *IRB: A Review of Human Subjects Research*, and the *Report and Recommendations: Institutional Review Boards and Appendix* (1978b), issued by the National Commission for the Protection of Human Subjects (nos. OS 78-0008 and OS 78-0009).

Summary

In biomedical research, subjects must be told everything required for the informed consent of patients (see chapter 2), plus the nature of the study and such details as might influence the consent of the subject. Particular attention must be paid to the autonomy of institutionalized patients and the elderly, as well as to poor persons who might be easily exploited. Risks must be taken only when necessary, must be minimized, and require justification from the humanitarian viewpoint and not merely from scientific good results.

Special problems exist in research that uses double-blind and randomized assignment to treatment and control groups.

THE ETHICS OF THE USER OF RESEARCH RESULTS

The health care professional is obliged to protect patients from harm insofar as this possible. This protection involves, among other things, a careful reading of research publications with two purposes in mind. First, the professional will want to be up to date on the latest in his or her field. Second, the professional will want to screen the research so that poor work is not used as a basis of health care practice. This second purpose demands a critical and informed reading of professional journals.

Some may object that a critical and informed reading of the journals is not required because the editors and, in the case of the better journals, the referees have read the article critically and in an informed way, culled out the poor articles, and put their seal of approval on those that are published.

In short, many professionals rely on the editors and referees. Unfortunately, some medical and nursing literature is not subject to peer review. Periodicals supported by advertisements from drug companies often solicit articles. Even in the case of those with peer review, research shows that this reliance is not always well founded. In addition, even when reliance is well-founded, a critical and informed reading is still required if the health care provider wishes to use the information intelligently and safely.

Reliance on the editors and referees is not an adequate safeguard in science in general or in medical research in particular. Broad and Wade (1982), Schoolman et al. (1968), and Sabine (1985) all speak to the errors and defects of methodology that regularly get by the editors and referees of even the best journals. Mosteller (1985) and Patterson and Bailar (1985) have studied the peer review process and the selection of papers and concluded that the reader still needs to proceed with care. Shapiro and Charrow (1985) write of "scientific misconduct in investigational drug trials." McDonald (1986) summarizes studies that indicate that as many as 75 percent of the papers examined may be flawed by some scientific misconduct. As many as 25 percent may be marked by *serious* scientific misconduct, such as publishing statements that are known to be misleading. In view of all this, it seems clear that the obligation to read critically remains in force.

Coping with the Biomedical Literature: A Primer for the Scientist and the Clinician (Warren, 1981) is an attempt to provide the basic tools for such critical reading. Duffy (1985) supplies a checklist for evaluating nursing research reports. *The New England Journal of Medicine* frequently publishes articles on research methodology intended to help the critical health care professional. We will not attempt to summarize any of this work, but will illustrate some of the simpler and more obvious points often neglected by readers.

The critical reading of a scientific paper requires that the reader know something about research methodology and the statistical methods used in reporting and analyzing data. The reader, for example, should be aware that generalizable conclusions cannot be drawn from a nonrandomized sample. An experiment done on seven volunteers from your medical ethics class will not produce results that you can then apply to all human beings, or even all Americans or all college students. The results might raise some interesting questions, but they would not provide you with any general truths that you could with honesty and safety apply to others.

The mere fact that the researchers fail to inform you of how they randomized the sample should create suspicions about the results. Not all methods that look random are random. For example, a method that involves taking every tenth name from a patient list after you have excluded those too sick to be interviewed is hardly a random process. But if the authors fail to tell the reader the crucial details, careless or unsophisticated readers may treat bad research as if it were well-designed and its results significant. In addition, good scientific writing demands that these important details be shared so that the study can be replicated. Failure to include pertinent details may thus show ignorance of or contempt for sound methodology.

Even when there is a properly drawn random sample, the results must be properly analyzed. Statistics, after all, do not give us certainty, only probabilities. The mere fact that one treatment produced better results than the other does not tell us much, unless we know what the chances are that the difference between treatments was due to more than mere chance.

We need to know the confidence level of the differences so that we can know how much weight to give the results. That is, we should know the probability that there is a type I error, which occurs when the observed results are attributed to treatment, but are merely due to chance. We would also like to know the probability of a type II error, which occurs when the effect is attributed to chance, but is actually an effect of treatment.

A good piece of research will tell us that P (the probability that the differences are due to chance) is less than a preselected number such as 0.05 or 0.10. The number 0.05 tells us that there is a 5 percent chance or less, that is, one chance in twenty or less, that the results were due to chance. If the number were 0.10, indicating a one out of ten chance that the results were due merely to chance, a clinician might not want to use the results or at least would be on her or his guard against the chance that the results were not valid in a given case. If nothing else, constant attention to the confidence level would keep practitioners aware that they are not dealing with certitude, but only with the odds. If no confidence level is given, beware.

Successful replication of an experiment is supposed to reduce the odds that the results, favorable or unfavorable, were due to chance. When the replication is unsuccessful, that is, when it reaches the opposite results of the original experiment (again with the chance that it too is due to chance), we are left very much in the dark. A classic case is presented in the *New England Journal of Medicine* (October 24, 1986). The *Journal* published two articles on postmenopausal estrogen therapy related to coronary heart disease (Stampfer et al., 1985; Wilson et al., 1985). Each article was based on impeccable scientific research, but the results were contradictory. The results of one or both of the studies were due to chance. Neither of them should be followed in practice until additional research clears up the matter.

Unfortunately, there is not enough replication in medical research, and the replication that exists is most often not published if it achieved negative results. In general, scientists do not submit and scholarly journals do not publish studies with negative results. As a consequence, valuable negative information is lost, while "successful" but erroneous or misleading research is accepted, published, and acted on.

Outcome Research

Outcome research looks at how a treatment performs in real life when used by hundreds of doctors on a diverse population. It thus goes beyond trials performed when the therapy was still experimental. Outcome research looks not merely at mortality or reduction in tumor size, but at the impact on the patient's daily life. This involves interviewing patients over time in order to determine long-range as well as short-range effects of treatment. These real life effects interest patients, who must make decisions about refusing or accepting treatment. In time, such research may also reduce health care costs by eliminating treatments that, while technically effective, do not noticeably improve the patient's life.

As this research becomes more widely available, health care practitioners will have an ethical obligation to give it a critical reading and to advise patients of the results of valid research projects.

The Double-Blind

The critical reader of health care research will want to know not only about randomization, confidence levels, and replication, but about the existence or nonexistence of a double-blind. Because medical researchers as well as patients are subject to biases, the researcher will want to guard against this by the use of the double-blind, a method that ensures that neither the researcher nor the subject knows who is getting the experimental treatment. When there is no double-blind, the reader will have to be on his or her guard against all sorts of biases and psychological effects that arise from the patients' getting extra attention or believing that they are receiving a miracle drug.

All this comes down to saying that health care professionals need to understand and use statistics and research methodology. If they lack such knowledge, they are not capable of a critical reading of the research and should be both ethically and professionally inhibited from using research that they do not fully understand.

When There Is No Research

Although health care is supposed to be based on scientific study, in many cases no clinical research exists to justify the treatment. This is particularly true of surgical procedures. For many years, male children were routinely circumcised. Research has now shown that there was no necessity for the procedure. Indeed, it exposed male babies to unnecessary risks. At one time, tonsils were extracted in wholesale fashion. Now we know that this should be done only rarely and for very serious reasons. Unfortunately, there is no organized vehicle for detecting such errors, and it may take a long time for reform to occur. Even when the error is detected, it takes time for health care providers to unlearn their errors (Robin, 1984).

In view of this, the health care provider should constantly ask to see the scientific basis and the carefully controlled clinical trials that justify practice, and not merely assume that accepted and professional approved practice is justified practice. A critical attitude will save more lives than a blind acceptance of health care professional group think.

When the Research Is Disregarded

The careless reading of research or the reliance on fads among peers can lead to disastrous results. The best known case involved diethylstilbestrol (DES). From the 1940s to the early 1970s, this drug was given to pregnant women. Between 4 and 6 million daughters of the women who received the drug have had problems. These range from clear-cell carcinomas to benign vaginal conditions associated with, among other problems, various forms of cancer.

The drug was designed for women who had serious medical problems and who had repeatedly miscarried. The research indicated that it did nothing positive for healthy women or even slightly increased their incidence of reproductive difficulties. Despite this, it became a fad and was used indiscriminately, with grave consequences for DES daughters. A critical reading of the research and a resistance to faddish thinking could have saved much heartache and illness. Similar questions have been raised about the use of research on borderline high blood pressure (Guttmacher et. al., 1981) and radical mastectomy (Katz, 1984).

When the Research Is Dishonestly Presented

In a long-used media campaign, the American Cancer Society promotes the idea that one of ten women will be a victim of breast cancer. They do not inform the reader or viewer that this rests on the assumption that all women will live to be 110 years old (Kelley, 1991). When confronted with the unlikelihood of this assumption, they disregarded the question of truth and argued that the advertising encouraged women to seek breast examinations. This is deceptive advertising, and while it may have fine intention, it remains an example of the misuse of truth. The society is limiting the ability of patients to make informed decisions about the risks of breast cancer by manipulating the information that it provides.

Results of Nazi Research

There is a dispute about whether it is ethical to use the results of very unethical Nazi medical research. One side says it is unethical to use the results of even properly designed Nazi research, lest the mantle of respectability be cast over the cruel and inhuman investigations performed on prisoners in the concentration camps. On the other side are those who say that, if the results of unethical but methodologically correct research can help anyone, the results can be used ethically. Indeed, the proponents of this approach note that using the results from such research can be a memorial to its victims.

Strong emotions can cloud the issues, but the authors are inclined to say that the results should be used, dedicated as a memorial to the victims and accompanied by continued reminders that we must be eternally vigilant lest the madness of the Nazis capture the minds of contemporary scientists.

Summary

The health care provider has an ethical obligation to read research critically. This requires a knowledge of statistics and research methodology. In addition, practitioners should beware lest they follow accepted practice when it is not based on sound clinical trials or, worse yet, follow professional fads that run counter to research.

FETAL RESEARCH

The ethical problems connected with fetal research are particularly thorny because they raise issues that cut to the heart of the relationship, not to mention the tension, between ethical considerations and scientific presumption. American culture has long nurtured the idea that scientific progress is inevitable and therefore unfettered scientific research can only be beneficial. Fetal research, and the genetic research discussed later in this chapter, pits these assumptions about science against our struggle to identify and protect human dignity, and does so in the areas where we are most desirous of success: health and longevity. A further problem is the increasing opportunity and willingness to commercialize both human tissue and genetic information, by patenting and selling these as products. There are several types of fetal research, but two are particularly important: research on fetal tissue and research on fetal development *in utero*. In evaluating the ethical correctness of both types it is important to look again at the moral status of the fetus (see chapter 8) , and to look clearly and unemotionally at the promise of these research projects.

A central concern of the ethics of fetal research is the moral status of the fetus. In its recommendations issued in 1994, the National Institutes of Health's Human Embryo Research Panel suggested that the preimplantation human embryo could be the subject of research because it lacks individuation, its lacks the possibility of sentience and other human psychological qualities, and it has a high rate of mortality. They suggest the development of the primitive streak as a marker for personhood. In their recommendations, research with the promise of significant benefit for human health could be done prior to the development of the primitive streak, but they reserve approval for, or simply disapprove of, research that is not directed toward some sort of therapy or that involves germline manipulation. The concerns that ground their reservations are based on respect for the fetus, the protection of those born, the protection of scientific research from public outcry, and the protection of our sense of humanity and family (National Institutes of Health, 1994). Their position has been the basis for a limited resumption of fetal research supported by the federal government, but it has proven controversial for several reasons.

The federal panel's selection of the primitive streak as a marker for personhood has struck many as arbitrary, and its call for respect for the preimplanatation embryo has been criticized as unclear and possibly vacuous (Callahan, 1995). As we argued in chapter 8, there is no clear, universally accepted answer to when the fetus becomes a person, and as a result there is no clear marker that would indicate personhood.

The issue is the protection of the fetus's serious right to life. That obligation to protect must be balanced against other goods, but those other goods must be sufficiently real and sufficiently weighty to justify any harm or risk to the fetus. The use of fetal tissue in therapy became a reality in 1992 when three experimental studies indicated that transplantation of fetal tissue lessened the symptoms of Parkinson's disease and so reduced the need for increased doses of drugs. Considering the devastating nature of Parkinson's symptoms, these results show us where there may be a proportionate reason of some experimental work with fetal tissue. The difficulties with clarifying our obligations to the fetus are magnified by increasingly suggestive research results using fetal tissues. Subsequent success will further change the proportionality even when the research is nontherapeutic. However, everyone involved must be careful to recognize that research is based only on the hope and substantiated expectation of positive results. No one knows whether the research will succeed and produce the benefits hoped for. Thus, when evaluating the ethical correctness of a research project we must remember that the knowledge it *might* produce must be weighed against the *known worth* of a human being and our *known obligation* to protect the fetus.

A further concern is that in the absence of clear guidelines for the respect of the fetus, the business applications of this research can take over and the most powerful motive for the research becomes commercial profit. Proposals to patent the results of fetal tissue research (see the following discussion on stem cells), even to patent our knowledge of the human genome, have far-reaching implications for our understanding of human dignity, our goals of health care, and our ability to justly distribute health care.

Embryonic Stem Cells

Embryonic stem cells are primordial cells harvested from either the inner mass of a blastocyst (a stage in the development of a fetus that occurs approximately four days after fertilization) or from the gonadal tissue of aborted fetuses. These cells are pluripotent, that is, they have the potential to develop into many different types of human cells, and the cell line is immortal, which means it can be cultured indefinitely into a limitless supply of cells. There are numerous potential uses for stem cells, including tissue transplantation, in which a failing organ could be rejuvenated by an injection of stem cells; pharmaceutical testing; embryology; and gene therapy.

Several problems exist regarding the development and use of stem cells. The main problem that is the original source of these cells is a fetus. As in fetal tissue research, this raises the problem of the moral status of the fetus. Does the harvesting of these cells involve sacrificing a person for scientific research? At this stage, it cannot be said that this research guarantees successful treatments. So these cells will be used for research, not treatment. Should the need to protect the fetus (as discussed in chapter 8) be dropped in favor of exciting research?

A problem that is also significant is the nature and moral status of these cells. They have been removed from the blastocyst and cultured in a laboratory. What was the blastocyst? What are the stem cells? Are they persons or are they tissue? What effect has the scientific alteration of the cells had on their meaning and significance (McGee and Caplan, 1999)? Can stem cells be patented and sold as a product, or do their human origins require that they be treated with more respect (Knowles, 1999)? But, if greater respect is required, what does that mean? These questions raise difficult metaphysical problems regarding the difference between the person and nature, and between the person and the thing made. In the isolation of stem cells, we have taken what might be a person (the embryo or blastocyst) and taken it apart to make things (the stem cells). Society will have to decide if the risk of harm to human dignity is outweighed by the possibility that someday stem cells may be useful in medical treatments. There is the possibility in this that we will lose our respect for ourselves as human beings and simply see ourselves as consumer products like any other machine. In chapter 9, we discussed the charge of artificiality, and this concern with fetal research is perhaps the most dramatic example of the issues that artificiality raises. This also raises the question of property (Nelkin and Andrews, 1998). Who owns fetal tissue: The woman who donates the egg? The man who donates the sperm? The researcher? Again, it is the direct responsibility of society to answer these questions, to provide itself with the legal guidelines for behavior. But working to find these answers will sorely try the ability of both the United States and the global community to come to agreement.

The Fetus *In Utero*

A second type of concern is with regard to research on the fetus *in utero*. This raises some familiar issues, but nevertheless calls for great caution to ensure the protection of all concerned. First, consent of the mother is necessary whether the fetus is destined for abortion or not. Second, the right of the mother to change her mind should be protected. Third, even when dealing with a nonviable fetus, there must be a proportionate good to be attained. In this context, we note that therapeutic research directed to the good of the fetus is often permissible. This would include research on fetal surgery to cure obstructive hydrocephalus and obstructive uropathy. Similarly, therapeutic research directed toward the mother would also be permissible if the fetus were placed at risk only to the extent necessary to protect the health of the mother.

Assuming informed consent of the mother, the following scenarios seem reasonable as examples:

1. Research directed to the fetus *in utero* when (a) there is no anticipation of abortion, the risks are minimal, and the knowledge can be obtained by no other means or (b) there is an anticipation of abortion but the risks are minimal.
2. Nontherapeutic research on the pregnant woman if the risks to the fetus are minimal.
3. Nontherapeutic research directed to the fetus *in utero* when (a) abortion is not anticipated, the risks are minimal, and the knowledge is not obtainable in any other way or (b) there is anticipation of abortion and the risks are minimal.
4. Nontherapeutic research directed toward the fetus during the abortion and nontherapeutic research directed toward the nonviable fetus *ex utero*, provided the fetus is at less than twenty weeks gestational stage and no significant changes made in the interests of the research alone are introduced into the process.
5. Research directed toward a possibly viable fetus is permitted when there are no additional risks to the infant and when the knowledge cannot be obtained by any other means.

Yet, the following questions can and should be raised about these scenarios. First, does the fact that abortion is anticipated justify doing away with the requirement that the knowledge not be obtainable in any other way? Has the fact of an anticipated abortion suddenly made this fetus less equal? Second, does the fact that the aborted fetus is not viable justify doing away with the condition that the knowledge cannot be obtained in any other way? To put it another way, does the fact that a fetus is doomed, whether by nature or someone's choice, give it a different moral status?

The authors do not know the answers to these questions, although they are inclined to answer all of them with a "No." The questions deserve carefully considered answers. There are, however, several important points to be made in the discussion of these questions. The fact that a society that seems to permit all sorts of abortions still limits research on the fetus indicates that we are still groping our way toward a consensus about the moral status of the fetus. The limits on research certainly indicate a sense that great harm could result if everyone were free to do as she or he wanted in this area.

GENETIC THERAPY

With the exception of trauma, every disease humans suffer has a genetic component (Collins, 1999). Some diseases are caused by a dominant gene (monogenic), while for most diseases the individual's genetic make-up to some degree provides or denies the opportunity for environmental factors to trigger its occurrence. Up to the present, there has been no cure for genetically caused diseases and in most cases no way of stopping their transmission except by abstinence, birth control, or abortion. Some dramatic human experimentation has, however, brought medical science to a point where it appears possible to remedy some of these conditions and even to prevent their transmission. As might be expected with any new and experimental treatments, there are ethical problems. We shall return to these shortly. First, however, let us look at a few scientific facts.

A gene is the basic unit of inheritance and is composed of DNA, with a location on one of the chromosomes found in every living cell. Human beings have twenty-three pairs of chromosomes, with an estimated 50,000 gene locations on each set of chromosomes. As soon as the year 2000, it is anticipated that 90 percent of the human genome will be mapped, and these maps will be available for anyone to use as a basis for research (Collins, 1999). Of course, merely mapping will not lead directly to treatment. First, although some traits and diseases are monogenic, others are polygenic, that is, result from several genes acting together. Second, in most cases the environment is known to affect the expression of the trait. This is called multifactorial inheritance and is seen in such situations as height and IQ, where environment, including nutrition, together with genetic endowment, enters into the final result. Third, in some cases the manifestation of the characteristic, probably polygenic or multifactorial, must cross a certain *threshold of liability* before the disease appears. Diseases like cleft palate and neural tube defects appear to be of this sort. In these cases, a certain number of defective alleles (genes that occupy corresponding positions on the paired chromosomes) must be present to pass the threshold and produce the disease.

Ethical Problems of Mapping and Screening

Lippman (1991) raises a series of ethical problems that arise out of the ability to map genes. First, the media and with it society has a tendency to reduce many diseases to a genetic problem in spite of the fact that environment and social conditions are important in causing or preventing the appearance of the gene-linked disease. When we fail to consider social and environmental factors, not only are we medically wrong, but we often find ourselves discriminating against a new class of people: those who have socially undesirable results in genetic tests. We falsely substitute a genetic trait for the more complex reality. In this way, mapping, and the screening it makes possible, often praised as a way of giving patients more choices, actually narrows their options and exploits their weakness.

For example, the discovery that the genes BRCA 1 and BRCA 2 can be indicators for a susceptibility for breast cancer has been widely discussed and has been the focus of the development of many genetic screening opportunities available to the public. Yet, while BRAC 1 and 2 *may* account for 80 percent of hereditary breast cancer, hereditary breast cancers are only 5 to 9 percent of breast cancers in the general population (Koenig, 1998). The overwhelming major of breast cancers are either environmentally caused or the true cause is still undiscovered. Even when a BRAC 1 or 2 test is positive, there is only a strong possibility that the woman will develop breast cancer. Further, insurance companies have been reported to deny individuals insurance because of the results of genetic screening, occasionally claiming that genetic defects are pre-existing conditions (Kolata, 1997a). In light of these statistics, dramatic responses to the genetic tests , such as prophylactic surgery (e.g., removing the breasts to avoid the future development of the cancer), would be an issue for only a very small number of women, and even providing the genetic test itself is of very questionable medical value to the patient.

Equally important, as Lippman notes, is the question as to who is to decide what is normal and what is abnormal. The definition will not only dictate medical practice, but will create pressures on patients, often pregnant women, to follow a definition and a social practice that hides the social and political elements in what are, at first glance, biological questions. This could give rise to a new eugenics and to an emphasis on prenatal diagnosis that presupposes that certain fetal conditions are intrinsically not bearable. It is, for example, already the case that in China there are legal requirements that physicians sterilize patients with serious genetic conditions (Rosenthal, 1998). Lippman (1991, p. 25) fears that "It is, perhaps, not unreasonable to ask if the 'imperfect' will become anything we can diagnose."

Ethics of Genetic Enhancement Interventions

At the very start we wish to distinguish between genetic disease therapy and genetic interventions that merely enhance a trait. The enhancement interventions are not ordinarily therapies, for they do not aim at curing or ameliorating a disease. Davis (1990) notes that the use of *enhance-*

ment procedures to improve "normal genes" raises problems like those resulting from the use of hormones to improve athletic performance. At this time, there is no scientifically proven way to accomplish this, but there is both great anticipation and fear that this can be done. There might, for instance, be a temptation to use such techniques so as to increase height in an effort to produce superior basketball players. In such cases, we are not dealing with therapy or healing; rather, we are reinforcing social interests or prejudices. We may also be furthering the degradation of the health professions as they become tools to manipulate the bodies of patients for commercial exploitation. Finally, and most importantly from an ethical point of view, it is unjust to allocate scarce resources to enhancement procedures when there are serious diseases that may ultimately be cured or controlled by true gene therapy. The Recombinant DNA Advisory Committee (RAC) of the National Institutes for Health as early as 1983 gave notice that it would not approve germ-line therapy or enhancement therapy (Nicholas, 1990: p. 176). The European Medical Research Councils (1988) have also forbidden such interventions.

The possible social consequences of enhancement interventions raise questions about the future. Neither individuals nor society know what traits will be necessary or even useful in future generations for the simple reason that we cannot predict the future. If a large number of people opt for a given trait, not only may this be a threat to biodiversity, but it may have more mundane effects that are nevertheless disruptive: for example, we may end up needing to redesign houses, furniture, and automobiles to accommodate the new traits. If society intervenes to produce superior soldiers or assembly-line workers or bureaucrats (all long-standing themes of science-fiction writers), we may end up with even bigger problems. Reasonable goals and prudent risks must be identified before we embark on these nontherapeutic journeys.

Ethics and Somatic Gene Therapy

Genetic therapies can be divided into somatic gene therapy and germ-line therapy. We shall first treat somatic gene therapy, which is basically *the insertion into a body cell (not an egg or a sperm) of a functioning gene to supplement a damaged one.*

Somatic therapies are or can become part of the practice of medicine. Recent scientific advances have caused physicians and scientists to move toward somatic gene therapy as feasible for disorders of the bone marrow, liver, and central nervous system, as well as some kinds of cancer and deficiencies of circulating enzymes, hormones, and coagulation factors (Lyon and Gorner, 1995).

The current difficulty with gene therapy is that for the most part it is research, and not true therapy. In other words, proposed gene therapies have not been proven to work, and scientists are still at the beginnings of such discoveries. The longest successful therapy was begun in 1992, and we still do not know the long-term success of this procedure, nor do we know the long-term side effects or other consequences of this therapy. Most efforts to date have been failures. One particular side-effect has been the difficulties involved with introducing the altered gene into the body. The device intended to do this is called a vector, and some of the greatest dangers to the patient are caused by these vectors. At this time, the most common vector is an adenovirus, similar to what causes the common cold. In September of 1999 a patient died of respiratory complications after receiving gene therapy using the adenovirus as a vector (Stolberg, 1999a). It is not know what the effect of the gene therapy might have been, but the effect of the vector was fatal. This presents a serious problem for the continuation of research, since the first concern (as discussed earlier in the chapter) must be the protection of the patient. Knowledge is not more important than the human person, whom that knowledge is to serve.

In the final analysis, if the research on genetic therapy does go forward, the ethicalness of validated somatic gene therapy is to be judged by *the medical indications principle*, keeping in mind that medicine is not dedicated to producing supermen and superwomen. Thus, if, *in a particular case*, somatic gene therapy is judged to produce more good than harm, it would be medically indicated and so ethical. On the other hand, for example, there would appear to be no medical indication for its use as a heroic measure in premature neonates whose life would be prolonged only at the price of misery and at great expense. Because of the risks, it appears that, at present, even somatic gene therapy will be medically indicated only in desperate cases. However, this could change as techniques are perfected and risks reduced. At present, even medically indicated treatment is experimental and requires approval of the National Institutes of Health.

One additional concern that strongly influences decisions in this area is the potential for money-making. We have mentioned earlier the ethical difficulties with looking at fetal tissue as a commercial product, and gene therapy may also be viewed this way. So great are the commercial possibilities that a start-up gene therapy company with no useful results, i.e., no product, was sold for $315 million (Stolberg, 1999b). Under pressure from this kind of expectation, scientific objectivity and ethical prudence can easily if unintentionally be set aside.

Ethics and Germ-Line Therapy

Germ-line therapy is effected by changing either the sperm or the egg for a single-cell zygote, or by altering the zygote itself. This produces changes that, unlike those resulting from somatic gene therapy, can be passed on to future generations. This has already been accomplished in animals and, particularly in conjunction with *in vitro* fertilization, this could be accomplished in humans. In theory, this would be a dramatic treatment for all monogenic human diseases. The highly polygenic nature of many important traits makes it doubtful that science will, in the short run, be able to modify them usefully by either somatic or germ-line therapy. Multifactorial inheritance obviously would pose problems that could not be fully addressed in this way.

The ethical arguments against germ-line therapy begin with a concern that meddling with the results of evolution can produce results that may be catastrophic or that may not appear for generations. Additional arguments, such as the possibility that in correcting one defect we may cause another or that the research necessary to develop the therapy may cause more harm than the good, are also very serious. At this stage, when scientific knowledge and technique are incomplete, the danger of such side effects must be prominent in discussions of the hoped for medical indications. As yet, with only animal studies to work from, we have no empirical knowledge of the risk or the lack of risk in humans and we have no real knowledge of medical benefit. Any such use of human germ-line therapy would appear to be a case of flying blind. These remarks apply to somatic gene therapy as well, but with the proviso that in urgent cases somatic therapy may be medically indicated.

The fact that germ-line therapy would occur at an early stage of development (in a fetus in the case of humans) is of particular concern to some (Davis, 1990) who feel that "risk of a new defect is less acceptable in a yet unborn person than in an already sick individual." This concern reflects the possibility that we will further diminish the protection of the fetus because the scientific manipulation makes the fetus more invisible than it already is.

If individuals want to use germ-line engineering, we are faced with the problem of distinguishing merely cosmetic enhancements from the prevention of crippling and devastating disease. We do not agree with Davis (1990) that the goal of germ-line therapy can be simply and inexpensively attained by prenatal diagnosis and abortion. This utterly disregards the ethical problems of abortion and the rights of women, and does not allow room for germ-line therapy to eventually become safe and inexpensive for those fetuses known to be seriously defective. In other words, openness to future development appears ethically required.

Friedmann (1989) and Anderson (1990) argue that, for both somatic and germ-line therapy, the ethical cutting edge separates those procedures that cure a defect and those that enhance a trait. We agree and believe that the medical indications principle is still primary, although institutions receiving federal funds still require the permission of the National Institutes of Health. This permission for somatic therapy has been given rarely and only after rigorous and far-reaching review. Human germ-line "therapy" has not been approved by the National Institutes of Health up to the present. The European Councils warn that even somatic therapy requires more research and should be done only on an individual basis and, for the near future, should be limited to those who have an invariably fatal or life-threatening disease, provided there is informed consent and no other treatment is available. We take this to be a broad statement of the medical indications principle at the present state of our knowledge.

CLONING

The announcement in March of 1997 that scientists had successfully cloned a sheep captured the world's attention (Kolata, 1997b). There were immediate speculations about a future full of many identical versions of the most desirable individuals of all the species, especially humans. With few legal limits, the future seemed to consist of sports teams composed of clones of the greatest athletes and universities populated with identical twins of history's smartest and most creative intellects (Jacobs, 1997). Cloning, growing a mature adult from a single cell obtained from another adult, has been well known for years; the cloning of frogs dates to the 1950s. In 1993, scientists cloned human embryos but made no attempt to bring those embryos to term. The recent cloning of a sheep is notable because it is the first successful birth of a healthy mammal from an adult cell. Yet there are unique attributes to the development of the embryos of sheep that suggest that the prospect of human cloning is quite some time away.

There are a variety of advantages to cloning animals; in medicine these are mostly associated with transgenic animals which will produce hormones or organs useful in the medical treatment of human beings. There is a larger ecological problem of biodiversity that is relevant to the discussion of the cloning of animals, but that is beyond our scope here. The primary health care ethical problems with cloning involve the possibility of cloning humans. As we have seen, there are several different types of problems in this area of research. First and foremost, it is to be remembered that any research on cloning humans is research on beings with a serious right to life and a fundamental dignity. There must be a proportionate reason to justify such research and it is hard for these authors to imagine what such a reason would be. Not only are there problems with individuals choosing to replicate themselves identically, but there are debates about the wisdom of removing the family from concerns with reproduction (see chapter 10) and the possible use of cloned embryos for research (Kass and Wilson, 1998).

Second, we have an ethical obligation to be accurate in our evaluation of what can be accomplished. To identically replicate the genetic nature of one individual is not to replicate that individual. A person is in large measure a result of his or her social history, and this history, this nurturing, can enhance or diminish tendencies presented by the genes. The clone of a great athlete will not grow up in the same environment with the same influences that the athlete had, and consequently may not even be an athlete at all. Much of the popular discussion of cloning is inflated by ignoring this point.

Finally, cloning introduces additional possibilities of genetic defects, and enhances the defects that are already present in the cell. As with germline therapy, there are serious threats to the gene pool when in our ignorance we introduce a genetic variant the long-term implications of which we do not understand.

While most ethicians have serious reservations about the cloning of human beings, fascination with the possibility is likely to drive researchers to continue to work on its accomplishment. Ethicists face a difficult task in fully articulating the cases for and against cloning, and in working with the public to achieve a consensus before the ability to clone humans becomes a reality too prevalent to control.

SUMMARY

Ethical research must be based on well verified conceptual and animal studies, and must have a reasonable chance of producing a good proportionate to the evils risked or permitted. The central concern must always be the protection of the human subject. Problems of informed consent are particularly delicate, since whole classes of potential subjects live in coercive environments and may be exploited as research subjects out of proportion to their numbers in the population. Scientific method can pose ethical problems when the *a priori* odds of success for the control and experimental groups are not equal.

In addition, the health care provider who uses the results of research has an obligation to read research critically. The user of biomedical research cannot simply rely on the editors of journals, but needs enough basic knowledge of statistics and research methodology to understand more than the mere conclusions of research. Further, health care personnel should be aware of the fact that much supposedly validated practice is not based on scientific research and cannot simply be followed with good conscience. Critical thinking is required even here.

Such critical areas as fetus research and genetic engineering are not simply matters of pursuing scientific discovery, but require careful distinctions to be made to protect the fetus or the patient, and the human community. All these new areas, especially genetic research, raise very serious ethical issues that can easily be forgotten in the midst of a passion for startling scientific accomplishment. The full participation of the public is necessary to develop and maintain an ethical and political consensus for the proper control of these possibilities. We must always remember that science and medicine both gain their real purpose from their ability to serve ethical human ends.

CASES FOR ANALYSIS _____

1. (This case is based on James J. McCartney's "Encephalitis and ARA-A: An Ethical Case Study," *Hastings Center Report*, Vol. 8(6) (December), 1978, pp. 5-7, and a letter from the researchers in *Hastings Center Report*, Vol. 9(4) (August), 1979, pp. 4, 46, and the reply of McCartney, pp. 46-47.

Herpes simplex viral encephalitis has a rapid onset. It is a severe clinical disease during the acute phase. There is a high percentage of seizures, regardless of age. Seventy percent of those who contract it die, many of the survivors are left with neurological deficits, and some have to be institutionalized. The researchers in this case, however, say that studies indicate mortality rates varying from 13 to 70 percent.

A definitive diagnosis requires a brain biopsy, with culturing of the sample. The biopsy, however, can miss the focus point of the involvement and give false negatives; that is, the test can indicate that no disease is present when the disease is actually present.

The research in question sought to discover whether the experimental drug ARA-A (adenine arabinoside, brand name Vira A) would be an effective treatment. ARA-A had already proved effective in the treatment of herpes simplex infections and disseminated herpes simplex infections in newborns. It had also been approved by the FDA for the treatment of herpes keratitis, a localized infection that produces inflammation of the cornea. Within the antiviral dosage range, there was no demonstrated hepatic, renal, or hematologic toxicity. The researchers noted, however, that there had been no controlled studies demonstrating this and, furthermore, that ARA-A could be very toxic and cause bone marrow depression and damage to the liver and kidneys.

The research involved a controlled, double-blind clinical trial with the subjects randomly assigned. Twenty-eight subjects had a positive biopsy. The biopsy-positive subjects received either ARA-A for ten days or a placebo. The biopsy-negative subjects got either ARA-A for five days or a placebo.

The subjects were not told that the disease was 70 percent fatal nor of the effectiveness of ARA-A in the case of the other herpes simplex infections. They were not told that the biopsy involved making a hole in the scalp and taking tissue from the brain. Nor were they told why a brain biopsy was necessary for this clinical trial. The researchers note that they changed the consent form after the first years of the test and used oral presentation. They do not, however, specify the changes.

Of the eighteen biopsy-positive cases who were on ARA-A for ten days, five (27.9 percent) died and seven (38.8 percent) recovered to lead normal lives. Of this last group four (22.23 percent of the eighteen) recovered completely. Six (33.3 percent) had serious drug-related or brain damage, perhaps because the treatment was started too late. Of the ten biopsy-positive subjects who were on the placebo, seven (70 percent) died while two (20 percent) recovered to lead a reasonably normal life. The study was stopped when the deaths in this placebo control group reached the normal mortality figures for the disease.

In view of the available historical base line, was a control group needed in this trial? What is to be said of the experimenter's ethics, since the *a priori* odds were not equal for the two groups? What is the ethical significance of the fact that there were no studies of the toxicity of the drug in the antiviral dose?

2. Willowbrook was an institute for the mentally retarded near a major metropolitan area. It had grown rapidly from 200 patients in 1950 to 6,000 patients in 1965. Four thousand of the patients were severely retarded, with IQs of less than 20. Over half of the patients were not toilet trained and had to be diapered. The institution was understaffed, and it was difficult to change diapers. As a result, the patients often sat in their own feces for hours. Since hepatitis is spread by the anal-oral route, this led to nearly every patient getting hepatitis within the first six to twelve months at Willowbrook. This was particularly true for those patients who were in the three to ten year-old range.

The study in question artificially exposed the subjects to the mild Willowbrook strain of hepatitis to achieve a better understanding of the disease and to develop methods of immunization.

Even when regular admissions to Willowbrook had been stopped because of overcrowding and understaffing, patients were still admitted to a special hepatitis unit with the written permission of the parents. The parents had been informed by letter or by personal interview or in groups. Children who were wards of the state were not included.

Many of the parents were desperate to have their child admitted because they could no longer care for the child, either because of the seriousness of the child's needs or their own inability to cope.

In the special ward, children were also protected from other infectious diseases and often developed immunity to hepatitis. The research had been approved by various local, state, and federal agencies.

Over the years, including the years when regular admissions had been stopped, approximately 800 out of 10,000 admissions were involved in the research project.

Is this research ethical if its only purpose was to increase understanding of the disease? Is there any ethical significance to the fact that the children "often developed immunity"? Was it ethical to continue the experiment after it was clear that the procedures generally did not lead to immunity? In view of their emotional situation and the child's need for care, were the parents free and so competent to give consent? Was admittance to the unit in the best interest of the children? How does this case illustrate the problem of the ethics of resource allocation?

3. This is a simplified case inspired by the sophisticated case by Peter Sordillo and Kenneth Schanffner, "Case Studies: The Last Patient in a Drug Trial," *Hastings Center Report* (1981) Vol. 11(6) pp. 21-23.

An experimental design calls for a test to end after the nineteenth patient. The drug being tested has proved ineffective in the first eighteen cancer patients used as subjects. The drug has caused the usual side effects: nausea and vomiting for about forty-eight hours after taking it. Some patients developed sores and nearly all have had temporary, but severe, decreases in their blood counts. John , a patient on whom all other treatments for this cancer have failed, is admitted to the hospital conducting the research. If John is used, they can, *unless John responds favorably*, conclude the experiment with a clearly negative conclusion. John is desperate and wants to be treated.

What are the experimenters obliged to tell John? Is more information required now than at the beginning of the experiment? In view of the side effects, is it ethical to admit additional patients to the test, even if they are terminal?

4. Bill, who holds a doctorate in education and has taken the advanced course in therapeutic touch, wishes to study the effect of therapeutic touch on patients with persistent headaches. He gets volunteers from the clinic in which he works. The sample is largely female and largely composed of people who are on welfare. There are also a disproportionate number of blacks and Hispanics in the sample. He randomly assigns them to a test group and a control group. The test group is given the therapeutic touch. With the control group, the experimenter goes through the motions of therapeutic touch, but withholds the intention of transferring energy, which is the soul of therapeutic touch. His results show that the experimental group reported a significant reduction in the severity of their headaches and that the difference between the two groups has a 95 percent confidence level; that is, there is only a 5 percent chance that the results are due to chance. On the basis of this research, he applies therapeutic touch to all patients with headaches.

If Bill is neither a licensed psychologist nor trained in psychological research, what is the ethical significance of this case? What does the nature of the sample tell us about the limits of research and so the ethics of costs? Does research that involves withholding an "intention" meet scientific standards? On the basis of this research, would it be ethical to use therapeutic touch for persistent headaches?

5. As part of a nontherapeutic research, researchers intend to inject dead cancer cells into seriously ill patients. There is no danger from the dead cancer cells other than the minimal danger of infection at the injection site. They feel that if they reveal the nature of the injection, patients and their surrogates will refuse consent. Even the word *cancer* creates fear in most people. As a result, the doctors do not reveal the nature of the injection on the consent form. They justify this on the grounds that there is no real danger to the patients and that the research is aimed at gaining knowledge that ultimately might help thousands of people.

Were the researchers ethical in suppressing the fact that they were using cancer cells? Did they obtain informed consent from their subjects? What should they have done?

6. The ABC Drug Company wants to test drug Q as a relief for high blood pressure. Tests have shown that the drug is not toxic in the doses required by the research protocol. Animal tests indicate that drug Q has fewer undesirable side effects than the existing treatments. Drug Q works by opening up the veins and uses a chemical compound produced by the heart itself. It promises to be far superior to present treatments because it uses a chemical that is found naturally in the body.

All this, including the side effects, has been explained to the prospective subjects, who understand that they will be randomly assigned to one of three groups. Some will receive drug Q, some an accepted treatment, and some a placebo. They are also informed that this will be a double-blind experiment.

The results show that drug Q is more effective than the accepted treatment and has fewer side effects, but the significance of this is not clear, since the probability that the difference is due to chance is less that 10 percent and the researchers had originally decided on 5 percent as the cutoff figure. Despite this, they publish an article concealing the difference in probabilities by simply not mentioning it.

Is it ethical to hide a key bit of information that would aid in interpreting the results? Are further tests needed to see if the drug meets the requirements? What is the utility of publishing studies with negative results? (Would they be read? Are they a way of making sure that unfavorable replications are known?)

REFERENCES

Abel, Ernest L. 1990. *Fetal Alcohol Syndrome*. Oradell, NJ: Medical Economic Books.

Abood, Richard R. 1989. Physician Dispensing: Issues of Law, Legislation and Social Policy, *American Journal of Law and Medicine*, 14:4, pp. 307-352.

Ackerman, Felicia. 1991. "The Significance of a Wish," *Hastings Center Report*, 21:4, pp. 27-29.

American Civil Liberties Union. 1998. *Mandatory Pre-Marital HIV Testing: A Record of Failure (An American Civil Liberties Union Report)*. ACLU AIDS Project. 30 Jan. 2000 <http://www.aclu.org/issues/aids/premarital.html>.

American College of Physicians. 1984. "Ethics Manual," *Annals of Internal Medicine*, 101, pp. 129-137, 263-274.

American Hospital Association. 1985. *Values in Conflict: Resolving Issues in Hospital Care: Report of the Special Committee on Biomedical Ethics*. Chicago: American Hospital Association.

———. 1992. *Patient Bill of Rights*. Chicago: American Hospital Association.

American Medical Association. Council on Ethical and Judicial Affairs. 1996a. *Current Opinions of the Judicial Council of the American Medical Association*. Chicago: American Medical Association.

———. 1994a. "Physician-Assisted Suicide," *Issues in Law and Medicine*, 91, p. 92.

———. Board of Trustees. 1994b. "Euthanasia/Physician-Assisted Suicide: Lessons in the Dutch Experience," *Issues in Law and Medicine* 10:81.

———. Inter-Council Task Force on Quality Care at the End of Life. 1995. Quality Care at the End of Life, *Journal of the American Medical Association*.

———. Council on Scientific Affairs. 1996b. "Good Care of the Dying Patient," *Journal of the American Medical Association*, 275: 474, 477.

———. 1996c. "Brief of the American Medical Association, The American Nurses Association, and the American Psychiatric Association, et al., as Amici Curiae in Support of Petitioners in State of Washington v. Glucksberg, et al. in the Supreme Court of the United States."

American Nurses Association. 1985. *Code for Nurses with Interpretive Statements.* Kansas City, MO: American Nurses Association.

———. 1990. "ANA Issues Position Statement on Support for Confidential Notification Services and a Limited 'limited privilege to disclose,'" *The Pennsylvania Nurse*, January, p. 8.

American Psychiatric Association, Ethics Committee. 1995. *Opinions of the Ethics Committee on the Principles of Medical Ethics: With Annotations Especially Applicable to Psychiatry.* Washington, DC: American Psychiatric Association.

American Psychological Association. 1982. *Ethical Principles in the Conduct of Research with Human Subjects.* Washington, D.C.: American Psychological Association.

Anders, George. 1994. "State Boards Disciplined More Doctors Last Year, Stepping Up Their Vigilance," *Wall Street Journal*, April 13, p. 19.

Anderson, W. F. 1989. "Human Gene Therapy: Why Draw the Line?" *Journal of Medicine and Philosophy*, 14:6, pp. 681-693.

———. 1990. "Genetics and Human Malleability," *Hastings Center Report*, 20:1, pp. 21-24.

Andrews, Lori B. 1986. "My Body, My Property," *Hastings Center Report*, 16:5, pp. 28-38.

Angell, Marcia. 1993. "The Doctor as Double Agent," *Kennedy Institute of Ethics Journal*, 3:3, pp. 279-287.

Annas, George J. 1975. *The Rights of Hospital Patients: The Basic ACLU Guide to a Hospital Patient's Rights.* New York: Avon Books.

———. 1981. "Contracts to Bear Child," *Hastings Center Report*, 11:2, pp. 23-24.

———. 1984. "Redefining Parenthood and Protecting Embryos: Why We Need New Laws," *Hastings Center Report*, 14:4, pp. 50-52.

———. 1986. "The Baby Broker Boom," *Hastings Center Report*, 16:3, pp. 30-31.

Arendt, Hannah. 1958. *The Human Condition.* Chicago: University of Chicago Press.

Aristotle, 1975. *Nicomachean Ethics.* Trans. by H. Rackham. Cambridge, Massachusetts: Harvard University Press.

Asch, D.A. 1996. "The Role of Critical Care Nurses in Euthanasia and Assisted Suicide," *New England Journal of Medicine*, 334:21, pp. 1374-1402.

Ashley, Benedict M., and Kevin D. O'Rourke. 1978. *Health Care Ethics: A Theological Analysis.* St. Louis, MO: Catholic Health Care Association of the United States.

Baillie, Harold. 1988. "Learning the Emotions," *The New Scholasticism*, 62:2, pp. 221-227.

Baillie, Harold, and Thomas Garrett. 1991. "The Ethics of Social Commitment," pp. 11-28 in *Biomedical Ethics Review: 1990.* Clifton, NJ: Humana Press.

Barnes, Mark, et al. 1990. "The HIV Infected Health Care Professional: Employment Policy and Public Health." *Law, Medicine and Health Care*, 18:4, pp. 311-330.

Baumrin, Bernard, and Benjamin Freedman, eds. 1983. *Moral Responsibility and the Professions*. New York: Haven Publications.

Bayles, Michael D. 1984. *Reproductive Ethics*. Englewood Cliffs, NJ: Prentice Hall.

Beauchamp, Tom L., and Laurence B. McCullough. 1984. *Medical Ethics: The Moral Responsibilities of Physicians*. Englewood Cliffs, NJ: Prentice Hall.

Beauchamp, Tom L., and Seymour Perlin, eds. 1978. *Ethical Issues in Death and Dying*. Englewood Cliffs, NJ: Prentice Hall

Becker, Carl B. 1990. "Buddhist Views of Suicide and Euthanasia," *Philosophy East and West*, 40:4, pp. 543-556.

Beis, Edward B. 1984. *Mental Health and the Law*. Rockville, MD: Aspen.

Benesch, K. 1994. "Risk Management: Emerging Theories of Liability for Negligent Credentialing in HMOs, Integrated Delivery and Managed Care Systems," *Trends in Health Care Law and Ethics*, 9:4, pp. 1-4, 28, 45-46.

Berger, Debra N. 1989. "The Infant With Anencephaly: Moral and Legal Dilemmas," *Issues in Law and Medicine*, 5:1, pp. 67-86.

Berrio, Margaret W., and Maureen Levesque. 1996. "Advanced Directives: Most Patients Don't Have One. Do Yours?" *American Journal of Nursing*, 96:8, pp. 25-28.

Bia, M. J. 1999. "Geriatric issues in renal transplantation," *Geriatric Nephrology and Urology*, 9:2, pp. 109-113.

BioLaw: A Legal and Ethical Reporter on Medicine, Health Care and Bioengineering. 1986. Ed. By James F. Childress, et al. Frederick, MD: University Publications of America.

BioLaw: Updates and Special Sections. 1987. Ed. By James F. Childress, et al. Frederick, MD: University Publications of America.

Blakiston's Gould Medical Dictionary. 1972. 3rd ed. Ed. By Arthur Osol. New York: McGraw Hill Book Company.

Bok, Sissela. 1979. *Lying: Moral Choice in Public and Private Life*. New York: Vintage Books.

———. 1984. *Secrets: On the Ethics of Concealment and Revelation*. New York: Vintage Books.

Breitowitz, Yitzchok. 1996. "Does Judaism Ever Sanction Suicide, and May a Physician or Third Party Facilitate It?" *Moment*, December, pp. 26-27.

Brier, A., et al. 1993. "Clozapine Treatment of Outpatients with Schizophrenia: Outcome and Long-Term Response Patterns," *Hospital and Community Psychiatry*, 44:12, pp. 1145-1149.

Broad, William, and Nicolas Wade. 1982. *Betrayers of Truth: Fraud and Deceit in the Halls of Science*. New York: Simon and Schuster.

Brody, Barunch. 1975. *Abortion and the Sanctity of Human Life: A Philosophical View*. Cambridge, MA: MIT Press.

———. 1987. *Life and Death Decision Making*. New York: Oxford University Press.

Buchanan, Allen E., and Dan W. Brock. 1989. *Deciding for Others: The Ethics of Surrogate Decision Making*. New York: Cambridge University Press.

Burkins, Glenn. 1996. "Health Costs Growth Rate Slows Further," *Wall Street Journal*, August 1, p. A15.

Bursztajn, Harold, et al. 1981. *Medical Choices, Medical Chances: How Patients, Families, and Physicians Can Cope With Uncertainty*. New York: Merloyd Lawrence Book.

Busuttil, R. W., et al. 1991. "Liver Transplantation in Children," *Annals of Surgery*, 213:1, pp. 48-57.

Cahill, Lisa Sowle. 1977. "A 'Natural Law' Reconsideration of Euthanasia," *Linacre Quarterly*, 44, pp. 47-63.

Calderone, R. R., et al. 1996. "Cost of medical care for postoperative spinal infections," *Orthopedic Clinics of North America*, 27:1, pp. 171-182.

Callahan, Daniel. 1991. "Medical Futility, Medical Necessity: The Problem Without a Name," *Hastings Center Report*, 21:4, pp. 30-35.

———. 1995. "The Puzzle of Profound Respect," *Hastings Center Report*, 25:1, pp. 39-40.

Callahan, Sidney, and Daniel Callahan, eds. 1984. *Abortion: Understanding Differences*. New York: Plenum Press.

Caplan, Arthur L. 1985. "Some Reflections Regarding Organ Transplants," *Ethics Center Update* 1:3 pp. 3-6.

———. 1986. "Baby Jesse and Beyond," *Ethics Center Update*, 2:3, pp. 1-2.

Capron, Alexander Morgan. 1987. "Anencephalic Donors: Separate the Dead from the Dying," *Hastings Center Report*, 17:1, pp. 5-8.

Carey, Benedict. 1991. "Sperm Inc.," in *Health*, 5:4 pp. 50-56.

Carlton, Wendy. 1978. *In Our Professional Opinion: The Primacy of Clinical Judgment Over Moral Choices*. Notre Dame, IN: University of Notre Dame Press.

Catholic Health Association Task Force on Pain Management. 1993. "Pain Management: Theological and Ethical Principles Governing the Use of Pain Relief for Dying Patients," *Health Progress*, Jan-Feb., pp. 30-39, 65.

CEMAT (Canadian Early and Mid-trimester Amniocentesis Trial Group). 1998. "Randomized trial to assess safety and fetal outcome of early and midtrimester amniocentesis," *Lancet*, 351:9098, pp. 242-247.

Centers for Disease Control and Prevention. 1998. "Trends in HIV and AIDS Epidemic, 1998," *CDC's National Center for HIV, STD & TB Prevention*. 30 Jan. 2000 <http://www.cdc.gov/nchstp/hiv_aids/stats/hasr1106pdF>.

———. 1999. "Assisted Reproductive Technology Success Rate: National Summary and Fertility Clinic Reports," 24 Jan. 2000 <http://www.cdc.gov/nccdphp/drh/art97/index.htm>.

Chervenak, Frank A., and Laurence B. McCullough. 1985. "Perinatal Ethics: A Practical Method of Analysis of Obligations to Mother and Fetus," *Obstetrics and Gynecology*, 66:3, pp. 442-446.

Christopherson, Lois K. 1982. "Heart Transplants," *Hastings Center Report*, 12:1, pp. 18-21.

Cohen, Barbara. 1984. "Surrogate Mothers: Whose Baby Is It?", *American Journal of Law and Medicine*, 10:3, pp. 243-286.

Cohen, Cynthia B. 1996. "Give Me Children or I Shall Die! New Reproductive Technologies and Harm to Children," *Hastings Center Report*, 26:2, 19-27.

Colburn, Don. 1996. "Survey Reveals Differences on Doctor Assisted Suicide," *Washington Post*, July 2, p. Z08.

Collins, Francis S. 1999. "Shattuck Lecture: Medical and Societal Consequences of the Human Genome Project," *New England Journal of Medicine*, 341:1, pp. 28-37.

Compassion in Dying v. Washington. 1996. 79 F.3d 790, p. 813-814.

Congregation for the Doctrine of the Faith. 1987. *Instruction on Respect for Human Life in Its Origin and on the Dignity of Procreation: Replies to Certain Questions of the Day.* Boston, MA: Pauline Books & Media.

Cowdrey, Michael L. 1984. *Basic Law for the Allied Health Professional.* Monterey, CA: Wadsworth Health Sciences.

Cox, Stephen S. 1987. "Is Dehydration Painful?" *Ethics and Medics,* 12:9, 1987.

Craig, Paul. 1990. "Health Maintenance Organization Gatekeeping Policies: Potential Liability for Deterring Access to Emergency Medical Services," *Journal of Health and Hospital Law,* 23:2, pp. 135-146.

Cranford, Ronald E. 1988. "The Persistent Vegetative State: The Medical Reality (Getting the Facts Straight)." *The Hastings Center Report,* 18:1, pp. 27-32.

————. 1991. "Helga Wanglie's Ventilator," *Hastings Center Report,* 21:4, pp. 23-24.

Culver, Charles M., and Bernard Gert. 1982. *Philosophy in Medicine: Conceptual and Ethical Issues in Medicine and Psychiatry.* New York: Oxford University Press.

Cushing, Maureen. 1984. "Wronged Rights in Nursing Homes," *American Journal of Nursing,* 84:10, pp. 1213-1218.

Danis, Marion, et al. 1991. "A Prospective Study of Advance Directives for Life-sustaining Care," *New England Journal of Medicine,* 324:882-888.

Davis, Iwan. 1985. "Contracts to Bear Children," *Journal of Medical Ethics,* 11, pp. 61-65.

"Death with Dignity Act." 1997. ORS 127.880-1278 97.

Department of Health, Education and Welfare. 1981. *Rules and Regulations: 45 CFR 16, The Federal Register,* January 26, 1981, 46:16.

Department of Health, Education and Welfare. 1983. "Guidelines on Fetal Research," *Code of Federal Regulations,* March 8, 45/cfr 46.

Department of Health and Human Services. 1985a. *Organ Transplantation: Questions and Answers.* Rockville, MD: Superintendent of Documents, No. HE20.9002: OR3.

————. 1985b. "Baby Doe Rule," 45 CFR Part 1340, *Federal Register,* April 15, pp. 14878- 14901.

————. 1986. *Report of the Task Force on Organ Transplantation, Organ Transplantation: Issues and Recommendations.* U.S. Government Printing Office, HE20.9002: OR3/2.

Diller, Lawrence H. 1996. "The Run on Ritalin: Attention Deficit Disorder and Stimulant Treatment in the 1990s," *Hastings Center Report,* 26:2. pp. 12-18.

Dixon, Nicholas. 1998. "On the Difference between Physician-Assisted Suicide and Active Euthanasia," *Hastings Center Report,* 28:5, pp. 25-29.

Drickamer, Margaret A., Melinda A. Lee, and Linda Ganzini. 1997. "Practical Issues in Physician-Assisted Suicide," *Annals of Internal Medicine,* 126:2, pp. 146-151.

Duffy, Mary E. 1985. "A Research Appraisal Checklist for Evaluating Nursing Research Reports," in *Nursing and Health Care,* 6:10, pp. 539-547.

Duncan, Ronald, and Miranda Weston-Smith, eds. 1984. *The Encyclopedia of Medical Ignorance: Exploring the Frontiers of Medical Knowledge,* Oxford: Pergamon Press.

Edmonson, A. S. 1990. "Recertification: One Orthopedic Surgeon's View," *Clinical Orthopedics* 257, pp. 35-37.

Ehrenreich, Barbara, and Deidre English. 1979. *For Her Own Good*. Garden City, NY: Anchor Press/Doubleday.

Eichelman, B. and A. Hartwig. 1990. "Ethical Issues in Selecting Patients for Treatment with Clozapine: A Commentary," *Hospital and Community Psychiatry*, 41:8, pp. 880-882.

Eidelman, Arthur L. 1986. "Caring for New Borns: Three World Views: In Israel Families Look to Two Messengers of God," *Hastings Center Report*, 16:4 pp. 18-19.

Emanuel, Ezekiel J., and Linda Emanuel. 1992. "Proxy Decision Making for Incompetent Patients," *Journal of the American Medical Association*, 267:15, pp. 2067-2071.

Emanuel, Ezekiel J., et al. 1996. "Euthanasia and Physician Assisted Suicide: Attitudes and Experiences of Oncology Patients, Oncologists, and the Public," *Lancet*, 347, pp. 1805-1810.

Emanuel, Linda L., et al. 1991. "Advance Directives in Medical Care—A Case for Greater Use," *New England Journal of Medicine*, 324:889-895.

Engelhardt, H. Tristam, Jr. 1985. *The Foundations of Bioethics*. New York: Oxford University Press.

English, Jane. 1975. "Abortion and the Concept of a Person," *Canadian Journal of Philosophy*, 5, pp. 233-243.

European Medical Research Councils. 1988. "Recommendations of European Medical Research Councils," *Lancet*, 8597, pp. 1271-1272.

Fackelmann, Kathy A. 1994. "Cloning Human Embryos: Exploring the Science of a Controversial Experiment," *Science News*, 145, pp. 92-95.

Faden, Ruth R., Tom L. Beauchamp, and Nancy M. P. King. 1986. *A History and Theory of Informed Consent*. New York: Oxford University Press.

Fauci, A. S. 1993. "Multifactorial nature of human immunodeficiency virus disease: implications for therapy," *Science*, 262, pp. 1011-1018.

Federation of State Medical Boards. 1999. *Summary of Board Actions: 1998* . 30 Jan. 2000 <http://www.fsmb.org/baction.htm>.

Feinberg, Joel. 1975. "Legal Paternalism." In *Today's Moral Problems,* ed. Richard Wasterstrom. New York: Macmillan.

Fickeissen, Janet L. 1990. "Fifty-Six Ways to Get Certified," *American Journal of Nursing*, 90:3, pp. 50 - 57.

Field, Martha A. 1989. "Controlling the Woman to Protect the Fetus." *Law, Medicine and Health Care*, 17:2, pp. 114-129.

Fletcher, John, Norman Quist, and Albert Jonsen, eds. 1989. *Ethics Consultations in Health Care*. Ann Arbor MI: Health Administration Press.

Fletcher, John C., and Diane E. Hoffman. 1994. "Ethics Committees: Time to Experiment with Standards," *Annals of Internal Medicine*, 120, pp. 335-338.

Fortess, Eric E., and Marshall B. Kapp. 1985. "Medical Uncertainty: Diagnostic Testing and Legal Liability," *Law, Medicine and Health Care*, 13:5, pp. 213-218.

Foster, L.E. and J. Lynn. 1988. "Predicting Life Span for Applicants to Inpatient Hospice," *Archives of Internal Medicine*, 148, pp. 2540-2543.

Frieden, Joyce. 1991. "Genetic Testing: What Will It Mean for Health Insurance," *Business and Health*, 9:3 pp. 40-46.

Friedmann, T. 1989. "Progress Toward Human Gene Therapy," *Science,* June 16, pp. 1275-81.

————. 1990. "The Human Genome Project Some Implications of Extensive 'Reverse Genetic' Medicine." *American Journal of Human Genetics,* 46:3, pp. 407-414.

Gallagher, James. 1985. "Reflections Regarding William Barting: Siding with Life," *Ethics Center Update* (Winter), 1:2, pp.3-4.

Garrett, Thomas M. 1963. *Ethics in Business.* New York: Sheed and Ward.

Garrett, Thomas M., and Richard J. Klonoski. 1986. *Business Ethics.* 2d ed. Englewood Cliffs, NJ: Prentice Hall.

Garrett, Thomas M., Richard J. Klonoski, and Harold W. Baillie. 1993. "American Business Ethics and Health Care Costs," *Health Care Management REVIEW,* 18:4, pp. 44-50.

George, J. R. and G. Schochtman, eds. 1994. *AIDS Testing: A Comprehensive Guide to Technical, Medical, Social, Legal, and Management Issues.* New York: Springer Verlag.

Gianelli, D. M. 1987. "ACOG issues guidelines on maternal, fetal rights," *American Medical News,* August 28, p. 7.

Gifford, Fred. 1996. "Outcomes Research and Practice Guidelines," *Hastings Center Report,* 26:2, pp. 38-44.

Gilbert, Dianne E. 1991. "Increasing Access to Long-Term Care Through Medicaid Antidiscrimination Laws," *Journal of Health and Hospital Law* (April), 24:4, pp.105-111.

Glaser, John W., et al. 1993. *Health Care Ethics Committees: The Next Generation,* Chicago: American Hospital Publishing Co.

Glendon, Mary Ann. 1987. *Abortion and Divorce in Western Law.* Cambridge, MA: Harvard University Press.

Goffman, Erving. 1963. *Stigma: Notes on the Management of the Spoiled Identity.* Englewood Cliffs, NJ: Simon and Schuster.

Goodman, Madeleine J., and Lenn E. Goodman. 1982. "The Over-Selling of Genetic Anxiety," *Hastings Center Report,* 12:5, pp. 20-27.

Gostin, Larry, and William Curran, eds. 1990. "The Harvard Model Aids Legislation Project." *American Journal of Law and Medicine,* 16:1 and 16:2, pp. 1-266.

Graber, Glenn C., et al. 1985. *Ethical Analysis of Clinical Medicine.* Baltimore, MD: Urban and Schwarzenberg.

Greenberg, David F. 1974. "Interference with a Suicide Attempt," *New York University Law Review,* 49, pp. 227-269.

Gross, Michael L. 1999. "Autonomy and Paternalism in Communitarian Society: Patients' Rights in Israel," *Hastings Center Report,* 29:4, pp. 13-20.

Hachney, Virginia A. 1991. "The National Practitioner Data Bank: A Step Toward More Effective Peer Review," *Journal of Health and Hospital Law,* 24:7, pp. 201-209.

Hanley, Robert. 1988. "Surrogate Deals for Mothers Held Illegal in New Jersey," *New York Times,* Feb. 4, pp. A1, B6.

Hansen, Hugh J., Samuel R. Caudill, and Joe Boone. 1985. "Crisis in Drug Testing: Results of CDC Blind Study," *Journal of the American Medical Association,* 253:16, pp. 2382-2387.

Harris, John. 1992. *Wonderwoman and Superman: The Ethics of Human Biotechnology.* New York: Oxford University Press.

Hartlaub, Paul P., Alan S. Wolkenstein, and Herbert F. Laufenburg. 1993. "Obtaining Informed Consent: It Is Not Simply Asking 'Do You Understand?'" *The Journal of Family Practice*, 36:4, pp. 383-384.

Hastings Center. 1987. *Guidelines on the Termination of Life Sustaining Treatment and the Care of the Dying.* Briarcliff Manor, NY: The Hastings Center.

Helminski, F. 1993. "Near the Conflagration: The Wide Duty to Warn," *Mayo Clinic Proceedings*, 68:7, pp. 709-710.

Henkelman, Wallace J. 1994. "Inadequate Pain Management: Ethical Considerations," *Nursing Management* 25:1, pp. 48a-49a.

High, Dallas M. 1994. "Families' Roles in Advance Directives," *Hastings Center Report*, 24:6, pp. S16-S18.

Hlatky, Mark A. 1986. "Evaluation of Diagnostic Tests," *Journal of Chronic Diseases*, 39:5, pp. 357-358.

Honigfeld, G., and J. Patin. 1990. " A Two-Year Clinical and Economic Follow-Up of Patients on Clozapine," *Hospital and Community Pscyhiatry*, 41:8, pp. 882-885.

Horner, Susan L. 1990. "The Health Quality Improvement Act of 1986: History, Provisions, Applications, and Implications," *American Journal of Law and Medicine*, 16:4, pp. 463-465.

Hornstra, Deborah. 1998. "A Realistic Approach to Maternal-Fetal Conflict," *Hastings Center Report*, 28:5, pp. 7-12.

Hoover, Erin, and Gail Kinsey Hill. 1998. "Two Die Using Suicide Laws," *The Oregonian*, March 26, pp. 1.

Hudson, Therse. 1991. "Hospitals Work to Provide Advance Directives Information," *Hospitals*, 65:3, pp. 26-32.

Hull, Richard T. 1985. "Informed Consent: Patient's Right or Patient's Duty?," *Journal of Medicine and Philosophy*, 10:2, pp. 182-197.

Illich, Ivan. 1976. *Medical Nemesis: The Expropriation of Health.* New York: Bantam Books.

Ingelfinger, Joseph A. et al. 1981. "Reliability of the Toxic Screen in Drug Overdose," *Clinical Pharmacology and Therapeutics*, 29:5, pp. 570-575.

International Council of Nurses. 1973. *Code for Nurses.* Reaffirmed in 1989. Geneva: ICN.

Iverson, K. R., R. V. Heimly, and T. I. Lundgren. 1995. "Implementing Security in Computer Based Patient Records: Clinical Experiences," *Medinfo*, 8:1, pp. 657-660.

Jacobs, Margaret A. 1997. "Legal Beat: Cloning Faces New Legal Barriers for Now," *Wall Street Journal*, Feb. 25, p. B8.

Jeffrey, Nancy Ann. 1996. "HMOs May Not Always Be Best for Long-Term Ills," *Wall Street Journal*, October 6, p. C1.

Jenkins, Holman W., Jr. 1996, "Managed Care Suffers a Bad Case of Politics," *Wall Street Journal*, July 16, p. A11.

Jonas, Steven, et al. 1981. *Health Care Delivery System.* 2d ed. New York: Springer Publishing.

Jonsen, Albert R., Mark Siegler, and William J. Winslade. 1986. *Clinical Ethics: A Practical Approach to Ethical Decisions in Clinical Medicine*, 2d ed. NY: Macmillan Publishing Co.

Jonsen, Albert R., et al. 1988. *The Abuse of Casuistry: A History of Moral Reasoning*, Berkeley: University of California Press.

Jordan, Kenneth G. 1987. "Let's Replace 'Do Not Resuscitate' with 'Care for the Dying,'" *Ethics Center Update*, 3:2, pp. 4-6.

Jordan, Shannon M. 1985. *Decision Making for Incompetent Persons: The Law and the Morality of Who Shall Decide*. Springfield, IL: Charles C. Thomas.

Kant, Immanuel. 1963. *Lectures on Ethics*, trans. Louis Infield. New York: Harper and Row.

Kass, Leon R. 1975. "Regarding the End of Medicine and the Pursuit of Health," *The Public Interest*, 40, pp. 10-42.

———. 1983. "Professing Ethically: On the Place of Ethics in Defining Medicine," *Journal of the American Medical Association*, 249:10, pp. 1305-1310.

———. 1991. "Why Doctors Must Not Kill," *Commonweal*, 118, pp. 8-12.

———, and James Q. Wilson. 1998. *The Ethics of Human Cloning*. Washington, D. C.: The AEI Press.

Katayama, K. Paul, and Mark R. Roesler. 1986. "Five Hundred Cases of Amniocentesis Without Bloody Tap," *Obstetrics and Gynecology*, 68:1, pp. 70-73.

Katz, Jay. 1984. *The Silent World of Doctor and Patient*. New York: The Free Press.

Kelly, Patricia. 1991. *Understanding Breast Cancer*. Philadelphia: Temple University Press.

Kettlekamp, D. B., and J. N. Herndon. 1990. "Recertification in Orthopedics." *Clinical Orthopedics*, 257, pp. 29-34.

Kieiman, Dena. 1985. "Hospital Care of the Dying: Each Day, Painful Choices," *New York Times*, January 14, pp. A1-B4.

King, P. A. 1992. "Twenty Years After: The Legacy of the Tuskegee Syphilis Study, The Dangers of Difference," *Hastings Center Report*, 22:6, pp. 35-38.

Knowles, Lori. 1999. "Property, Progeny, and Patents," *Hastings Center Report*, 29:2, pp. 28-40.

Koenig, Barbara, et al. 1998. "Genetic Testing for BRCA1 and BRCA2: Recommendations of the Stanford Program in Genomics, Ethics, and Society," *Journal of Women's Health*, 7:5, pp. 531-545.

Kolata, Gina Bari. 1980. "Mass Screening for Neural Tube Defects," *Hastings Center Report*, 10:6, pp. 8-10.

———. 1997a. "Advent of Testing for Breast Cancer Genes Leads to Fears of Disclosure and Discrimination," *New York Times*, Feb. 4, pp. C1, C3.

———. 1997b. "Scientist Reports First Cloning Ever of Adult Mammal," *New York Times*, Feb. 25, p. A1.

Krimmel, Herbert T. 1983. "The Case Against Surrogate Parenting," *Hastings Center Report*, 13:5, pp. 35-39.

Krugh, Timothy R. 1990. "Is COBRA Poised to Strike? An Analysis of Medical COBRA." *Journal of Health and Hospital Law*, 23:6, pp. 161-175.

Kuczewski, Mark G. 1996. "Reconceiving the Family: The Process of Consent in Medical Decisionmaking," *Hastings Center Report*, 26:2, 30-37.

Kuhse, Helga. 1986. "The Case for Active Involuntary Euthanasia," *Law, Medicine and Health Care*, 14:3-4, pp. 145-148.

LaFleur, William R. 1990. "Contestation and Consensus: The Morality of Abortion in Japan," *Philosophy East and West*, 40:4, pp. 529-542.

Lancet. 1984. "Review of Mortality Results in Randomized Trials in Early Breast Cancer," 2:8414, p. 1205.

Langsley, D. G. 1990. "Medical Specialty Credentialing in the United States." *Clinical Orthopedics*, 257, pp. 22-88.

Leong, G.B., S. Eth, and J.A. Silva. 1992. "The Psychotherapist as Witness for the Prosecution: The Communalization of Tarasoff," *American Journal of Psychiatry*, 148:8, pp. 1011-1015.

Leventhal, R. I., et al. 1990. "Liver Transplantation: Initial Experience in the Veterans Administration," *Digestive Diseases and Sciences*, 156:6, pp. 673-680.

Levine, Carol. 1984. "Questions and (Some Very Tentative) Answers about Ethics Committees," *Hastings Center Report*, 14:3, pp. 9-12.

Levine, Carol, Joyce Bermel, and Paul Homer, eds. 1987. "Biomedical Ethics: An Multinational Review, Special Supplement," *Hastings Center Report*, 17:3, p. 36.

Liberman, Trudy. 1996. "Health Care Special report: How Good Is Your Health Plan?" *Consumer Reports*, August, pp. 28-42.

Lippman, Abby. 1991. Prenatal Genetics Testing and Screening: Constructing Needs and Reinforcing Inequities," *American Journal of Law and Medicine*, 17:1-2, pp. 15-50.

Lo, Bernard. 1987. "Promises and Pitfalls of Ethics Committees," *New England Journal of Medicine*, 317:1, pp. 46-49.

Lombardo, Paul A. 1981. "Consent and Donations from the Dead," *Hastings Center Report*, 11:6, pp. 9-11.

Lynn, Joanne, and James F. Childress. 1983. "Must Patients Always Be Given Food and Water?" *Hastings Center Report*, 13:5, pp. 17-21.

Lyon, Jeff, and Peter Gorner. 1995. *Altered Fates: Gene Therapy and The Retooling of Human Life.* New York: W. W. Norton and Co.

MacIntyre, Alasdair. 1988. *Whose Justice? Which Rationality?* Notre Dame, IN: University of Notre Dame Press.

Macklin, Ruth, and Gerald Friedland. 1986. "AIDS Research: The Ethics of Clincal Trials," *Law, Medicine and Health Care*, 14:5-6, pp. 273-280.

Mahowald, Mary B. 1993. *Women, Children and Health Care*, New York: Oxford.

Mahowald, Mary B., Jerry Silver, and Robert A. Ratcheson. 1987. "The Ethical Options in Transplanting Fetal Tissue," *Hastings Center Report*, 17:1, pp. 9-15.

Manuel, Patricia, and Kristine Alster. 1994. "Unlicensed Personnel: No Cure for an Ailing Health Care System," *Nursing and Health Care*, 15:1, pp. 18-21.

Markowitz, Sally. 1990. "Abortion and Feminism." *Social Theory and Practice*, 16, pp. 1-17.

Marquis, Don. 1989. "Why Abortion is Immoral." *Journal of Philosophy*, 86:3, pp. 183-202.

Massachusetts Task Force on Organ Transplantation. 1984. *Report of the Task Force.* Boston: Department of Public Health. Reprinted in *Law, Medicine and Health Care*, 1985, 13:1, pp. 8-26.

Mattingly, Susan S. 1992. "The Maternal-Fetal Dyad: Exploring the Two-Patient Obstetric Model," *Hastings Center Report*, 22:1, pp. 13-18.

May, William F. 1983. *The Physician's Covenant: Images of the Healer in Medical Ethics*. Philadelphia: Westminster Press.

Mayer, Klemens B., and Stephen G. Pauker. 1987. "Screening for HIV: Can We Afford the False Positive Rate?" *New England Journal of Medicine*, 317:4, pp. 238-240.

McCartney, James J. 1980. "The Development of the Doctrine of Ordinary and Extraordinary Means of Preserving Life in Catholic Moral Theology Before the Karen Quinlan Case," *The Linacre Quarterly*, August, pp. 215-224.

McCartney, Scott. 1994. *Defying the Gods: Inside the New Frontiers of Organ Transplants*. New York: MacMillan Publishing Co.

McCormick, Richard A. 1981. *How Brave a New World: Dilemmas in Bioethics*. Garden City, NY: Doubleday.

———. 1984. "Ethics Committees: Promise or Peril?" *Law, Medicine and Health Care*, 4:4, pp. 150-155.

McCormick, Richard A., and Paul Ramsey, eds. 1978. *Doing Evil to Achieve Good: Moral Choice in Conflict Situations*. Chicago: Loyola University Press.

McDonald, Kim. 1986. "Misconduct by Scientists Said to Be More Common Than Many Believe in Scholarship," *Chronicle of Higher Education*, May 21, pp. 7, 10.

McDowell, Theodore N., Jr. 1990. Physician Self Referral Arrangements: Legitimate Business or Unethical "Entrepreneurialism." *American Journal of Law and Medicine*, 15:1, pp. 61-110.

McGee, Glenn, and Arthur L. Caplan. 1999. "What's in the Dish?" *Hastings Center Report*, 29:2, pp. 36-38.

McGovern, Margaret M., Jules D. Goldberg, and Robert J. Desnick. 1986. "Acceptability of Chorionic Villi Sampling for Prenatal Diagnosis," *American Journal of Obstetrics and Gynecology*, 155:1, pp. 25-29.

McMorris, Frances A. 1996. "Courts Are Giving New Rights to Fetuses," *Wall Street Journal*. September 4, B1.

Mechanic, David. 1986. *From Advocacy to Allocation: The Evolving American Health Care System*. New York: The Free Press.

Medical Letter on Drugs and Therapeutics. 1987. "Serum Cholesterol Determinations," 29:738, pp. 41-42.

Meisel, Alan. 1989, supp. 1991. *The Right To Die*. New York: John Wiley and Sons.

Meisel, Alan, and Mark Kuczewski (1996). "Legal and Ethical Myths About Informed Consent," *Archives of Internal Medicine*, 156, pp. 2521-2526.

Meltze, Herbert Y., et al. 1990. "Effects of Six Months of Clozapine Treatment on the Quality of Life of Chronic Schizophrenic Patients," *Hospital and Community Psychiatry*, 41:8, pp. 892-997.

Mendelsohn, Robert S. 1981. *Male Practice: How Doctors Manipulate Women*. Chicago: Contemporary Books.

Miles, Steven H. 1992. "New Business for Ethics Committees," *H.E.C. Forum* 4:2, pp. 97-102.

Miller, Franklin G., and Howard Brody. 1995. "Professional Integrity and Physician-Assisted Death," *Hastings Center Report*, 25:3, pp. 8-17.

Morreim, E. Haavi. 1991. *Balancing Act: The New Medical Ethics of Medicine's New Economics*. Massachusetts: Kluwer Academic Publishers.

———. 1996. "Lifestyles of the Risky and Infamous: From Managed Care to Managed Lives," *Hastings Center Report*, 25:6, pp. 5-12.

Morrissey, James M., Adele D. Hoffmann, and Jeffrey C. Thorpe. 1986. *Consent and Confidentiality in the Health Care of Children and Adolescents: A Legal Guide*. New York: The Free Press.

Morse, Robert A., and Renee M. Popovits. 1989. "Stark's Crusade: The Ethics in Patient Referrals Act of 1989," *Health and Hospital Law*, 22:7, pp. 208-216, 224.

Moskop, John C. 1987. "The Moral Limits to Federal Funding for Kidney Disease," *Hastings Center Report*, 17:2, pp. 11-15.

Mosteller, Frederick. 1985. "Selection of Papers by Quality of Design, Analysis, and Reporting," pp. 98-116 in Kenneth S. Warren, ed., *Selectivity in Information Systems: Survival of the Fittest*. New York: Praeger.

Murdock, George P. 1949. *Social Structure* New York: MacMillan Co.

Murphy, Catherine, and Huner Howard. 1983. *Ethical Problems in the Nurse-Patient-Relationship*. Boston: Allyn and Bacon.

Murphy, Patricia. 1980. "Dilemmas in Practice: Deciding to Blow the Whistle," *American Journal of Nursing*, pp. 169-72.

Murray, Thomas H. 1985. "The Final, Anticlimactic Rule on Baby Doe," *Hastings Center Report*, 15:3, pp. 5-9.

———. 1987. "Gifts of the Body and the Needs of Strangers," *Hastings Center Report*, 17:2, pp. 30-38.

National Commission for the Protection of Human Subjects of Biomedical and Behavioral Research. 1976. *Report and Recommendations: Research on the Fetus*, DHEW Publication, No. 0S, 76-127.

———. 1977. *Research Involving Children: Report and Recommendations*. Washington, DC: U.S. Government Printing Office.

———. 1978a. *The Belmont Report: Ethical Guidelines for the Protection of Human Subjects of Research*. Washington, DC: DHEW, No. OS, 78-0012 and Appendixes A and B, No. OS, 78-0013-14.

———. 1978b. *Report and Recommendations: Institutional Review Boards and Appendix*. Washington, DC: Department of Health and Human Services, Nos. OS 78-0008 and OS 78-0009.

———. 1978c. *Report and Recommendations: Research on the Fetus*. Washington, DC: Department of Health and Human Services, DHEW Publication, No. OS 76-127.

National Conference of the Commissioners on Uniform State Laws. 1989. *Uniform Rights of the Terminally Ill Act*.

National Conference of Commissioners on Uniform State Laws. 1988. *Uniform Status of Assisted Conception Act* 988 U.L.A. Supp. 87.

National Institutes of Health. 1994. *Research Guidelines*. 30 Jan. 2000 <http://www.nih.gov/grants/oprr/humansubjects/guidance/hsdc94-01.htm>.

National Institutes of Health, Human Embryo Research Panel (Ad hoc Group of Consultants to the Advisory Committee to the Director). 1994. *Report*, 1.1, September. Bethesda, MD: US National Institutes of Health.

National Institutes of Health, National Heart, Liver, and Blood Institute. 1995. *Consensus Guidelines.* NIH Publication No. 95-3045, Bethesda, MD: US National Institutes of Health.

Neale, Heidi. 1990. Mother's Rights Prevail: In re A.C. and the Status of Forced Obstetrical Intervention in the District of Columbia. *Journal of Health and Hospital Law*, 23:7, pp. 208-213.

Nelkin, Dorothy and Lori Andrews. 1998. "*Homo Economicus*: Commercialization of Body Tissue in the Age of Biotechnology," *Hastings Center Report*, 25:5, pp. 30-39.

Nelson, Laurence J., and Nancy Milliken. 1990. "Compelled Medical Treatment of Pregnant Women: Life, Liberty and Law in Conflict," in *Ethical Issues in the New Reproductive Technologies*, Richard T. Hull, ed., Belmont, CA: Wadsworth Publishing Co., pp. 224-240.

Newman, Stephen A. 1989. "Baby Doe: Congress and the States: Challenging the Federal Treatment Standards for Impaired Infants," *American Journal of Law and Health Care*, 15:1, pp. 1-60.

New York State Task Force on Life and the Law. 1986. "Do Not Resuscitate Order: The Proposed Legislation," *New York State Journal of Medicine*, 86:1, pp. 3-8.

Nicholas, Eve K. 1990. *Human Gene Therapy.* Cambridge, MA: Harvard University Press.

Noonan, John T. ed., 1970. *The Morality of Abortion: Legal and Historical Perspectives.* Cambridge, MA: Harvard University Press.

"Nuremberg Code of Ethics In Medical Research," 1948-9. *Trials of War Criminals before the Nuremberg Military Tribunals under Control Council Law.* 10:2, pp. 181-182. Washington, D.C.: U.S. Government Printing Office.

Nussbaum, Martha C. 1986. *The Fragility of Goodness: Luck and Ethics in Greek Tragedy and Philosophy.* Cambridge: Cambridge University Press.

Office of the Surgeon General. 1991. "HIV-Infected Surgeons: Behringer v. Medical Center," *Journal of American Medical Association*, 266:268, pp. 1134-1137.

Olson, Ellen et al. 1994. "Early Experiences of an Ethics Consult Team," *Journal of the American Geriatrics Society*, 42, pp. 437-441.

Omnibus Budget Reconciliation Act. 1990. "Patient Self-Determination Act," Sections 4206 and 4751, Public Law 101-508.

Oppenheimer, Gerald M., and Robert A. Padug. 1986. "AIDS: The Risk to Insurers, the Threat to Equity," *Hastings Center Report*, 16:5 pp. 18-27.

Oppl, Hubert, and Ernst von Kardorff. 1990. "The National Health Care System in the Welfare State," *Social Science Medicine*, 31:1, pp. 43-50.

Oregon Death with Dignity Act.

O'Rourke, Kevin. 1996. "Federal Courts Approve Physician Assisted Suicide," *Health Care Ethics USA*, 4:3, pp. 4-5.

Ozar, David T. 1985. "The Case Against Thawing Unused Frozen Embryos, *Hastings Center Report*, 15:4, pp. 7-12.

Panner, Morris J., and Nicolas A. Christakis. 1986. "The Limits of Science in On-the-Job Screening," *Hastings Center Report*, 16:6, pp. 7-12.

Patterson, Kay, and John C. Bailar, III. 1985. "A Review of Journal Peer Review," in Kenneth S. Warren, ed., *Selectivity in Information Systems: Survival of the Fittest.* New York: Praeger, pp. 65-82.

Paulson, R. J. and M. V. Sauer. 1990. "Factors Affecting Embryo Implantation after In Vitro Fertilization: A Hypothesis." *American Journal of Obstetrics and Gynecology*, 163 (6:Pt 1), pp. 2020-2023.

Pellegrino, Edmund D. 1979a. *Humanism and the Physician*. Knoxville, TN: University of Tennessee Press.

———. 1979b. "Toward A Reconstruction of Medical Morality," *Journal of Medicine and Philosophy*, 4:1, pp. 32-56.

Pellegrino, Edmund D., and David Thomasma. 1981. *The Philosophical Basis of Medical Practice: Toward an Ethic of the Healing Profession*. New York: Oxford University Press.

———. 1987. *For the Patient's Sake*. New York: Oxford University Press.

Perspectives: The Blue Cross and Blue Shield Magazine. 1985. "Second Surgical Opinions: Struggles to Get Out of a Political Box," Fall, pp. 19-25.

Peters, David A. 1986. "Protecting Autonomy in Organ Procurement Procedures: Some Overlooked Issues," *The Milbank Quarterly*, 64:2, pp. 241-270.

Peterson, Lynn M. 1989. "AIDS: Ethical Dilemma For Surgeons," *Law, Medicine and Health Care*, pp. 139-144.

Planned Parenthood of Southeastern Pennsylvania v. Robert P. Casey, et al., etc. Slip Opinion, Docket No. 91-744, 29 June 1992.

Polonoff, David B., and Michael J. Garland. 1979. "Oregon's Premarital Blood Test: An Unsuccessful Attempt at Repeal," *The Hastings Center Report*, 9:6, pp. 5-6.

Popovits, Rene M. 1991. "Criminalization of Pregnant Substance Abusers," *Journal of Health and Hospital Law*, 24: pp. 169-181.

President's Commission for the Study of Ethical Problems in Medicine and Biomedical and Behavioral Research. 1981. *Defining Death: Medical, Legal and Ethical Issues in the Determination of Death*. Washington DC: U.S. Government Printing Office.

———. 1982. *Making Health Care Decisions: The Ethical and Legal Implications of Informed Consent in the Patient-Practitioner Relationship* I, Report, Washington, DC: The President's Commission.

Pritchard, J.A., P.C. MacDonald, and N.F. Grant. 1986. *Williams Textbook of Obstetrics*. East Norwalk, CT: Appleton, Century, Crofts.

Qui, Ren-Zong, Chun-Zhi Wand and Yuan Gu. 1989. "Can Late Abortion Be Ethically Justified?" *The Journal of Medicine and Philosophy*, 14, pp. 343-350.

Quickel, K. E., Jr. 1996. "Diabetes in a Managed Care System," *Annals of Internal Medicine*, 124 (1pt2): pp. 160-163.

Quill v. Vacco. 1996. 117 S.Ct., p. 2293.

Quill, Timothy. 1991. "Death and Dignity: A Case of Individualized Decision Making," *New England Journal of Medicine*, 324, pp. 691.

Quinn, Carroll A., and Michael D. Smith. 1987. *The Professional Commitment: Issues and Ethics in Nursing*. Philadelphia: W.B. Saunders.

Rachels, James. 1975. "Active and Passive Suicide," *New England Journal of Medicine*, 292:2, pp. 78-80.

Ramsey, Paul. 1978. *Ethics on the Edges of Life: Medical and Legal Intersections*. New Haven, CT: Yale University Press.

Rawls, John. 1971. *A Theory of Justice*. Cambridge, MA: Belknap Press of Harvard University Press.

Regan, Tom. 1983. "Nursing Complaints: Going Public is Risky," *The Regan Report on Nursing Law*, 24:4, p. 1.

———. 1984. *The Case for Animal Rights*. Berkeley, CA: University of California Press.

Reid, William H. 1990. "Access to Care in the Public Sector." *Hospital and Community Psychiatry*, 41:8, pp. 870-873.

Reiser, Stanley Joel. 1994. "The Ethical Life of Health Care Organizations," *Hastings Center Report*, 24:6, pp. 28-35.

Rhoden, Nancy K. 1986. "Treating Baby Doe: The Ethics of Uncertainty," *Hastings Center Report*, 16:4, pp. 34-42.

Rideout v. Hershey Medical Center, PICS Case No. 96-5260 (Dec. 29, 1995) Thurgeon, J. 41 pages.

Robertson, John A. 1983. "Surrogate Mothers: Not So Novel After All," *Hastings Center Report*, 13:5, pp. 28-34.

———. 1996. "The Case of the Switched Embryos," *Hastings Center Report*, 25:6, pp. 13-19.

Robin, Eugene D. 1984. *Medical Care Can Be Dangerous to Your Health: A Guide to the Risks and Benefits*. New York: Harper and Row.

Rodes, Ned D. et al. 1986. "The Impact of Breast Cancer Screening on Survival: A 5- to 10-Year Follow Up Study," *Cancer*, 57, pp 581-585.

Roe v. Wade (1973). 410 U.S. 113, S. C.T. 705, 35 L.ED.2D. 147.

Rogers v. South Carolina Department of Health. 1989. 377 S.E. 2nd 125 and S.C. Ct. appeals 1989.

Rosenberg, Charles. 1979. "The Therapeutic Revolution: Medicine, Meaning, and Social Change in Nineteenth-Century America," in Morris J. Vogel and Charles E. Rosenberg, eds. *The Therapeutic Revolution: Essays in the Social History of American Medicine*. Philadelphia, PA: University of Pennsylvania Press.

Rosenberg, Stephen A. et al. 1988. "Use of Tumor-Infiltrating Lymphocytes and Interleuken-2 in the Immunotherapy of Patients with Metastatic Melanoma," *New England Journal of Medicine*, 319:25, p. 1676-1680.

Rosenfeld, Albert. 1984. "At Risk for Huntington's Disease: Who Should Know What and When," *Hastings Center Report*, 14:3, pp. 5-8.

Rosenthal, Carolyn J. et al. 1980. *Nurses, Families and Patients*. New York: Springer.

Rosenthal, Elisabeth. 1998. "Scientists Debate China's Law on Sterilizing the Carriers of Genetic Defects," *New York Times*, August 16, p. A14.

Rosoff, Arnold J. 1981. *Informed Consent: A Guide for Health Care Providers*. Rockville, MD: Aspen.

Rosovsky, Fay A. 1984. *Consent to Treatment, A Practical Guide*. Boston: Brown, Little and Co.

Rothman, William. 1983. *Strikes in Health Care Organizations*. Owings Mills, MD: National Health Publishing.

Ruffenbach, Glenn. 1991. "CDC Proposes That Hospital Patients Undergo Screening for the Aids Virus," *Wall Street Journal*, September, 20, p. B3.

Rundle, Rhonda L. 1996. "Salick Pioneers Selling Cancer Care to HMOs," *Wall Street Journal*, August, 12, pp. B1-B2.

Sabine, John R. 1985. "The Error Rate In Biological Publication: A Preliminary Survey," in *BioScience*, 35:6, pp. 358-363.

Sauer, Mark V., Richard J. Paulson, and Rogerio A. Long. 1990. "A Preliminary Report on Oocyte Donation Extending Reproduction Potential for Women Over 10," *New England Journal of Medicine*, 123:17, pp. 1157-1160.

Schoeman, Ferdinand. 1985. "Parental Discretion and Children's Rights: Background and Implications for Medical Decision Making," *Journal of Science and Medicine*, 10:1, pp. 45-61.

Schoolman, Harold M., et al. 1968. "Clinical and Experimental Statistics in Medical Reserach: Principles versus Practices," *Journal of Laboratory and Clinical Medicine*, 71:3, pp. 357-367.

Shannon, T. A. 1990. "Ethical Issues Involved with in Vitro Fertilization." *AORN Journal*, 52:3, pp. 627-631.

Shapiro, Martin F., and Robert P. Charrow. 1985. "Special Report: Scientific Misconduct in Investigational Drug Trials," *New England Journal of Medicine*, 312:11, pp. 731-736.

Shaw, Margery W., and A. Edward Doudera. 1983. *Defining Human Life: Medical, Legal and Ethical Implications*. Ann Arbor, MI: AUPHA Press.

Shelp, Earl E., ed. 1985. *Virtue and Medicine: Explorations in the Character of Medicine*. Boston, MA: D. Reidel Publishing.

Siegler, Mark. 1986. "Ethics Committees: Decisions in Bureaucracy," *Hastings Center Report*, 16:3, pp. 22-24.

Singer, Lawrence E. 1989. "Review and Analysis of Federal 'Anti-dumping' Legislation: Practical Advice and Unanswered Questions." *Journal of Health and Hospital Law*, 22:5, pp. 145-156.

Singer, Peter. 1985. "Making Laws on Making Babies," *Hastings Center Report*, 15:4, pp. 5-6.

Sordillo, Peter P., and Kenneth F. Schaffner. 1981. "The Last Patient in a Drug Trial," *Hastings Center Report*, 11:6, pp. 21-23.

Spector, Rachel E. 1985. *Cultural Diversity in Health and Illness*. 2d ed. Norwalk, CT: Appleton-Century-Crofts.

Stampfer, Meir J. et al. 1985. "A Prospective Study of Post-Menopausal Estrogen Therapy and Coronary Heart Disease," *New England Journal of Medicine*, 313:17, pp. 1044-1049.

1986 "Standards and Guidelines for Cardiopulmonary Resuscitation (CPR) and Emergency Cardiac Care (ECC)." *Journal of the American Medical Association*, 255:21, pp. 2905-2985.

Starr, Paul. 1982. *The Social Transformation of American Medicine*. New York: Basic Books.

Starzl, Thomas E. 1985. "Will Live Organ Donations No Longer Be Justified?" *Hastings Center Report*, 15:2, p. 5.

Stolberg, Sheryl Gay. 1999a. "The Biotech Death of Jesse Gelsinger," *New York Times Magazine*, November 24; pp. 136-140, 149-150.

———. 1999b. "The Long Horizon of Gene Therapy," *The New York Times*, December 12; sec 3, p. 4.

Sullivan, Thomas D. 1977. "Active and Passive Euthanasia: An Impertinent Distinction?" *Human Life Review*, 3:3, pp. 40-46.

SUPPORT Principle Investigators. 1995. "A Controlled Trial to Improve Care for Seriously Ill Hospitalized Patients: The Study to Understand Prognoses and Preferences for Outcomes and Risks of Treatments (SUPPORT)," *Journal of the American Medical Association.* 274:20, pp. 1591-1598.

Szasz, Thomas. 1977. *The Theology of Medicine: Political-Philosophical Foundations of Medical Ethics.* New York: Harper and Row.

Taranto, Richard B. 1986. "The Psychiatrist-Patient Privilege and Third Party Payers: Commonwealth v. Korbin," *Law, Medicine and Health Care,* 14:1, pp. 25-29.

Tarasoff v. Regents of the University of California. 1976. 551 P.2d 334, 17 Cal.3d 425.

Taub, Sheila. 1985. "Surrogate Motherhood and the Law," *Connecticut Medicine,* 49:10 pp. 671-674.

Tegtmeir, James W. 1990. "Ethics and Aids: A Summary of the Law and a Critical Analysis of the Individual Physician's Ethical Duty to Treat," pp. 249-266 in Larry Gostin and William Curran, eds. *The Harvard Model Aids Project, American Journal of Law and Medicine,* 16:1, pp. 1-2.

Terkelsen, Kenneth G., and Rene C. Grosser. 1990. "Estimating Clorazin's Cost to the Nation." *Hospital and Community Psychiatry,* 41:8, pp. 863-870.

Terry, Don. 1996. "In Wisconsin, a Rarity of a Fetal-Harm Case," *New York Times,* August 17, Sec. 1, p. 6.

Thompson, J., et al. 1987. "Retaining Rights of Impaired Elderly," *Journal of Gerontological Nursing,* 13:3, pp. 2-25.

Thomson, Judith Jarvis. 1971. "A Defense of Abortion," *Philosophy and Public Affairs,* 1:1, pp. 47-66.

Tomlinson, Tom, and Diane Czlonka. 1995. "Futility and Hospital Policy," *Hastings Center Report,* 25:3, pp. 28-35.

Tooley, Michael. 1972. "Abortion and Infanticide," *Philosophy and Public Affairs,* 2, pp. 137-165.

Truog, Robert D., Joel E. Frader, and Allan S. Brett. 1992. "The Problem with Futility," *New England Journal of Medicine,* 326:23, pp. 1560-1564.

Uhlmann, Richard F. et al. 1987. "Medical Management Decisions in Nursing Home Patients," *Annals of Internal Medicine,* 106, pp. 879-885.

Uniform Determination of Death Act. 12 Uniform Laws Annotated 320 (1990 Supp).

Uniform Law Commissioners. 1988. *Uniform Model Health Care Consent Act,* 6,9 U.L.A., 67, 76-77, 70-71, (supp. 1990).

Uniform Law Commissioners. 1989. *Uniform Rights of the Terminally Ill Act.* Chicago: National Conference of Commissioners on Uniform State Laws.

United Nations Commission on Human Rights. 1948. "Universal Declaration of Human Rights," in Ian Brownlie, ed. *Basic Documents on Human Rights.* Oxford: Oxford University Press, 1975.

Van der Maas, P.J. et al. 1991. "Euthanasia and Other Medical Decisions Concerning the End of Life," *Lancet,* 338, pp. 669-674.

VanDeVeer, Donald. 1986. *Paternalistic Intervention: The Moral Bounds on Benevolence.* Princeton, NJ: Princeton University Press.

Veatch, Robert M. 1972. "Models for Ethical Practice in a Revolutionary Age," *Hastings Center Report,* 2:3, pp. 5-7.

————. 1978. "Defining Death Anew: Technical and Ethical Problems," pp. 18-38 in Tom L. Beauchamp and Seymour Perlin, eds., *Ethical Issues in Death and Dying*. Englewood Cliffs, NJ: Prentice Hall.

————. 1981a. *A Theory of Medical Ethics*. New York: Basic Books.

————. 1981b. "Nursing Ethics, Physician Ethics and Medical Ethics," *Law Medicine and Health Care*, 9:5, pp. 17-19.

————. 1986. "DRG's and the Ethics Allocation of Resources," *Hastings Center Report*, 16:3, pp. 32-40.

————. 1987. *The Patient as Partner: A Theory of Human-Experimentation Ethics*. Bloomington, IN: Indiana University Press.

————. 1989. *Cross Cultural Perspectives in Medical Ethics*. Boston: Jones and Bartlett, Publishers.

Waldholtz, Michael. 1996. "Precious Pills: New AIDS Treatment Raises Tough Questions of Who Will Get It," *Wall Street Journal*, July 3, p. 1.

Warren, Kenneth S., ed. 1981. *Coping with the Biomedical Literature: A Primer for the Scientist and the Clinician*. New York: Praeger.

Warren, Mary Anne. 1973. "On the Moral and Legal Status of Abortion," *The Monist*, 57:1, pp. 43-61.

Wass, Debbie M., et al. 1986. "Chorionic Villus Sampling: Clinical Experience in 50 Diagnostic Cases," *Australian and New Zealand Journal of Obstetrics and Gynaecology*, 26:65, pp. 65-70.

Weber, Leonard J. 1995. "When to Excuse Employees from Work Responsibilities," *Health Progress*, November/December, pp. 51-53.

Webster v. Reproductive Health Services. 1989. 57 U.S.L.W. 5203.

Weil, F. (1993). "Releasing the Treating Psychiatrist from Confidentiality," *Medicine and Law*, 12:3-5, pp. 249-255.

Wermiel, Stephen. 1991. "High Court Says Hospital Review Panels May Face Lawsuits on Antitrust Grounds." *Wall Street Journal*, May 29, p. A3.

Williams Obstetrics. 1996. 20th ed., F. Gary Cunningham, ed., Boston, MA: McGraw-Hill Publishing Co.

Wilson, James Q. 1998. "Sex and Family," in Leon Kass and James Q. Wilson, eds. *The Ethics of Human Cloning*, Washington, DC: The AEI Press.

Wilson, Peter W. F. et al. 1985. "Postmenopausal Estrogen Use, Cigarette Smoking and Cardiovascular Morbidity in Women over 50: The Framingham Study," *New England Journal of Medicine*, 313:17, pp. 1038-1043.

Winslade, W. J. 1981. "Surrogate Mothers—Private Right or Public Wrong?" *Journal of Medical Ethics*, 9, pp. 153-154.

Winslade, W.J., and Judith Wilson Ross. 1986. *Choosing Life or Death: A Guide for Patients, Families and Physicians*. New York: The Free Press.

Winslow, Ron. 1991. "Liver Transplant Researchers Challenge Assigning Top Priority To Sickest Patients." *Wall Street Journal*, May 22, p. B4.

————. 1996a. "Heart Research Hurt by Funding Cuts, Managed Care Growth, Scientists Say," *Wall Street Journal*, July 15, p. B4.

————. 1996b. "Managed Care Acts to Mollify Clients, Doctors," *Wall Street Journal*, December 17, p. B1.

Wolf, Sidney M. 1999. "Public Citizen's Health Research Group Ranking of State Medical Board's Serious Disciplinary Actions in 1998," *Public Citizen*. 30 Jan. 2000 <http://www.citizen.org/hrg/PUBLICATIONS/1478.htm#table1>.

Wolf, Susan M. 1986. "Ethics Committees in the Courts," *Hastings Center Report*, 16:3, pp. 12-15.

———. 1994. "Health Care Reform and the Future of Physician Ethics," *Hastings Center Report*, 24:2, pp. 28-41.

Wolf-Devine, Celia. 1989. "Abortion and the 'Feminine Voice'." *Public Affairs Quarterly*, 3:3, pp. 81-87.

Woolfrey, Joan. 1998. "What Happens Now? Oregon and Physician-Assisted Suicide," *Hastings Center Report*, 25:3, pp. 9-17.

World Medical Association. 1975. Declaration of Helsinki. Geneva: World Health Organization, in *Biomedical Ethics*, Thomas A. Mappes and Jane S. Zembaty, eds., Boston, MA: McGraw-Hill Publishing Co.

Yoon, Mimi. 1990. "The Uniform Status of Children of Assisted Conception Act: Does It Protect the Best Interests of the Child in a Surrogate Arrangement?" *American Journal of Law and Medicine*, 16:4, pp. 525-580.

INDEX